CAMPUS CRIME

Third Edition

CAMPUS CRIME

Legal, Social, and Policy Perspectives

Edited by

BONNIE S. FISHER

School of Criminal Justice
University of Cincinnati

and

JOHN J. SLOAN, III

Department of Justice Sciences
University of Alabama – Birmingham

CHARLES C THOMAS • PUBLISHER, LTD.
Springfield • Illinois • U.S.A.

Published and Distributed Throughout the World by

CHARLES C THOMAS • PUBLISHER, LTD.
2600 South First Street
Springfield, Illinois 62704

© 2013 by CHARLES C THOMAS • PUBLISHER, LTD.

ISBN 978-0-398-08857-6 (hard)
ISBN 978-0-398-08858-3 (paper)
ISBN 978-0-398-08859-0 (ebook)

Library of Congress Catalog Card Number: 2012035558

First Edition, 1995
Second Edition, 2007
Third Edition, 2013

With THOMAS BOOKS *careful attention is given to all details of manufacturing
and design. It is the Publisher's desire to present books that are satisfactory as to their
physical qualities and artistic possibilities and appropriate for their particular use.*
THOMAS BOOKS *will be true to those laws of quality that assure a good name
and good will.*

Printed in the United States of America
SM-R-3

Library of Congress Cataloging-in-Publication Data

Campus crime : legal, social, and policy perspectives / edited by Bonnie S.
Fisher and John J. Sloan III. -- 3rd ed.
     p. cm.
Includes bibliographical references and index.
ISBN 978-0-398-08857-6 (hard) -- ISBN 978-0-398-08858-3 (pbk.) -- ISBN
978-0-398-08859-0 (ebook)
1. College students--Crimes against--United States. 2. Universities and col-
leges--Security measures--United States. 3. Campus police--Legal status, laws,
etc.--United States. I. Fisher, Bonnie, 1959- II. Sloan, John J.

HV6250.4.S78F57 2013
364.973--dc23
                                                                    2012035558

ABOUT THE CONTRIBUTORS

Andrea Allen is a Ph.D. Candidate in the Department of Criminology and Criminal Justice at the University of South Carolina and a Part-time Instructor of Criminal Justice and Criminology at Georgia State University. She received her M.S. in criminal justice from the University of Alabama. Her research explores the drug-crime relationship, how it is policed, and to what effect. Her work has been published in *Crime & Delinquency.*

Joanne Belknap is Professor of Sociology at the University of Colorado-Boulder. She received her Ph.D. in criminal justice from Michigan State University. Her primary research focus is on the trajectory of trauma to offending, an area in which she has numerous scholarly publications and most of which examine violence against women and girls, and incarcerated women and girls. She has secured almost two million dollars in grant money to conduct research on women, girls, and crime. Her current project, funded by the Bureau of Justice Statistics, is a study of the onset of trauma, mental illness, and offending among women in jail. She is also working on the fourth edition of her book, *The Invisible Woman: Gender, Crime, and Justice* to be published by Cengage. Dr. Belknap has won numerous research, teaching and service awards, and is president-elect of the American Society of Criminology.

Kristie R. Blevins is Associate Professor in the Department of Criminal Justice at Eastern Kentucky University. She received her Ph.D. in criminal justice from the University of Cincinnati. Her research interests include crime prevention, corrections, school safety, and the occupational reactions of criminal justice employees. Her recent work can be found in the *Journal of Offender Rehabilitation, Criminal Justice Policy Review, American Journal of Criminal Justice, Deviant Behavior,* and *International Journal of Police Science and Management.*

Max L. Bromley is Associate Professor *Emeritus* and Director of the graduate program in Criminal Justice Administration at the University of South Florida (USF). He received his Ed.D. from Nova Southeastern University. He has 25 years of experience in campus law enforcement, including serving as Associate Director of Public Safety at USF and helping develop and establish the first set of law enforcement accreditation standards for the State of Florida. His primary research interests include campus crime, campus law enforcement, and community policing. He is author of *Department Self-Study: A Guide for Campus Law Enforcement Administrators,* used at over 1,000 institutions of higher education in the U.S.; co-author of *Crime and Justice in America* (6th ed.) and *College Crime Prevention and Personal Safety Awareness;* and co-editor *Hospital and College Security Liability.* His research has appeared in such journals as *Policing, Police Quarterly, Criminal Justice Policy Review,* and *Journal of Contemporary Criminal Justice.*

Jennifer M. Burke is a doctoral student in Criminology at the University of Cincinnati. Ms. Burke earned her law degree *magna cum laude* from the Boston College Law School in 2001, where she was the Solicitations Editor of the *Boston College Environmental Affairs Law Review.* She is a former Associate in business litigation at the law firm of Thompson Hine, LLP. Ms. Burke has been adjunct faculty member in the School of Criminal Justice at the University of Cincinnati, where she taught undergraduate criminal justice courses, and in the Department of Political Science at John Carroll University in Cleveland, OH. Ms. Burke's research interests include regulatory crime prevention, survey research, and professional ethics.

Nancy Chi Cantalupo is an Abraham L. Freedman Fellow at the Beasley School of Law at Temple University. She received her J.D. *cum laude* from the Georgetown University Law Center. Her research interests include using various legal regimes to combat gender-based violence, including U.S. civil rights, tort and criminal law, as well as international and comparative regimes. She has practiced education law with the Washington DC firm of Drinker Biddle & Reath; served as director of a campus women's center and as an Assistant Dean at the Georgetown University Law Center where she was "Faculty Counsel" for student complainants in campus disciplinary proceedings. Her work has appeared in the *Loyola University-Chicago Law Journal,* the *Journal of College and University Law,* and the *Georgetown Journal of Gender and Law.*

Francis T. Cullen is Distinguished Research Professor of Criminal Justice and Sociology at the University of Cincinnati. He received his Ph.D. in sociology from Columbia University. Dr. Cullen has published over 200 works in the areas of criminological theory, corrections, public opinion, white-collar crime, and sexual victimization. His recent works include *Correctional Theory: Context and Consequences, Unsafe in the Ivory Tower: The Sexual Victimization of Women* (with Bonnie Fisher and Leigh Daigle), and *The Oxford Handbook of Criminological Theory.* His current research focuses on the organization of criminological knowledge and on rehabilitation as a correctional policy. He is a Past President of both the American Society of Criminology (ASC) and the

Academy of Criminal Justice Sciences (ACJS). In 2010, he received ASC's *Edwin H. Sutherland Award.*

Leah E. Daigle is associate professor of Criminal Justice and Criminology at Georgia State University. She received her Ph.D. in criminal justice from the University of Cincinnati. Her most recent research has centered on repeat sexual victimization of college women and the responses that women use during and after being sexually victimized. Her other research interests include the development and continuation of offending over time and gender differences in the antecedents to and consequences of criminal victimization and participation across the life-course. She is coauthor of *Unsafe in the Ivory Tower: The Sexual Victimization of College Women* (with Bonnie Fisher and Francis Cullen) and *Criminals in the Making: Criminality Across the Life-Course* (with John Wright and Stephen Tibbits), and author of *Victimology: A Text/Reader.* Her research has appeared in various professional journals including *Justice Quarterly, Victims and Offenders, The Journal of Quantitative Criminology,* and *The Journal of Interpersonal Violence.*

George W. Dowdall is Professor of Sociology at Saint Joseph's University in Philadelphia. He received his Ph.D. in sociology from Brown University. His research and teaching interests include substance use, mental health, and research methods. His publications include *College Drinking: Reframing a Social Problem / Changing the Culture* (2013), *Adventures in Criminal Justice Research* (2008), *Finding Out What Works and Why: A Guide to Evaluating College Prevention Programs and Policies* (2002), *The Eclipse of the State Mental Hospital* (1996). His work has appeared in the *Journal of the American Medical Association,* the *American Journal of Public Health,* and *Social Problems,* among others. He is a member of the *Pennsylvania Advisory Council on Drug and Alcohol Abuse* and also of the Board of Directors of the *Clery Center for Security on Campus.* During 1999–2000, he was an American Sociological Association Fellow in the office of then Senator Joseph R. Biden, Jr.

Edna Erez is Professor of Criminology, Law, and Justice at the University of Illinois at Chicago. She received her LL.B. degree from Hebrew University of Jerusalem and Ph.D. in sociology from the University of Pennsylvania. Her research interests include victimization and victims in the criminal justice system, gender in crime and justice, and women in terrorism. Her work has been funded by federal and state agencies in the U.S. and overseas. Professor Erez has published over 100 scholarly works, including journal articles, book chapters, and grant reports. She serves as coeditor of *International Review of Victimology,* associate editor of *Violence and Victims,* and on the editorial board of other criminology and legal studies journals. Her most recent coauthored grant reports of research supported by the National institute of Justice (NIJ) include *Jihad, Crime and the Internet* (2011), and *GPS Monitoring Technologies and Domestic Violence: An Evaluation Study* (2012).

Bonnie S. Fisher is Professor of Criminal Justice in the School of Criminal Justice at the University of Cincinnati (UC), where she also is a Fellow of the Graduate School. She received her Ph.D. in political science from Northwestern University. Her research interests include the sexual victimization of college women, repeat victimization, fear of crime, and bystander intervention effectiveness. Her work has appeared in outlets including *Criminology, Justice Quarterly*, and *Violence Against Women* and has been funded by the U.S. Department of Justice. Her most recent books are *The Dark Side of the Ivory Tower: Campus Crime as a Social Problem* (Cambridge University Press, 2011) with John Sloan and *Unsafe in the Ivory Tower: The Sexual Victimization of College Women* (SAGE Publications, Inc., 2010) with Leah Daigle and Frances Cullen. She was recently honored with the 2012 *George Reiveschl Jr. Award* for Creative and/or Scholarly Works from UC.

Dennis E. Gregory is an Associate Professor of Higher Education at Old Dominion University (ODU) and Director of the Higher Education Graduate Programs. He received his Ed.D. from the University of Virginia. Prior to joining the faculty at Old Dominion, Dr. Gregory served in various student affairs positions in the Southeast from 1974 to 2000. He is a past president of the Association for Student Judicial Affairs and served in a wide variety of professional leadership positions, including his current service as Associate Editor of the *NASPA Journal* and on the Board of Directors of the Council for the Advancement of Standards in Higher Education (CAS). He has presented over 100 programs, speeches, teleconferences, seminars, and keynote addresses on student affairs and legal topics and authored or coauthored over fifty articles, book chapters, monographs, and other publications. His most recent book is *The Administration of Fraternal Organizations on North American Campuses: A Pattern for the New Millennium*, which was published in 2003 by College Administration Publications.

Timothy C. Hart is a faculty member in the Department of Criminal Justice at the University of Nevada Las Vegas (UNLV) and Director of the State of Nevada's *Center for the Analysis of Crime Statistics*. He received his Ph.D. in criminology from the University of South Florida. His areas of interest include survey research, applied statistics, geographic information systems (GIS), and victimization. Prior to joining the UNLV faculty, Dr. Hart was a Statistician for the Bureau of Justice Statistics; a Program Analyst for the Drug Enforcement Administration; and a Research Analyst for the Hillsborough County (FL) Sheriff's Office. Dr. Hart's work has been published in such journals as *Criminal Justice and Behavior, Criminal Justice Policy Review*, and the *Journal of Quantitative Criminology*. The second edition of his book (with Clayton J.

Mosher and Terance D. Miethe), *The Mismeasure of Crime,* was published in 2010 by SAGE Publications Inc.

Scott Jacques is Assistant Professor of Criminal Justice and Criminology at Georgia State University. He received his Ph.D. in criminology and criminal justice from the University of Missouri-St. Louis. His research focuses on victimization, social control among drug dealers, and theories of offender-based research. He has served as Assistant Editor of the *British Journal of Sociology* and as an Advisory Editor to *Oxford Bibliographies Online.* His research has been funded by Proctor & Gamble and by the Dutch Police and Science Program. His articles have appeared in outlets such as *Criminology, Crime & Delinquency, The Journal of Research in Crime & Delinquency,* and *Justice Quarterly.* He is currently working on two books dealing with suburban drug markets and qualitative methods.

Steven M. Janosik is Associate Professor of Educational Leadership and Chair of the Department of Educational Leadership and Policy Studies at Virginia Polytechnic Institute and State University (Virginia Tech). He received his Ed. D. from Virginia Tech. Dr. Janosik has more than 20 years of experience in college administration and is the author or coauthor of more than 70 refereed journal articles, book chapters, and policy reports on the topics of campus crime, college administration, higher education law and policy, liability and risk management, professional standards and ethics, residence life, and student development. His work has been recognized by Commission III of the American College Personnel Association, and by the Association of College and University Housing Officers International. He is a member of the media board of the American College Personnel Association and serves as Associate Editor for the *Journal of Student Conduct Administration.*

Heather M. Karjane is a consultant, after serving as sexual harassment officer for a state court system and a research scientist in public health non-profits. She received her Ph.D. from the University of Massachusetts at Amherst. Dr. Karjane has specialized in issues related to gender, sexual victimization, violence and, increasingly, institutional accountability for over 25 years. As a research scientist, her work has been funded by the National Institute of Justice and the Centers for Disease Control and Prevention. As a consultant, she has advised the U.S. Air Force, U.S. Department of Defense, the Children's Safety Network, the National Suicide Prevention Resource Center and Media Education Foundation. Her work has been published by the National Institute of Justice and appeared in such publication as *The Journal of Forensic Science.*

Alison Kiss is the Executive Director of the *Clery Center for Security On Campus* (formerly Security On Campus, Inc.). She is completing her Ed.D. in Higher Education Administration at Northeastern University. Ms. Kiss has provided expert witness services in campus sexual assault cases, and is affiliated with various professional organizations including Rapid Response Expert Network; Violence Against Women On-line Resources (VAWnet); and Expanded Partners Network. She also served on the 2008 National Attorneys General *Task Force on School and Campus Safety.* Her most recent work includes a book chapter on campus crime in Michele A. Paludi and Florence L. Denmark's (2010) *Victims of Sexual Assault and Abuse: Resources and Responses for Individuals and Families.*

Samuel C. McQuade, III is the Professional Studies Graduate Program Director at the Rochester Institute of Technology (RIT). He received his Ph.D. in public policy from the George Mason University. Dr. McQuade's research interests include cybercrime, professional communications, integrative learning, critical thinking, problem solving, and ethical reasoning. From 2006–2011 he worked with educators throughout New York State to survey over 40,000 students in grades K–12, along with hundreds of parents and teachers, to identify ways that youth misuse information technology and are victimized online. That research contributed to new laws, policies, curriculum and professional development training for educators. His most recent books include *Understanding and Managing Cybercrime; The Encyclopedia of Cybercrime;* and *Cyber Bullying: Protecting Kids and Adults from Online Bullies.* He is coauthor of the forthcoming *Handbook on Cyber Bullying* and *Online and Electronic Gaming: Fun, Abuse, Crime and Addiction,* as well as Editor of the five-volume *World of Cybercrime: Issues, Cases and Responses.*

Elizabeth Ehrhardt Mustaine is Professor of Sociology at the University of Central Florida. She received her Ph.D. in sociology and criminology from The Ohio State University. Her research interests include criminal victimization and its risks; violence against women; registered sex offenders; child abuse; crime locations, sources, and patterns; and academic publishing in criminology and criminal justice. Dr. Mustaine is currently working with the Brevard County (FL) Sheriff's Office to launch a program whereby victims of child sexual abuse are paired with therapy dogs to help them successfully navigate the criminal justice process. Her work has appeared in such journals as the *American Journal of Criminal Justice, Deviant Behavior,* and *Crime and Delinquency.* Her most recent book (with Jana Jasinski, Jennifer Wesley, and James Wright) is *Hard Lives, Mean Streets: Violence in the Lives of Homeless Women* (Northeastern University Press, 2010).

Eugene A. Paoline, III is Associate Professor of Criminal Justice in the Department of Criminal Justice at the University of Central Florida. He earned his Ph.D. in criminal justice from the University at Albany, State University of New York (SUNY). His research interests include police culture, police use of force, and occupational attitudes of criminal justice practitioners. He is the author of *Rethinking Police Culture* (2001) and his research has appeared in a variety of peer-reviewed journals including *Criminology, Justice Quarterly,* and *Police Quarterly.* His most recent project was a National Institute of Justice (NIJ) funded study of variation in American police departments' policies concerning less lethal use of force, and various outcomes associated with these different policies.

Matthew B. Robinson is Professor of Government and Justice Studies at Appalachian State University in Boone, NC, where he is also Coordinator of the undergraduate program in Criminal Justice. He received his Ph.D. in criminology and criminal justice from Florida State University. His research interests include criminological theory, crime prevention, capital punishment, national drug control policy, and injustices of the criminal justice system. He is the author of dozens of articles and chapters as well as 12 books, including most recently *Crime Prevention: The Essentials* (Bridgewater Education, 2012). He is a past president of the North Carolina Criminal Justice Association and of the Southern Criminal Justice Association.

Sunghoon Roh is Assistant Professor of criminology at the Korean National Police University. He earned his Ph.D. in criminal justice from Sam Houston State University. Dr. Roh is a former Chief Officer assigned to the Crime Prevention Division, Criminal Investigation Unit and Combat Police Force Unit in South Korea. His research interests include ecological criminology, spatial distribution of crime, crime prevention, race/ethnicity issues in crime, and fear of crime. His research has been funded by the National Research Foundation of Korea and the Korean National Police Agency. His work has appeared in such journals as *Journal of Criminal Justice, Policing, Police Quarterly, Journal of Drug Issues,* and numerous Korean scholarly outlets.

Shannon A. Santana is Assistant Professor in the Department of Sociology and Criminology at the University of North Carolina Wilmington. She received her Ph.D. in criminal justice from the University of Cincinnati. Her research interests include violence against women, the effectiveness of self-protective behaviors in violent victimizations, workplace violence, and public attitudes towards crime and criminal justice. Her work has appeared in *Violence and Victims, Justice System Journal, Crime and Delinquency,* and *Security Journal.* In addition, she has also coauthored chapters in several books including *Female Crime Victims: Reality Reconsidered* and *Public Opinion and Criminal Justice.*

John J. Sloan, III is Professor of Criminal Justice and Sociology and Chairman of the Department of Justice Sciences at the University of Alabama at Birmingham, where he is also Co-Director of the Computer Forensics and Security Management graduate program and Associate Director of the *Center for Information Assurance and Joint Forensics Research* (CIA|JFR). He received his

Ph.D. in sociology from Purdue University. His research interests include crime and related issues on college and university campuses, fear and perceived risk of victimization, specialized police agencies, and criminal justice policy. His work has appeared in such outlets as *Criminology, Criminology and Public Policy,* and *Justice Quarterly* and been funded by the U.S. Department of Justice and state and local agencies in Alabama. His most recent book (with Bonnie S. Fisher) is *The Dark Side of the Ivory Tower: Campus Crime as a Social Problem* (Cambridge University Press, 2011).

Megan Stewart is Assistant Professor of Criminal Justice at Georgia Gwinnett College. She earned her Ph.D. in criminal justice from the University of Cincinnati. Her primary areas of research interest include violence against women and college student victimization. Her work has appeared in *Victims & Offenders.* Dr. Stewart has been a hotline counselor and rape crisis advocate, as well as worked for the University of Cincinnati Police Department (UCPD).

Richard Tewksbury is Professor of Justice Administration at the University of Louisville. He received his Ph.D. in sociology from The Ohio State University. Professor Tewksbury has served as Research Director for the National Prison Rape Elimination Commission; as Visiting Fellow with the Bureau of Justice Statistics; and as editor of both the *American Journal of Criminal Justice* and *Justice Quarterly.* His research interests include societal responses to sex offenders, community violence, correctional institution administration, and the construction and management of deviant, stigmatized identities. He has published more than 250 articles, chapters, and reports, and his books include *Criminological Theory* (Prentice Hall, 3rd ed., 2011), *Introduction to Gangs in America* (CRC Press, 2011) and *Introduction to Criminal Justice Research Methods* (Charles C Thomas, 2008).

To Nick, Olivia, and Camille with many thanks for their endless encouragement and inspiration.

B.S.F.

To Tavis, with thanks for the support and understanding.

J.J.S.

Thank you to all our students who over the years have listened to our respective campus crime lectures and been an invaluable source of "new" thinking about campus crime and security.

J.J.S.
B.S.F.

PREFACE

This volume is the third edition of *Campus Crime: Legal, Social, and Policy Perspectives*. That a third edition is warranted – more than 15 years after publication of the first edition in 1995 – underscores that interest in the legal, social, and policy contexts of campus crime has not waned. Congress, and to a lesser extent the states, have maintained their interest in campus crime and security through passage of, and amendments to, laws addressing these issues. Scholars from a variety of disciplines continue to publish peer-reviewed research examining the full spectrum of campus crime and security topics, ranging from the extent and nature of student victimization to postsecondary institutional compliance with federal and state legislative mandates. Campus law enforcement and security professionals face not only traditional challenges such as how to best serve and protect the campus community 24 hours a day seven days a week, but new challenges involving the security of sensitive information routinely compiled by universities, not to mention planning for and responding to a mass casualty event such as an active shooter on campus or a bombing.

Among the purposes for assembling a third edition of *Campus Crime: Legal, Social, and Policy Perspectives* is our desire to share with readers the advancements that have occurred in understanding campus crime, especially the dynamics of college student victimization, and efforts to effectively address campus security issues. For the sake of continuity with the first and second editions, we maintain the three sections to the volume: Part I – The Legal Context of Campus Crime, Part II – The Social Context of Campus Crime, and Part III – The Security Context of Campus Crime. Within each section are chapters that address what we believe are the most pressing crime and security issues confronting postsecondary institutions at the dawn of the new millennium. Some of these chapters address "long-standing" topics such as the sexual victimization of college women and the role of campus police departments in securing postsecondary institutions. Other chapters address "new" issues in campus crime and security, such as the challenges posed by "high-tech" crimes such as cybercrime, cyberstalking, and identity theft that involve campus community members as both victims and offenders.

Nearly 25 years have passed since Congress passed landmark campus crime legislation, now known as the *Jeanne Clery Disclosure of Campus Security Policy and Campus Crime Statistics Act* (20 U.S.C. 1092[f]). *Clery's* requirements have generated both critical discussion and empirical analyses that raise questions about the legislation's effectiveness at reducing campus crime and enhancing campus security as stated goals of the legislation. Researchers continue to unravel the dynamics surrounding college student victimization, particularly the key role played by students' lifestyles and routines, including the use (and abuse) of alcohol. While this body of research has answered many questions about college student victimization, it has also given rise to still more questions that need answers before researchers fully understand the extent, nature, and spatial aspects of student victimization. Further, state legislatures and Congress have criminalized two behaviors, stalking and "high-tech" abuses such as computer hacking and identity theft, which pose both unique victimization risks and opportunities for offending, and create security and policing challenges for campus administrators far different from "traditional" types of violent and property crime. Finally, the burgeoning use of intelligence-led or intelligence-based policing on many campuses has ushered in a new era which gives rise to new training, practices, and challenges.

Section I of the book examines the legal context of campus crime by presenting five chapters whose focus is on *Clery* and its state-level progenies. *Clery* and its state-level counterparts created important obligations for postsecondary institutions including annually reporting campus crime statistics and publicly reporting institutional processes designed to enhance campus security and provide assistance to campus crime victims. The chapters acquaint the reader with: (1) the genesis and evolution of *Clery;* (2) the current state of research concerning public awareness of *Clery* and its impact; (3) results and implications of the only national-level evaluation of the sexual assault reporting requirements of *Clery*, the *National Campus Sexual Assault Policy Study;* (4) how *Clery, Title IX of the Higher Education Amendments of 1972,* and case law have shaped the responses of postsecondary institutions to peer-related on-campus sexual assaults; and (5) a national-level comparative analysis of state-based *Clery*-style legislation.

Part II examines the social context of campus crime. The six chapters contained within Part II describe and explain the extent and nature of college student victimization by addressing salient topics of interest to researchers, campus administrators, and students and their parents. The chapters address topics such as whether college students suffer higher rates of victimization than nonstudents; the utility of routine activities and lifestyle theories for explaining college student victimization; how alcohol use (and abuse) are key correlates to college student victimization; the on-campus spatial distribution of frequently occurring offenses such as alcohol and drug violations, and vandalism; an overview of the extant literature on the sexual victimization of college women; and an analysis of the extent, nature, and impact of stalking and cyberstalking behaviors perpetrated against and by college students.

Section III of the book focuses on the security context of campus crime and consists of four chapters. Two of these chapters focus on the evolution, organization, and practices of campus law enforcement agencies, while one chapter addresses the challenges faced by campus law enforcement in enforcing alcohol laws. The final chapter in the section examines the challenges posed to campus security and campus law enforcement by high-tech crimes and offers suggestions for how postsecondary institutions can address new forms of illegal behavior involving the Internet, information systems, and technology.

Although we added new topics to and updated others for this edition, we remain committed to providing as timely a compilation of topics as possible to an audience of students, parents, academicians, practitioners, service providers, and postsecondary administrators. In organizing the chapters, our goal was to bring together authors who could provide a current picture and a critical analysis of issues concerning the legal, social, and policy contexts of campus crime and security. We believe the chapters found in this volume offer critical analyses and insightful discussion, raise relevant policy questions, and provide plausible explanations for and responses to campus crime and security, a social problem that continues to affect students, their parents, and postsecondary institutions on a daily basis throughout the year

Bonnie S. Fisher
John J. Sloan, III
August 1, 2012

ACKNOWLEDGMENTS

We again thank our editor, Michael Payne Thomas, for his guidance and patience with us in putting together this third edition. We are also grateful to each of our contributors, both returning and new, for producing high-quality chapters and adhering to our deadlines with not only professionalism but also a sense of humor. Their enthusiasm for this volume and dedicated efforts in producing their chapters give us hope that future researchers can better inform the development and implementation of effective proactive and preventive responses to campus crime.

John thanks Tavis for her enduring support and his colleagues at UAB, both past and present, for their willingness to serve as sounding boards and informal reviewers. I also want to thank Frank Cullen for serving as a superb role model, and Bonnie Fisher for her wonderful friendship and fabulous collaboration over the years. It has been an honor to know them both.

Bonnie thanks Nick for encouraging her to follow her passion for engaging in college student victimization and prevention research. She thanks her daughters, Olivia and Camille, for their insights, for helping her understand how the world works from a teenager's perspective and for making her laugh aloud and think critically every day. She thanks her "campus victimization" colleagues for their insights and support throughout the years, especially her coauthors, Emily Clear, Ann Coker, Frank Cullen, Leah Daigle, Suzanne Swan, and Corrine Williams. Many thanks also to her undergraduate and graduate students for providing her ideas about and insights into *why* and *how* college student victimization occurs. Also, many thanks to John Sloan whose passion for conceptualizing ideas and eloquent writing has influenced her professional development over their 20-year collaboration.

CONTENTS

CAMPUS CRIME

Chapter 1

CAMPUS CRIME POLICY: LEGAL, SOCIAL, AND SECURITY CONTEXTS

BONNIE S. FISHER AND JOHN J. SLOAN, III

INTRODUCTION

In 1990, Congress passed and President George H.W. Bush signed into law the landmark *Student Right-to-Know and Campus Security Act of 1990* (20 U.S.C. 1092[f]). This legislation, for the first time in history, required postsecondary institutions to, among other mandates, annually report crimes known to campus police and other authorities. Subsequently this act was renamed the *Jeanne Clery Disclosure of Campus Security Policy and Campus Crime Statistics Act* (20 U.S.C. 1092[f]; henceforth *Clery*) in 1998, in remembrance of Jeanne Clery who was murdered by a fellow student while she slept in her dorm room at Lehigh University in 1986. The legislation has been amended multiple times and created additional requirements for postsecondary institutions since its initial passage. The 1990s also saw colleges and universities being held liable for "foreable" criminal victimizations occurring in dormitories or other on-campus locations, while state legislatures began passing their own *Clery*-type legislation. Since the early 1990s, colleges and universities not only professionalized their campus security and law enforcement agencies, but also began experimenting with new technologies such as crime mapping and hot spots analyses. Finally, social science researchers began systematically studying crime and security issues on postsecondary institutions. Their findings revealed startling realities about life in the "ivory tower" and underscored the importance of further investigation into the legal, social, and security issues that are at the nexus of understanding and effectively addressing campus crime and security.

These events form the backdrop of what we describe as the legal, social, and security contexts of campus crime and form the basis for campus administrators to develop, implement, and evaluate policy relating to campus crime. Importantly, a change in one of these three contexts often affects the others, thus making them inextricably linked. For example, research shows that a sizeable portion of college students, especially college women, experience criminal victimization while on campus (the social context). This fact, in part, became the rationale for passage of *Clery* to require postsecondary institutions to report their crime data and create prevention programs and procedures for dealing with victims (the security context). Another example is research that examines postsecondary institutional compliance with state and federal legislation relating to campus crime and security (the legal context). Thus, while one is certainly able to examine each context separately, being mindful of linkages among them and of their relationship to campus crime policy is equally important.

This chapter presents an updated overview of the legal, social, and security contexts of campus crime. Our two goals for the chapter are to give readers a broad-based overview of key issues we see related to each context and show readers important linkages among these contexts. By doing this, we introduce readers to the kinds of issues that are identified in the remaining chapters of the book.

We begin the chapter by updating the legal context of campus crime which includes activities occurring in both the judicial and legislative arenas. Here, we examine leading state court decisions since 2007 that have repeatedly held colleges and universities liable under civil law for criminal victimizations occurring on campus and examine the prominent legal theories used to justify holding schools liable. We then examine legislative developments relating to campus crime and security issues at the federal and state levels of government. Next, we examine the social context of campus crime which includes important social scientific studies of campus crime and security. Following this, we examine the security context of campus crime which includes examining administrative models for campus law enforcement agencies, issues relating to their development, and the increasingly important role that information technology security plays on college campuses. We conclude the chapter by presenting important linkages across the three contexts.

The Legal Context of Campus Crime

The legal context of campus involves activities arising from the judicial and the legislative branches of government. In the former instance, the courts have helped shape campus crime policy via their rulings in lawsuits filed by students (and/or by their parents) over on-campus victimizations. In the latter instance, legislation passed by the states and Congress also helps shape policy by imposing various mandates on postsecondary institutions relating to campus crime statistics, student disciplinary proceedings arising from on-campus victimizations, security plans, or crime prevention activities.

Since the late 1970s, state courts have been increasingly willing to hold colleges and universities liable for on-campus victimizations using several different legal theories involving the legal duties owed by schools to their students. In some instances, the courts have held that common-law based theories of negligence are sufficient to hold schools liable while in other cases, the courts have relied more on contract law (see Burling, 2003; Lake 2001). In the legislative arena, Congress continues to amend *Clery*, while the U.S. Department of Education has become more involved in enforcing *Clery* through various regulations it passed and sanctions levied on schools for failing to follow the law's mandates. Simultaneously, media reporting of campus victimizations, victims' testimony at Congressional hearings, and campus advocacy groups (which came to forefront during the late 1980s and early 1990s), continue to influence legislative responses to campus crime (Fisher, Hartman, Cullen, & Turner, 2002; Fisher, Sloan, Cullen, & Lu, 1998; Sloan & Fisher, 2011). To better understand these issues, below we review recent developments in the legislative and judicial arenas of campus crime and explore their policy implications.

The Judicial Arena: Institutional Liability

Student victims of campus crime and their parents have repeatedly sued postsecondary institutions for damages resulting from injuries received during the criminal incident. Smith (1995) indicates that these lawsuits first began appearing in the late 1970s, but that postsecondary institutions did not feel a significant impact from this litigation until the 1980s. By the end of the 1980s, according to Smith (1995), this type of litigation had become more frequent at least in part because plaintiffs were winning their lawsuits. By the 1990s and into the first decade of the new millennium, colleges and university responded to the threat of such lawsuits by changing institutional practices. Throughout the period, legal scholars argued over which of the principles courts were using in these cases were most appropriate.

THEORIES OF LIABILITY. Lawsuits arising from on-campus victimizations of students will typically claim the institution knew – or should have known – about conditions that were in place that would likely give rise to the incident, and failed to address them (Burling, 2003). Because of this failure, the student suffered physical injury and/or loss of property. In short, the claim being made is the college or university (or its representative(s)) had acted *negligently*.

To prevail in a case claiming negligence on the part of the institution, the plaintiff's attorney must prove four elements: (1) the university *owed the student a duty of care;* (2) the university *breached that duty;* (3) the *student suffered damages* (e.g., injury, death, property loss, etc.) and (4) the *breach caused the damage* (Yeo, 2002). The greatest obstacle facing student plaintiffs in these cases is with establishing the existence of a duty owed them by the postsecondary institution against whom the lawsuit is being filed. Importantly, determining whether the duty existed is a question of law and is thus decided by the judge – not the jury (Burling, 2003). For the trial to commence, the judge must first rule that, *as a matter of law,* the institution owed a duty to the student. Remaining questions, including a weighing of the evidence, become matters of fact for the jury to decide (Burling, 2003; Yeo, 2002). The issue that has generated a nontrivial amount of discussion among scholars of higher education law is the legal principle(s) courts have used to guide them when determining that a duty is owed by a postsecondary institution to the on-campus victim (Lake, 2001).

IN LOCO PARENTIS. Until the 1960s, all postsecondary schools in the U.S. operated under the legal doctrine of *in loco parentis* ("in the place of the parents") (Melear, 2002). As Swartz (2010) notes, this meant colleges and universities were free to create and enforce any rule or regulation that pertained to student conduct, especially those relating to students' social lives. *In loco parentis* resulted in the courts deferring to the institution in determining what was best for students in cases involving suspension, dismissal, or other sanction and limited judicial intervention since doing so ". . . could undermine school authority and impinge the student-university relationship" (Swartz, 2010, p. 109). Courts were, however, willing to impose a legal duty on colleges and universities ". . . to protect the morals and personal safety of their students" (Yeo, 2002, p. 79).

The turbulent 1960s eventually resulted in a dismantling of *in loco parentis* and the legal duties it had established beginning with a 1961 landmark decision by the Fifth U.S. Circuit Court of Appeals in the case *Dixon v. Alabama State Board of Education* (294 F.2d 150). In *Dixon,* the court ruled that college students were entitled to various due process rights when facing expulsion, including the right to notice of the hearing and the right to present evidence on their behalf. Over the course of the next two decades, state courts repeatedly ruled postsecondary institutions had a duty to *not* interfere with students' speech, behavior, etc. and to interfere would result in negative consequences for the institution. Some legal scholars (e.g., Bickel & Lake, 1999; Lake, 2001) describe this period as one in which courts decided that colleges and universities would assume a new legal role as "bystander" in the lives of students, such that no legal duty toward the student was legally assumed by the institution (Bickel & Lake, 1999; Lake, 2001; Yeo, 2002).

ESTABLISHING A DIFFERENT STANDARD. Beginning in the 1980s, decisions by various state courts established a new principle that under certain, specific conditions, colleges and universities had an "affirmative duty" to ensure students' safety (Burling, 2003; Lake, 2001; Swartz, 2010; Yeo, 2002). Some held that the duty arose on the basis of a "landlord-tenant" or "landlord-invitee" relationship that existed between institution and student. In these decisions, the courts ruled that as "landlords" colleges and universities had a duty to protect students from criminal activity that was "foreseeable" including offenses such as rape, robbery, and assault occurring in campus housing. According to Burling (2003, pp. 5–6), *foreseeability* involves a twofold test: was the conduct that injured the plaintiff within the range of possibilities *knowable* to the institution and do the facts show the institution knew (or should have known) about the risks to which the plaintiff was exposed? If the judge decides the conditions leading to the injury were foreseeable, the jury then decides if the institution knew (or should have known) about the conditions causing the plaintiff's injuries and awards damages to the plaintiff.

A second line of reasoning in these decisions was based on the theory that postsecondary institutions assumed a legal duty for students' safety because they had entered into a *special relationship* with students (*Furek v. University of Delaware*, 594 A 2d 506 as cited by Burling, 2003, p. 7). Courts adopting this reasoning held colleges and universities liable for failing to (1) educate students about dangerous behavior (e.g., hazing; alcohol use); (2) warn students about unsafe conditions on or near the campus (e.g., reports of crimes occurring in a particular dormitory); and (3) protect students from injuries arising from those conditions (Burling, 2003; Swartz, 2010; Yeo, 2002).

Finally, state courts also adopted a third line of reasoning in these cases which held that liability flowed from an expressed or implied *contract* between the school and the plaintiff (Burling, 2003; Lake, 2001). According to this logic, if a college or university provided housing to students, it could be liable for a lack of security under an implied contract or warranty of hospitability, grounded in the housing contract signed by both parties. Postsecondary institutions producing brochures or pamphlets detailing the school's security may form an implied contract with students to provide specific types of security services to them, such as an attendant present in a dormitory who is responsible for monitoring visitors. If the measures are either not provided or incorrectly implemented and a criminal victimization occurs, a school may then be held liable for damages suffered by the plaintiff as a result of breach of contract.

For more than 30 years, state courts have used various legal principles to hold colleges and universities liable for on-campus criminal victimizations. The decisions all indicate that *under certain circumstances* postsecondary institutions have a legal duty to protect students from on-campus victimizations, and failure to fulfill that duty *may* lead to liability for damages arising from the victimization. However, as Burling (2003) and others (Lake, 2001) have noted, no clearly established legal principle has consistently been used by courts in these cases. Rather, as one moves from state to state, one finds different courts using differing logic in their decisions. Indeed, one of the most unsettled aspects of this area of postsecondary civil liability for on-campus victimizations is the lack of a clearly articulated duty that schools may have to students. Depending on the court, the facts in the case, and the particular judge involved, different principles may be applied or the judge may simply decide the school owes no duty whatever to students. As Burling (2003, p. 21) argued, state court decisions determining when and under what circumstances a postsecondary institution will be held liable for on-campus victimizations constitute "a maze of conflicting and inconsistent analysis" and that ". . . what is worse, there is no clear line of cases leading to a coherent analysis."

In summary, state courts continue to wrestle with the problem of what legal duties are owed by colleges and universities to their students who suffer criminal victimizations. No clearly demarcated line of reasoning exists when reviewing decisions in this area other than *in loco parentis* is no longer viable as a guiding principle. Theories of negligence and those arising from contract law have been relied upon by judges, while other judges are just as willing to rule that no duty exists between school and student. Thus, no general precedent exists and such precedent is unlikely to arise until the federal courts become involved and clarify what specific duty or duties are owed by postsecondary institutions to students who suffer criminal victimizations while on campus.

The Legislative Arena: Campus Crime and Security Acts

The other component of the legal context of campus crime involves state legislatures and Congress which develop, debate, and pass legislation intended to address issues relating to campus crime/security. Some of these statutes, such as *Clery*, are considered by proponents as "ground breaking" while others are little more than examples of symbolic politics (Edelman 1964, 1977, 1988) where laws passed to address a problem have little chance of substantive impact. Finally, some of these statutes supplement court rulings on postsecondary institutional liability while others may impose new rules/regulations on schools relating to campus crime and security.

CLERY AND ITS PROGENIES. According to supporters, *Clery* and its progenies at the state level of government (Burke & Sloan, 2013) share common goal: increase student and parental awareness about, and discussion of, crime on campus (Carter & Bath, 2007; Kiss, 2013; Sloan & Fisher, 2011). As Part I of this volume reveals, *Clery* requires all Title IV institutions to annually gather and disseminate information to the public on campus crime and security. The legislative intent behind the *Clery* and its state-level progenies was to force postsecondary administrators to take appropriate steps (ranging from increased police patrols to Internet-based crime incident reporting systems) to lower the risk of criminal victimization happening on campus and providing effective services to victims and raise awareness among members of the public about the problem of campus crime.

During its nearly 25 year existence, *Clery* greatly expanded the responsibilities of postsecondary institutions in addressing crime and security on campus. From an initial focus on preparing and annually distributing a general security report that contained crime statistics and security policies *Clery* evolved — via amendments and changes in federal regulations — into a complex and far more expansive piece of legislation with increasingly detailed reporting, programming, and procedural requirements (Security on Campus, 2012; Sloan & Fisher, 2011). In fact, in response to concerns expressed by postsecondary officials over possible unintentional noncompliance due to the complexity of *Clery's* reporting requirements, several years ago the U.S. Department of Justice began sponsoring training around the country for campus officials responsible for completing *Clery* reporting requirements. Additionally, the U.S. Department of Education also released *The Handbook for Campus Safety and Security Reporting* (hereafter, the *Handbook*) in 2005, updated it in 2008, and revised it further in 2011. The *Handbook* provides step-by-step instructions to campus officials for completing *Clery's* reporting requirements and includes multiple examples and illustrations to facilitate accurate, complete, and timely reporting (United States Department of Education, 2011).

Clery, its amendments, and related legislation such as the *Higher Education Opportunity Act of 2008* (P.L. 110-315), as well as amendments or revisions to other, related legislation such as the *Family Educational Rights and Privacy Act* (20 U.S.C. § 1232g; 34 CFR Part 99) have enhanced Congressional efforts to require postsecondary institutions to "come clean" with their crime statistics and security policies. *Clery* has evolved to the point where it now requires extremely detailed reporting from schools who are also required to report their crime data each fall to the U.S. Department of Education using a Web-based data-entry portal. Schools must also identify mechanism(s) they use to send "timely warnings" to the campus community of ongoing threats to public health and safety. For schools with campus police or security departments, *Clery* now requires them to keep and make available a daily crime log of reported incidents occurring on campus. Other *Clery* requirements include schools outlining in their annual security reports, specific victims' rights in student disciplinary hearings arising from on-campus rapes or sexual assaults. Included here is the school developing a *Program Participation Agreement* (PPA) that requires disclosure of the results of disciplinary proceedings to victims of violence or nonforcible sex offenses, as well as removing results of campus disciplinary proceedings from protections afforded students by the *Family Educational Rights and Privacy Act* (FERPA). Schools also are allowed to disclose information concerning registered sex offenders enrolled as students or working on the campus without prior written or other consent from the student.

CRITIQUES OF *CLERY*. Student advocacy and campus watchdog groups have hailed legislative efforts to make campuses safer. However, academicians interested in campus crime and safety issues have identified inherent limitations to *Clery* and its mandates. Research has provided ample empirical evidence which questions the usefulness of *Clery* in addressing campus crime.

Several researchers, some using results of national-level studies, have questioned the ability of *Clery* statistics to provide valid and reliable information about the true occurrence of crime on college campuses. The reason for this is because *Clery* does not require postsecondary institutions to compile and report statistics on commonly occurring offenses such as theft, simple assault, and stalking. Fisher et al. (1998), based on results of the first ever national-level study of student victimization, reported that rates of student victimization involving theft and vandalism were much higher than were rates of rape/sexual assault, robbery, and aggravated assault. Hart (2003, 2013), using data collected by the *National Crime Victimization Survey* showed that simple assaults were the most frequently occurring type of violent crime committed against college students, with rates much higher than those of rape/sexual assault, robbery, and aggravated assault. Further, results from the *National College Women Sexual Victimization Study* (NCWSV; see Fisher, Cullen, & Turner, 2000) show that about 13 percent of college women experienced a stalking victimization during a typical academic year. Yet, statistics on the crimes that touch large portions of college and university students are not required by *Clery* to be included in annual security reports prepared by postsecondary institutions (Fisher et al., 2000). As a result, interested parties are receiving, at best, incomplete information that does not include the actual types of crimes most likely to touch a student's daily life.

Aside from omitting various crimes, for a crime to be included in the annual security reports victims must first report the offense to campus officials or law enforcement. Considering the types of crime that *Clery* mandates must be included in annual crime reports, a sizeable body of victimization research repeatedly shows substantial numbers of college students *do not* report their victimizations to anyone for a variety of reasons (Belknap & Erez, 2013; Fisher et al., 2000; Shafer, 2007). As a result, such incidents are not included in reported campus crime statistics which again leads to a distorted picture.

To illustrate the magnitude of this issue, using data collected from a national-level study of college student victimization, Sloan, Fisher, and Cullen (1997) reported that 75 percent of the on-campus burglaries during the 1994–

1995 academic year went unreported to either campus police or other campus officials. Hart (2003) reported that 1995–2000 NCVS data reveal 47 percent of all robberies and 52 percent of all aggravated assaults involving college students went unreported to police. Using data collected in the NCWSV, Fisher et al. (2000) showed that 95 percent of rapes involving college students were not reported to the police, an estimate comparable to the 1995–2000 NCVS's estimate of 86 percent of rape/sexual assault incidents not being reported to police. The important point here is that publicly reported postsecondary crime statistics (mandated by *Clery*) significantly underreport the true amount of campus crime.

Researchers such as Gregory and Janosik (2013) have questioned whether students and parents, specifically targeted by *Clery,* are even *aware* of the legislation. Should this be true, it is especially important because *Clery* supporters have claimed students and their parents use the information in the mandated annual reports to decide which school to attend. Research has also shown that even those who work closely with student victims have reservations that students actually read the annual security reports (Gregory & Janosik, 2013). Collectively, results of these and other studies suggest that more work needs to be done to make all interested parties, including campus personnel, aware of the availability of (and the limitations to) campus crime information.

There remain significant flaws and limitations with current legislation mandating postsecondary institutions to "come clean" with their crime statistics and to report what they are doing to address campus crime. These problems seriously hamper the potential impact of federal and state legislation on campus crime and security. There is, however, some good news: interest and activism by campus advocates, watchdogs groups, and researchers with an interest in campus crime and student victimization is not waning, but growing. Their sustained interest, as evident by the chapters in Part I of this volume, has led to several evidence-based recommendations to address the noted limitations and weaknesses of *Clery* and state-level *Clery*-style legislation. Lawsuits filed by campus crime victims or their parents continue and have resulted in advances in the development of liability law for postsecondary institutions. These efforts helped focus attention on and created the impetus for further analysis of issues concerning the legal context of campus crime and the development of recommendations for change and enhancement of campus security.

The Social Context of Campus Crime

Violence, vice, and victimization on college and university campuses have been a part of their landscape since the first colleges were created in America during the seventeenth century (Sloan & Fisher, 2011). Similar to the evolution of the legal context, understanding the social context of campus crime has developed (and continues to develop) into providing much needed information into campus crime. Campus crime as a field of both scientific study and practice of prevention and interventions is evolving, especially as the enrollment in postsecondary institutions increases annually.

For our purposes, the social context of campus crime has two components. The first component is characterized by the social scientific research that describes and explains the scope of college student victimization and why these students and their property are victimized. The second component is prevention and interventions aimed at reducing the incidence of campus crime and published evaluations of the effectiveness of countless programs and designed to address campus crime. Here, we present a brief overview of the evolution of the current state of the social context of campus crime.

The Evolution of Interest in Student Victimization

Academic interest in college student victimization was initially sparked by two pioneering studies. Early case studies by Kirkpatrick and Kanin (1957) and Kanin (1967, 1970, 1977) into sexual aggression by college men against college women at a single campus was among the first empirical analyses of campus crime. Koss, Gidycz, and Wisnieski's (1987) national-level study of the sexual victimization experiences of female college students in the early 1980s remains the most widely cited study of campus crime. Their findings revealed that not only had a substantial proportion of college women been sexually victimized since the age of 14 but many had experienced "hidden" rapes – those committed by persons known to the victim (e.g., boyfriends, dates, and acquaintances). Until Koss and colleagues' study, many thought that strangers were the most likely perpetrators. Their use of behaviorally specific questions to estimate the prevalence and incidence of different forms of sexual victimization (e.g., rape, sexual coercion) called into question the validity and reliability of past survey instruments. Koss and colleagues' findings and methods influenced subsequent generations of campus crime researchers, especially those interested in sexual victimization, not to mention responses by campus administrators and policy makers to the problem of the sexual victimization of college women.

It was not until the 1990s, influenced by several factors – the momentum of the feminist movement, rape-law reforms, successful lawsuits filed against colleges and universities, student activism, and federal crime reporting mandates – academics from different disciplines began conducting large-scale and significant research on the victimization experiences of college and university students. During the mid-1990s, the U.S. Department of Justice funded three national-level studies that examined general student victimization patterns, sexual victimization, and stalking among college women, and nonfatal violence, including rape and sexual assault, against college women (Fisher et al., 1998; Fisher et al., 2000). Among the contributions of these studies to the social context of campus crime was their adoption and testing of opportunity theories, particularly lifestyle-exposure and routine activities, to explain and predict college student victimization (Fisher et al., 1998).

These studies sparked interested into identifying predictors or correlates of college student victimization. Published results from numerous case studies and studies using small samples of college campuses also appeared during the 1990s and focused on estimating the extent of student victimization and further testing opportunity theories to explain these experiences (Mustaine & Tewksbury, 2013). It is these smaller scales studies that have defined much of the campus crime field of study rather than the national scale studies.

The Bureau of Justice Statistics was also involved in helping define the social context of campus crime. During the 1990s, the *National Crime Victimization Survey* (NCVS), one of two official sources of national-level data on crime in the U.S., added a question to its main survey that asked respondents whether they were a college student for the express purpose of developing average annual victimization rates for college students compared to nonstudents of similar ages (Hart, 2013).

Criminologists were not the only parties interested in the social context of campus crime. During the 1990s, public health researchers, particularly Henry Wechsler and his colleagues at Harvard University, advanced the study of college student victimization by examining the relationship between substance abuse – alcohol and illegal drugs – and victimization, and reported a positive association between binge drinking and victimization (Dowdall, 2013). Public health researchers heavily influenced the perception that college student victimization is not only a criminal justice and personal safety issue but also involves psychological harm and physical injuries in need of medical responses and interventions. These two paradigms – criminal justice and public health – are evident in the prevention and intervention programs implemented on campuses nationally as well as in campus police responses (Allen & Jacques, 2013).

Interest in college student victimization has not waned with the arrival of the new millennium. Researchers continue to publish numerous studies examining the scope and predictors of a range of types of student victimization, including violence, theft, stalking, intimate partner violence, identity theft, and computer crimes (see Part II of this volume for representative scholarship; also see McQuade, 2013). Researchers' interest in the social context of campus crime more recently has extended to different types of cybervictimization – harassment, stalking, and sexting – among college students (Reyns,

Burek, Henson, & Fisher, 2011).

Sexual assault – physically forced, drug facilitated, and incapacitated rape – has been at the forefront of researchers' attention since Kanin's first studies (Kilpatrick, Resnick, Ruggiero, Conoscenti, & McCauley, 2007; Krebs, Lindquist, Warner, Fisher, & Martin, 2007). Interest in sexual assault will likely to continue for two primary reasons. First, recent studies document the grim reality that a substantial proportion of the college women experience not only sexual victimization but also are repeatedly victimized during their college tenure (Fisher, Daigle, & Cullen, 2010). Second, in April 2011, the Office for Civil Rights in the Department of Education issued a *Dear Colleague Letter* to all colleges and universities detailing their obligations under *Title IX* regarding sexual violence, which includes taking prompt and effective steps to end the violence, preventing its recurrence, addressing its impact, and using the preponderance of evidence in its grievance procedure (Fisher et al., 2013).

Understanding the social context of campus crime continues to evolve due to multidisciplinary researchers' efforts, the Department of Education's actions concerning the implantation and evaluation of the *Clery Act* and *Title IX*, and administrators' responses to both. What appears unchanged is that violence, vice, and victimization on college and university campuses will remain part of their landscape. Reducing its occurrence (as well as the associated liability for schools) also will continue to characterize postsecondary administrators' efforts.

Classifying the Campus Crime Research

We divide published campus crime research into three categories: (1) studies that *describe the extent and nature of student victimization,* (2) studies that *explain the correlates and predictors of victimization* among students, and (3) studies that *evaluate the effectiveness of responses to campus crime, including education or prevention programs.* Each category has produced a substantial body of research, which, in turn, has begun informing campus-level crime prevention, education, and policing programs and practices.

DESCRIPTIVE STUDIES. Descriptive studies *describe* the amount and type of student victimization and the nature of their experiences. These studies address fundamental issues such as developing improved measures of victimization, as well as exploring how much of which types of victimization happened among members of the campus community and where these victimizations occur. While these studies are important because they produce estimates (hopefully ones that are valid and reliable) of the extent and nature of crime against students, because they are descriptive, they cannot establish the direction and magnitude of relationship between factors, say lifestyle or routine activities and student victimization.

EXPLANATORY STUDIES. Explanatory studies use existing theory to guide *empirical tests of hypotheses about how and why student victimization* occurs. Here, researchers have modeled the dynamics of student victimization and presented a deeper understanding of how and why students are at risk of experiencing different types of victimization using theories such as lifestyle and routine activities or self control, and advanced quantitative statistical techniques (Dowdall, 2013; Mustaine & Tewksbury, 2013; Stewart & Fisher, 2013). These studies not only have identified individual- and campus-level factors associated with different types of victimization, but present statistical models that predict students' risk of experiencing victimization. Coupled with these empirical studies of individuals are studies examining "hot spots" of crime on campus; that is, identifying specific places on campus where most crime occurs and explaining these spatial patterns (Robinson & Roh, 2013). Collectively, findings from these studies primarily have defined the focus of study of campus crime, but their findings have also established the need for further investigation into how and why college students and their property are victimized.

EVALUATION STUDIES. Evaluation studies assess program processes or program outcomes (or both) of policies designed to reduce victimization, increase campus safety, or reduce levels of fear of victimization. Studies of this type are infrequently published in academic journals, partly because few evaluations of campus programs or policies have occurred (see Vladutiu, Martin, & Macy, 2011). Ironically, there are also only a handful of published evaluations of campus rape prevention programs even though Congress allocated monies for the Office of Violence against Women to annually fund grants to establish education and prevention programs and more than 6,500 Title IV postsecondary institutions have implemented rape prevention programs as mandated by the *Clery Act*. These evaluations of campus rape prevention are limited in generalizability because they are largely characterized by a single site with a small convenience sample, and rarely use a before-or-after research design or a comparison group (Lonsway et al., 2009).

In the late 1990s, Congress attempted to remedy this situation by commissioning a national-level evaluation, the *National Campus Sexual Assault Policy Study* (Karjane, Fisher, & Cullen, 2002, 2005), to assess how America's postsecondary institutions have responded to reports of sexual assaults. The study also evaluated institutional compliance with *Clery* mandates directed at sexual assault (Fisher et al., 2013).

In April of 2011, Vice President Biden renewed awareness and promotion of effective rape prevention efforts when he outlined new federal guidelines to combat rape on campus, including bystander intervention programs. These programs include discussions about how students can actively prevent a crime from happening when they observe a risky situation, such as an intoxicated person being led to a secluded room at a party. Bystander programs are aimed at teaching students skills about how to intervene successfully and safely and how to respond to the situations that could lead to violence, including rape. Recently, evaluations of these types of programs have been published, including work by Barnyard, Moynihan, and Plante (2007) and Coker et al. (2011) and report promising results in increasing students' bystander behaviors. Programs are currently being evaluated to determine whether such behaviors reduce the risk of student victimization.

Examples of each study type – descriptive, explanatory, and evaluation – appear in Part II of this volume, and some of the chapters represent more than one type of study. Regardless of study type, each chapter contributes to the evolving body of social scientific research on campus crime. The accumulated body of knowledge represented in these chapters has produced a better understanding of the correlates of, and causal mechanisms underlying, student victimization and is informing prevention efforts on campus. More research informed by current campus policies and practices and their evaluation and translation research (translating research into practical measures) are needed so that the cost of being a college student does not include being a target for violence, vice, and victimization and for a substantial number of students, being a repeat victim.

Unfortunately, much of this cost remains hidden from college administrators and is not addressed by *Clery's* mandates. Another part of the social context is that victims, especially those sexually victimized, rarely report their experience to law enforcement or seek help. These victims' secrets mean that few receive services and campus officials have little opportunity to respond. Unfortunately, the costs experienced by these students remain hidden, but they must be anticipated in light of the findings presented in the social context section. Students need to be aware and reminded of on campus prevention programs and legal and medical services tailored to victims' needs. Hopefully both students' use of prevention and services will help to reduce their hidden costs of attending college.

The Security Context of Campus Crime

As discussed above, postsecondary institutions face potential liability over foreseeable victimizations resulting from security lapses not addressed in a timely manner. Liability issues relate directly to the third context of campus crime: campus security.

As shown in Figure 1.1, campus security specifically encompasses three related sets of activities: those relating to physical security (e.g., controlling access to buildings), those relating to law enforcement activities, and those relating to information technology security (such as infrastructure protection).

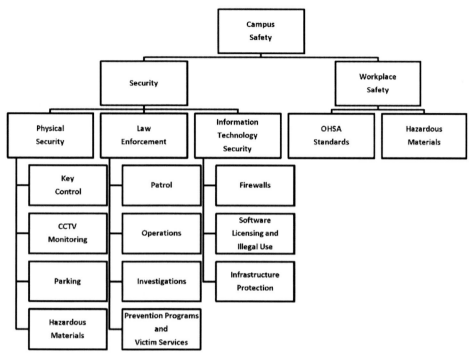

Figure 1.1. The multifaceted nature of campus safety.

Part III of this volume presents chapters addressing campus policing and information system security, with reference made to physical security.

As per requirements of *Clery,* postsecondary institutions must annually report not only campus crime statistics, but also their security policies and the power and authority of campus security/police departments. *Clery* has thus put an even greater onus on colleges and universities to develop modern security/law enforcement departments who can adequately protect and respond to the security needs of the campus community.

The Professionalization of Campus Security

The past 20 or so years has seen a key development in the context of campus security: the *professionalization* of individuals and departments charged with the sometimes daunting task of reducing opportunities for on-campus victimization, responding to calls for assistance, and providing services to victims. This professionalization has touched almost all aspects of campus security and has resulted in significant changes in, and upgrades to, security policies.

When one looks at the history of campus security, one finds that for most of the past century, universities primarily geared security toward protecting property – preventing and responding to break-ins, addressing vandalism, or insuring doors were locked. As a result, until very recently, an organized police presence on college campuses was an unknown. Rather, "night watchmen" (so-called because women did not occupy such roles) would "patrol" campus in search of physical plant problems, violations of student codes of conduct, etc. and address the problems discovered.

During the early 1970s, changes occurred when college and university administrators realized that the campus unrest of the late 1960s and other issues would likely result in the presence of armed, local police officers on their campuses if they did not take action to deal with the problems confronting them. The action they took was to create a new department on the campus, the campus police department.

Campus administrators put these early departments in the charge of an experienced police officer from a municipal department, who usually occupied an upper rank in that department (e.g., precinct commander or deputy chief). Campus administrators gave these individuals the responsibility of designing, staffing, and overseeing an on-campus operation whose mission not only was to protect property and person, but to enforce the law. Made possible by state-level enabling legislation, campus police departments with sworn officers soon became common.

During the 1980s, these operations sought legitimacy from their municipal police colleagues by largely "copying" existing organizational, tactical, and operational components of city agencies. Campus agencies also sought legitimacy by requiring new recruits to complete POST (Peace Officer Standards Training) training offered at the same academies attended by municipal police recruits. Beginning in the 1990s and moving into today, campus police departments adopted new organizational models that revolve around problem solving, establishing partnerships with stakeholders in the campus community, adopting new tactics, and making greater use of technology (Paoline & Sloan, 2003).

As the chapters by Bromley (2013) and Paoline and Sloan (2013) report, recent years have seen campus agencies adopt an organizational model known as *Community-Oriented Policing* (or COP) (Colorado Regional Policing Institute, n.d.). This model stresses community partnerships and problem solving, and police in a variety of activities designed to enhance police/community relations, empower officers, and prevent crime (e.g., Cordner, 1996, 1997). Campus police officers have entered an era in which partnerships with students, faculty, and staff members; interacting with people on campus; engaging in foot and bicycle patrol; and participating in programs such as "campus watch," are stressed. Through these tactics, campus police departments are partnering with members of the campus community to identify and eliminate common problems.

Additionally, campus police agencies, like their municipal counterparts, have begun experimenting with greater use of information technology including crime mapping, geographic information systems (GIS) and global positioning systems (GPS), statistical analyses of crime patterns on campus (commonly referred to as COMPSTAT or "compare statistics" (Dabney, 2010), "hot spots" analyses (Robinson & Roh, 2013), and to engage in "intelligence led" policing (Ratcliffe, 2003). These strategies seek to use large amounts of information routinely collected by campus officers to make departments more efficient and effective at addressing problems relating to crime, fear of victimization, and related issues on campus.

A growing concern for campus law enforcement and security personnel involves information security. We now discuss this increasingly important aspect of campus security.

Information Security and Infrastructure Protection

The past decade has seen an explosion of new technology relating to the storage, retrieval, and compilation of information. Computers and other devices, including tablets, iPads, and cellular telephones, perceived as the stuff of science fiction as recently as 25 years ago, are commonplace on college campuses. Additionally, campus-based computer networks that link hundreds (if not thousands) of personal computers are standard. Students "surf the 'net" to conduct research while faculty use computers not only for their research, but also for student record keeping. Many faculty members increasingly find themselves teaching "online" courses which also present challenges relating to information security.

Such fundamental changes in gathering, using, and securing information have created enormous problems for colleges and universities. Because of computer-based networks, it is now possible for intruders ("hackers") to access personally identifiable information (including social security numbers) of students and employees stored in large-scale databases. Students can "pirate" copyrighted materials such as recordings, videos, and software from various sites on the Internet or share these copyrighted materials with one another via file sharing software. Students also have the ability to "cyber-stalk" peers and send obscene or threatening email messages to them and to faculty members. Unscrupulous individuals send "junk" email ("spam") to students and employees that may contain hidden programs (malware) designed to "take control" of their computers. Thus, the tremendous advances in communication and information retrieval that have come via the Internet and through personal computers and other digital devices have created both positive results, such as the ability for a graduate student to conduct a literature review in a topical area in a few minutes or a faculty member to meet in real time online with a colleague thousands of miles away, as well as tremendous opportunities for illicit, deviant, and outright illegal behavior. College and university administrators thus face significant challenges in the realm of information security.

Increasingly, colleges and universities must be both *reactive* and *proactive* in their information security efforts. They must identify potential threats and quickly react to actual attacks on, or breaches of, information technology infrastructures, while simultaneously develop strategies designed to keep "one step ahead" of those seeking to misuse the technology, including students, faculty members, and staff (not to mention outsiders). The stakes are enormous by any measure.

Consider the following scenario: A hacker penetrates firewalls at State University which allows her to gain access to all of the student records stored in the Registrar's database. This individual now has access to thousands of social security numbers and he or she can use them for a variety of illegal purposes. The implications of such an event are overwhelming; such an event also raises the specter of institutional liability issues.

Additionally, there are crossover implications of the misuse of technology that directly involve campus law enforcement. For example, imagine that a student uses a university-issued computer to "capture" and store social security numbers of other students by hacking into university databases. Campus law enforcement is informed of this situation and must now respond, which means the department must have appropriate expertise in computer forensics to press charges against the student and testify in court to obtain a conviction. Information security must address these and other scenarios that McQuade (2013) and others (Meier, 2005) have described in some detail.

In summary, the security context of campus crime not only involves physical security and law enforcement, it also involves "digital security." Not only must colleges and universities address traditional kinds of security issues, such as preventing burglaries and thefts, but must also address the abuse of information technology for monetary gain or other reasons. While campus law enforcement agencies seek greater connections with the campus community, information security professionals wrestle with new and increasingly dangerous threats by "cyber criminals" to computer networks and electronic databases housed on university campuses. Both campus law enforcement and security professionals must develop reactive responses and proactive strategies to the challenges they face. No longer is campus security solely a matter of insuring that doors to research laboratories are locked. Increasingly, campus security involves not only the protection of property and person, but the protection of information as well.

Campus Crime Policy:
Linking the Legal, Social, and Security Contexts

This chapter explored the legal, social, and security contexts of campus crime. It presented to readers a broad overview of the evolution of the campus crime field over the past 20 or so years and where it may be headed. Included in this overview were glimpses into each of the contexts.

As we observed earlier, there are important linkages across the three contexts: *Clery* mandates the annual reporting of campus crime statistics, but social science research shows that common forms of student victimization, theft, stalking, and simple assault, are not included in the *Clery* reporting requirements. Research into victimization of college students had led to the development of new institutional protocols for providing law enforcement and related services to victims, especially victims of sexual assault. Enabling legislation at the state level of government allows colleges and universities to create campus police agencies, staffed by sworn officers with wide ranging arrest powers. These officials also have the responsibility for complying with the reporting requirements of *Clery* and state-level mandates.

Throughout this and the remaining chapters in this volume, there is an implicit acknowledgement of the fact there is an circular relationship between the legal, social, and security contexts of campus crime and campus crime policy: each context influences policy and policy influences each context. This is true whether the policy context is national, state, or that found on a single campus. Federal or state legislation requires colleges and universities to develop policies to address crime victimization; successful lawsuits filed by students or their parents result in new policies concerning security on the campus; threats to the campus information technology infrastructure lead to new policies concerning student, staff, or faculty member access to key databases.

Policy, in short, is the overarching concept that not only links the individual contexts – legal, social, security – of campus crime examined in this volume, but which also serves as an instrument of change. Without policy development, changes, and evaluations, the contributions made by researchers, campus administrators, law enforcement and security personnel, and student advocates concerned about campus crime would count little toward making campuses safer. Thankfully, that has not been the case, and the policy aspects of campus crime continue to remain "front and center" among each of these interested parties.

REFERENCES

Allen, A., & Jacques, S. (2013). Policing alcohol-related crime among college students. In B. S. Fisher & J. J. Sloan (Eds.), *Campus crime: Legal, social, and policy perspectives* (3rd ed.). Springfield, IL: Charles C Thomas.

Banyard, V. L., Moynihan, M. M., & Plante, E. G. (2007). Sexual violence prevention through bystander education: An experimental evaluation. *Journal of Community Psychology, 35,* 463–481.

Belknap, J., & Erez, E. (2013). The acquaintance and date rape, sexual harassment, and intimate partner abuse of college women. In B. S. Fisher & J. J. Sloan (Eds.), *Campus crime: Legal, social, and policy perspectives* (3rd ed.). Springfield, IL: Charles C Thomas.

Bickel, R., & Lake, P. (1999). *The rights and responsibilities of the modern university: Who assumes the risks of college life?* Charlotte, NC: Carolina Academic Press.

Bromley, M. (2013). The evolution of campus policing: An update to different models for different eras. In B. S. Fisher & J. J. Sloan (Eds.), *Campus crime: Legal, social, and policy perspectives* (3rd ed.). Springfield, IL: Charles C Thomas.

Burke, J., & Sloan, J. (2013). State-level Clery Act initiatives: Symbolic politics or substantive policy? In B. S. Fisher & J. J. Sloan (Eds.), *Campus crime: Legal, social, and policy perspectives* (3rd ed.). Springfield, IL: Charles C Thomas.

Burling, P. (2003). *Crime on campus: Analyzing and managing the increasing risk of institutional liability* (2nd ed.). Washington DC: National Association of College and University Attorneys.

Carter, S., & Bath, C. (2007). The evolution and components of the *Jeanne Clery Act:* Implications for higher education. In B. S. Fisher & J. J. Sloan (Eds.), *Campus crime: Legal, social, and policy perspectives* (2nd ed.) (pp. 27–44). Springfield, IL: Charles C Thomas.

Coker, A. L., Cook-Craig, P. G., Williams, C. M., Fisher, B. S., Clear, E. R., Garcia, L. S., & Hegge, L. M. (2011). Evaluation of Green Dot: An active bystander intervention to reduce sexual violence on college campuses. *Violence Against Women, 17,* 777–796.

Colorado Regional Policing Institute. (n.d.). The key elements of Community-Oriented Policing. Retrieved from http://dcj.state.co.us/crcpi/KeyElements.html.

Cordner, G. (1996). *Principles and elements of community policing.* Washington, DC: National Institute of Justice.

Cordner, G. (1997). Community policing: Elements and effects. In R. Dunham & G. Alpert (Eds.), *Critical issues in policing: Contemporary readings* (pp. 432–449). Prospect Heights, IL: Waveland Press.

Dabney, D. (2010). Observations regarding key operational realities in a *Compstat* model of policing. *Justice Quarterly, 27,* 28–51.

Dowdall, G. (2013). The role of alcohol abuse in college student victimization. In B. S. Fisher & J. J. Sloan (Eds.), *Campus crime: Legal, social, and policy perspectives* (3rd ed.). Springfield, IL: Charles C Thomas.

Edelman, M. (1964). *The symbolic uses of politics.* Urbana, IL: University of Illinois Press.

Edelman, M. (1977). *Political language: Words that succeed and policies that fail.* Chicago: Academic Press.

Edelman, M. (1988). *Constructing the political spectacle.* Chicago: University of Chicago Press.

Fisher, B., Hartman, J., Cullen, F., & Turner, M. (2002). Making campuses safer for students: The *Clery Act* as a Symbolic Legal Reform. *Stetson Law Review, XXXII,* 61–89.

Fisher, B., Karjane, H., Cullen, F., Santana, S., Blevins, K., & Daigle, L. (2013). Reporting sexual assault and the *Clery Act:* Situating findings from the *National Campus Sexual Assault Policy Study* within college women's experiences. In B. S. Fisher & J. J. Sloan (Eds.), *Campus crime: Legal, social, and policy perspectives* (3rd ed.). Springfield, IL: Charles C Thomas.

Fisher, B., Cullen, F., & Turner, M. (2000). *Sexual victimization of college women.* Washington, DC: Bureau of Justice Statistics.

Fisher, B. S., Daigle L. E., & Cullen, F. T. (2010). *Unsafe in the ivory tower: The sexual victimization of college women.* Thousand Oaks, CA: Sage.

Fisher, B., Sloan, J., Cullen, F., & Lu, C. (1998). Crime in the ivory tower: The level and sources of student victimization. *Criminology, 36,* 671–710.

Gregory, D., & Janosik, S. (2013). The research on the *Clery Act* and crime reporting: Its impact on the literature and administrative practice in higher education. In B. S. Fisher & J. J. Sloan (Eds.), *Campus crime: Legal, social, and policy perspectives* (3rd ed.). Springfield, IL: Charles C Thomas.

Hart, T. (2003). *National Crime Victimization Survey, 1992–2000: Violent victimization of college students.* Washington DC: Bureau of Justice Statistics. Retrieved from http://www.ojp.usdoj.gov/bjs/pub/pdf/vvcs00.pdf.

Hart, T. (2013). The violent victimization of college students: Findings from the National Crime Victimization Survey. In B. S. Fisher & J. J. Sloan (Eds.), *Campus crime: Legal, social, and policy perspectives* (3rd ed.). Springfield, IL: Charles C Thomas.

Kanin, E. (1967). An examination of sexual aggression as a response to sexual frustration. *Journal of Marriage and the Family, 29,* 428–433.

Kanin, E. (1970). Sex aggression by college men. *Medical Aspects of Human Sexuality, 4,* 25–40.

Kanin, E. (1977). Sexual aggression: A second look at the offended female. *Archives of Sexual Behavior, 6,* 67–76.

Karjane, H., Fisher, B., & Cullen, F. (2002). *Campus sexual assault: How America's institutions of higher education respond.* Final Report, NIJ Grant No. 99-WA-VX-0008. Retrieved from http://www.ncjrs.org/pdffiles1/nij/grants/196676.pdf.

Karjane, H., Fisher, B., & Cullen, F. (2005). *Sexual assault on campus: What colleges and universities are doing about it.* United States Department of Justice, NIJ Research for Practice Series. Retrieved from http://www.ncjrs.gov/pdffiles1/nij/205521. pdf.

Kilpatrick, D., Resnick, H., Ruggiero, K., Conoscenti, L., & McCauley, J. (2007). *Drug-facilitated, incapacitated, and forcible rape: A national study.* Retrieved from http://dx.doi.org/10.3886/ICPSR20626.

Kirkpatrick, C., & Kanin, E. (1957). Male sex aggression on a university campus. *American Sociological Review, 22,* 52–58.

Kiss, A. (2013). The *Jeanne Clery Act:* A Summary of the Law and its Evolution in Higher Education. In B. S. Fisher & J. J. Sloan (Eds.), *Campus crime: Legal, social, and policy perspectives* (3rd ed.). Springfield, IL: Charles C Thomas.

Koss, M., Gidycz, C., & Wisniewski, N. (1987). The scope of rape: Incidence and prevalence of sexual aggression and victimization in a national sample of higher education students. *Journal of Consulting and Clinical Psychology, 55,* 162–170.

Krebs, C., Lindquist, C., Warner, T., Fisher, B., & Martin, S. (2007). Campus sexual assault (CSA) study: Final report. Retrieved from https://www.ncjrs.gov/App/Publications/abstract.aspx?ID=243011.

Lake, P. (2001). The special relationship(s) between a college and a student: Law and policy ramifications for the post *in loco parentis* college. *Idaho Law Review, 37,* 531–554.

Lonsway, K., Banyard, V., Berkowitz, A., Gidycz, C., Katz, J., Koss, M., Schewe, P., & Ullman, S. (2009). Rape prevention and risk reduction: Review of the research literature for practitioners. Retrieved from http://www.vawnet.org.

McQuade, S. (2013). High tech abuse and crime on college and university campuses: Evolving forms of victimization, offending, and their interplay in higher education. In B. S. Fisher & J. J. Sloan (Eds.), *Campus crime: Legal, social, and policy perspectives* (3rd ed.). Springfield, IL: Charles C Thomas.

Melear, K. (2002). From *in loco parentis* to consumerism: A legal analysis of the contractual relationship between institution and student. *Journal of Student Affairs Research and Practice, 40,* 124–148.

Meier, T. (2005). Information security technology. Retrieved from http://www.corp.att.com/edu/docs/article_info_security.pdf.

Mustaine, E., & Tewksbury, R. (2013). The routine activities and criminal victimization of students: Lifestyle and related factors. In B. S. Fisher & J. J. Sloan (Eds.), *Campus crime: Legal, social, and policy perspectives* (3rd ed.). Springfield, IL: Charles C Thomas.

Paoline, E., & Sloan, J. (2003). Variability in the organizational structure of contemporary campus law enforcement agencies: A national level analysis. *Policing: An International Journal of Police Strategies and Management, 26,* 612–639.

Paoline, E. A., & Sloan, J. J. (2013). Community oriented policing (COP) on university campuses: New directions? In B. S. Fisher & J. J. Sloan (Eds.), *Campus crime: Legal, social, and policy perspectives* (3rd ed.). Springfield, IL: Charles C Thomas.

Ratcliffe, J. (2003). Trends and issues in crime and criminal justice. Retrieved from http://www.aic.gov.au/publications/current%20series/tandi/241-260/tandi248/view%20paper.aspx.

Reyns, B., Burek, M., Henson, B., & Fisher, B. (2011). The unintended consequences of digital technology: Exploring the relationship between sexting and cybervictimization. *Journal of Crime and Justice,* DOI:10.1080/0735648X.2011.641816.

Robinson, M., & Roh, S. (2013). Crime on campus: Spatial aspects of campus crime at a regional comprehensive university. In B. S. Fisher & J. J. Sloan (Eds.), *Campus crime: Legal, social, and policy perspectives* (3rd ed.). Springfield, IL: Charles C Thomas.

Security on Campus. (2012). Summary of the *Jeanne Clery Act.* Retrieved from http://www.securityoncampus.org/summary-jeanne-clery-act.

Shafer, L. (2007). Women, gender, and safety on campus: Reporting is not enough. In B. Fisher & J. Sloan (Eds.), *Campus crime: Legal, social, and policy perspectives* (2nd ed.) (pp. 87–101). Springfield, IL: Charles C Thomas.

Sloan, J. J., & Fisher, B. S. (2011). *The dark side of the ivory tower: Campus crime as a social problem.* New York: Cambridge University Press.

Sloan, J., Fisher, B., & Cullen, F. (1997). Assessing the *Student Right-to-Know and Campus Security Act of 1990:* An analysis of the victim reporting practices of college and university students. *Crime and Delinquency, 43,* 148–168.

Stewart, M., & Fisher, B. (2013). Vulnerabilities and opportunities 101: The extent, nature, and impact of stalking and cyberstalking among college students and implications for campus policy and programs. In B. S. Fisher & J. J. Sloan (Eds.), *Campus crime: Legal, social, and policy perspectives* (3rd ed.). Springfield, IL: Charles C Thomas.

Smith, M. (1995). Vexatious victims of campus crime. In B. S. Fisher & J. J. Sloan (Eds.), *Campus crime: Legal, social, and policy perspectives* (pp. 25–37). Springfield, IL: Charles C Thomas.

Swartz, J. (2010). The revivification of *in loco parentis* behavioral regulation in public institutions of higher education to combat the obesity epidemic. *New England Law Review, 45,* 101–137.

United States Department of Education, Office of Postsecondary Education. (2011). *The Handbook for Campus Crime Reporting.* Washington, DC: United States Department of Education.

Vladutiu, C. J., Martin, S. L., & Macy, R. J. (2011). College- or university-based sexual assault prevention programs: A review of program outcomes, characteristics, and recommendations. *Trauma, Violence, & Abuse, 12,* 67–86.

Yeo, S. (2002). The responsibility of Universities for their students' safety. Retrieved from http://www.austlii.edu.au/au/journals/SCULawRw/2002/5.pdf.

Part I

THE LEGAL CONTEXT
OF CAMPUS CRIME

Part I

THE LEGAL CONTEXT OF CAMPUS CRIME

INTRODUCTION

The legal context of campus crime consists of two related arenas: the legislative and judicial. In both these arenas, policy has been developed to address the problems of crime and security issues on college campuses. As we did in the second edition of *Campus Crime,* we devote the chapters in Part I of the third edition to the *Student-Right-to-Know and Campus Security Act of 1990* (20 U.S.C. 1092[f]), renamed in 1998 as the *Jeanne Clery Disclosure of Campus Security Policy and Campus Crime Statistics Act* in memory of Jeanne Clery who was raped and murdered in her dormitory room at Lehigh University in 1986. Over 20 years have passed since Congress enacted that legislation in response to intense lobbying by well-meaning advocates about perceived rampant crime levels occurring on postsecondary campuses, combined with lax security at many colleges and universities. By requiring postsecondary institutions to "come clean" and publically and annually report their campus crime statistics and security policies, supporters of the legislation believed campus crime and security information would prove useful to both current and prospective members of the campus community, especially students and their parents. The chapters that follow address the legal context of campus crime by focusing on the *Clery Act* and its progenies, including related federal-level and state-level legislation, case law, and research.

Chapter 2, by Allison Kiss, documents the genesis and evolution of the *Clery Act* from its inception. Given the importance of the *Clery Act* mandates for postsecondary institutions, she outlines the *Clery Act* compliance requirements and discusses companion legislation including the *Campus Sexual Assault Victims' Bill of Rights, Violence Against Women Act,* and the *Campus SaVE Act* that also involve postsecondary institutional efforts to address crime and security issues on campus.

29

Over 20 years have passed since the *Clery Act* was signed into law and yet a simple question remains unanswered: what impact has the legislation had on campus crime and safety? In Chapter 3, titled "Research on the *Clery Act* and Crime Reporting: Its Impact on the Literature and Administrative Practice in Higher Education," higher education scholars Dennis Gregory and Steven Janosik answer that question by presenting results of their analysis of source materials on the impact of *Clery* – including doctoral dissertations, master's theses, research articles, law reviews, and white papers – found in electronic bibliographic databases such as *Google Scholar*™ and *Lexis-Nexis Legal*™. Given their interests in higher education administration, the authors also present results from their own work that has explored the perceptions of student affairs personnel concerning the impact of the *Clery Act* on higher education administration. They conclude that the *Clery Act* has not had anywhere near the impact its sponsors had hoped, and had marginal effects at best on postsecondary student affairs personnel.

Bonnie Fisher and colleagues, in Chapter 4 titled "Reporting Sexual Assault and the *Clery Act:* Situating Findings from the National Campus Sexual Assault Policy Study within College Women's Experiences," question the validity of *Clery Act* mandated statistics on the sexual victimization of college women. Using results from past research and their *National Campus Sexual Assault Policy Study,* Fisher and colleagues discuss on-campus barriers to victim reporting and explain how these barriers contribute to institutional underreporting of sexual victimizations. They also offer policy recommendations that campus administrators and campus safety advocates should consider implementing and evaluating.

In Chapter 5, titled "'Decriminalizing' Institutional Responses to Peer Sexual Violence, attorney and legal scholar Nancy Cantalupo examines student judicial proceedings stemming from peer-to-peer sexual victimization. Cantalupo reviews *Title IX, Clery Act* and case law regarding the due process rights of students accused of misconduct warranting suspension or expulsion, all of which makes clear that colleges and universities should not treat student disciplinary proceedings like criminal trials. She argues that doing so diminishes the effectiveness of *Title IX, Clery,* and institutional responses to sexual violence. Further, she argues that colleges and universities should seek not only to decriminalize their disciplinary procedures but also their reporting mechanisms. Cantalupo concludes decriminalizing both ends of the process could occur either through amending *Title IX* or *Clery,* or by adopting new federal regulations under either statutory blanket.

We conclude Part I with a chapter by Jennifer Burke and John Sloan titled "State-Level *Clery Act* Initiatives: Symbolic Politics or Substantive Policy?" which analyzes the content of state-level, *Clery Act*-type campus crime and security legislation and compares state-level requirements to those found in key

Clery Act provisions. Their findings lead Burke and Sloan to conclude that state-level *Clery Act* initiatives offer little substantive impact and, as a result, constitute symbolic public policy in legislative efforts to address campus safety and security.

In summary, Part I of the book presents the legal context of campus crime by describing the evolution and requirements of the *Clery Act* and comparable state-level initiatives. The section provides insights into the evolution of the *Clery Act* and describes its mandates. Informed by research findings, the contributors also identify and critically discuss how weaknesses and limitations inherent in the *Clery Act* and state-level *Clery*-like statutes undermine their potential effectiveness at making campuses safer. Together, the chapters in Part I show that campus crime and security issues remain despite passage of well-intentioned campus crime legislation and case law decisions.

Chapter 2

THE *JEANNE CLERY ACT:*
A SUMMARY OF THE LAW AND ITS
EVOLUTION IN HIGHER EDUCATION

ALISON KISS

INTRODUCTION

On April 5, 1986, Jeanne Ann Clery, a freshman at Lehigh University, was brutally raped and murdered in her dormitory room by another student, Josoph Henry, whom she did not know. Henry crept into her room through a series of propped open and unlocked doors intending to steal items from students' rooms. Jeanne's parents, Connie and Howard Clery, were devastated to learn of the brutal murder of their daughter. In fact, the Clerys believed they had been prudent when selecting a college with Jeanne. Jeanne at first had chosen to attend Tulane University in New Orleans, from which her two brothers had graduated. However, shortly after her acceptance, the Clerys learned a co-ed had been murdered off-campus and they decided to look for a "safer" campus for Jeanne. Eventually, the Clerys selected Lehigh University for Jeanne to attend. As Connie Clery remembered, "Jeanne fell in love with the campus" (Clery, 2011).

The Clerys assumed Lehigh was as safe as it looked, but after Jeanne's death, they learned that Lehigh had only 12 security guards for its 5,400 students and that 38 violent offenses, including rape, robbery, and assault, had occurred on the campus around the time of Jeanne's admission. They obtained this information from the FBI's Uniform Crime Reports, an annual compilation of crimes reported to police including those occurring on selected campuses. Howard Clery stated "what citizen gets the FBI crime report when they're trying to decide where their children should go to college? Who would even think of doing that?" (Fine & Gross, 1990). The Clerys' anger and frustration extended beyond the trial of Josoph Henry when they learned of lapses occurring in Lehigh's security protocols (which were probably not unique to Lehigh). On learning of the lapses, the Clerys brought a lawsuit against Lehigh for negligence and ultimately settled the suit for an undisclosed amount. They then used the award, along with personal funds, to found the national nonprofit organization Security On Campus, Inc. (SOC) in 1987 (renamed the *Clery Center for Security on Campus* in 2012).

Almost immediately, SOC successfully lobbied the Pennsylvania state legislature and later Congress to pass legislation that would require colleges and universities to publish their crime statistics (Sloan & Fisher, 2011). Pennsylvania became the first state to pass comprehensive campus crime legislation in 1989 (see Burke & Sloan, 2013), while Congress passed the *Student Right to Know and Campus Security Act of 1990* (20 USC 1092 [f]), and renamed the law in 1998 as the *Jeanne Clery Disclosure of Campus Security Policy and Campus Crime Statistics Act* (hereafter, *Clery Act*) in memory of Jeanne Clery. This landmark federal legislation requires colleges and universities eligible to receive federal financial aid funds to annually report their crime statistics and security policies along with other crime-related information.

More than two decades later, the face of campus safety and security has changed dramatically. According to Hefling (2011), Terry Hartle, Senior Vice President at the American Council on Education recently commented that the *Clery Act* has forced postsecondary institutions to significantly expand and professionalize their campus security operations, while the U.S. Department of Education, tasked with overseeing *Clery Act* compliance, has not hesitated to use the *Clery Act* as a "blunt instrument" against institutions. He further stated, "I think the *Clery Act* has resulted in every institution in higher education taking campus security far more seriously than was the case twenty years ago."

In 2006, Connie Clery stated ". . . there is no way that campuses and their students can be safe unless institutions tell the truth about campus crime" (Clery, 2006) and five years later, she noted in a keynote address on campus safety and security held at Lehigh University, "The best education in the world is useless if a student does not survive with a healthy mind and body" (Clery, 2011). These words, spoken five years apart and two decades after Jeanne's murder, embody both the spirit and letter of the *Clery Act*. Although some critics refer to the *Clery Act* as overly complicated and a burden on postsecondary institutions (see National Association of College Business Officers, 2008), the intent behind the original legislation was to encourage transparency among institutions of higher education through disclosure of crime statistics and campus security policy. Connie Clery recalled the effort it took lobbying for federal legislation and the resistance she and Howard experienced from the higher education community and even from personal friends: "[T]hey fought us tooth and nail (lobbyists for higher education groups) and many friends of mine, alumni of prominent colleges and universities, stopped speaking to Howard and I [sic]" (Clery, 2011).

This chapter examines the evolution of the *Clery Act* and its impact on campus crime prevention, interventions, and policy. Topics covered include the core elements of the *Clery Act,* notable amendments to the legislation that have occurred since 2008, on-going needs as revealed by specific program reviews, and a discussion of the future of campus safety.

The *Jeanne Clery Act*

The *Student Right to Know and Campus Security Act of 1990* (Title II of Public Law 101–542) (henceforth, the *Clery Act*) was signed into law by President H. W. Bush on November 8, 1990 and became the first piece of federal legislation specifically designed to provide public access to campus crime information. Current and prospective students, their parents and postsecondary institutional employees now would have access to information about crime on campus when considering attending or working at a particular college or university.

The *Clery Act's* key requirements for all postsecondary institutions include:

- Disclosure of an annual security report with crime statistics and security policy;
- Disclosure of timely information through public crime log and warnings issued about ongoing threats to the health/safety of the campus community;
- Insure the protection of certain basic rights for both the accused and accuser in sexual assault cases adjudicated by campus disciplinary proceedings.

All institutions of higher education, private and public alike, eligible to participate in any federal student aid program under Title IV of the *Higher Education Act of 1965,* are subject to the reporting and program requirements stipulated in the *Clery Act.* The U.S. Department of Education oversees compliance with the *Clery Act,* investigates complaints of *Clery Act* violations, and, if needed, determines the sanction (e.g., fines) when a school fails to comply with the *Clery Act's* mandates.

Annual Security Report

The *Clery Act* mandates that postsecondary institutions must publish and distribute an annual security report by October 1st each year. The report contains statistical compilations of crimes reported to campus authorities for the three most recent calendar years, as well as abridged versions of campus security policies including those relating to institutional handling of sexual assault complaints and policies regarding timely warnings and emergency notification to students and employees, and details about where students should go to report crimes. The institution must make this report available automatically to all current students and employees, and notify prospective students and employees of its existence and provide them an opportunity to receive a copy of the report. Per the U.S. Department of Education guidelines the annual security report can be distributed via a website as long as the institution provides a paper copy if one is requested.

The crime statistics reported are for seven major categories of crime as defined by the FBI's *Uniform Crime Reporting Program* (e.g., Federal Bureau of Investigation, 2004), with several subcategories included: (1) homicide (murder, nonnegligent and negligent manslaughter); (2) sex offenses broken down by forcible (including rape) and nonforcible offenses; (3) robbery; (4) aggravated assault; (5) burglary; (6) motor vehicle theft; and (7) arson. Institutions are also required to report the following three types of incidents if they resulted in either an arrest or if a campus disciplinary referral is undertaken (if both occur, for reporting purposes only the arrest is counted): liquor law violations, drug law violations, and illegal weapons possession. The annual security report must also indicate if any of the reported crimes were "hate crimes," again based on *Uniform Crime Reporting Program* definitions. If this is the case, the report must contain a narrative specifying what category of motivation was behind the offense including race, gender, religion, sexual orientation, ethnicity, or physical disability (Federal Bureau of Investigation, 2004, pp. 74–77). Using *Uniform Crime Reporting Program* guidelines helps insure uniformity in collecting and reporting crime statistics across institutions within the same state, as well as across the states.

The statistics also are broken down geographically into the following locations including "on-campus," "residential facilities for students on campus," "non-campus buildings," or "public property" such as streets and sidewalks immediately adjacent to or running through a campus. Many institutions, although not required to do so, use a map to denote these areas.

A Deeper Look into "Campus Security Authorities"

The obvious source for campus crime statistics would be to obtain them from campus police or security departments. However, other campus officials – such as residence hall personnel, faculty members, or staff – hold reporting responsibility as well. Among campus officials obligated to report campus crime are those with "significant responsibility for student and campus activities, including, but not limited to, student housing, student discipline, and campus judicial proceedings" (U.S. Department of Education, 2011, p. 74). This group of officials also includes students serving in roles such as on campus residence hall advisors.

An illustration of the extent campus security authorities are supposed to be involved in reporting on-campus offenses became clear in late 2011 after public revelations of alleged sexual assaults of boys by an assistant football coach on the staff of the Pennsylvania State University (Penn State) athletics department. In December, 2011, the U.S. Department of Education announced a review of Penn State's compliance with the *Clery Act* after public outcry occurred over the Penn State revelations that was coupled with demands for stronger enforcement of the *Clery Act* for preventing violent crimes and enhancing overall safety on college campuses (Duncan, 2011; Gifford, 2011; Meehan, 2011).

The issue of campus security was at the forefront of the Penn State investigation which focused on the lack of a formal crime reporting structure, coupled with an alleged institutional cover-up of serial sex offenses by the assistant football coach. As the story was splashed across print and electronic media outlets, the public learned that a campus graduate assistant had informed the then head coach, Joe Paterno, of a specific incident of sexual assault of a child the graduate assistant had a witnessed. Mr. Paterno, a "Campus Security Authority" as defined under the *Clery Act,* reported the crime to his supervisor, Tim Curley, who was then Director of Athletics. Mr. Curley reported the incident to then Vice President for Administration, Gary Schultz. While the *Clery Act* allows for a chain of command reporting by campus security authorities, in this instance, the report never made it to campus police, resulting in a national scandal that brought attention from the United States Department of Education and United States Congressman Patrick Meehan (R-PA) to call for a investigation of whether Penn State violated *Clery Act* reporting requirements (Duncan, 2011; Gifford, 2011; Meehan, 2011).

In November of 2011, Congressman Meehan asked U.S. Secretary of Education Arne Duncan to fully investigate Penn State's compliance with the *Clery Act.* The Congressman wrote to Mr. Duncan that ". . . the failure to report the 2002 allegations (the year the alleged abuses began) would appear to break Penn State's own reporting methods for sexual abuse on campus" (Meehan, 2011). Later that month, then Penn State President Graham Spanier received a letter from the U.S. Department of Education informing the university that the department was conducting a *Clery Act* compliance audit, and it needed to provide the department with over 10 years worth of *Clery Act* related documents and information. The audit formally commenced on November 28, 2011, and key stakeholders for campus safety were directed to be available for interviews: security, policing, judicial affairs, residence life, student affairs, athletics, Greek organizations, etc. (Gifford, 2011). As of this writing, the audit has not been completed.

The recent Penn State scandal may have a positive impact on officials' commitment to campus safety. Moreover, the Penn State *Clery Act* audit may alter former interpretations of compliance. As Secretary Duncan noted in a November 9, 2011 statement:

> If these allegations of sexual abuse are true then this is a horrible tragedy for those young boys. If it turns out that some people at the school knew of the abuse and did nothing or covered it up, that makes it even worse. Schools and school officials have a legal and moral responsibility to protect children and young people from violence and abuse. (Duncan, p. 1, 2011)

Tangential to the Penn State investigation, crime victim advocates and violence prevention educators focused attention on the need to augment awareness and services for crime victims on campus, embracing both the letter and spirit of the *Clery Act*. As Jackson Katz has written:

> Finally, the sad events unfolding at Penn State demonstrate clearly that the tide is turning. The voices of sexual abuse victims – girls *and* boys, women *and* men – are breaking through the walls of silence that powerful men have built to advance their interests and protect their privilege. Look at the institutions that have been rocked to their core in just the past decade. The Catholic Church. The U.S. military. And now Joe Paterno and Penn State football. (Katz, 2011, p. 1)

Clery Act stipulations regarding campus security authorities indicate that "a dean of students, director of athletics, team coach, and faculty advisor to a student group" would be required to report crimes, but due to different hierarchies and programs at institutions throughout the country, the rules do not specify exact job titles. The U.S. Department of Education stipulates that current "definitions and guidance reflect the reality that on college campuses, officials who are not police officials or acting as event security at student or campus events, nevertheless are responsible for students' or campus security" (Student Assistance General Provisions, 1999). Institutions may not only collect statistics from campus police or security, there must also be an effort to collect statistics from other campus officials, as well as a good faith effort to gather statistics from local law enforcement agencies.

In amendments to the *Higher Education Act* (Public Law 105-244, §951) that occurred in 1998, a change in that law specifically prohibited the re-disclosure of any "privileged information" by campus officials. For this reason, mental health and pastoral counselors are considered exempt from all reporting obligations.

Public Crime Logs

One of the most significant requirements of the *Clery Act* is that public and private institutions with campus police or security departments must maintain "public crime logs." Institutions are required to log any reported crime occurring on campus or within the patrol jurisdiction of the campus police or security departments (the legislation allows institutions already maintaining a public crime log under state law to use that log to comply with this requirement). As long as all other minimum requirements of the *Clery Act* are met, schools may use state crime definitions for offenses compiled in the log which is required to include the nature, date, time, general location of each crime, and its disposition. Reported incidents are to be logged within two business days but may withhold certain limited information to protect victim confidentiality.

Timely Warning Requirements

As a result of recent amendments to the *Clery Act*, institutions are required to provide "timely warnings" for incidents threatening the health and/or the safety of the campus community. It is this requirement that most likely affects the day-to-day lives of students. The timely warning requirement is somewhat subjective and triggered when the senior institution officials consider a crime to pose an ongoing threat to students and employees. As part of the amendments, campuses are required to "immediately notify" the campus community as soon as an emergency is confirmed on the campus unless doing so would compromise efforts to contain it. The emergency notification requirement covers a broad array of threats, not just *Clery Act* reportable crimes.

Federal Legislation Relating to the *Clery Act*

Several other pieces of federal legislation seek additional protection of campus community members beyond that of the *Clery Act*. Each related law is described below.

Campus Sexual Assault Victims' Bill of Rights

The late Frank Carrington, then Chief Counsel to SOC, developed the *Campus Sexual Assault Victims' Bill of Rights* to prevent the re-victimization of on-campus survivors of sexual assault. In 1991, Mr. Carrington boarded an airplane and was reviewing the legislation in his seat. Congressman Jim Ramstad (R-MN) was sitting next to him and inquired about his research. He then asked if he could read Mr. Carrington's draft of the law. Congressman Ramstad was so impressed with the intent of the law that he wanted to help get it passed. He and Congresswoman Susan Molinari (R-NY) worked alongside the staff at SOC to obtain passage of the law in 1992 (Sloan & Fisher, 2011).

In 1992, Congress enacted the *Campus Sexual Assault Victims' Bill of Rights* (hereafter, *Bill of Rights*) as part of the *Higher Education Amendments of 1992* (Public Law 102-325, §486 (c)). The legislation was originally introduced in May of 1991 by Congressman Ramstad and has been referred to as the *Ramstad Act*. The *Bill of Rights* articulates policies, procedures, and services for all victims of sexual assault occurring at postsecondary educational institutions, and that result in disciplinary proceedings being convened in the case. The law is designed to ensure that victims and offenders are both afforded the same rights throughout the student disciplinary process, as follows:

- The accuser and accused must have the same opportunity to have others present at campus disciplinary hearings;
- The institution shall inform both parties of the outcome of any disciplinary proceeding;
- The institution shall inform survivors of their options to notify law enforcement and assist them in doing so, if requested;
- The institution shall notify all survivors of counseling services; and
- The institution shall notify survivors of options for changing academic and living situations.

SOC is currently working with multiple nonprofit, victim service organizations to pass the *Campus Sexual Violence Elimination Act (SaVE Act)* as an amendment to the *Clery Act* to include dating violence, domestic violence, and stalking in the legislation. The bipartisan Campus *SaVE Act* would help colleges and universities to educate, to respond, and prevent multiple forms of sexual violence. In early December of 2011, Senator Patrick Leahy (D-VT) and Mike Crapo (R-ID) included the Campus *SaVE Act* in a bipartisan bill to reauthorize the *Violence Against Women Act (VAWA)*. The provisions included in VAWA would update the *Clery Act's* two-decade-old campus sexual violence prevention and response provisions. The *SaVE Act* provides a baseline for colleges and universities to develop procedures addressing victim support services. Institutions will also receive guidance on primary prevention initiatives. The *Campus SaVE Act* was included in the Senate version of the VAWA that passed in May of 2012, but was intentionally excluded from the House version that passed in May 2012 for jurisdictional reasons.

Family Education Rights and Privacy Act

Institutions of higher education have their own student judiciary system (variously referred to as "community standards," "judicial affairs," or "discipline" depending on the institution). The process is designed to address violations of student codes of conduct including allegations of plagiarism, copyright infringement, underage drinking, and other problem behaviors. The processes also address on-campus violent student misconduct like sexual assault and hazing. Results of these proceedings then become a permanent part of the student perpetrator's educational records.

The *Family Educational Rights and Privacy Act (FERPA)* (20 U.S.C. § 1232g; 34 CFR Part 99) is a Federal law that protects the privacy of student education records. The law applies to all schools that receive funds under an applicable program of the U.S. Department of Education. *FERPA* gives parents certain rights with respect to their children's education records. These rights transfer to the student when he or she reaches the age of 18 or attends a school beyond the high school level. *FERPA,* however, does not apply to law enforcement records nor to certain student disciplinary records.

Amendments and clarifications occurring in 1992 and 1998 relate directly to *FERPA's* confidentiality protections and are relevant to the *Clery Act.* The Foley Amendment, which passed in 1998 and named after its sponsor Congressman Mark Foley (R-FL), changed *FERPA* rules to permit postsecondary institutions to publicly disclose the results of campus disciplinary hearings in cases of violent crime where there is a finding of responsibility. The victim and witness names remain confidential unless they authorize the release in writing; further stating that institutions may, but are not required to, release the records upon request from third parties. The disclosure of a disciplinary proceeding's results must include only the name of the offender, the violation committed, and any sanction imposed by the institution against the student.

Campus Sex Crimes Prevention Act

The *Campus Sex Crimes Prevention Act* (1601, Public Law 106-386) *(CSCPA)* was enacted on October 28, 2000 and allows the tracking of convicted, registered sex offenders enrolled as students at institutions of higher education or working/volunteering on campus. The *CSCPA* amended federal sex offender registration requirements to provide that any registrant already required to register in a state must also provide additional notice to each institution where the person is a student or employed. Each institution must issue a statement, in addition to other disclosures, advising the campus community where to find the information concerning registered sex offenders on campus (*Campus Sex Crimes Prevention Act,* 1601, Public Law 106-386, 2000).

Complaints Alleging *Clery Act* Violations

Information on complaints relating to *Clery Act* noncompliance and findings relating to these complaints is public information and available through the U.S. Department of Education (ED). The U.S. Department of Education rules indicate that citizens must file complaints regarding alleged violations of the *Clery Act* to the regional office overseeing the state where the violation allegedly occurred. A review (*Clery Act* audit) may then be initiated by a complaint, a media story about a crime, or if an institution's individual audit raises concerns. The review can be part of a general financial aid audit or can be a specific campus security review.

Between 1997 and 2005, the Department of Education conducted 14 *Clery Act* audits. Between 2006 and 2011, however, the number more than doubled to 34 audits. This change in activity potentially indicates that more citizen complaints are being received by the Department of Education, which it is then investigating, and/or the Department is being more proactive in pursuing audits of schools it suspects are not in compliance with *Clery Act* mandates.

Campus Community Responsibility

Crime response and prevention on a college campus is a community responsibility. College women face a rate of sexual assault much higher than is found in the larger population of women. According to one United States Department of Justice funded study, one in five females are the victim of a completed or attempted rape or sexual assault (Kilpatrick, McCauley, Ruggiero, & Resnick, 2007, p. 3). Furthermore, 90 percent of sexual assault victims on college campuses know their assailants (Fisher, Cullen, & Turner, 2000). The reality is that many campus sexual assaults are perpetrated by someone known to the victim. For this reason, as well as a result of *Clery Act* mandates, the field of higher education health education and prevention has recently shifted more toward a primary prevention approach to sexual assault through on-campus education programs. This new approach involves tiers of prevention based on a public health orientation. Primary prevention programs target potential perpetrators and bystanders, while secondary prevention programs target at-risk groups, and tertiary prevention programs enhance safety networks for victims.

Recent research provides insight about the importance of involving the broader community in prevention efforts, including the role of community norms (Fabiano, Perkins, Berkowitz, Linkenbach, & Stark, 2003). Lisak and Miller (2002) found through detailed interviews with "undetected rapists" that predators use community contexts, including social events with alcohol, to facilitate their crimes. Based on this research, prevention programs aimed at building skills among members of the campus community to serve as intervening bystanders are becoming more common. The *Clery Act* requires crime prevention, crime awareness, and sexual assault prevention education. Institutions must take this requirement a step further and truly scan their campus climate to determine what evidence-based approaches are needed.

Recent amendments to the *Clery Act,* including requirements specific to emergency notification, demand a need for collaboration among the various components of the campus community. Campus safety is not the sole responsibility of campus law enforcement. Instead, collaboration is needed among multiple departments on campus, and students and faculty must understand their roles in prevention and intervention. SOC recently received a grant from the Justice Department's Office for Victims of Crime to create a four-module training program to assist postsecondary institutions achieve *Clery Act* compliance. The training contains sections on counting, collecting, and classifying crime data; on-going disclosure; victim support services; and the annual security report. A multidisciplinary team representing areas on campus including campus law enforcement, faculty members, student conduct, and victim advocacy developed this curriculum.

Conclusion

Postsecondary institutions must embrace both the letter and spirit of the *Clery Act* to build safer campus communities that hopefully translate into a more civil academic environment. Various official and unofficial sponsors of the *Clery Act* have stressed the importance of an enhanced ethical commitment to campus safety that extends beyond mere technical compliance with the law. In September of 2011, SOC partnered with Lehigh University to present *Proceeding in Partnership: The Future of Campus Safety.* Connie Clery, in her welcome speech, stated:

> In collaboration, we can do many things *and* make a tremendous difference. We can and must continue to change the culture of high-risk drinking and sexual assault. These institutions, leaders and you can't do it all. We *must* engage the students — we have to reach *them*. Respect and responsibility need to come back and stay in style. Young people today live in a different world where there is a lot of fear and terror. Students can feel empowered by helping one another to take ownership of their campus's safety. This Summit gives me hope that we have people working on solutions. I am quite confident that the event today will help continue to spread Jeanne's gift of safety on college campuses. (September 29, 2011, p. 1)

It is collaborations like the one Connie described that will hopefully transform how campus crime is addressed in the future and thereby help to prevent crime from being committed both by and against college students.

REFERENCES

Beder, M. (2007). Eastern Michigan University faces largest ever fines for failure to report crime. *Student Press Law Center.* Retrieved from http://www.splc.org/news/newsflash.asp?id=1661.

The Campus Sex Crimes Prevention Act. Public Law 106-386, § 1601 (2000).

Clery, C. (2011). Welcome Speech delivered at *Proceeding in partnership: The future of campus safety summit.* Lehigh University, Bethlehem, PA.

Clery, C. (2006). Personal communication. September 29, 2006.

Duncan, A. (2011). U.S. Department of Education to investigate Penn State's handling of sexual misconduct allegations. Retrieved from http://www.ed.gov/.

Eastern Michigan University. (2006). EMU student passes away; EMU community mourns. Retrieved from http://www.emich.edu/univcomm/releases_archived/121606statement.html.

Fabiano, P. M., Perkins, H. W., Berkowitz, A., Linkenbach, J., & Stark, C. (2003). Engaging men as social justice allies in ending violence against women: Evidence for a social norms approach. *Journal of American College Health, 52,* 105–114.

Federal Bureau of Investigation. (2004). *Uniform Crime Reporting Handbook.* Washington, DC: United States Department of Justice, pp. 74–77.

Fine, A., & Gross, K. (1990). After their daughter is murdered at college, her grieving parents mount a crusade for campus safety. *People, 33,* 113–115.

Fisher, B. S., Cullen, F., & Turner, M. (2000). *The sexual victimization of college women.* NIJ Research Report. Washington, DC: U.S. Department of Justice.

Gifford, N. P. (2011). Penn State Clery Act review request. Retrieved from http://www.psu.edu/ur/2011/DoE_Letter_110911.pdf.

Hefling, K. (2011). Ed. Dept. uses law to investigate campus crimes. Retrieved from http://articles.boston.com/2011-11-10/sports/30383088_1_clery-act-dorm-room-jeanne-clery.

Higher Education Amendments of 1992, Public Law 102-325, section 486 (c) (1992).

Higher Education Amendments, Public Law 105-244, section 951 (1998).

Higher Education Opportunity Act, Public Law 110-315, (2008).

How to File a Jeanne Clery Act Complaint. (2012). Retrieved from, http://www.securityoncampus.org/students/clerycomplaint.html.

Janosik, S. M., & Gregory D. E. (2009). The Clery Act, campus safety, and the perceptions of senior student affairs officers. *NASPA Journal, 46,* 208–227.

Jeanne Clery Disclosure of Campus Security Policy and Campus Crime Statistics Act. (1998). 20 U.S.C. § 1092 [f].

Katz, J. (2011). There are victims in the Penn State tragedy, not "accusers." *The Huffington Post.* Retrieved from http://www.huffingtonpost.com/jackson-katz/penn-state-victims_b_1098571.html.

Kilpatrick, D. G., McCauley, J., Ruggiero, K., & Resnick, H. (2007). *Drug-facilitated, incapacitated, and forcible rape: A national study.* Washington, DC: National Institute of Justice.

Layton, L. (2012). $55k fine against Va. Tech overturned. Retrieved from http://www.washingtonpost.com/local/education/55k-fine-against-va-tech-overturned-timing-of-warning-during-rampage-was-questioned/2012/03/30/gIQADswOmS_story.html.

Lisak, D., & Miller, P. (2002). Repeat rape and multiple offending among undetected rapists. *Violence and Victims, 17,* 73–82.

McCaffrey, J. (2006). Senators call for help in *Clery Act* enforcement. *The Philadelphia Evening Bulletin.* Retrieved from http://www.theeveningbulletin.com.

Meehan, P. (2011). Meehan calls for federal investigation into Sandusky matter. Retrieved from http://meehan.house.gov.

Moxley, T. (2011).Virginia Tech's *Clery* hearing opens. Retrieved from http://www.roanoke.com/news/roanoke/wb/302095.

Nash, A. (2007). Police contradict EMU in slaying. Retrieved from http://www.emutalk.org/2007/03/police-contradict-emu-in-slaying.

National Association of College Business Officers. (2008). Record fine levied for *Clery Act* violations. Retrieved from http://www.nacubo.org/Business_and_Policy_Areas/Risk_Management/Risk_Management_News/Record_Fine_Levied_for_Clery_Act_Violations.html.

Regulations to revise the current Student Assistance General Provisions. (1998). 34 CFR, § 668.

Security On Campus, Inc. (2007). Eastern Michigan University to pay largest ever *Clery Act* fine of $350,000. Retrieved from http://www.securityoncampus.org/index. php?option=com_content&view=article&id=154.+&Itemid=75.

Student Assistance General Provisions: Final Rules (1999). *Federal Register, 64,* 59063.

Student Press Law Center. (2009). Covering crime. *Student Press Law Center Report,* p. 4–26. Retrieved from http://www.splc.org.

U.S. Department of Education. (2012). Clery Act reports. Retrieved from http://federal studentaid.ed.gov/datacenter/cleryact.html.

U.S. Department of Education, Office of Postsecondary Education. (2001). *The incidence of crime on the campuses of U.S. postsecondary education institutions.* Washington, DC.

U.S. Department of Education, Office of Postsecondary Education. (2005). *The handbook for campus crime reporting.* Washington, DC.

U.S. Department of Education, Office of Postsecondary Education. (2011). *The handbook for campus safety and security reporting.* Washington, DC.

Chapter 3

RESEARCH ON THE *CLERY ACT* AND CRIME REPORTING: ITS IMPACT ON THE LITERATURE AND ADMINISTRATIVE PRACTICE IN HIGHER EDUCATION

DENNIS E. GREGORY AND STEVEN M. JANOSIK

INTRODUCTION

The *Jeanne Clery Disclosure of Campus Security Policy and Campus Crime Statistics Act* (2000) (hereafter the *Clery Act,* the *Act,* or *Clery*) has sparked a number of questions regarding crime and safety on college and university campuses. Although these questions range from asking about the usage of *Clery Act* crime statistics to the *Act's* effects on campus security policies, the longstanding question underlining all these queries is quite simple: Are college and university campuses in the United States safer today because of *Clery?*

This question is of major concern to college administrators, faculty, staff, students, parents, lawmakers, and others around the country. While we have added some material that updates our chapter from the last edition of this book, we find our conclusions are still primarily the same, relatively speaking, there is little, though an increasing amount, of scientific research in the higher education literature that provides quantitative or qualitative studies of the *Clery Act* and its impact on campus crime. While the amount of research has increased, there is still much that can be examined related to the *Clery Act*. As noted above, we have added several studies related to the *Clery Act* and crime on campus which were not reported in our earlier chapter. We recommend that you refer back to that chapter to examine earlier studies. We also found several studies which we did not report in the earlier chapter and commend them to you for study as well.

The purpose of this chapter is to provide a review of the current state of the research literature on the *Clery Act,* note several books which have been written on crime issues related to campus, and describe a number of studies that demonstrate how the impact of the *Act* is being studied. We, however, as noted above, believe that there has been relatively little research conducted on this topic. While there has been a growing amount of research on campus crime, and there has certainly been much commentary, particularly in the periods after each tragic incident, there has been little research on the *Act* and its impact and implementation.

The *Clery Act* in the Literature

The *Clery Act* sprang from the death of Jeanie Clery who was raped and murdered in her residence hall room on the Lehigh University campus. The Clery family received an out of court settlement in its suit against the university and pushed to have a campus safety act passed, first in Pennsylvania, and ultimately by Congress in 1990. Congress passed the *Act* not only because of this tragedy, but because legislation was viewed as a necessity due to perceived increases in juvenile crime in society as a whole and a perceived increase in crime on college campuses. There were, however, no means at the time to determine whether this presumption about campus crime was accurate (Gregory & Janosik, 2003).

With the concern among the public, the press and watchdog groups such as the *Clery Center for Security on Campus,* about the safety of college campuses, it is surprising that so little formal research has been done on how the *Act* has been implemented, how campus officials have perceived its impact, and how effective it has been. In fact, the "literature" on the topic is replete with news stories and law review and other articles that opine about the *Act's* level of importance and enforcement. Most of the source material one finds is popular press-based, largely because the media appear fascinated by lurid reports of crimes such as the murder of Patricia Guardado on the University of Arkansas Little Rock in 2009 (Fear on campus, 2011), the killing of Virginia Tech police officer Deriek Crouse (Quigley & Durante, 2011), the murders at Oikos University (Sander, 2012), and other high profile crimes. *The Morning Call,* the newspaper of the Lehigh Valley in Pennsylvania, has a website which is an index of campus crime articles (Morning Call, nd). On Ask.com, blogger Jackie Burrell (2009) commented on a list complied by the *Daily Beast,* which provided a list of the 25 campuses with the highest crime rates, which she called the "Worst Colleges" regarding campus crime. ABC News (nd) has a series on line called "Murdered at College," which provides pictures and small snippets on 11 women who died violently while college students. While these crimes are certainly troubling and indicate that higher education faces many challenges, there is little evidence that such crimes are the norm on American college and university campuses particularly when campus crime is compared with crime in the larger society . Unfortunately, such news outlets have little incentive to place these incidents in an objective context (Wood & Janosik, in press).

Gregory and Janosik (2002) described the tone and content of much of the literature related to the *Clery Act* that appeared during the 1990s. This content included media commentary about the results of campus crime, reports of institutions that failed to accurately report crime, and criticisms of campuses that failed to be adequately open about the crime on and around their campuses. This literature also included legal journal articles that described the *Act,* its content, its strengths and its weaknesses as well as several books on the topic (see Fisher & Sloan, 1995; Gregory & Janosik, 2002; Smith, 1988, 1989; Smith & Fossey, 1995). The quantity of literature has changed little since 2007.

Method

To examine the number, content, and variety of published material relating to the *Clery Act* and review that material, we conducted Google™ and Google Scholar™ searches, followed by searches of *Lexis-Nexis™ Academic* and *ProQuest™*. These sources provided a broad overview of recent writings concerning the *Clery Act* and its impact. The databases we selected are available to, and understandable by, people seeking information about the *Act,* such as parents, students, police officials, and scholars. We also conducted broad Internet searches using the same search terms. While not exhaustive, our review provides a reasonable summary of what consumers and others with an interest in the *Act* might find.

We first conducted a Google™ search using the term "Clery Campus Safety Act" that returned 76,000 citations, some 100,000 fewer citations than we found in 2007. As before, we reviewed the first 30 pages of citations returned and found the vast majority included references to electronic versions of campus security reports and related documents from various colleges and universities in the United States. The remainder of the citations were primarily electronic postings relating to the *Clery Center for Security on Campus* (an advocacy group involved with insuring colleges and universities properly implement the *Clery Act*), the U.S. Department of Education, and news reports from campus and other newspapers covering crimes on specific campuses. We also, unlike 2007, found listings for companies selling campus safety and emergency notification products and equipment, campus safety consulting companies , and a reference to the U.S. Department of Education's revised campus safety manual: *Department of Ed Releases Updated Campus Safety Guide,* 2011. While we expected such a search would likely provide sources such as those found, with

76,000 citations returned, we also expected to find citations to research, including master's theses and doctoral dissertations posted online.

We next conducted a search on Google Scholar™ using the same search term and found 2340 "hits." Of these, we found Gregory and Janosik, and their coauthors were mentioned in 15 of the first 20 references returned and another reference mentioned one of the editors of this volume and her colleagues (Fisher, Hartman, Cullen, & Turner, 2002). Few of the "hits" included quantitative or qualitative research on issues that related directly to the *Clery Act* and other studies' issues related to campus crime more broadly. References were returned for research on related issues such as sexual assault on campus, alcohol abuse, fraternal organization violence and the like, but most of the references were for reports similar to those found in the Google™ database.

Using the same term, we next conducted a search of popular news sources for the last several years found in the LexisNexus™ Academic Database using the "Search the News" search. We undertook this search specifically to examine how the popular and legal press has covered the *Clery Act*. Our search returned 86 citations from campus and commercial newspapers. Sixty-four of the stories were written in 2007 or earlier and only two were from 2012. We examined the articles and found the majority described issues related to the Virginia Tech Killings, Eastern Michigan University, and issues around Penn State, Jerry Sandusky, and Joe Paterno. There were also several obituaries of Howard Clery, whose daughter's murder resulted in passage of the *Clery Act*. There was also listed a story written by Nina Bernstein of the *New York Times* in November of 2011 entitled "On Campus, a Law Enforcement System to Itself" (Bernstein, 2011). As previously noted, the Google™ database contained sources almost exclusively from the popular and legal press and as a result, we did not expect the database to yield academic research articles.

We followed our search of popular press sources with a search of law journals/law reviews using the LexisNexis™ Academic Database using the search term "Clery Campus Safety Act." The search produced only one return, a 2005 law review article by Seidman and Vickers published in the *Suffolk University Law Review,* which dealt with victim's rights in sexual assault cases, so we revised our search using the term *"Clery Act"* and located 22 additional citations. Among these, eight were on unrelated topics, two dealt with issues related to guns on campus, and seven dealt with sexual assault and related topics. Only one of these (Ahn, 2010) related directly to the *Clery Act,* in that it recommended revision of the *Act* to improve reporting of acts of sexual assault. Three of the citations were from a special issue of the *Stetson University Law Review* from 2002 (these are discussed elsewhere in this chapter and other chapters in the book). One article by Griffin (2007) dealt with "recent cases regarding the legal duty American colleges and universities have to protect the student community from harm or injury resulting from safety or security breaches." A second article by Griffin (2009) dealt with how incident command system management has impacted the development of organizational frameworks to manage emergency incidents. The article also reviews selected case law regarding campus safety and state and federal statutory responses designed to minimize threats to campus safety. Another search using the term *"Jeanne Clery Disclosure of Campus Security Policy and Campus Crime Statistics Act"* yielded no citations.

The final search we conducted was of the *ProQuest*™ Electronic Database for Education Theses and Dissertations using the search term "Clery Campus Safety Act." Results of the search yielded seven dissertations which have been written since 2007, as well as several theses and dissertations that addressed the *Clery Act* and/or related campus crime issues from other sources.

Thus, while the searches we conducted were not the type of exhaustive research that may be necessary for a doctoral dissertation, using several electronic databases available to both the casual user as well as scholars, we found relatively little content that could be reasonably be considered analytical, qualitative, or quantitative research on the *Clery Act*. As a result, we suggest the way people inside and outside of higher education view campus crime is based on views espoused by the press and not academic research.

Below, we review the research our searches discovered. Much of this work has been conducted by a small group of scholars, including the two of us and authors of other chapters in this volume (e.g., Sloan, Fisher, Mustaine, & Tewksbury).

Clery Act Research

As previously mentioned, scientific research on the impact of the *Clery Act* on campus crime has been limited. We now turn our attention to reviewing the substance of the dissertations, theses, articles, and research reports found in our searches. We arrange the studies by type of publication rather than by substantive content focus for ease of reference. We also report on several books that have been published recently which dealt with the *Clery Act* or campus crime. Finally, our review does not reveal a single set of conclusions from these studies as a whole, since their content focus, methodologies, subject populations, and research questions differed widely. There are, however, common themes we will describe in the concluding section of this chapter.

Doctoral Dissertations

The search of the *ProQuest*™ Electronic Database found dissertations by Patton (2010), Dagler (2009), Barnes (2009), Kerkhoff (2008), Talesh (2007),

Olszewska (2007), and Aliabadi (2007). These studies particularly focused on whether colleges or universities complied with various requirements of the *Act* (e.g., crime statistics, timely warnings, reports of security policies and procedures); on perceptions of fear of victimization on campus; and on the efficacy of training and compliance efforts and whether such efforts were effectively reduced campus crime and increased campus safety.

In a study currently under way, White (2012) is examining the impact of *Clery* training on campus officials' ethical commitments to campus safety, using Noddings' (2003) ethic of care theory. According to the author,

> This study aims to evaluate the influence of *Clery*-related training on the participants' ethical commitment to campus safety beyond compliance at their respective institutions. In consideration of Nel Noddings' ethic of caring theory, the researcher frames this qualitative study in connection to caring; educational decision-making; and one's responsibility for morality, fidelity, and true concern for individuals. By surveying, examining institutional documents, and interviewing, the researcher intends to explore the influence of *Clery Act* Training Seminars on participants' devotion to the letter and spirit of the law. (pp. iii–iv)

Patton (2010) examined perceptions of students from Virginia community colleges regarding their fear of campus crime. He surveyed students from all 23 Virginia community colleges and found that students felt least safe in parking lots and bathrooms, and that they had the greatest fear of being a victim of a robbery, despite the fact that no robberies had occurred on the campuses in 10 years. He also studied whether the perception of safety varied on several demographic factors, as well as on the rurality of the institutions and whether the institutions had police, security, or no form of campus safety force. Finally, he questioned whether best practices established by the Virginia Crime Commission have been implemented at the schools and whether these practices had any impact on perceptions of safety at the campuses identified as "most" and "least" safe in his study.

Dagler (2009) also conducted a study related to fear of crime. He used a mixed methods design to survey and interview both international and American students to determine whether the two groups differed in levels of fear of sexual assault and property crime. He found that international students were, in fact, more fearful of both types of crime compared to their American counterparts. He also noted that both domestic and international students shared common perceptions about crime, and that international students became less fearful over time.

Barnes (2009) studied crime in Virginia institutions of higher education and did comparisons of crime at institutions that had campus police and campus security departments. She used a rate of the number of crimes per 100 students similar to the crimes per 100,000 used by Janosik and Gregory (2003b).

Her findings suggested that crime in the communities which surround these campuses needed to be better focused upon by campus officials; suggested that the campus buildings, layout, structure, and capacity need to be examined when campus crime was compared across campuses; and noted that her study examined:

> . . . the general categories of campus crime utilized in the multivariate models (total, violent/personal, and property offenses reported per 100 student), future researchers are cautiously encouraged to determine a valid, reliable way to examine specific crime categories. However, based on the experience gained from the current research, the utility of examining any type of sexual assault is questionable due to inherent underreporting. (Barnes, 2009, p. 173)

Kerkhoff (2008) studied the impact of the Virginia Tech tragedy on safety policy in community colleges in Florida. She examined changes in campus safety policy related to student mental health policy and recommendations within the *Florida Task Force Report* (2007) and examined tort liability for campus crime. Kerkhoff also made a variety of suggestions for future research that may provide excellent guidance for future researchers, and concluded that:

> Ongoing assessment of crisis management teams should include audits to recommend improvement of internal procedures related to coordination, adequacy, and timeliness of actions, as well as the unit's efficiency in the follow up and tracking of students designated at risk. Agent-based modeling and social networking theories provide avenues for determining where dysfunction in communication relays exist. Policymaker should define safety and the goals sought to be achieved. (pp. 151–152)

Talesh (2007), in a qualitative study, explored the experiences of senior student affairs officers (SSAO) facing the leadership challenges of implementing external legislation on their campuses. Nine current or retired SSAOs shared their stories and insights about the *Clery Act* and provided reflections on the leadership challenges and issues they faced when the legislation was enacted. Talesh (2007) found that senior student affairs officers examined considerations of legal and crime related issues using four conceptual "frames," including the *structural, human resources, symbolic,* and *political.* He also noted that the most important leadership skills needed by the SSAO when considering these issues were communication and relationship building; that SSAOs had to rely on colleagues and professional associations for support and assistance; and that collaboration among campus leaders improved when working on *Clery*-related issues.

Olszewska (2007) studied whether there was a difference in crime rates between institutions that did or did not request information about students' disciplinary records during the admissions process. According to Olszewska (2007):

The primary independent variable was the practice of gathering disciplinary background information; the secondary independent variables were control of the institution, ratio of students living on-campus, gender distribution of the undergraduate student population, and size of the city in which the institution was located; and the dependent variable was the rate of campus crime.

She found that items such as an applicant's criminal record, student conduct record while in high school and military discharge records were likely not effective measures to mitigate campus crime. She found no statistically significant difference in the campus crime rates between institutions which sought this information and those that did not.

Aliabodi (2007), in a mixed methods study, investigated whether students at three California universities were changing their safety/crime prevention behaviors over time as a result of knowledge about the *Clery Act*. Aliabodi (2007, pp. 126–127) reached the following conclusions:

1. The *Clery Act* is changing student behaviors in some ways. . . . It is causing students to reflect upon the issue [of campus crime] more often, however it is not enough. It is up to the institution to teach students methods they can use to protect themselves.

2. Student behaviors are not changing between their first and fourth year at the given institutions because of the *Clery Act* alone. The knowledge students gain from the *Clery Act* is useful and does make a difference, but it is only one of many factors that illicit change. Over time students become more acclimated to the university at large, they develop more friendships, and they develop new outlooks on what is important in life.

Master's Thesis

In addition to the above listed dissertations, we found one master's thesis related to the *Clery Act* that was written since 2007. Walters (2010) conducted a qualitative study including personal interviews and document reviews at three California universities. She noted the personal perceptions of compliance by those for responsibility for such compliance and examined both campus crime reports and crimes reported to the Department of Education to determine whether they were identical. While she found that the reports were identical, she also found the three institutions were in varying levels of compliance in other areas, and that training seminars were sometimes lacking.

Books and Journal Articles

In addition to the dissertations and theses previously described, researchers have conducted studies on various aspects of the *Clery Act* that have appeared in books, professional journals, and other forums. Many of the articles are foundational and are often cited in the dissertations, theses, articles, and other materials that have followed. There are several themes running through much of this research, which is not surprising since a relatively small group of scholars has produced much of this work. Further, surveys conducted by some of these scholars contained common items. In general, the studies found that large percentages of study participants believed their campuses and the surrounding areas to be "safe" or "very safe." Students, parents, and administrators indicated they did not study *Clery Act* crime statistics, and even when they did review the statistics, they did not use them to decide which school to attend. Only very small percentages of the administrative groups believed that campus officials were intentionally hiding crime on campus, and few among any study group reported that the *Clery Act* had any appreciable affect on lowering crime rates or making campuses safer. As the research beyond the foundational work of Gearing (e.g., Gearing & Galloway, 1997), Gregory (e.g., Gregory & Janosik, 2002, 2003, 2006) and Janosik (e.g., Janosik, 2001, 2004) has occurred, a broader examination of campus crime and the *Clery Act* has also occurred.

BOOKS. While, as with the dissertations and theses, we do not claim that we have provided an exhaustive list of books on the *Clery Act* and related topics. We describe two books that have recently dealt with issues of campus crime.

Perhaps the book most relevant to this chapter is Hemphill and LeBanc's (2010) *Enough Is Enough: A Student Affairs Perspective on Preparedness and Response to a Campus Shooting*. This edited volume has chapters, authored primarily by student affairs professionals at Northern Illinois University, and consists of nine chapters that examine such issues as murder on college campuses, mental health issues among college students, planning for and managing campus crises, the role of counseling centers during campus crises, and other important issues for student affairs professionals.

Another book on a related topic is *Violence Goes to College* (2010). According to a review by Gregory (2012, p. 174), the metaphor of "violence as a virus," or at least an illness on the campus, is woven throughout the book and the primary authors, as well as several chapter authors, give a nod to this metaphor throughout. The authors assist the reader in understanding campus violence and where it comes from; discuss ways to recognize, prevent, and prepare for campus violence; and then identify and examine those types of violence that are most prevalent on American campuses. Gregory (2012) also notes that while the book is interesting and draws attention to various issues that face campuses, it is not what many would identify as "scholarly research."

JOURNAL ARTICLES. Hart and Colavito (2011) interviewed 160 students at the University of Nevada at Las Vegas to study the reporting of crime by college students to police. They sought to examine whether victimization reporting differed between college students and the general public. Using the theory of "collective efficacy," they found that social control influenced college students' reporting and that there was little correlation between reporting by college students and the general public except with regard to crime severity. While this article did not specifically refer to the *Clery Act,* we felt it was important to show that research related to the topic was occurring regrading college students.

Kaminiski, Koons-Witt, Thompson, and Weiss (2010) conducted interviews with students at the University of South Carolina before and after the mass shootings at Virginia Tech and Northern Illinois University to determine whether the levels of fear of crime increased as a result of these shootings. They found that there was a "modest" increase in fear generally but that levels of fear varied by type of fear measured and student demographics.

Janosik and Gregory (2009) studied the perceptions of 351 senior student affairs officers regarding their awareness of and the perceived efficacy of the *Clery Act* in informing parents and students about campus safety as well as reducing crime, and found the respondents to be very homogeneous in terms of age and other physical characteristics such as race, educational background, years of experience, etc. as well as in their opinions regarding the *Clery Act* in comparison to previous populations studied and found little difference between respondents from public and private institutions. The respondents almost universally reported they were aware of the *Act* and expressed the belief campus officials were not hiding crime. They had significant confidence that students were reading crime reports and would attend training programs on campus safety topics. Approximately 5 percent of the respondents expressed the belief that the *Clery Act* was having an impact on the reduction of campus crime.

Conclusion

Despite the presence of the *Clery Act* since 1990, prior to the first decade of the twenty-first century, there was little formal study regarding the legislation's impact. The studies reviewed in this chapter comprise the large majority of available research, particularly that occurring from 2007 to 2012, and from which several common themes and conclusions are recognized. These themes are continuations of the research which was reviewed in the last edition of this book.

First, while the *Clery Act* is an important piece of legislation, it has often been perceived as confusing and ill focused. Even now, after 22 years, some administrators, and to a lesser extent campus police officers may not fully understand some of the nuances of the *Act,* and "institutions still do not report crime data in a way fully consistent with Federal law" (U.S. Department of Justice, 2005, p. 4). Such difficulties prompted Karjane et al. (2002) to conclude that college administrators need more guidance on how to comply with *Clery*. While the U.S. Department of Education has provided more guidance since these statements were published, and a number of states have examined campus safety in the wake of the Virginia Tech tragedy and other high profile campus murders, there is still much confusion and relatively small amounts of scientific research being conducted on the law and its impact on campus safety more broadly. The lack of compliance with certain aspects of *Clery* is a theme echoed by several of the studies reviewed above.

The U.S. Department of Education has updated many of its resources to assist campuses to better understand and comply with the *Act.* In 2011, the U.S. Department of Education revised *The Handbook for Campus Safety and Security Reporting* (Westat, Ward, & Mann, 2011) it created in 2005 to assist campus officials comply with *Clery*. The updated publication provides significant guidance and training regarding the *Act.* The current version of the *Handbook* totals some 300 pages and contains many technical definitions that define reporting expectations. However, because additional reporting requirements have been added since 2005, there is still room for misunderstanding. Wood and Janosik (in press) argue that many of these provisions are overly prescriptive and onerous.

Second, *Clery* does not seem to have had the positive impact that its sponsors had hoped. There is no evidence that parents and students are using the *Act* to make decisions regarding where to attend college and there are no reports that the *Act* has had an impact on reducing crime. Early studies, indicated that less than 27 percent of students and parents know of the *Act* and fewer than 25 percent of students acknowledge reading the crime reports mandated by the legislation (Janosik & Gearing, 2003; Janosik, 2001). Fewer than 10 percent of parents and students use crime information contained in *Clery* mandated campus security reports to make college selection decisions (Janosik, 2004). Despite efforts by campus administrators to improve reporting, one has to wonder about the efficacy of such a strategy. We question whether such a strategy in and of itself is of any value. While these crime incident numbers may have changed since early reports such as those noted above, since there is no known research to confirm any changes, these earlier data are likely very similar to today's results. Perhaps Fisher et al. (2002) are correct and *Clery* is merely a symbolic effort to make campuses safer.

Third, though many critics indicate that campus crimes are still not being reported accurately and skepticism about the accuracy of campus crime statistics continues to exist among campus "watchdog" groups (e.g., Kerkstra, 2006), there is no evidence that the crime statistics reported per *Clery* mandates are in a broad way systematically and intentionally being manipulated by campus officials. A case can be made that the accuracy of *Clery* statistics is no greater or less than the accuracy of crime statistics generated by other agencies responsible for reporting crime. Most of the data seem to indicate that students, parents, and institutional officials believe that college administrators, for the most part, are being candid about campus safety issues and that very few administrators attempt to hide crime. While a number of the studies cited in this chapter and in the previous edition suggest that campus crime is underreported, particularly sexual assault, we would argue that much the same phenomenon is true in society as a whole.

Fourth, research by Gregory, Janosik, and their colleagues involving surveys of postsecondary institutional constituent groups showed members of these groups perceived their campuses to be at least as safe as the surrounding community and this perception is largely borne out by crime data. The fact is, campus crime, like crime in the general population in the United States, has been and continues to decline. The wave of youth crime predicted by criminologists in the 1990s never materialized (Greve, 2006), while studies by Fisher et al. (2002), Janosik and Gregory (2003b), Janosik et al. (2005), and Gregory et al. (2006) all report that the campuses they studied had lower crime rates than the communities that surrounded them. Almost none of these researchers, however, attribute this finding to the *Clery Act*. While certainly administrators have work to do to make campuses safer, particularly in the important areas of sexual assault, hate crimes, theft, assault, and substance abuse, campuses are implementing educational programs; have increased training for key personnel; have installed safety equipment, such as blue light safety phones; and since the Virginia Tech massacre, the number of various types of electronic alert systems for timely notices have skyrocketed.

Finally, we do believe that the *Clery Act* has had some positive effects on administrative practice in higher education. Clearly, college administrators of all types have had to devote resources to comply with the *Clery Act* and generate the mandated reports required by the *Clery Act*. This allocation of resources varies widely by school and is difficult to quantify with any precision (Janosik & Gregory, 2003a). As noted in several studies cited above, fear of crime is high (Dagler, 2009; Patton, 2010) and the knowledge level of campus officials is low (Gregory & Janosik, 2006: Janosik & Gregory, 2009).

Judicial officers and campus law enforcement officers report an increased consistency in crime reporting by colleges and universities. These two groups and counselors report a slight improvement in their working relationships with one another (Gregory & Janosik, 2003; Janosik & Gregory, 2003a). About one-quarter of administrative groups, parents, and students report an increased level of confidence in campus police officers (Gregory & Janosik, 2003; Janosik & Gregory, 2003a), and a majority of students report an increased willingness to report campus crime on their respective campuses (Janosik & Gearing, 2003; Janosik, 2001). Better relationships among key officials and increased confidence are likely to result in increased reporting of campus crime.

Beyond requiring college and university administrators to prepare mandatory reports, we believe the *Clery Act* has influenced student affairs practice only on the margins. Even in this respect, readers should remember that many colleges and universities reported crime statistics using the FBI's uniform crime reporting protocols long before the *Act* was passed. We encourage additional research in the area of campus safety, crime prevention, and improvements in the *Clery Act* to make it even more effective. We believe that this can occur.

REFERENCES

ABC News. (nd). "Murdered at college: Campus murders." Retrieved from http://abcnews.go.com/US/popup?id=8610849.

Ahn, K. (2010). The pendulum swings backwards: The Clery Act must be amended to address university policies that discourage rape reporting. *Womens' Rights Law Reporter, 31,* 514–535.

Aliabadi, S. (2007). *Understanding the effects of the Clery Act on college students' behaviors: How can student affairs professionals change the current practices of college students with regard to safety.* Ed.D. dissertation, University of Southern California, United States – California. Retrieved from Dissertations & Theses: Full Text. (Publication No. AAT 3330349).

Barnes, C. (2009). *Examining campus crime at Virginia's colleges and universities.* Ph.D. dissertation, Virginia Commonwealth University, United States – Virginia. Retrieved from Dissertations & Theses: Full Text. (Publication No. AAT 3388624).

Bernstein, N. (2011, November 12). On Campus, a Law Enforcement System to Itself. *New York Times.* Section A; Column 0; Metropolitan Desk; 1, http://www.lexisnexis.com.proxy.lib.odu.edu/hottopics/lnacademic/?.

Burrell, J. (2009, October 20). Campus crime: 25 worst colleges. Retrieved from http://youngadults.about.com/b/2009/09/20/campus-crime-25-worst-colleges.htm.

Department of Ed Releases Updated Campus Safety Guide. (2011, March 1). *Campus Safety Magazine* online. Retrieved from http://www.campussafetymagazine.com/Channel/University-Security/News/2011/03/01/Department-of-Education-Releases-Updated-Clery-Compliance-Guide.aspx.

Dagler, M. (2009). *A comparative study of fear of sexual assault and personal property theft between international and noninternational students on an urban university campus.* Ed.D. dissertation, Spalding University, United States – Kentucky. Retrieved from Dissertations & Theses: Full Text. (Publication No AAT 3359505).

Fear on campus after Ark. college student's killing. (2011, October 18). MSNBC. com. Retrieved from http://www.msnbc.msn.com/id/44952385/ns/us_news-crime_and_courts/t/fear-campus-after-ark-college-students-killing/.

Fisher, B. S., Hartman, J. L., Cullen, F. T., & Turner, M. G. (2002). Making campuses safer for students: The Clery Act as a symbolic legal reform. *Stetson Law Review, 32,* 61–89.

Fisher, B. S., & Sloan III, J. J. (Eds.). (1995). *Campus crime: Legal, social, and policy issues.* Springfield, IL: Charles C Thomas.

Florida's gubernatorial task force for university campus safety: Report on findings and recommendations. (2007, May 24). State of Florida. Retrieved from http://www.dcf.state.fl.us/campusSecurity/docs/finalReport052407.pdf.

Gearing, D. D., & Callaway, R. L. (1997). Compliance with the notice requirement of the Campus Security Act. *College and University, 73,* 13–18.

Gregory, D. E. (2012, January/February). Review of the book *Violence goes to college* for the *Journal of College Student Development, 53,* 174–175.

Gregory, D. E., & Janosik, S. M. (2002). The Clery Act: How effective is it? Perceptions from the field – The current state of the research and recommendations for improvement. *Stetson Law Review, 32,* 7–59.

Gregory, D. E., & Janosik, S. M. (2003). The effect of the Clery Act on campus judicial practices. *Journal of College Student Development, 44,* 763–778.

Gregory, D. E., & Janosik, S. M. (2006, July). The views of senior residence life and housing administrators on the Clery Act and campus safety. *The Journal of College and University Student Housing, 34,* 50–57. http://web.ebscohost.com/ehost/pdf?vid=4&hid=5&sid=ea2cd9a0-6a5d-4662-b26c-88525db2c6b5%40sessionmgr14.

Gregory, D. E., Janosik, S. M., Strayhorn, T. L., & Kalagher, S. S. (2006). Crime on college and university campuses in the southeastern United States: A more accurate method for examining campus crime statistics. A paper presented at the National Student Personnel Association conference. Washington, DC.

Greve, F. (March 9, 2006). Feared juvenile 'super-predators' never materialized. *Wisconsin State Journal,* A1, A7.

Griffin, O. R. (2007, April). Confronting the evolving safety and security challenge at colleges and universities. *Pierce Law Review, 5,* 413.

Griffin, O. R. (2009, Fall). Constructing a legal and managerial paradigm applicable to the modern-day safety and security challenge at colleges and universities. *Saint Louis University Law Journal, 54,* 241.

Hart, T. C., & Colavito, V. (2011). College Student Victims and Reporting Crime to the Police: The Influence of Collective Efficacy. *Western Criminology Review 12,* 1–19. Retrieved from http://www.readperiodicals.com/201111/2557787851.html.

Hemphill, B. O., & LaBanc, B. H. (Eds.). (2010). *Enough is enough: A student affairs perspective on preparedness and response to a campus shooting.* Published by NASPA and ACPA by Sterling, VA: Stylus.

Janosik, S. M. (2001). The impact of the Campus Crime Awareness Act on student behavior. *NASPA Journal, 38,* 348–360.

Janosik, S. M. (2004). Parents' views of the Clery Act and campus safety. *The Journal of College Student Development, 45,* 43–56.

Janosik, S. M., & Gearing, D. D. (2003). *The impact of the Jeanne Clery Act Disclosure of Campus Security Policy and the Campus Crime Statistics Act on student decision-making.* EPI Policy Paper No. 10. Blacksburg, VA: Virginia Tech.

Janosik, S. M., & Gregory, D. E. (2003a). The Clery Act and its influence on campus law enforcement practices. *NASPA Journal, 44,* 182–199.

Janosik, S. M., & Gregory, D. E. (2003b). *Crime on Virginia's college and university campuses, Annual report 2002.* EPI Policy Paper Number 14, Blacksburg, VA: Virginia Tech. Retrieved from http://filebox.vt.edu/chre/elps/EPI/VACC2002.pdf.

Janosik, S. M., & Gregory, D. E. (2006). Senior student affairs officer's perceptions of campus safety and the impact of the Clery Act. A paper presented at the National Student Personnel Association conference. Washington, DC.

Janosik, S. M., & Gregory, D. E. (2009). The Clery Act, campus safety, and the perceptions of senior student affairs officers. *NASPA Journal, 46,* Art. 5. Retrieved from http://journals.naspa.org/cgi/viewcontent.cgi?article=6039&context=jsarp.

Jeanne Clery Disclosure of Campus Security Policy and Campus Crime Statistics Act. 20 U.S.C. § 1092(f) (2000).

Kaminski, R., Koons-Witt, B. A., Thompson, N. S., & Weiss, D. (2010). The impacts of the Virginia Tech and Northern Illinois University shootings on fear of crime on campus. *Journal of Criminal Justice, 38,* 88–89.

Karjane, H. M., Fisher, B. S., & Cullen, F. T. (2002). *Campus sexual assault: How America's institutions of higher education respond.* Washington, DC: National Institute of Justice. Retrieved from http://www.ncjrs.gov/pdffiles1/nij/grants/196676.pdf.

Kerkhoff, J. L. (2008). *Assessing the development of campus safety policy in the community college following the Virginia Tech tragedy.* Ph.D. dissertation, University of Florida, United States – Florida. Retrieved from Dissertations & Theses: Full Text. (Publication No. AAT 3322927).

Kerkstra, P. (January 15, 2006). On campus, creating an illusion by crime data. *The Philadelphia Inquirer,* B16, 18.

Morning Call (nd). "Campus crime article index." Retrieved from http://www.msnbc.msn.com/id/44952385/ns/us_news-crime_and_courts/t/fear-campus-after-ark-college-students-killing/.

Nicoletti, J., Spencer-Thomas, S., & Bollinger, C. (Eds.). (2010). *Violence goes to college.* Springfield, IL: Charles C Thomas.

Noddings, N. (2003). *Caring: A feminine approach to ethics and moral education* (2nd ed.). Berkeley, CA: University of California Press.

Olszewska, M. J. V. (2007). *Undergraduate admission application as a campus crime mitigation measure: Disclosure of applicants' disciplinary background information and its relation to campus crime.* Ed.D. dissertation, East Carolina University, United States – North Carolina. Retrieved from Dissertations & Theses: Full Text. (Publication No. AAT 3255419).

Patton, R. C. (2010). *Student perceptions of campus safety within the Virginia community college system.* Ph.D. dissertation, Old Dominion University, United States – Virginia. Retrieved from Dissertations & Theses: Full Text. Publication No. AAT 3442173).

Quigley, R., & Durant, T. (2011, December 9). Pictured: The murdered police officer and father-of-five shot dead after gunman brings terror back to Virginia Tech campus. Retrieved from http://www.dailymail.co.uk/news/article-2071719/Virginia-Tech-shooting-2011-victim-Deriek-Crouse-Picture-murdered-police-officer.html#ixzz1ktKt3T4u.

Sander, L. (2012, April 3). After shootings at Oikos U., a scholar urges a nuanced look at stereotypes and bullying. *Chronicle of Higher Education.* Retrieved from http://chronicle.com/article/After-Shootings-at-Oikos-U-a/131421/.

Seidman, I., & Vickers, S. (2005) Beyond prosecution: Sexual assault victim's rights in theory and practice symposium: The second wave: An agenda for the next thirty years of rape law reform. *Suffolk University Law Review, 38* Suffolk U. L. Rev. 467.

Seng, M. (1995). The Crime Awareness and Campus Security Act: Some observations, critical comments and suggestions. In B. S. Fisher & J. J. Sloan, III (Eds.), *Campus crime: Legal, social, and policy perspectives* (pp. 38–52). Springfield, IL: Charles C Thomas.

Seng, M., & Koehler, N. (1993). The Crime Awareness and Campus Security Act: A critical analysis. *Journal of Crime and Justice, 16,* 97–110.

Sloan III, J. J., Fisher, B. S., & Cullen, F. T. (1997, April). Assessing the Student Right-to-Know and Campus Security Act of 1990: An analysis of the victim reporting practices of college and university students. *Crime and Delinquency, 43,* 146–168.

Smith, M. C. (1988). *Coping with crime on campus.* New York: American Council on Education: Macmillan.

Smith, M. C. (1989). *Crime and campus police: A handbook for police officers and administrators.* Asheville, NC: College Administration Publications.

Smith, M. C., & Fossey, R. (1995). *Crime on campus: Legal issues and campus administration.* Westport, CT: Greenwood Press.

Talesh, R. (2007). *The Clery Act: Leadership perspectives from Senior Student Affairs Officers.* Ed.D. dissertation, University of Southern California, United States – California. Retrieved from Dissertations & Theses: Full Text. (Publication No. AAT 3291800).

U.S. Department of Justice. (2005). *Sexual assault on campus: What colleges and universities are doing about it.* Washington, DC: Author.

Walters, M. W. (2010). *The Jeanne Clery Act:* Making campuses safer through compliance, collaboration and training. Unpublished Master of Arts Thesis. California State University at Sacramento. Retrieved from http://csusdspace.calstate.edu/xmlui/bitstream/handle/10211.9/414/WALTERS%20THESIS%20FINAL%204%2029%2010.pdf?sequence=2.

Westat, Ward, D., & Mann, J. L. (2011). *The handbook for campus safety and security reporting.* United States Department of Education. Washington, DC. Retrieved from http://www2.ed.gov/admins/lead/safety/handbook.pdf.

White, K. N. (2012). *The influence of "Clery Act training seminars" on participants' ethical commitment to campus safety beyond compliance in public and religious colleges and universities.* Ed.D dissertation proposal. Saint Joseph's University. Pennsylvania – United States. Author.

Wood, A. R., & Janosik, S. M. (in press). The *Clery Act:* Crime reporting concerns. *University Risk Management and Insurance Journal.*

Chapter 4

REPORTING SEXUAL ASSAULT AND THE *CLERY ACT:* SITUATING FINDINGS FROM THE NATIONAL CAMPUS SEXUAL ASSAULT POLICY STUDY WITHIN COLLEGE WOMEN'S EXPERIENCES

BONNIE S. FISHER, HEATHER M. KARJANE, FRANCIS T. CULLEN, SHANNON A. SANTANA, KRISTIE R. BLEVINS, AND LEAH E. DAIGLE

INTRODUCTION

Contrary to the traditional image of college and university campuses as safe havens, criminal violence, vice, and victimization have been a part of the collegiate landscape of postsecondary schools since the first schools were created in the United States during the seventeenth century (Sloan & Fisher, 2011). Media accounts, including in *The Chronicle of Higher Education* and *New York Times,* have documented heinous crimes committed against college students. The Center for Public Integrity's year-long investigation, entitled *Sexual Assault on Campus,* uncovered widespread underreporting and mishandling of allegations of sexual assault (Lombardi, 2010). Their collective efforts have stirred the public, state legislatures, and Congress to question whether college and university campuses are less idyllic ivory towers and more hot spots of crime scenes (see Fisher, Sloan, Cullen, & Lu, 1998; Mustaine & Tewksbury, 2013).

Numerous studies consistently have reported that a sizable proportion of female students experience a range of different types of sexual assault, including fondling, partner violence, rape, and stalking, during their college tenure (Belknap & Erez, 2013; Fisher, Cullen, & Turner, 2000; Kilpatrick,

Resnick, Ruggiero, Conoscenti, & McCauley, 2007; Stewart & Fisher, 2013). For a substantial number of these women, repeat sexual victimization is a grim reality during their college years; they experience a disproportionate amount of sexual incidents ranging from verbal threats to completed rape (Fisher, Daigle, & Cullen, 2010).

Issues concerning the extent and nature of the sexual assault[1] and stalking of college women have moved beyond scholarly attention and have attracted a much wider audience of interested parties. Of note, several movements emerged independently that influenced Congress' initial attention and ensuing (and sustained) legislative actions. First, on the heels of the feminist movement, Koss, Gidycz, and Wisniewski's (1987) path-breaking national study established that sexual victimization occurs with some frequency to a sizable proportion of college women. During the 1990s, alcohol consumption among college students, namely binge drinking, and its relationship to victimization was labeled as a public health problem by the Harvard School of Public Health's College Alcohol Study (Wechsler, Davenport, Dowdall, Moeykens, & Castillo, 1994). Second, an increasing number of the precedent-setting court decisions held institutions of higher education (IHEs) civilly liable for "foreseeable" crimes, including cases in which students had been raped (Burling, 2003). Institutional responses to sexual violence, including the due process rights of students, have come to the attention of the courts through lawsuits and the Office for Civil Rights in the Department of Education (ED) through *Title IX of the Education Amendments of 1972* requirements (see Ali, 2011; Cantalupo, 2013). Third, college student safety advocates, such as the Clery Center for Security on Campus (formerly Security On Campus, Inc.), continue to document and publicize postsecondary institutional disciplinary inactions in response to rape cases; campus rape reports being mishandled by school officials; and lax security that led to violent victimizations, most notably student homicides (Kiss, 2013). The Clery Center staff also continues to lobby Congressional members to introduce and vote for critical campus sexual violence prevention and response legislation.

In response to growing public pressure and lobbying by the then Security On Campus, Inc. and other interested parties, Congress passed the *Student Right-to-Know and Campus Security Act of 1990* (20 U.S.C. 1092) (Kiss, 2013; for state-level legislation see Burke & Sloan, 2013). As Kiss (2013) described in Chapter 2, the legislation required all Title IV eligible IHEs to issue an annual security report in which they publicly disclose (1) crime statistics and (2) the crime prevention and security policies and procedures that are in effect on their campuses. The law was amended in 1992 to require that IHEs afford victims specific rights and again in 1998 to emphasize reporting obligations regarding sexual assault on campus.[2] The 1998 amendments also renamed the legislation the *Jeanne Clery Disclosure of Campus Security Policy and Campus Crime*

Statistics Act (Pub. L. 101-542; commonly known as the *Clery Act* or *Clery*). The primary goal of the *Clery Act* is to require IHEs to develop and provide student safety prevention and response procedures as well as accurate safety and security information for each Title IV college or university. Proponents of the *Clery Act* believe that such information will furnish students and their parents with the basis to make informed decisions about safety and security risks on the campus the students now or will attend.

Despite the emergence of concern about sexual victimization among college students and the passage of the *Clery Act*, little systematic information or research exists about the degree to which Title IV IHEs comply with the requirements to publish campus statistics on reported forcible and nonforcible sex offenses and the content of their institutions' sexual assault policies, protocols, and programs (Gregory & Janosik, 2013). This was true when the second edition of this volume was published in 2007. Unfortunately, not much has changed since that time despite the fact that The Office on Violence Against Women (OVAW) of the U.S. Department of Justice has awarded numerous grants annually to fund the *Grants to Reduce Violent Crimes Against Women on Campus Program*. These grants are part of the federal *Violence Against Women Act of 1994* (42 U.S.C. 14039; commonly abbreviated as VAWA) that are available to colleges and universities so staff can implement a campus-wide response to domestic violence, dating violence, sexual assault, and stalking. No published evaluation of these campus-wide responses funded by OVAW could be located on either the OVAW website (see http://www.ovw. usdoj.gov/publications.html) or in other scholarly electronic bibliographic resources (e.g., *Criminal Justice Abstracts, SocIndex*).

At best, the current state of knowledge about compliance with the *Clery Act* is based primarily on single cases of noncompliant IHEs that have been brought to the attention of the U.S. Department of Education (ED) – the federal agency with jurisdiction over the *Clery Act*. For example, between January of 2006 and April of 2012, the ED issued 35 findings involving alleged violations of *Clery*. Nine of the findings resulted in fines, with Eastern Michigan University receiving the largest fine ever imposed for a *Clery* violation ($357,500 in fines for 13 individual violations). Six of the fines were negotiated through settlement agreements; three are under appeal (Moxley, 2012).

In the late 1990s, Congress mandated a national-level study to examine responses by Title IV IHEs to reports of campus sexual assaults. Under Public Law 105–244, Congress specifically mandated the ground breaking research to address nine issues. These issues covered a range of efforts mandated by the *Clery Act*, spanning from reporting of sexual offense statistics to sexual assault prevention programs to victim support services; sexual assault reporting and adjudication policies, procedures, and practices; perceived facilitators of and barriers to reporting; and adjudication follow-through in campus judicial and criminal courts. Among the goals was to provide baseline information about how IHEs address the sexual assault-related mandates of the *Clery Act*. This chapter draws on the results from the federally funded national-level *Campus Sexual Assault Study* (Krebs, Lindquist, Warner, Fisher, & Martin, 2007). Given the comprehensiveness of the project, this chapter presents only the results relating to the reporting of sexual assault on campus.

The chapter begins with a brief overview of the National Campus Sexual Assault Policy Study (Karjane, Fisher, & Cullen, 2002; 2005). We discuss the *Clery Act* and its requirements for IHE reporting of sex offenses that occur on their campuses. As we show, the statistics compiled under the *Clery Act* are inherently inaccurate because they include only those offenses that victims bring to the attention of law enforcement and campus officials and overlook the fact the vast majority of sexual victimizations are not reported. We present statistics on the extent to which sexual offenses, namely rape, are underreported.

In the remainder of the chapter, we draw on the findings of the Campus Sexual Assault Study (CSA) and related scholarly research in our efforts to explore why sexual victimization incidents are underreported. Specifically, we focus on two key issues: (1) factors affecting individuals' decisions not to report, and (2) the lack of sexual assault responses training of students and campus officials as barriers to reporting. We also discuss policies and practices that might increase the reporting of sexual victimization. The chapter ends with a discussion of the challenges facing IHEs in their efforts to understand and encourage the reporting of sexual assault incidents.

The National Campus Sexual Assault Policy Study

In 2000, researchers at the University of Cincinnati, Education Development Center, Inc., and the Police Executive Research Forum undertook the Campus Sexual Assault Policy Study.[3] Along with examining compliance with the crime statistics reporting mandates of the *Clery Act,* the larger study also collected information about prevention, reporting procedures, response policies, and practices and protocols for dealing with incidents of sexual assault on campus aimed toward students (rather than students, staff, and faculty).

The sheer breath and complexity of the issues included in the Congressional mandate demanded a rigorous and multimethod research design with a large representative sample of IHEs and their administrators. The national sample was comprised of 2,438 IHEs in the United States and Puerto Rico, including all Historically Black Colleges and Universities (HBCU; N=98) and all Native American tribal schools (N=28). All nine categories of schools eligible for Title IV funding were represented in the sample: four-year public, four-year private nonprofit, two- to four-year private for profit, two-year public, two-year private nonprofit, less-than-two-year public and private nonprofit, less-than-two-year private for profit, Native American tribal schools, and HBCUs. The final sample consisted of 1,015 IHEs and 1,001 campus administrators.

To comprehensively investigate the wide array of issues and institutional contexts mandated by Congress, multiple forms of data were collected and analyzed. These data included: (1) results of a content analysis of published sexual assault policy material from a nationally representative sample of randomly selected IHEs[4], (2) mail surveys of campus administrators from a nationally representative sample of IHEs[5], (3) field research at eight IHEs determined to be demonstrating promising practices related to sexual assault prevention and response policies and protocols[6], and (4) electronic focus groups conducted with campus administrators and advocates[7] (see Karjane et al., 2002, 2005). The results presented in this chapter are drawn from these four sources of information and data.

The *Clery Act* Sex Offenses Reporting Requirements

The *Clery Act* crime classifications include murder, sex offenses, robbery, aggravated assault, burglary, motor vehicle theft, manslaughter, arson, and violations relating to alcohol, drugs, and weapons as defined by the Uniform Crime Reporting program (UCR) of the Federal Bureau of Investigation (Kiss, 2013). The *Clery Act* further requires institutions to distinguish between forcible and nonforcible sex offenses. Forcible sex offenses, defined as "any sexual act directed against another person, forcibly and/or against that person's will or not forcibly or against the person's will where the victim is incapable of giving consent," include forcible rape, forcible sodomy, sexual assault with an object, and forcible fondling. Nonforcible sex offenses, defined as "unlawful, nonforcible sexual intercourse," include incest and statutory rape. Of the schools that responded to our request for materials, 78 percent sent – as requested – their annual security reports (ASR). The ASR is important because, under the *Clery Act,* Title IV-eligible institutions are required to report crime statistics, including separate statistics on forcible and nonforcible sex offenses as defined in the UCR. The large percentage of IHEs that sent us their ASRs suggests that a large proportion of IHEs are complying with this aspect of the *Clery Act*.

Over eight in 10 schools that provided ASRs included three years of crime statistics as mandated by the *Clery Act*. However, there was less compliance with the *Clery Act's* stipulation that IHEs divide sexual offenses into the categories "forcible" and "nonforcible." Only 37 percent of IHEs reported crime statistics in a manner fully consistent with the *Clery Act*. Nearly half (49%) of the four-year public schools and 43 percent of the four-year private nonprofit schools included forcible and nonforcible sexual offenses in their crime statistics. Between 19 percent to 31 percent of the other types of schools did not report separate statistics on forcible and nonforcible sexual offenses.

The *Clery Act* crime-statistics mandate – the core idea of the *Clery Act* – relies exclusively on data relating to crimes known to, and recorded by, law enforcement and other campus authorities. For IHEs, official statistics are those compiled by campus law enforcement, security departments, or campus officials, based on the reports by students or others (e.g., employees, visitors) victimized while on campus. The mandated reporting of specific crime statistics raises several important issues concerning the validity of these statistics, particularly sex offenses, as measures of the safety of any campus.

Underreporting Rape: Why Individuals Do Not Report Their Victimization

The Extent of Underreporting Rape

Complicating the effective application of the *Clery Act* is underreporting of sexual assaults by victims to campus officials. This underreporting results in gross underestimates of the "true" amount of on-campus sexual offenses. Indeed, the widespread phenomenon of underreporting of rape and other types of sexual assault is consistently well documented in the research (Fisher, Daigle, Cullen, & Turner, 2003a). For example, the Sexual Victimization of College Women study found that less than 5 percent of rape victims officially reported the incident to campus and/or law enforcement authorities (Fisher et al., 2000; 2003a; 2003b). The *National Drug-Facilitated, Incapacitated, and Forcible Rape Study* (Kilpatrick et al., 2007) showed that 11.5 percent of college women reported the incident to the police. Sixteen percent of the forcible rapes were reported to the police compared to 7 percent of the drug and alcohol-facilitated or incapacitated rapes. Interestingly, Kilpatrick and colleagues also found that college women were less likely to report all types of rape than their adult female counterparts.

The Victim-Offender Relationship

Researchers also have consistently documented that female college students are far more likely to report rape by a stranger than by a friend or classmate. However, contrary to cultural myths regarding rape, stranger rape represents only a small fraction of the on-campus rapes of students; the vast majority is perpetrated by men known to the victim (Belknap & Erez, 2013). To illustrate, the *National College Women Sexual Victimization* study (NCWSV; Fisher et al., 2000) reported that rape victims knew their attacker as classmates (36%), friends (34%), boyfriends or former boyfriends (24%), or acquaintances (3%). Zinzow and Thompson's (2011) study of undergraduate female sexual assault victims also reported a similar pattern of the victim-perpetrator relationship, with acquaintances accounting for the largest percentage (60%), followed by romantic partner (32%). Underreporting by victims of acquaintance sexual assault is one of the most, if not the most, significant factors in low reporting rates on IHE campuses (Fisher et al., 2000).

Individuals' Reasons for Not Reporting

A substantial majority of these victims do not define their experiences using legal terms. That is, even though the incident is legally a criminal offense, they do not call their victimization a "rape" (Fisher et al., 2003b). This is particularly true when weapons are absent, alcohol is present, and/or physical injury (e.g., choke marks, bruises) is not apparent – the characteristics that are most often found in nonstranger rapes (Bondurant, 2001). Victims not identifying and naming events that meet legal definitions of rape and sexual assault has serious implications for reporting campus sexual assault since one must conceptualize an event as a crime before she (or he) seeks justice or heals. These barriers to reporting become even more immediate to address in light of the strong positive correlation between forcible rape, incapacitated rape and drug-alcohol facilitated rape and posttraumatic stress disorder (PTSD) and depression among college women (Zinzow et al., 2010).

Those who have experienced rape do not report the incident for a range of reasons. To illustrate, results from the NCWSV study (Fisher et al., 2000; 2003a) indicated that the most common reasons given for not reporting a completed rape included: (1) not thinking it was serious enough to report (65%), (2) not wanting other people to know (47%), (3) not wanting family to know (44%), (4) not clear a crime had occurred or that harm was intended (44%), and (5) lack of proof an incident occurred (42%). College women gave some similar reasons and some different reasons as to why they did not report an attempted rape. These reasons included: (1) not thinking it was serious enough to report (77%), (2) not clear a crime had occurred or that harm was intended (40%), (3) believing that the police would not think the incident was serious enough (34%), (4) not wanting other people to know (32%), (5) not wanting family to know (32%). Noteworthy is that not knowing how to report a rape was cited as a reason for not reporting in 14 percent of the completed rape incidents and in 7 percent of the attempted rape incidents (Fisher et al., 2000; 2003a).

Women's reasons for not reporting to law enforcement in the *National Drug-Facilitated, Incapacitated, and Forcible Rape Study* (Kilpatrick et al., 2007) were similar to those given in the NCWSV study. Note, however, that the reasons for not reporting varied by type of rape. For example, 85 percent of drug and alcohol-facilitated or incapacitated victims said they were unclear crime or harm was intended, 76 percent indicated that they didn't think the act was serious enough, and 62 percent stated a lack of proof as a reason for not reporting to the police. In contrast, forcible rape victims gave different reasons for not reporting to the police: 74 percent of them stated that they did not want others to know, 73 percent didn't want family to know and 71 percent feared reprisal.

The perceived importance of barriers also shed some light on understanding both the common and different factors which can contribute to underreporting. Sable and colleagues examined college freshmen's perceptions of barriers to reporting sexual assault for females and males (Sable, Danis, Mauzy, & Gallagher, 2006). They reported gender differences as to the relative importance of perceived barriers to reporting rape and sexual assault. Issues related to fear of retaliation by the perpetrator, insufficient or lack of resources (e.g., financial dependence on the perpetrator, no resources to obtain help such as transportation, money, or insurance), and not wanting the perpetrator to be prosecuted were scored significantly higher for females victims than male victims. Issues related to personal dignity such as shame, guilt and embarrassment, confidentiality, and fear of not being believed scored significantly higher for male victims than female victims.

Lack of Training in Sexual Assault Responses as a Barrier to Reporting

The Need for Student Training

Another factor that may contribute to low reporting rates among college students may be the lack of responsiveness of IHEs in handling disclosure and formal complaints of sexual assault. In many cases, those who first hear of the sexual assault – whether they are Resident Assistants (RAs), faculty, staff, or other students – are not adequately trained to respond to students' disclosure and to make appropriate referrals, including recommending medical and mental health services and filing a formal complaint (Bohmer & Parrot, 1993). Results from the campus administrator survey of the Campus Sexual Assault Policy Study revealed that overall, 42 percent of the schools provided sexual assault reporting training for students, with over half of four-year public and private nonprofit schools (77% and 65%, respectively) and HBCUs (61%) doing so. In about half the IHEs (51%) where training is provided, this training is voluntary. In another 45 percent of the IHEs, this training is mandatory for student RAs. In a small percentage of IHEs, 14 percent, training was manda-tory for student security officers. Most often (64%), faculty and staff of the in-stitution provide the sexual assault response training, though it can also in-volve staff from a community agency (40%) or peer educator or trainer (23%). In IHEs where RAs and student security officers receive mandatory training, this is largely due to institutional rules rather than to state laws (see Karjane et al., 2002, Table 4.1).

What remains unclear from these data, however, is the extent and quality of sexual assault response training given to the average college student – pre-cisely the people most likely to learn about sexual assaults. Again, about 60 percent of the schools provide no training whatsoever to students, and it ap-pears that when training occurs, it is most often directed at RAs and student security officers. Accordingly, it seems that the lack of training given to the college student body is an issue that warrants further attention and action by college administrators.

The Need for Law Enforcement and Security Officer Training

When asked about providing security or law enforcement services on their campuses, almost half the campus administrators (48%) stated that they rely on local law enforcement agencies. Other options chosen by administrators (who could select more than one option) were sworn officers employed by the school (28%) and private security personnel employed by the school (8%). Sworn officers were common at four-year public schools and HBCUs (84% and 75%, respectively), while private security officers were more common at two- and four-year private, nonprofit schools. A majority of the remaining five types of schools relied on local law enforcement agencies (see Karjane et al., 2002, Table 4.2).

When campus administrators were asked whether campus law enforce-ment or security officers were "required by law or institutional policy to be trained to respond to reports of sexual assault," just over one-third (38%) of the administrators answered in the affirmative. The figures were higher for four-year public schools (more than 8 in 10) and HBCUs (more than 7 in 10). About half of the four-year private nonprofit and two-year public schools stat-ed that they required training. The key finding here is that while training is fairly standard at four-year public schools and HBCUs which rely primarily on sworn officers employed by the school, at many other institutions, training *is not provided to the very people most likely to receive formal complaints from victims.*

Although school administrators indicated that a variety of sources provide this training, IHEs most often rely on the state training academy (39%), which presumably provides training of a general nature to law enforcement person-nel who will serve in a variety of social settings. How specific this training is to the reporting of sexual victimization by college students is unknown. Other common sources of training for enforcement/security personnel – each used by about one in five schools – include the faculty or staff of the institution (23%), the faculty or staff of the law enforcement/security agency (22%), and specialized trainers (19%) (Karjane et al., 2002, Table 4.2).

Faculty and Staff Training

Another source in whom student victims may confide about their sexual assault are faculty members and staff. The survey of campus administrators also furnished information on IHE faculty member and staff training on how to respond to reports of sexual victimization. About half of all schools – including three in 10 public, four-year schools – provide no training to faculty and staff on appropriate responses to disclosures of sexual assault. Training is mandatory in about one in three schools, but voluntary in 17 percent of the other schools. Across all the schools when the training is required, it is because institutional policy mandates it. Finally, when training is supplied it is most often conducted by faculty members and staff of the institution rather than by outsiders (see Karjane et al., 2002, Table 4.3).

Barriers to Reporting Identified from Survey of Campus Administrators

Reporting Options

Reporting options also could influence whether or not students report their sexual assault to campus officials. Analysis of the campus administrator surveys revealed that IHEs utilize a variety of reporting options: confidential, anonymous, third party, and (anonymous) Internet reporting. A majority (84%) of all school types offer a confidential reporting option. An anonymous reporting option was available at less than one-half of small, nonresidential, nontraditional school types and at slightly more than one-half of four-year public and private schools (52%) and HBCUs (51%). Only a small fraction of schools (4%) offered anonymous Internet reports. This latter finding is salient because the recognition of an anonymous reporting option was found to be a promising practice as well as a policy that student activists, rape trauma professionals, and victims' advocates believed would facilitate reporting of the crime (see Karjane et al., 2002, Table 4.A and Chapter 8).

Also salient is the finding that third-party reporting by witnesses is recognized at only one in three schools, roughly, and only slightly more than half (53%) of four-year public IHEs offered this option. Given Fisher and her colleagues' (2000; 2003a) finding that most victims disclose their experience to their friends but do not report the crime to campus authorities or law enforcement, this omission may significantly impact reporting rates of the sexual assault.

Institutional Barriers

The *National Sexual Assault Policy Study* also asked campus administrators about types of institutional policies that might function to discourage or prevent reporting of sexual assaults on their campuses. Two important factors emerged from their responses. First, more than 80 percent of campus administrators indicated that a requirement that victims who file sexual assault complaints must "somewhat" participate in the adjudication process discourages victims from reporting assaults. This insight is consistent with site visit data as well as with research on female sexual assault victims and their low incidence of reporting these assaults to the police (Fisher et al., 2000; 2003a; National Victims Center, 1992). As previously noted, Fisher and her colleagues' (2000) research suggests that female college students do not want their families and other people to know about the victimization, are not certain they can prove that a victimization occurred, and are not convinced that the incident was "serious enough" to warrant a formal intervention. In this light, victims faced with participating in an adjudication process might not report a sexual assault if they wished to avoid public disclosure, were doubtful about proving they were assaulted, and/or did not believe that a formal hearing was the appropriate way to resolve the victimization.

The question remains, however, over the extent victims are informed of (1) their choices regarding informally and formally reporting their assault to campus and/or local criminal justice authorities and (2) how their confidentiality will be protected, if at all, in each type of action taken. Qualitative data collected in this study strongly suggest that any policy or procedure that compromises or, worse, eliminates the student victim's ability to make her or his own informed choices throughout the reporting and adjudication process not only reduces reporting rates, but may also be counterproductive to the victim's healing process. A second factor worth noting is the presence of a campus drug and/or alcohol policy. Typically, the aggressor and victim know each other and the assault frequently emerges from a social encounter in which one or both are drinking or drugging (see Abbey, Zawacki, Buck, Clinton, & McAuslan, 2004). If student victims know that they are in violation of a policy forbidding the use of drugs or alcohol, this might make them fearful to report a sexual assault.

Intrinsically related to this concern is the issue of victims' acknowledging (or failing to acknowledge) their assault as a crime. Research shows that drugs and/or alcohol are frequently present (and used by both perpetrators and victims) when college women are sexually assaulted (Abbey et al., 2004; Dowdall, 2013). Victims of rape and attempted rape who were drinking before the assault are far less apt to name their experience "rape" or "sexual assault" than victims who did not drink before the assault (Bondurant, 2001; Schwartz & Leggett, 1999). If victims do not name their experience, they do not have a crime to report. Thus, while the issue of a school's alcohol and drug policies may be related to the issue of drinking and its strong association with campus sexual assault, the two are analytically distinct.

Barriers to Reporting Identified from Field Research

Qualitative interviews – with rape crisis counselors, sexual assault nurse examiners, victims' advocates, deans of students, and students themselves – provided further insight into the reporting barriers issue. Again, these and related issues are situated within the context of the existing scholarship.

Developmental Issues

Students attending postsecondary institutions, especially traditional schools, are generally between the ages of 18 and 24. Developmentally, these young adults are testing themselves and their new (partial) independence from their parents. These youth feel like they can take care of themselves, or at least feel they should show their parents that they can. Being sexually assaulted may make them feel like they have failed to protect themselves, in the midst of their first autonomous living situation. Reporting the incident makes it more real in that their "failure" is documented. This feeling is further exacerbated when high-risk behavior such as drinking or drugging is involved.

Trauma Response Issues

Women who experience events that meet the legal definition of sexual assault frequently do not label their victimization as such, particularly when weapons are absent, alcohol is present, and/or physical injury (e.g., choke marks, bruises) is not apparent – the predominant scenario for nonstranger rape (Bondurant, 2001). While some victims deliberately minimize the importance of the assault as a way of mitigating its impact, most victims cannot avoid a traumatic response to what happened (Herman, 1992; Karjane, 2002; Kelly, 1988). Victims of sexual assault, whether acknowledged or not, may experience intense feelings of shame and self-blame and high levels of psychological distress (Belknap & Erez, 2013; Karjane, 2002).

Shame is the emotional response to a perceived or actual threat to social bonds (Scheff & Retzinger, 1991). Tragically, for student victims, the fear that people will hold them responsible for their own criminal victimization may be warranted. Tolerance for rape and sexual assault in intimate relationships is widespread in the general population and among college students, and largely because of this tolerance "blame the victim" attitudes flourish (Kershner, 2000; Kopper, 1996; Kormos & Brooks, 1994; Stormo, Lang, & Stritzke, 1997). Institutional authorities may (unintentionally) condone victim blaming (for example, by circulating materials that focus on the victim's responsibility to avoid sexual assault rather than on the perpetrator), and certainly the mass media play a part. Students, both prior and subsequent to being sexually victimized, can internalize these attitudes, further exacerbating their own sense of shame and stigmatization and inhibiting their ability to name their experience – and thus making an informed decision to report the assault more difficult. Victims of acquaintance rape have been found to have higher levels of self-blame than victims of stranger rape (Frazier & Seales, 1997; Katz, 1991). Studies show that student victims of on-campus acquaintance rape are far less likely to report their victimization to campus authorities than are victims of campus stranger rape (Belknap & Erez, 2013; Fisher et al., 2010).

Research has shown that the victim's ability to name the experience is dependent on the reactions of those to whom she or he first discloses the assault (Pitts & Schwartz, 1997; Bondurant, 2001; Schwartz & DeKeseredy, 1997). When asked during field research interviews what distinguishes those who report from those who do not report, victim advocates, police officers, and campus officials uniformly asserted that victims who report are encouraged to do so by their friends, who frequently accompany them when they make the report to campus and/or criminal justice authorities.

Finally, having just experienced a profoundly disempowering event, victims of sexual assault need to reassert control over basic aspects of their lives and environments (Herman, 1992; Janoff-Bulman, 1992). One way to regain this control is to avoid a lengthy adjudication process – whether through the campus or the criminal justice system – that threatens to dominate the victim's college experience. Some victims believe that if they keep the assault to themselves, they can focus on their academics and maintain their original reason for attending school. In addition, due to a lack of accurate knowledge about the system, victims fear that they will have no control over the reporting and adjudication process, for example, that their confidentiality will not be honored. Student victims often do not realize that reporting a rape or sexual assault is different from pursuing the case criminally or through campus adjudication boards. This need to regain control is an important part of the victim's healing process; reporting policies that disempower the victim – such as mandatory reporting requirements that do not include an anonymous reporting option – are widely viewed by sexual assault advocates as detrimental to this healing process.

Socio-Political and Social Support Issues

In terms of the politics of interpersonal relations, gender politics play a large role in social support. Self-acknowledgement of the rape politicizes the relationship in ways that make it difficult for many people to comprehend what happened (e.g., "he is my friend," "he cares about me," "yet he raped me") and to recognize themselves as victims of a crime (Karjane, 2002). Overall, campus sexual assault victims often have been violently assaulted by someone they know and someone whom their peers and professors know. When the victim acknowledges and names the experience "rape" or "sexual assault," the victim is, at the same time, naming a friend, boyfriend, or classmate a "criminal" – specifically, a "rapist." Historically, this act has different meanings and consequences for a white woman naming a white man a rapist and for a black woman naming a black man a rapist. As the criminal justice system incarcerates black men at rates highly disproportional to their share of the population compared to white men, black women need to contend with feelings of betraying their race in ways that other minority women and white women do not have to contend with (Crenshaw, 1991; Neville & Pugh, 1997; Wyatt, 1992).

Furthermore, whether victims of sexual assault see themselves as "victims" or as people who have been victimized but retain the ability to willfully act and protect themselves, the social conventions and institutional contexts within which they must name and claim their experience often construct them as victims. As such, others who know they have been raped perceive them as victims. Given that the social definition of "victim" entails a perception of a person who is weak, pitiful, and often blameworthy, and that these assumptions are taken to reflect a life stance rather than an experience, it is not surprising that people would seek to avoid the label of "rape victim" (Karjane, 2002).

Within IHEs, when allegations of rape and sexual assault occur, information is often spread through rumor, and campuses may become polarized. This is particularly true when campus, local, and national media cover the trial. Students fear that "ratting" on another student by filing a report with campus or local criminal justice authorities will result in social isolation or, worse, social ostracism. Based on field research, this fear appears to be especially strong at institutions with strong social cliques, such as campuses dominated by Greek life.

As one administrator described it, the campus works "like a microcosm of society where victims get punished for reporting." There does seem to be slight progress, at least among the schools noted to have promising practices regarding sexual assault response, in changing social attitudes toward non-stranger rape. In previous years, the frequent phrase used to describe – and condone – the criminal act of rape was "boys will be boys." Such a phrase negates the victim's perspective altogether, while it conflates a masculine per-spective with a rapist's perspective. In essence, this phrase classifies forms of criminal activity as normative in (hetero) sexual relations. Today, administra-tors almost uniformly use the phrase "It's a he said, she said," which ac-knowledges a (female) victim's perspective, yet still functions to trivialize the crime. This phrase is used by administrators to mean that evidence – foren-sic and even circumstantial – is frequently absent in sexual assaults commit-ted by "dates" or acquaintances, thus, the two versions of the events must be weighed against each other to establish truth. While certainly an improve-ment over "boys will be boys," this phrase implies a false equality to the per-spectives, thus trivializing the victim's experience.

In the face of this perceptual shift, it is disturbing that the Campus Sexual Assault Policy Study reported that once a student files a complaint of a sexu-al assault, only 26 percent of IHEs had an investigation or fact-finding stage for the gathering of information to determine if there is sufficient evidence to decide whether a sexual misconduct code violation has occurred. Lack of a fact-finding stage to gather evidence before a complaint moves to review dur-ing a hearing by the adjudication board or another decision-making entity al-most inevitably means that the vast majority of complaints of sexual assault stay at the level of the proverbial "he said, she said." It is highly likely, given the importance victims place on being believed, that this institutional barrier negatively impacts victim reporting decisions.

Confidentiality Issues

Given the loss of personal control the victim has just experienced, coupled with the way society perceives and individuals respond to "victims," confi-dentiality issues – that is, how or whether information regarding the student's victimization will circulate throughout the campus – function as important barriers to reporting and following through with adjudication procedures. As such, the use of mandatory reporters on campus and in the community and the establishment of reporting Memorandums of Understanding (MOU) be-tween a school and its local prosecutor's office that preclude the victim's con-sent are policies identified as reporting barriers during site visits.

In one national survey, 50 percent of women who had been raped re-sponded that they would be "a lot" more likely and 16 percent would be "somewhat" more likely to report to the police if there were a law prohibiting the news media from disclosing their names and addresses (National Victims

Center, 1992). Similarly, on postsecondary campuses, field research found that any policy or procedure that students (particularly student victims) perceived as a risk to their ability to control information about their victimization functioned as a barrier to reporting.

Criminal Justice Issues

While rape reform efforts in the United States have been somewhat successful in eradicating myths about stranger rape and their institutionalization within the criminal justice system, we have only just begun to acknowledge the far more prevalent problem of rape among acquaintances and intimates. As such, student victims still fear unsympathetic treatment by the police and local prosecutors, which inhibits them from reporting their criminal victimization.

Compounding this fear is the legal quandary of many acquaintance rape cases: lack of evidence to substantiate the crime. If a prosecutor is reticent or, more frequently, refuses outright to bring an acquaintance rape case to trial without sufficient evidence, victims often take that to mean the prosecutor does not believe their story. Furthermore, as one victim advocate from a sheriff's office observed, distrust of law enforcement is especially prevalent within some age and ethnic groups "because they're dealing with a criminal justice system that isn't [just] and a playing field that isn't level."

Student victims of campus sexual assault, especially when the assault is perpetrated by someone they know, do not report, in part, because they do not believe that the perpetrator will be punished. While this perception is somewhat accurate – given the slim likelihood of a perpetrator known to the victim being held accountable by the criminal justice system – IHEs are potentially more likely to punish perpetrators, as campus adjudication boards often operate with a "preponderance of the evidence" evidentiary standard rather than "beyond a reasonable doubt" standard that is used in criminal trials. This empirical issue deserves more attention, especially in light of the "Dear Colleague" letter issued by the ED's Office of Civil Rights on April 4, 2011. The letter stated that for a school's grievance procedure to be consistent with *Title IX* standards, the school must use the "preponderance of the evidence standard" (i.e., it is more likely than not that the sexual assault occurred) (Ali, 2011).

Finally, treatment and forensic evidence collection by a certified sexual assault nurse examiner, when available, because of funding structures is usually contingent on first filing a police report of the crime. Rape trauma professionals see the lack of choice involved in this policy as a barrier to reporting. The state-of-the-art Rape Treatment Center at the Santa Monica – UCLA Medical Center offers free treatment to *all* victims, whether or not they first file a police report. The forensic evidence that is collected is then preserved through a chain of custody established in consultation with the Los Angeles County crime lab and stored indefinitely so it will be available if the victim ever wishes to pursue criminal charges. Crime Lab Director Gail Abarbanel says that giving the victim the choice to be treated before filing the report frequently results in the victim ultimately filing a police report of the crime; the act of being treated and seeing that there is evidence of the crime seems important in victim decisions to file police reports.

Policies and Practices That Facilitate Reporting Victimization

Facilitators Identified through Campus Administrators' Survey

Campus administrators were also asked about the types of institutional policies that might function to encourage sexual assault reporting. Two findings emerge from these data. First, administrators believe that policies like providing services to potential victims, strategies to make campus personnel more responsive to reports of sexual assault, confidential reporting by victims, and targeted educational programs (for example, those aimed at fraternities and student-athletes) encourage reporting. If they are correct, then IHEs could combine a variety of strategies into a multimodal approach to increase the likelihood of victims reporting their assaults. It remains to be confirmed, of course, whether students in general and victims in particular see these factors as salient to the reporting decision. Still, the insights of the administrators at the very least, suggest strategies that might actually facilitate reporting.

Second, but on a less optimistic note, it appears that a large number of campuses have few of these policies in place. The exceptions are four-year public schools and HBCUs, where such policies are relatively common. Of these, the administrators' survey results revealed that only six policies are in place in more than half the campuses: confidential reporting options (84%)[8], new student orientation programs on sexual assault issues (68%), providing faculty and staff with information on who can help victims (67%), campus law enforcement protocols for responding to sexual assaults (52%), campus-wide publicity of high risk factors and/or past crimes on campus (51%), and a coordinated crisis response across the campus and community to provide victim services (50%). Noteworthy is that only three policies − confidential reporting, new student orientation programs, and providing faculty and staff with information − are in place in two-thirds of these campuses.

Facilitators Identified through Field Research

IHE administrators and rape trauma response professionals identified additional policies, protocols, and practices as facilitating victim reporting of campus rape and sexual assault.

EDUCATION AND SOCIAL SUPPORTS. Three main facilitators were identified through conversations with student rape trauma response team members, educators/activists, and victim advocates: on-campus presentations, information dissemination, and social support. Response team members noted that actively courting invitations for sexual assault-oriented presentations at ethnic and sexual minority group organizations increased reports, especially in the few weeks after the presentations were made. Such presentations can target the particular cultural myths surrounding rape and sexual assault in terms of prevalent community norms. Student educators/activists observed that students get the majority of their information through the Internet, word of mouth, and education programs provided by RAs and faculty. Therefore, disseminating information on what constitutes a violation of the school's sexual misconduct policy, describing administrative responses and sanctions, and, in particular, publicizing the knowledge that filing a report is different from pressing charges and noting the potential benefits from reporting the incident should increase reporting to campus law enforcement among college students (see also Zinzow & Thompson, 2011).

As previously noted, victim advocates state that the primary characteristic that distinguishes victims who report their assaults and access professional services and those who do not is the support they receive from their friends – who often accompany them to make the report. As one victim advocate noted, "Sometimes whole groups of kids come; they come with their posse." Witnesses who see the crime occur – or have a strong sense that a crime is about to occur – can provide social support to the victim, encourage the victim to make a report, or make a third-party report of their own. They can also be trained in active bystander techniques to interrupt the behavior (see Coker et al., 2011).

AN ANONYMOUS REPORTING OPTION. There was strong agreement among field interviewees that an anonymous reporting option increases reporting of campus sexual assault. A primary strength of this option is that the victim can seek out assistance, information, and support referrals without first having to take the step of identifying her- or himself and formally entering a system the victim does not yet have enough information to effectively negotiate. The anonymous reporting option allows student victims to come forward and talk to a trusted school official without the possibility of losing control of the process (e.g., mandated reporters at schools that do not offer anonymous reporting). This option allows victims to receive support and information on which to base informed decisions about filing a report in their own name, while also allowing the crime to be documented in the annual security report statistics if the student never feels comfortable with making a formal report. Allowing anonymous reporting also may have a secondary effect that should not be overlooked. Since reporting to police is the most significant predictor of who receives medical care, allowing anonymous reporting may increase the numbers of women receiving acute postrape medical care (Kilpatrick et al., 2007). This means that more college students who have been raped would receive not only standard medical treatment for injuries but also testing for HIV/AIDS, sexually transmitted diseases, and, for women, pregnancy.

A VICTIM-DRIVEN POLICY. An anonymous reporting option is a good example of a victim-driven policy. Sexual assault policies that emphasize criminal justice imperatives (e.g., to report disclosures of the crime against the victim's will) or higher education imperatives (e.g., to maintain the school's image as a safe haven) at the expense of the immediate and long-term needs of the rape victim are highly problematic. Policies that are sensitive to and respect the victim's needs (and ability) to make his or her own decision at each and every juncture in the process of seeking information, support, treatment, and, possibly, justice within the campus and/or the criminal justice system have been found to facilitate students coming forth and reporting the crime. As such, students and student victims ideally should receive explicit information about what to expect in each step of the process of seeking help from school administrators, including faculty and resident advisors. Publicizing information on how the different components of the school's sexual assault and reporting policies relate, are contingent on, or are separate from one another was also found to increase reporting. For example, providing students with information that explains that reporting an assault to campus authorities is different than going forward with an adjudication board hearing or campus and criminal prosecution within the criminal justice system.

Based on these findings, the challenge is two-fold. First, systematic evaluations should be undertaken to see which policies – whether alone or in combination – increase the very low rate of reporting sexual assaults that now exists on college campuses. Second, effective policies and combinations of strategies should be publicized to campus administrators across the nation. One option would be to develop a model sexual assault reporting document that outlines the best strategies – based on empirical evidence – for fostering the reporting of sexual victimization to law enforcement – both campus and local authorities.

Conclusion

The impetus for student-victim-oriented Congressional legislation throughout the 1990s, such as the *Clery Act,* was to ensure that IHEs employ strategies to prevent and respond to reports of sexual assault on campus in a proactive manner and to provide current and prospective students and their parents with an accurate idea of the level of violence on campuses. Both national studies and smaller-scale research have consistently found that one in five female students suffer rape and/or rape attempts during their college years, most frequently at the hands of their peers. As such, prevention, reporting, and response policies should be built on definitions of sexual assault – including different types of rape (e.g., forcible rape, drug- and alcohol-facilitated rape, and incapacitated rape) that make it clear that individuals known to the victim most frequently commit this crime.

A key issue confronted by postsecondary institutions is that the vast majority of students who experience sexual assaults – on and off campus – do not report them to campus or law enforcement officials. The reasons for not reporting victimizations, as discussed in this chapter, are complex and unlikely to be fully overcome but nonetheless, identifying both barriers and facilitators to reporting can be a starting point for change in policies and procedures (Fisher et al., 2003a, 2010; Kilpatrick et al., 2007; Zinzow & Thompson, 2011).

Bear in mind that the college community is affected by this underreporting in at least two significant ways, and these should not be overlooked. First, as the researchers cited above have reported, victims of sexual assault are unlikely to secure the medical care (e.g., sexual assault exam), psychological counseling and support they need to cope with and heal from this potentially traumatic event in their lives making it more probable that they will engage in "self-blame," self-medication (e.g., disordered eating and excessive drinking), and other self-destructive behaviors. The friends to whom they disclose their experience are also likely to be affected, having their own feelings of anger, fear, and/or helplessness. In this way, a single instance of sexual assault can have a ripple effect. Second, and of crucial importance unless sexual assaults are reported, students who sexually assault their classmates will not be subjected to appropriate disciplinary sanctions. Recent research on the "undetected rapist" on college campuses, that is those men who commit rape and are never reported to any authority, suggests that a majority of these unsanctioned rapists will go on to sexually victimize others, or the same person (Lisak & Miller, 2002).

Issues discussed in this chapter concerning the act of reporting a sexual assault raised other pertinent issues that campus administrators as well as campus safety advocates should proactively address (see Cantalupo, 2013). First, response and reporting policies should be designed to allow victims as much decision-making authority in the process as possible. This includes both the criminal justice options and the medical options. Victims fear losing control over the reporting and adjudication processes, which is a barrier to their coming forth and making the initial reports. Policies should be designed to allow victims to make the decision about moving forward, stopping, or slowing down the pace at each juncture of the disclosure, reporting, and adjudication process as well as choices about medical and psychological care. Explicit information regarding the policy and its different components – and the decisions to be made at each juncture – should be provided to only the victim to inform her or his decisions but also disseminated publically to the campus community so all are educated. Also, victims should be informed of how each junction in the process affects their confidentiality.

As recommended by Kilpatrick and his colleagues (2007), a system that allows for separation of the choice of whether to pursue legal action – criminal or civil – from the choice as to whether to receive medical care may lead to an increased number of college students who were raped to seek medical care. In this type of system, a sexual assault nurse examiner or medical personnel can gather forensic evidence at that time whether the person who has been raped decides to report the incident to the police. Such a system allows a decision about reporting or prosecution to be made at a later time but ensures immediate medical attention for injuries, sexually transmitted diseases, HIV/AIDS, and pregnancy.

Second, adjudication or grievance hearings should be fair to all parties (see Cantalupo, 2013) and in accordance with procedural requirements outlined by the ED's Office for Civil Rights' "Dear Colleague" letter including notice of nondiscrimination, presence of a designated *Title IX* coordinator, and adoption and publication of grievance procedures for prompt and equitable resolution of complaints of all forms of sexual harassment, including sexual violence (Ali, 2011). Per the "Dear Colleague" letter, grievance procedures include giving notice of grievance procedures; adequate, reliable and impartial investigation of complaints; designated and prompt time frames; and notice of outcomes.

Victims of campus crime often seek acknowledgment of and justice for their experience; they seek respect within the campus system. One way to ensure that respect is to provide campus adjudication hearings that are fair to both parties. Operational rules and responsibilities should be explicit, unbiased, communicated to both parties, and adhered to. Current litigation instigated by students found responsible for sexual misconduct often centers on due process rights not being consistently applied.[9] As these suits threaten the validity of the board's determination of responsibility, the needs of student victims are also compromised (see Cantalupo, 2013).

Third, response and reporting policies and policy materials should be gender-neutral and refer to the person who has experienced an assault as a "survivor," the term used by many victims of sexual assault in an effort to reclaim their lives. This term connotes the strength of living through and beyond the traumatic experience as opposed to focusing on the implied weakness in not being able to adequately protect oneself. Response policies should provide strategies to empower victims, rather than revictimize them by taking choices away or withholding information.

Fourth is a recommendation proposed by Kilpatrick and colleagues (2007) in which they suggest that it may also be useful to encourage reporting based on the reasons given by the small numbers of victims who reported their incident to the police. These women's primary reason for reporting was to "prevent crime against others," followed by "because it was a crime," and/or "to catch or find the assailant." Kilpatrick and colleagues (2007) suggest building on these altruistic motives by stressing the beneficial public safety outcomes as well as the individual outcomes of reporting.

Fifth, sexual assault definitions, protocols and policies should be widely distributed every term, written in lay terms, and explicitly supported by administration so that all students are aware of their rights and options before they need the system. Distribution of materials should be made every term to ensure that students (and faculty and staff) are reminded of their rights and options.

Further research needs to determine the most effective ways to increase reporting sexual victimization. Zinzow and Thompson (2011, p. 722) have suggested that research is needed to determine whether interventions that decrease self-blame, increase acknowledgement of rape as crime, increase positive reactions from support networks and emphasize confidentiality will increase reporting rates. Findings from this line of research, along with that suggested by the findings from the National Campus Sexual Assault Policy Study, are much needed to better understand the barriers to reporting to law enforcement. These findings can then inform the development, implementation, and evaluation of efforts to increase reporting.

Addressing the reporting issues discussed in this chapter by implementing and evaluating the recommendations outlined are critical first steps toward better understanding campus sexual assault within the context of college students' experiences. Reducing the barriers to college students' reporting and documenting which strategies "work" to increase reporting is an evidence-based approach to comprehensively and sensitively addressing nonreporting that characterizes a large proportion of sexual assault incidents. As noted, these barriers to reporting undermine not only the effectiveness of the *Clery Act* but the safety of the entire campus community, especially students who are at high risk for different types of sexual assault.

NOTES

1. Federal reporting requirements define "rape" as a set of crimes that constitute non-consensual forcible or non-forcible sexual penetration (e.g., unwilling forcible vaginal intercourse). In recent years, rape reform law has moved toward expanding the definition of rape to include various forms of sexual abuse and degrees of severity (e.g., forcible non-consensual oral intercourse, non-forcible non-consensual fondling). This expansion has taken place through the codification of multiple forms of sexual abuse in federal and state law. The term "sexual assault" refers to a range of sexually oriented criminal acts defined federally by the Federal Bureau of Investigation as well as by state statute. Rape is a form of sexual assault.

2. *The Campus Sex Crime Prevention Act* was enacted 28 October 2000. As changes pertaining to this act did not go into effect until 28 October 2002, they are not reflected in the reported study's results.

3. This project was supported by Grant No. 1999-WA-VX-0008 awarded by the National Institute of Justice, Office of Justice Program, U. S. Department of Justice. Points of view in this chapter are those of the authors and do not necessarily represent the official position or policies of the U.S. Department of Justice.

4. The policy materials response rate ranged from 20 percent (two- and four-year private for profit IHEs) to 88 percent (four-year public IHEs) (average response rate, 42%) (see Karjane et al., 2002, Table 2.5).

5. The survey of campus administrators response rate ranged from 29 percent (two- and four-year for profit IHEs) to 54 percent (four-year public IHEs) (average response rate, 41%) (see Karjane et al., 2002, Table 2.6).

6. See Karjane et al., 2002 pages 32–40 for description of the field research, including the selection criteria, and names and location of these eight IHEs.

7. Focus group participants were recruited by various means. Health care professionals were recruited through the Student Health Services on-line mailing list operated by the American College Health Association. Campus law enforcement professionals were chosen from a list maintained by the Police Executive Research Forum and individually invited via e-mail. Resident life directors were recruited primarily by word of mouth. A notice was also posted on the DISCUSS on-line mailing list, a "members only" forum maintained by the Association for Student Judicial Affairs and the American College Personnel Association.

8. A discrepancy regarding the rates of schools offering a confidential reporting option exists in our findings. This discrepancy results from our differing data sources: content analysis of sexual assault policies and/or ASRs indicate that 84 percent of IHEs offer a confidential reporting option at their school; the administrator survey indicates 75 percent of IHEs offer a confidential reporting option. Given that the administrators' survey was self-report, the researchers believe that the figure drawn from the content analysis of written sexual assault policies is the more valid, thus accurate measure.

9. The Campus Sexual Assault Policy Study reported that only 37 percent of IHEs offer procedures for due process for those accused of sexual assault.

REFERENCES

Abbey, A., Zawacki, T., Buck P., Clinton, M., & McAuslan, P. (2004). Sexual assault and alcohol consumption: What do we know about their relationship and what types of research are still needed? *Aggression and Violent Behavior, 9,* 271–303.

Ali, R. (2011). Dear Colleague Letter. U.S. Department of Education: Office for Civil Rights, Office of the Assistant Secretary. Retrieved from http://www2.ed.gov/about/offices/list/ocr/letters/colleague-201104.html.

Belknap, J., & Erez, E. (2013). The sexual harassment, rape, and intimate partner abuse of college women. In B. S. Fisher & J. J. Sloan (Eds.), *Campus crime: Legal, social, and policy perspectives* (3rd ed.). Springfield, IL: Charles C Thomas.

Bohmer, C., & Parrot, A. (1993). *Sexual assault on campus: The problem and the solution.* New York: Lexington Books.

Bondurant, B. (2001). University women's acknowledgement of rape: Individual, situational, and social factors. *Violence Against Women, 7,* 294–314.

Burke, J. M., & Sloan, J. J., III. (2013). State-level *Clery Act* initiatives: Symbolic politics or substantive policy? In B. S. Fisher & J. J. Sloan (Eds.), *Campus crime: Legal, social, and policy perspectives* (3rd ed.). Springfield, IL: Charles C Thomas.

Burling, P. (2003). *Crime on campus: Analyzing and managing the increasing risk of institutional liability* (2nd ed.). Washington DC: National Association of College and University Attorneys.

Cantalupo, N. C. (2013). "Decriminalizing" our institutional responses to campus peer sexual violence. In B. S. Fisher & J. J. Sloan (Eds.), *Campus crime: Legal, social, and policy perspectives* (3rd ed.). Springfield, IL: Charles C Thomas.

Coker, A. L., Cook-Craig, P. G., Williams, C. M., Fisher, B. S., Clear, E. R., Garcia, L. S., & Hegge, L. M. (2011). Evaluation of Green Dot: An active bystander intervention to reduce sexual violence on college campuses. *Violence Against Women, 17,* 777–796.

Crenshaw, K. (1991). Mapping the margins: Intersectionality, identity politics, and violence against women of color. *Stanford Law Review, 43,* 1241–1299.

Dowdall, G. (2013). The role of alcohol abuse in college student victimization. In B. S. Fisher & J. J. Sloan (Eds.), *Campus crime: Legal, social, and policy perspectives* (3rd ed.). Springfield, IL: Charles C Thomas.

Fisher, B., Cullen, F., & Turner, M. (2000). *The sexual victimization of college women.* Washington, DC: National Institute of Justice and Bureau of Justice Statistics.

Fisher, B., Daigle, L., & Cullen, F. (2010). *Unsafe in the ivory tower: The sexual victimization of college women.* Thousand Oaks, CA: Sage.

Fisher, B., Daigle, L., Cullen, F., & Turner, M. (2003a). Reporting sexual victimization to the police and others: Results from a national-level study of college women. *Criminal Justice and Behavior, 30,* 6–38.

Fisher, B., Daigle, L., Cullen, F., & Turner, M. (2003b). Acknowledging sexual victimization as rape: Results from a national-level study. *Justice Quarterly, 20,* 401–440.

Fisher, B., Sloan, J., Cullen, F., & Lu, C. (1998). Crime in the ivory tower: The level and sources of student victimization. *Criminology, 36,* 671–710.

Frazier, P., & Seales, L. (1997). Acquaintance rape is real rape. In M. D. Schwartz (Ed.), *Researching sexual violence against women: Methodological and personal perspectives* (pp. 54–64). Thousand Oaks, CA: Sage.

Gregory, D., & Janosik, S. (2013). The research on the *Clery Act* and crime reporting and its impact on the literature and student affairs practice. In B. S. Fisher & J. J. Sloan (Eds.), *Campus crime: Legal, social, and policy perspectives* (3rd ed.). Springfield, IL: Charles C Thomas.

Herman, J. (1992). *Trauma and recovery: The aftermath of violence, from domestic abuse to political terror.* New York: Basic Books.

Janoff-Bulman, R. (1992). *Shattered assumptions: Toward a new psychology of trauma.* New York: The Free Press.

Karjane, H., Fisher, B., & Cullen, F. (2002). *Campus sexual assault: How America's institutions of higher education respond.* Retrieved from https://www.ncjrs.gov/pdffiles1/nij/205521.pdf.

Karjane, H. (2002). The communication of trauma in media culture: A Poststructural analysis of women's experience of gender-based violence and healing (Doctoral dissertation, University of Massachusetts at Amherst, 2002). *Dissertation Abstracts International, 63,* 3407.

Karjane, H., Fisher, B., & Cullen, F. (2005). *Sexual assault on campus: What colleges and universities are doing about it.* U.S. Department of Justice, NIJ Research for Practice Series. Retrieved from http://www.ncjrs.gov/pdffiles1/nij/205521.pdf.

Katz, B. (1991). The psychological impact of stranger versus nonstranger rape on victims' recovery. In A. Parrot & L. Bechhofer (Eds.), *Acquaintance rape: The hidden crime* (pp. 251–269). New York: John Wiley & Sons.

Kelly, L. (1988). *Surviving sexual violence.* Minneapolis, MN: University of Minnesota Press.

Kershner, R. (2000). Adolescents' beliefs about rape: A preliminary study. *The Prevention Researcher, 7,* 8–9.

Kilpatrick, D. G., Resnick, H. S., Ruggiero, K. J., Conoscenti, L. M., & McCauley, M. S. (2007). *Drug-facilitated, incapacitated, and forcible rape.* Final report submitted to U. S. Department of Justice.

Kiss, A. (2013). The *Jeanne Clery Act:* A summary of the law and its evolution in higher education. In B. S. Fisher & J. J. Sloan (Eds.), *Campus crime: Legal, social, and policy perspectives* (3rd ed.). Springfield, IL: Charles C Thomas.

Kopper, B. (1996). Gender, gender identity, rape myth acceptance, and time of initial resistance on the perception of acquaintance rape blame and avoidability. *Sex Roles, 34,* 81–93.

Kormos, K. C., & Brooks, C. I. (1994). Acquaintance rape: Attributions of victim blame by college students and prison inmates as a function of relationship status of victim and assailant. *Psychological Reports, 74,* 545–546.

Koss, M., Dinero, T., Seibel, C., & Cox, S. (1988). Stranger and acquaintance rape: Are there differences in the victims' experience? *Psychology of Women Quarterly, 12,* 1–24.

Koss, M., Gidycz, C., & Wisniewski, N. (1987). The scope of rape: Incidence and prevalence of sexual aggression and victimization in a national sample of higher education students. *Journal of Consulting and Clinical Psychology, 55,* 162–170.

Lisak, D., & Miller, P. M. (2002). Repeat rape and multiple offending among unde-tected rapists. *Violence & Victims, 17,* 73–84.

Lombardi, K. (2010). A lack of consequences for sexual assault. Washington DC: Cen-ter for Public Integrity. Retrieved from http://www.iwatchnews.org/accountabili-ty/education/sexual-assault-campus.

Moxley, T. (2012, March 31). Virginia Tech wins appeal of $55,000 in Clery Act fine. Retrieved from http://www.roanoke.com/news/roanoke/wb/306872.

Mustaine, E., & Tewksbury, R. (2013). The routine activities and criminal victimiza-tion of students: Lifestyle and related factors. In B. S. Fisher & J. J. Sloan (Eds.), *Campus crime: Legal, social, and policy perspectives* (3rd ed.). Springfield, IL: Charles C Thomas.

National Victims Center (1992). *Rape in America: A report to the nation.* Crime Victims Research and Treatment Center, Charleston, SC: Medical University of South Carolina.

Neville, H., & Pugh, A. (1997). General and culture-specific factors influencing African American women's reporting patterns and perceived social support fol-lowing sexual assault. *Violence Against Women, 3,* 361–381.

Pitts, V., & Schwartz, M. (1997). Self-blame in hidden rape cases. In M. Schwartz (Ed.), *Researching sexual violence against women: Methodological and personal perspectives* (pp. 65–70). Thousand Oaks, CA: Sage.

Sable, M. R., Danis, F., Mauzy, D. L., & Gallagher, S. K. (2006). Barriers to reporting sexual assault for women and men: Perspectives of college students. *Journal of American College Health, 55,* 157–162.

Scheff, T., & Retzinger, S. (1991). *Emotions and violence: Shame and rage in destructive con-flicts.* Lexington, MA: Lexington Books.

Schwartz, M., & DeKeseredy, W. (1997). *Sexual assault on the college campus: The role of the male peer model.* Thousand Oaks, CA: Sage.

Schwartz, M., & Leggett, M. (1999). Bad dates or emotional trauma? The aftermath of campus sexual assault. *Violence Against Women, 5,* 251–271.

Sloan, J. J., III, & Fisher B. S. (2011). *The dark side of the ivory tower: Campus crime as a social problem.* New York: Cambridge University Press.

Stewart, M., & Fisher, B. S. (2013). Vulnerabilities and opportunities 101: The extent, nature, and impact of stalking and cyberstalking among college students and im-plications for campus policy and programs. In B. S. Fisher & J. J. Sloan (Eds.), *Campus crime: Legal, social, and policy perspectives* (3rd ed.). Springfield, IL: Charles C Thomas.

Stormo, K., Lang, A., & Stritzke, W. (1997). Attributions about acquaintance rape: The role of alcohol and individual differences. *Journal of Applied Social Psychology, 27,* 279–305.

Wechsler, H., Davenport, A., Dowdall, G., Moeykens, B., & Castillo, B., (1994). Health and behavioral consequences of binge drinking in college: A national sur-vey of students at 140 campuses. *Journal of the American Medical Association, 272,* 1672–1677.

Wyatt, G. (1992). The sociocultural context of African American and White Ameri-can women's rape. *Journal of Social Issues, 48,* 77–91.

Zinzow, H. M., Resnick, H. S., McLauley, J. L., Amstadter, A. B., Ruggiero, K. J., & Kilpatrick, D. G. (2010). The role of rape tactics in risk for posttraumatic stress disorder and major depression: Results from a national sample of college women. *Depression and Anxiety, 27,* 708–715.

Zinzow, H. M., & Thompson, M. (2011). Barriers to reporting sexual victimization: Prevalence and correlates among undergraduate women. *Journal of Aggression, Maltreatment and Trauma, 20,* 711–725.

Chapter 5

"DECRIMINALIZING" CAMPUS INSTITUTIONAL RESPONSES TO PEER SEXUAL VIOLENCE[1]

NANCY CHI CANTALUPO

INTRODUCTION

Peer sexual violence – when one student sexually harasses another in a manner that includes physical contact[2] – is an epidemic on campuses across the nation. Estimates[3] are that some 20–25 percent of college women are victims of attempted or completed nonconsensual sex during their time in college, overwhelmingly at the hands of someone they know (see: Benson, Gohm, & Gross, 2007; Bohmer & Parrot, 1993; Fisher, Cullen, & Turner, 2000; Krebs, Lindquist, Warner, Fisher, & Martin, 2007). Moreover, college and university women are particularly vulnerable to sexual violence, since "[w]omen ages 16 to 24 experience rape at rates four times higher than the assault rate of all women . . . [and] college women are more at risk for rape and other forms of sexual assault than women the same age but not in college" (Sampson, 2003, p. 2).[4] Between 6 percent and 15 percent of college men "report [having engaged in] acts that meet legal definitions for rape or attempted rape" (Lisak & Miller, 2002, p. 73); a small number of repeat perpetrators commit most of the sexual violence and likely contribute to other violence problems as well (Lisak & Miller, 2002, p. 73). College men can also be victims of sexual violence, but because so few male victims report instances of abuse, there is a limited amount of information about the extent of campus peer sexual violence against men. Despite the low rate of male victim reporting, statistics do show that when men are raped, it is usually done by other men (Bohmer & Parrot, 1993, p. 6; Sampson, 2003, p. 3).

90

These statistics show not only epidemic rates of violence, but because they are drawn from studies conducted as early as the mid-1980s (Warshaw, 1988) and as late as 2007 (Benson, et al., 2007; Krebs, et al., 2007), they also show the persistence of this problem. Indeed, as early as the 1950s, researchers documented high levels of sexual victimization among female university students (Fisher & Cullen, 2000, pp. 335–336), whereas a comprehensive journalistic account of campus peer sexual violence published in 2009–10 by Kristen Lombardi of the Center for Public Integrity ("CPI") shows that we are now moving into our seventh decade of dealing with this problem (Center for Public Integrity, 2009).

While there are relatively few studies that give some insight into the causes of both the problem and its persistence, a series of studies have used Routine Activities Theory (Cohen & Felson, 1979) to posit that sexual violence occurs on college campuses because there are a surfeit of "motivated offender[s] [and] suitable target[s] and an absence of capable guardians all converg[ing] in one time and space" (Cass, 2007, p. 351). Two studies, which the authors describe as using a feminist version of the Routine Activities Theory, suggest that all three of these elements must be present for there to be a significant crime problem and that the failure of schools to act as "capable guardians" elevates the influence of peer support on "motivated offenders" (i.e., college men) to assault "suitable targets" (i.e., college women) (Mustaine & Tewksbury, 2002, p. 101; Schwartz, DeKeseredy, Tait, & Alvi, 2001, pp. 630, 646).

In light of this theory, other studies can be viewed as elucidating different parts of the "suitable target," "motivated offender" and "incapable guardian" triangle. For instance, studies have focused on the "suitable targets" when studying the high rate of victim nonreporting and on "the motivated offenders" when studying the widespread presence of sexual harassment- and rape-supportive attitudes among college students as serious contributing factors to the campus peer sexual violence problem. Such studies estimate that 90 percent or more of survivors of sexual assault on college campuses do not report the assault (Fisher et al., 2000, p. 24) for a number of reasons including fear of hostile treatment or disbelief by legal and medical authorities (Bohmer & Parrot, 1993, p. 63; Fisher et al., 2000, p. 23; Warshaw, 1988, p. 50); not thinking a crime had been committed or that the incidents were serious enough to involve law enforcement (Fisher et al., 2000, p. 23); not wanting family or others to know (Fisher et al., 2000, p. 24); lack of proof (Fisher et al., 2000, p. 24); and believing that no one will believe them and nothing will happen to the perpetrator (Bohmer & Parrot, 1993, p. 63; Fisher et al., 2000, p. 23; Warshaw, 1988, p. 50). These fears are not surprising, when on-campus incidents regularly appear in the news such as the infamous Yale fraternity pledge chant of "No means yes! Yes means anal!" (Kimmel, 2010) and sociological studies confirm wide subscription to such attitudes among college men, including finding significant peer support for sexual violence (Schwartz et al., 2001, p. 641), that 35 percent of college men indicate some likelihood that they would rape if they could be assured of getting away with it (Bohmer & Parrot, 1993, p. 21), and that 50 percent of men in general would "force a woman into having sex" if they would not get caught (Warshaw, 1988, p. 97). Many studies regarding the role of alcohol in campus peer sexual violence focus on both the "suitable targets" and "motivated offenders" (Benson et al., 2007). Yet relatively few studies have focused on the role of the "(in)capable guardians" (i.e., the colleges and universities), and how their institutional responses factor into the persistent campus peer sexual violence problem.

Despite this lack of attention, however, institutional responses are a key factor in the peer sexual violence epidemic. As the studies on this violence cumulatively show, the rate of campus peer sexual violence and the high nonreporting rate perpetuate a cycle whereby perpetrators commit sexual violence because they think they will not get caught or because they actually have not been caught. Then, because survivors do not report the violence, perpetrators are not caught, continue to believe they will not get caught, and continue to perpetrate. Moreover, because victim nonreporting is closely linked to the documented disbelieving and/or hostile reactions of others, particularly those in authority, the choice of institutional response when victims do report has the potential either to break the cycle of violence and nonreporting or to feed that cycle. Therefore, responses likely to break the cycle need to be designed, on the front end, to encourage victim-reporting as well as other sources of information about violence occurring at that institution, and, on the back end, to hold perpetrators accountable, including through some kind of effective disciplinary process.

For a variety of complicated reasons, at the current time and at many colleges and universities, neither of these responses is generally occurring. Instead, as the cases, journalistic accounts, and empirical studies reviewed in this chapter suggest, on the front end, many institutions do their best to avoid knowledge of the peer sexual violence, both in general and in specific cases, and on the back end, they adopt disciplinary procedures that make it more difficult to find students accused of sexual violence responsible for that violence. In between these two points exist any number of other, largely unhelpful and often harmful, institutional responses. As a result, many institutions truly are incapable guardians and provide the critical third leg in the "motivated offender" – "suitable target" – "lack of capable guardian" tripod.

Yet evidence suggests that these unhelpful/harmful institutional responses are motivated or encouraged not so much by direct anti-survivor animus, but by other incentives, including "false" incentives born of various myths about sexual violence. Chief among these myths is that sexual violence is not just a crime, but a particular kind of crime: one committed by strangers on victims whom they do not know. In the public imagination, a rapist is still a depraved criminal who jumps a woman in a dark alley, late at night, someone who she has never seen before and may never see again, depending on whether he is caught (Sampson, 2003, p. 9). Yet in reality – a reality that has been confirmed repeatedly in the college context – the vast majority of sexual violence perpetrators are those who are known to the victims: acquaintances, dates, friends, husbands, family members, religious officials, employers, supervisors, and others (Rape, Abuse and Incest National Network, 2009) none of whom need to jump a woman in a dark alley. Instead, they have access to her home, her room, her workplace. They are around her when she is most vulnerable and when the least amount of force, if any at all, is needed to overcome her will and lack of consent.

Because of the myth of sexual violence as a stranger crime, the responses adopted by many policymakers at institutions of higher education suggest that these policymakers believe they should respond to such violence in a manner similar to the criminal justice system both on the front end and on the back end. Thus, on the front end, institutions' reporting mechanisms generally require students to report sexual violence to campus police, who for the most part take a traditional law enforcement approach to that report, often with all of the well-documented deficiencies of that traditional approach in the sexual violence context. On the back end, institutions create disciplinary procedures that adopt standards of proof, evidentiary, and due process requirements provided to criminal defendants, an approach that has been criticized for its lack of fit with the purposes of student discipline and the institution's powers.

These responses are not only not solving the problem, as already indicated, but they are also contrary to both the spirit and letter of the applicable law – particularly three areas of federal law: *Title IX* of the *Educational Amendments of 1972*, the *Jeanne Clery Disclosure of Campus Security Policy and Campus Crime Statistics Act (Clery)*, and case law regarding the due process rights of students at state institutions when they stand accused of any offense that could result in their suspension or expulsion.

Accordingly, the remainder of this chapter will look at these three areas of law to see how these laws encourage institutions to adopt certain methods of dealing with campus peer sexual violence. It will ultimately conclude that, both to comply with their legal obligations and ultimately to end the violence, institutions need to "decriminalize" their institutional responses to the problem, both on the front end and on the back end. Finally, it will make two recommendations of specific methods that institutions can use to begin the decriminalization process.

Laws Applicable to Institutional Responsibilities Regarding Campus Peer Sexual Violence

The three legal regimes listed above constitute the three areas of national law applicable to a higher education institution's responsibilities to respond to incidents of campus peer sexual violence. *Title IX* and *Clery* are federal statutes with accompanying administrative and court enforcement structures that focus mainly on how an institution responds to victims and reports of violence. The due process precedents are based on U.S. Supreme Court and federal courts of appeals interpretations of the U.S. Constitution and focus on the institution's obligations to students accused of perpetrating violence. It is important to note that, in any given case, various state laws may also be applicable, but those laws are beyond the scope of this chapter. This section will discuss each set of federal laws in turn and demonstrate that, with regard to the back end of an institution's responses, not only do none of these legal regimes require institutions to imitate the criminal justice system in their disciplinary procedures, but they also often affirmatively require institutions to respond in a way that is significantly different from a criminal approach. In addition, this section will show that, on the front end, these laws are largely ineffective in addressing the campus peer sexual violence problem because these laws – largely through silence – inadvertently encourage institutions to take a criminal justice system-like approach to victim reporting and gathering information about campus peer sexual violence.

Title IX

Title IX provides a good example of mixed legal incentives that collectively show that imitating the criminal justice system on either the front end or the back end of an institution's response will be ultimately ineffective in solving the campus peer sexual violence problem and may actually perpetuate it. As the review below shows, *Title IX's* requirements for institutions' responses to a report of sexual violence are both quite protective of student survivors' rights and do not encourage schools to take a "criminal" approach to their investigations and hearings regarding such reports. However, because current enforcement of *Title IX* does not account for the victim-nonreporting problem discussed above, *Title IX* does not intervene in front end institutional responses related to reporting, and allows – even provides incentives – for institutions to adopt a criminal approach to reporting. This approach acts as an obstacle to institutions preventing and ending peer sexual violence because, if the studies discussed above are any judge, the criminal approach is a significant deterrent to victim reporting.

Title IX prohibits sexual harassment in schools as a form of sex discrimination (Office for Civil Rights, 2001, p. 2). Peer sexual violence is generally considered a case of hostile environment sexual harassment that is "so severe, pervasive, and objectively offensive that it effectively bars the victim's access to an educational opportunity or benefit" (*Davis v. Monroe County Board of Education*, 1999, p. 632). Because of the severity of sexual violence, generally, even a single instance of violence will be considered hostile environment sexual harassment (Office for Civil Rights, 2001, p. 6).

Title IX is enforced in two ways when peer sexual violence is at issue: first, through a survivor's private right of action against her school (*Cannon v. University of Chicago*, 1979; *Franklin v. Gwinnett County Public Schools*, 1992), and second, through administrative enforcement by the Office for Civil Rights ("OCR") of the Department of Education ("ED") (Office for Civil Rights, 2001, p. i). Both enforcement jurisdictions derive from the fact that schools agree to comply with *Title IX* in order to receive federal funds (Office for Civil Rights, 2001, p. 2–3).

The private right of action requires a plaintiff/survivor to reach the standard set out by two Supreme Court cases, *Gebser v. Lago Vista Ind. Sch. Dist.* (1998) and *Davis v. Monroe County Bd. of Educ.* (1999). In order to make out a violation of *Title IX,* this standard requires that a school act with "deliberate indifference" in the face of "actual knowledge" of an incident of sexual violence (*Vance v. Spencer County Public School District*, 2000, p. 258–59). If a plaintiff can meet that standard, the damages that the school could be required to pay are quite significant. While most cases settle out of court, the settlements give a sense of what both sides anticipate the damages awarded by a jury would be. The largest settlement in a *Title IX* case to date was in *Simpson v. University of Colorado – Boulder* (2007), when two college women were gang-raped as a part of an unsupervised football recruiting program that the university had evidence was leading to sexual violence. The university ultimately paid $2.85 million to the plaintiffs, hired a special *Title IX* analyst and fired some 13 university officials, including the President and football coach (Rosenfeld, 2008, p. 418). Other large settlements include six-figure settlements by *Arizona State University* (Muggeridge, 2009) and the *University of Georgia* (Rosenfeld, 2008, p. 420).

Beyond these high-profile cases, there have been instances where courts have allowed a *Title IX* claim to proceed to a jury for a determination as to whether the school violated the statute. Schools have been found to have acted with deliberate indifference for the following general categories of institutional responses to a report of sexual violence:[5]

1. The school does nothing at all (e.g., *McGrath v. Dominican Coll.*, 2009; *Rinsky v. Boston Univ.*, 2010);

2. The school talks to the alleged perpetrator, who denies the allegations, makes no determination as to which story is more credible (*S. S. v. Alexander,* 2008), and then does nothing, including nothing to protect the victim from any retaliation from the alleged perpetrator or his friends as a result of her report (e.g., *Doe v. Erskine Coll.,* 2006; *Patterson v. Hudson Area Sch.,* 2009);

3. The school waits or investigates so slowly that it takes months or years for the survivor to get any redress (e.g. *Albiez v. Kaminski,* 2010; *Williams v. Bd. of Regents,* 2007);

4. School officials investigate in a biased way, such as through their treatment of the survivor or characterization of her case (e.g., *Babler v. Arizona Bd. of Regents,* 2010; *Kelly v. Yale Univ.,* 2003);

5. The school determines or acknowledges that the sexual violence did occur, but fails to or minimally disciplines the assailant or other students engaging in retaliatory harassment, or also disciplines the victim of the violence (e.g., *Doe ex rel Doe v. Coventry Bd. of Educ.,* 2009; *Terrell v. Del. State Univ.,* 2010);

6. School officials investigate and determine that the sexual violence did occur and proceed to remove the victim from classes, housing, or transportation services where she would encounter her assailant, resulting in significant disruption to the victim's education but none to the assailant's (*Siewert v. Spencer-Owen Cmty. Sch. Corp.,* 2007; *James v. Indep. Sch. Dist. No. 1-007,* 2008).

7 The school requires or pressures the survivor to confront her assailant or to go through mediation with him before allowing her to file a complaint for investigation (*S. S. v. Alexander,* 2008).

In addition, the case law in this area increasingly gives a sense of when school responses *are* adequate under *Title IX,* since two clear trends emerge from cases where courts *have* granted schools' motions for summary judgment or to dismiss the plaintiffs' *Title IX* claims. First, once a school has knowledge of an incidence of sexual violence, the case law suggests that separating the students involved (e.g., by moving the alleged perpetrator, suspending him, or both) can help a school avoid a "deliberate indifference" finding (e.g., *Theriault v. Univ. of S. Me.,* 2004). Second, a smaller group of schools have avoided being found deliberately indifferent because they expelled the perpetrators after determining them to be responsible for peer sexual violence (e.g., *Doe v. North Allegheny Sch. Dist.,* 2011).

These cases show that schools can face significant liability if they respond to a report of sexual violence in a way that is not protective of student survivors. This is a significant difference from the criminal justice system, which is not particularly protective of victims, who are not considered parties on par with the state and the defendant, and whose interests are therefore not at the center of a criminal proceeding. Moreover, the focus of *Title IX* case law is forward-looking, scrutinizing whether the school's institutional responses avoided or led to further risk for or actual occurrence of harassment or violence against a survivor. Such responses often require actions generally not associated with the criminal justice system, such as moving an accused student out of housing or classes prior to an investigation or determination as to the "truth" of the victim's report.

However, these cases obscure times when the victim was not able to successfully show the school had "actual knowledge" of the violence, due to three problems with the "actual knowledge" standard and how it has been applied by the courts as a whole. First, the actual knowledge prong requires that *the school* has actual knowledge of the harassment, raising the question of who represents the school. Some courts allow teachers to count as the school in peer sexual harassment, including sexual violence, cases (e.g., *Jones v. Ind. Area Sch. Dist.*, 2005), but this is not guaranteed (e.g., *M. v. Stamford Bd. of Educ.*, 2008), and others who would seem to be in similar positions of authority as teachers, such as bus drivers (*Staehling v. Metro. Gov't of Nashville & Davidson County*, 2008), coaches (*Halvorson v. Indep. Sch. Dist. No. I-007*, 2008), and other school professionals or "paraprofessionals" (e.g. *Noble v. Branch Intermediate Sch. Dist.*, 2002) have been judged to be "inappropriate persons." This leads to confusing variation, requiring survivors to know and parse through school hierarchies in specific and diverse contexts based on the identities of the perpetrators and the relationships between the person with knowledge and the harasser.

Second, variation has emerged as to what kind of knowledge constitutes actual knowledge. If a school is aware of a student's harassment of other students besides the victim who is reporting in a given case, must the school have actual knowledge of the harassment experienced by that particular victim? Courts have resolved the issue in different ways. In a review of the peer harassment cases where this question was posed, the decisions are fairly evenly split between courts that find that the school must have actual knowledge of the harassment experienced by the particular survivor bringing the case (e.g., *Ross v. Mercer Univ.*, 2007), those that state that the school's knowledge of the peer harasser's previous harassment of other victims is sufficient to meet the actual knowledge standard (e.g., *J. K. v. Ariz. Bd. of Regents*, 2008), and ambiguous decisions (e.g., *Ostrander v. Duggan*, 2003).[6]

Finally, the actual knowledge standard, as Justice Stevens noted in his dissent in *Gebser v. Lago Vista Ind. Sch. Dist.* (1998, p. 296), encourages schools to avoid knowledge rather than set up procedures that allow survivors easily to report what happened to them. This is in contrast to the constructive knowledge standard, which asks whether the defendant knew, or reasonably should have known, that a risk of harassment existed (*Gebser v. Lago Vista Ind. Sch.*

Dist., 1998, p. 296). A constructive knowledge standard creates incentives for schools to set up mechanisms likely to flush out and address harassment, since there is a substantial risk that a court will decide that the school "should have known" about the harassment anyway. In addition, the rule adopted by the Supreme Court in the sexual harassment in employment cases caused many employers to adopt sexual harassment policies and procedures (Grossman, 2003, p. 4). Employers did so because under this standard, if they have such policies and procedures in place, but a plaintiff fails to use them, the employer has a defense against liability for the harassment (*Faragher v. City of Boca Raton,* 1998, p. 807; *Burlington Industries, Inc. v. Ellerth,* 1998, p. 764).

A decade plus of experience with the actual knowledge standard demonstrates that these are not the incentives created by the standard. In fact, as already noted, doing nothing at all is both most schools' response of choice and the response that is most likely to qualify as a violation of a different prong of the same review standard. Unlike with the behavior encouraged by the standard used in the employment context, there has not been a rush to develop policies, procedures, and training on sexual harassment and sexual violence among schools as there has been among employers. In addition, we are now left with the unjust result that *children* and young people with fewer resources to deal with sexual harassment and violence are less protected at their schools – where their attendance for at least the early years is *compulsory* – than their *adult* parents are at their *noncompulsory* workplaces.

Thus, the actual knowledge standard does not encourage schools to address the victim-nonreporting problem and, if anything, gives schools incentives to suppress reporting, at least passively. Moreover, because, fear of hostile treatment by police and other authority figures is the most common reason listed by student victims for not reporting, as suggested by the statistics presented above, such passive suppression is easily done just by making no changes to the traditional criminal justice, policing approach to reports of sexual violence.

Fortunately, the Office for Civil Rights (OCR) uses a constructive knowledge standard when it investigates schools for violations of *Title IX* in peer sexual harassment cases, including those involving sexual violence, in part because student victims complaining to OCR can compel a school to take various actions, such as changing its policies and procedures, but will not get monetary damages for violations of their rights. OCR enforcement generally takes place as a result of a complaint being filed regarding a school's response to a sexual harassment case, which causes OCR to undertake a fairly comprehensive investigation of that school's response system (Office for Civil Rights, 2001, p. 14). This investigation often includes a close review of institutional policies and procedures, as well as the steps the school took to resolve a complaint (Office for Civil Rights, 2001, p. 14). In addition, in a website entitled

How the Office for Civil Rights Handles Complaints, OCR specifies that it will look at all files relating to past sexual harassment cases and interview those involved, particularly relevant school personnel (U.S. Department of Education, n.d.). OCR cases are generally resolved through a "letter of finding" ("LOF").

As a result, OCR's approach is both more comprehensive and more exacting than is possible in a private lawsuit, especially under the *Gebser/Davis* standard. Schools can be, and often are, required to change their entire response system to peer sexual violence and harassment, including but not limited to policies, procedures, and resource allocations. Thus, in addition to the list of institutional responses that have gotten schools in trouble in private lawsuits, each category of which includes investigations where schools have been found in violation of *Title IX*, OCR has additionally found *Title IX* violations when a school's policies and procedures did not follow OCR's requirements, such as when schools create fact-finding procedures and hearings with significantly more procedural rights for the accused than the survivor (e.g., Coleman, 2007; Criswell, 2010; Osgood, 2011); adopt a standard of proof more exacting than "preponderance of the evidence" (e.g., Goldbecker, 2004; Jackson, 1995); have policies or procedures that are contradictory, confusing and/or not coordinated (e.g., Hibino, 2012; Stephens, 2004); do not provide clear time frames for prompt resolutions of complaints (e.g., Kallem, 2004; Palomino [Sonoma State], 1994; Palomino [University of California, Santa Cruz], 1994); or violate more "technical" *Title IX* requirements (e.g., Howard-Kurent, 2001). Thus, even more so than the "deliberate indifference" cases noted above, the responses required by OCR are decriminalized, with explicit rejection of the criminal "beyond a reasonable doubt" standard of proof and an elevation of the student survivor's rights in hearings and other procedures above the status of victims in the criminal system.

Despite this good news, OCR's enforcement, like enforcement of *Title IX* in the court context, has significant problems that encourage schools to avoid, passively or actively, knowledge of campus peer sexual violence generally and of specific cases particularly. First, very few students seem to be aware of OCR's complaint process. Only a single page entitled *How to File a Discrimination Complaint with the Office for Civil Rights* is posted on the OCR website (U.S. Department of Education, n.d), and OCR's own guidance and an April 2011 "Dear Colleague Letter" ("*DCL*") regarding sexual violence never explain how one would go about initiating an investigation or where one might file a complaint, even while referring to OCR investigations (Office for Civil Rights, 2001, pp. i, iii, 5–6, 8, 10, 11, 14–15, 20–22; Ali, 2011, pp. 9–12, 16). The CPI's series on campus sexual violence confirms that "few students know they have the right to complain" and "the number of investigations into sexual assault-related cases is 'shockingly low'" (Jones, 2010).

Second, and more critically, lack of publicity regarding OCR's resolution of the complaints that it does receive diminishes the reach of those resolutions because schools that have not been investigated cannot learn from previous investigations and proactively fix any problems with their own response systems. The only way that anyone other than a complainant or the school being investigated can see the resolution of most cases is through filing a Freedom of Information Act ("FOIA") request. If schools or individuals wish to see various OCR LOFs but do not know which ones in particular, they must file a blanket FOIA request for all of the LOFs in a particular timeframe, against a particular school, or similar category. With the exception of a couple of recent cases, links of which are available from a website entitled *Recent Resolutions* (U.S. Department of Education, n.d.), the letters are not available in ED's public FOIA reading room. Moreover, even though the only way a member of the public can read the LOFs is through filing a FOIA request, the request process is particularly lengthy for these documents (see also Cantalupo, 2011, pp. 236–239). This means that the vast majority of school officials will not wait the months or expend the labor involved in filing and receiving results from a blanket FOIA request that might not even contain a case that is on point. Thus, although OCR's more exacting "knew or should have known" standard has the potential to fix some of the problems with the "actual knowledge" standard required in private lawsuits, general ignorance about OCR's complaint process and investigation results fails to create incentives for schools to seek out knowledge of peer sexual violence – or at the very least not to avoid that knowledge.

Therefore, both court and OCR's enforcement of *Title IX* provides mixed incentives to schools with regard to their institutional responses. On the back end, schools are encouraged to decriminalize their responses, but on the front end, *Title IX's* enforcement structure encourages schools to keep in place traditional law enforcement approaches to victim reporting.

The Clery Act

Like *Title IX,* the *Clery Act* deals with the rights of student survivors in campus disciplinary proceedings, primarily through a set of provisions referred to as the *Campus Sexual Assault Victim's Bill of Rights* ("CSAVBR") (20 USC § 1092 (f)(8) (2008)). Unlike *Title IX, Clery* also deals with the front end, reporting aspect of the campus sexual violence problem, requiring colleges and universities to report to the public any "forcible and non-forcible sex offenses" reported to the college/university, according to the FBI's definitions of such offenses. However, because, as its full title suggests, the *Clery Act* conceives of campus peer sexual violence as merely one form of campus crime, its reporting procedures unsurprisingly tend to encourage "criminalization" of institutional responses. As such, it has been less effective than *Title IX* in encouraging schools to use decriminalized reporting procedures on the front end. It is also less effective than *Title IX* on the back end because there is no right to private enforcement under *Clery*, so victims can only get injunctive relief (e.g. requiring the school to change its policies or take other actions on a going forward basis) but no monetary compensation for *Clery* violations (20 USC § 1092 (f)(8)(C) (2008)).

Nevertheless, the enforcement of *Clery*, particularly with regard to CSAVBR, has been more protective of surviving students' rights than the criminal justice system is, and violating the *Clery Act* can still be quite expensive for schools, since ED has the power to fine schools for violating *Clery*, whereas OCR has no fining capability. CSAVBR requires schools to publish policies that inform both on-campus and off-campus communities of the programs designed to prevent sexual violence provided by the school, as well as the procedures in place to respond to sexual violence once it occurs. It further specifies that a school's educational programs should raise awareness of campus sexual violence. Also, procedures adopted to respond to such violence must include: procedures and identifiable persons to whom to report; the right of victims' to notify law enforcement and to get assistance from school officials in doing so; instructions as to how to preserve evidence of sexual violence; notification to students regarding options for changing living and curricular arrangements and assistance in making those changes; and student disciplinary procedures that explicitly treat both accuser and accused equally in terms of their abilities "to have others present" at hearings and to know the outcome of any disciplinary proceeding.

Probably the most visible sexual violence case involving the *Clery Act* was the 2006 rape and murder of Laura Dickinson in her dormitory room at Eastern Michigan University ("EMU") by a fellow student. The school initially told Dickinson's family that her death involved "no foul play," then informed the family over two months later of the arrest of the student since convicted of raping and murdering her (Menard, 2007; Williams, 2008). As a result of a complaint filed against EMU for violations of the *Clery Act* (Menard, 2007), the school eventually agreed to pay $350,000 in fines for 13 separate violations of the *Clery Act*, the largest fine ever paid in a sexual violence case according to publicly available information, and settled a state law-based tort case with Dickinson's family for $2.5 million (Larcom, 2008). The case eventually led to the President, Vice President for Student Affairs, and Director of Public Safety being fired (Schultz, 2007), and an estimated $3.8 million in costs from the fines, the settlement with the Dickinson family, and "severance packages, legal fees and penalties" (Schultz, 2007).

According to publicly available information, before EMU, the largest fine levied against a school was $200,000 against Salem International University

(SIU) (Loreng, 2001) for not reporting five sex offenses, not regularly providing counseling and other victim support services, "actively discourag[ing vic-
tims] from reporting crimes to law enforcement or seeking relief through the
campus judicial system" (Loreng, 2001), and responding to survivors' reports
with "threats, reprisals, or both" (Loreng, 2001). Furthermore, the school
would not make accommodations for new living and academic arrangements
for victims following an assault, and survivors were inadequately informed of
their rights to pursue disciplinary action against the assailant (Loreng, 2001).
The next highest fine was apparently $27,500 to Miami University of Ohio
(Susman & Sikora, 1997), again for a combination of underreporting various
crimes, including sex offenses, and "fail[ing] to initiate and enforce appropriate procedures for notifying both parties of the outcome of any institutional
disciplinary proceeding brought alleging a sex offense" (Carter, 2004). Lastly,
in 2000, Mount St. Clare College was evidently the first school to be fined
$15,000, in part for two rapes that were reported to police but did not appear
in the school's reports since the perpetrators were never criminally charged
(Leinwand, 2000). As both the provisions of CSAVBR and these four cases
demonstrate, like *Title IX* but unlike the criminal justice system, *Clery* gives
sexual violence survivors' procedural rights on par with accused students, and
requires schools to provide services to victims that are not contemplated in a
criminal case.

Unfortunately, and despite *Clery's* attempts to the contrary, the reporting
system created by the statute does not similarly encourage institutions to decriminalize their front end reporting-related responses to sexual violence. The
primary purpose of the *Clery Act* was to increase transparency around campus
crime so that prospective students and their parents could make more knowledgeable decisions about which schools to attend (Rep. Gooding, 1990, p. 1).
Therefore, the *Clery Act's* focus is on establishing requirements for schools to
report and publish certain categories of crime that occur on campus, including sex offenses. However, *Clery's* reporting requirements do not adequately
account for the differences between campus peer sexual violence and other
kinds of criminal activity. For instance, *Clery* adopts definitions of criminal acts
used in the Federal Bureau of Investigation's *Uniform Crime Reporting Handbook,* which, until very recently, defined forcible sex offenses as "carnal knowledge of a female forcibly and against her will" (Federal Bureau of Investigation, 2004). *Clery* also considers a crime "reported" – and thus necessary for
the institution to disclose – if it is brought to the attention of a "campus security authority" or the local police, but excludes faculty, campus physicians, or
counselors (mental health, professional, and pastoral) from the definition of
"campus security authority" (Office of Postsecondary Education, 2005, pp. 23,
51; Office of Postsecondary Education, 2011, pp. 73, 77–8). Even more fundamentally, *Clery's* approach draws from the stranger rape myth discussed

above. Institutions are required to report crimes based on four factors: (1) where the crime occurred; (2) the type of crime; (3) to whom the crime was reported; and (4) when the crime was reported (Office of Postsecondary Education, 2005, p. 23; Office of Postsecondary Education, 2011, p. 11). Thus, rather than requiring an institution to count criminal acts that take place between its students at any location, the *Clery Act* only counts criminal acts occurring on school property. In doing so, it assumes that an institution can protect students from sexual violence through its control of facilities and traditional policing and security methods, such as campus lighting (no dark alleys for those stranger rapists to hide) and blue light phones (to get police protection when fleeing the stranger rapist). In light of where, how, and at whose hands most campus sexual violence actually occurs, this assumption is likely to spur institutions to adopt ineffective traditional policing and security responses to the violence.

As a result, despite its greater focus than *Title IX* on the front end reporting of sexual violence, *Clery* does no better – likely worse – than *Title IX* in creating incentives for schools to develop decriminalized reporting procedures. While it does encourage decriminalized back end disciplinary procedures, its criminalized conception of reporting undercuts the message of CSAVBR and the results of the four investigations discussed above.

Due Process Rights of Accused Students

The case law regarding the due process rights of students accused of conduct warranting suspension or expulsion from a public school further supports the idea that colleges and universities are not required to imitate the criminal justice system in structuring their student disciplinary processes. This case law, of course, is not applicable to the front end reporting structure because it only comes into play once a report has been made, and the institution's disciplinary procedures are operating. However, on the back end, the case law confirms that there are no legal requirements that institutions treat accused students like criminal defendants with the full panoply of due process rights to which criminal defendants are constitutionally entitled.

All accused students have some due process rights; the variation is in "what process is due" (*Morrissey v. Brewer,* 1972). Although the Supreme Court has never decided a case involving expulsion from a public institution, in *Goss v. Lopez* (1975), the court considered a 10-day suspension, without a hearing, of a group of public high school students involved in a series of demonstrations and protests (*Goss v. Lopez,* 1975, p. 579). The Court decided that the students were entitled to due process consisting of "*some* kind of notice and afforded *some* kind of hearing" (*Goss v. Lopez,* 1975, p. 579). The *Lopez* Court also cited approvingly to *Dixon v. Alabama State Board of Education,* where the 5th Circuit

Court of Appeals defined what was required for cases involving expulsion (*Goss v. Lopez,* 1975, p. 576). In *Dixon,* a group of students were expelled without a hearing from the Alabama State College for Negroes for unspecified misconduct after they had all participated in a sit-in at an all-white lunch counter and possibly had engaged in other civil rights protests and demonstrations (*Dixon v. Alabama State Bd. of Educ.,* 1961, p. 152). *Dixon* set forth the requirements for due process before a state school can expel a student, including notice "of the specific charges and grounds which, if proven, would justify expulsion" (*Dixon v. Alabama State Bd. of Educ.,* 1961, p. 158), "the names of the witnesses . . . and an oral or written report on the facts to which each witness testifies" (*Dixon v. Alabama State Bd. of Educ.,* 1961, p. 159) and a hearing, "[t]he nature of [which] should vary depending upon the circumstances of the particular case" (*Dixon v. Alabama State Bd. of Educ.,* 1961, p. 158). The hearing must provide "an opportunity to hear both sides in considerable detail" (*Dixon v. Alabama State Bd. of Educ.,* 1961, p. 159) and must give the accused student an opportunity to present "his own defense against the charges and to produce either oral testimony or written affidavits of witnesses in his behalf" (*Dixon v. Alabama State Bd. of Educ.,* 1961, p. 159). These requirements fall short of "a full-dress judicial hearing, with the right to cross-examine witnesses" (*Dixon v. Alabama State Bd. of Educ.,* 1961, p. 159) nor do they "require opportunit[ies] to secure counsel, to confront and cross-examine witnesses . . . or to call . . . witnesses to verify [the accused's] version of the incident" (*Dixon v. Alabama State Bd. of Educ.,* 1961, p. 153). While both *Lopez* and *Dixon* are decades old and deal with high school students, because they involve rights under the U.S. Constitution and have not been superseded by later Supreme Court cases, they currently apply to other public schools, including public colleges and universities, throughout the nation.

Because constitutionally-based due process rights apply generally only to actions by government entities, for private institutions, the requirements are even less onerous. While courts have reviewed private institutions for expelling or suspending students in an arbitrary and capricious manner (*Abbariao v. Hamline Univ. Sch. of Law,* 1977; *Rollins v. Cardinal Stritch Univ.,* 2001), most courts review private schools disciplinary actions under "the well settled rule that the relations between a student and a private university are a matter of contract" (*Dixon v. Alabama State Bd. of Educ.,* 1961, p. 157). Therefore, private institutions are mainly bound by what they have promised students in the school's own policies and procedures, and courts will review disciplinary actions according to the terms of the contract (*Centre College v. Trzop,* 2004; *Schaer v. Brandeis Univ.,* 2000).

In a representative selection of cases where students have challenged expulsions, courts have steadfastly refused to intervene in school disciplinary decisions as long as they follow the minimal requirements laid out by *Lopez,*

Dixon, and the school's own policies and procedures. They have upheld expulsions for a wide range of student behaviors, including smoking (*Flint v. St. Augustine High Sch.,* 1975); drinking beer in the school parking lot (*Covington County v. G. W.,* 2000); engaging in consensual sexual activity on school grounds (*B. S. v. Bd. of Sch. Trs.,* 2003); participating in but withdrawing, prior to discovery, from a conspiracy to shoot several students and school officials (*Remer v. Burlington Area Sch. Dist.,* 2002); and being found by two female students in a dormitory room with two other male students and the female students' roommate, who was inebriated, unconscious, and naked from the waist down (*Coveney v. President & Trs. of Holy Cross Coll.,* 1983).

In the sexual violence context, research has uncovered only three cases where a court found a college to have violated an accused student's due process rights (*Fellheimer v. Middlebury Coll.,* 1994; *Marshall v. Maguire,* 1980; *Doe v. University of the South,* 2011) and in only the *Doe* case did the court require the institution to pay any damages, although these were only a small fraction of the amount for which the accused student asked, basically amounting to a tuition refund (South, 2011). This research has uncovered no case where a court has overturned a school's decision to sanction a student for peer sexual violence, even in the *Doe* case, where the court allowed the case to go to a jury to determine whether the university failed to comply with its own procedures in a sexual assault case but explicitly refused to offer an "opinion as to whether a sexual assault occurred, whether any such acts were consensual, or who, as between John Doe and the Complainant is credible" (*Doe v. University of the South,* 2011, p. 755). Courts have, however, rejected challenges to the admissibility of certain witnesses and evidence (e.g., *Brands v. Sheldon Cmty. Sch.,* 1987; *Cloud v. Trs. of Boston Univ.,* 1983); the right to know witnesses' identities and to cross-examine them (e.g., *Coplin v. Conejo Valley Unified Sch. Dist.,* 1995); the right to an attorney (e.g., *Ahlum v. Administrators of Tulane Educ. Fund,* 1993); discovery (e.g., *Gomes v. Univ. of Maine Sys.,* 2005); *voir dire* (e.g., *Gomes v. Univ. of Maine Sys.,* 2005); and appeal (e.g., *Gomes v. Univ. of Maine Sys.,* 2005). They have also allowed a victim to testify from behind a screen (e.g., *Cloud v. Trs. of Boston Univ.,* 1983) and have consistently reiterated the distinction between disciplinary hearings and criminal proceedings (e.g., *Granowitz v. Redlands Unified School Dist.,* 2003; *Ray v. Wilmington College,* 1995).

Moreover, these cases demonstrate that schools may even take actions prior to notice and a hearing without running afoul of due process requirements. Indeed, *Goss v. Lopez* itself acknowledges that it might be necessary for a school to act quickly and prior to notice and a hearing under certain circumstances: "Students whose presence poses a continuing danger to persons or property or an ongoing threat of disrupting the academic process may be immediately removed from school. In such cases, the necessary notice and rudimentary hearing should follow as soon as practicable" (*Goss v. Lopez*, 1975). Courts have relied on this language to allow schools to take measures protecting victims and accusers, including allowing them to submit witness statements instead of appearing at the hearing (*Coplin v. Conejo Valley Unified Sch. Dist.*, 1995), protecting them from retaliation (*B. S. v. Bd. of Sch. Trs.*, 2003), and, in cases of peer sexual violence, suspending or otherwise separating accused students from the school and survivor prior to notice and a hearing (*Jensen v. Reeves*, 1999; *J. S. v. Isle of Wight County Sch. Bd.*, 2005).

These cases clearly demonstrate that courts do not require schools, regardless of level of education, to treat accused students like criminal defendants. Moreover, this makes sense in light of the different goals of student disciplinary proceedings compared to criminal trials and the limited powers of schools compared to courts. As these precedents implicitly acknowledge, the deprivations of property involved in a school expulsion are not comparable to sending someone to jail and potentially requiring registration as a sex offender. In fact, schools lack even much less coercive powers such as the subpoena. To the extent that high standards of proof, the treatment of the victim as a complaining witness as opposed to a party, and unequal rights to discovery and disclosures of evidence are all procedural protections provided in the criminal law context because of the state's coercive powers, it is inappropriate to copy them wholesale in a context where those coercive powers are not present.

Instead, as literature in the student discipline area acknowledges (e.g., Stoner, 2000), the goals of a school in conducting student disciplinary proceedings are quite different. As Stoner (2000, p. 7) explains, the central goal of student disciplinary systems is helping:

> to create the best environment in which students can live and learn . . . [a]t the cornerstone [of which] is the obligation of students to treat all other members of the academic community with dignity and respect – including other students, faculty members, neighbors, and employees.

Stoner (2000) reminds school administrators and lawyers that this goal means that *"student victims are just as important as the student who allegedly misbehaved"* (emphasis in original) (Stoner, 2000, p. 7), a principle that "is critical" to resolving "[c]ases of student-on-student violence" (Stoner, 2000, pp. 7–8). In doing so, he points out that this principle of treating all students equally "creates a far different system than a criminal system in which the rights of a person facing jail time are superior to those of a crime victim" (Stoner, 2000, p. 7). Therefore, he advises that student disciplinary systems use the "'more likely than not' standard [of proof] used in civil situations" and avoid describing student disciplinary matters with language drawn from the criminal system (Stoner, 2000, p. 10).

Thus, the need to decriminalize institutional responses to student misconduct, including peer sexual violence, is widely acknowledged, even when the focus is upon the rights of the student accused of misconduct. When combined with the requirements of *Title IX* and the *Clery Act* with regard to victims' rights in disciplinary proceedings, the mandate, both legal and policy-based, that institutions decriminalize their responses to sexual violence is clear in terms of institutions' back end responses once a report is filed. Moreover, the student disciplinary literature, as well as guidelines from the Office on Violence Against Women at the U.S. Department of Justice (Office on Violence Against Women, 2012), provide specific strategies and recommendations for institutions to use in the decriminalization process (see also Cantalupo, 2009, pp. 665–90). However, because the due process precedents and literature regarding student disciplinary systems provide no additional insight into the front end victim-reporting problem, and *Title IX* and the *Clery Act* deal with that problem inadequately, we still need to generate some methods for decriminalizing the reporting process. The next and final section of this chapter turns to that task.

Recommendations for Decriminalizing Reporting

Because of the *Clery Act's* focus on reporting as well as a number of the amendments that have been made to it since it was first passed, we should start on the decriminalization process by amending the *Clery Act* to enable two new approaches to the sexual violence and victim-non-reporting problems (for additional "decriminalization" recommendations of both reporting and disciplinary procedures, see Cantalupo, 2009, pp. 680–90; Cantalupo, 2011, pp. 252–66). In fact, a recent set of amendments to *Clery* were proposed in the 112th Congress via the *Campus SaVE Act* (Sieben, 2011), so additional changes to *Clery* are already on the table, presenting a good moment to add these methods to the list of changes already being proposed. Alternatively, these approaches might be adopted through new regulations under either *Clery* or *Title IX*.

The first approach is to require schools to collect information about campus peer sexual violence (and any other violent criminal behavior with similar non-reporting problems) in a manner more likely to produce useful information that will both make it impossible for a campus to avoid (passively or actively) knowledge of peer sexual violence and provide the school with the information it needs to address the violence problem properly. More specifically, schools should be required to administer to all students a standard survey developed by ED or a contractor working for ED every four years or a similarly appropriate interval via a method that would guarantee a high response rate (e.g., requiring a response to the survey in order to graduate or to register for classes). The survey would ask students questions designed to determine the incidence of sexual violence without depending on individual survivors to come forward to report, and schools would submit results of the survey to ED and publish it in the campus crime report. ED could also do statistical comparisons of survey results from schools and ideally make those available to the public. Many schools already participate voluntarily in similar surveys, and these often include such compilations, which are given to schools confidentially for their own use (e.g., American College Health Association, National College Health Assessment II, n.d.). Schools generally use information from these surveys to inform themselves of what students are experiencing and to develop policies and programs for responding to those experiences. As helpful as such surveys can be, even with a comparatively small group of schools participating (e.g., 180–200 schools per academic year in recent National College Health Assessments [American College Health Association, Participation History, n.d.]), imagine the wealth of information about students that schools and the public could obtain from a survey in which all schools must participate.

Because such a survey would not depend on a traditional policing model, it would solve or bypass a number of difficulties that plague the current traditional system, including both the perception and the reality of police or school officials who are hostile or otherwise lack expertise in the dynamics of sexual violence. A survey would essentially remove the institution from its current "middle-man" position, where students report to the institution and then the institution reports to the public, and would enable students to report directly to the public what is happening among students on every campus across the country. School officials would receive campus-specific information that is easily comparable to national incidence rates. With such a survey in place, institutions would simply have no incentives to minimize reporting either passively or actively and would gain valuable information about what their students are experiencing so that the institution can better address any problems that are present.

In addition, because such a survey would be required of all schools, it would remove an ethical dilemma for schools that is created by the large victim nonreporting problem. That is, when a school creates better responses to victim reporting and survivors begin to report the violence as a result, a strange thing happens: the campus suddenly looks like it has a serious crime problem. In fact, what is known about the problem indicates that every campus currently has this serious crime problem at a similar rate, a rate that tracks the national incidence (American College Health Association, Publications and Reports, n.d.). The nonreporting phenomenon and how it is created, however, means that the schools that ignore the problem have fewer reports and look safer, whereas the schools that encourage victim reporting have more reports and look less safe. Appearances in this case are completely the opposite of reality, and the correct conclusion to draw from the number of reports of peer sexual violence on a campus is entirely counterintuitive. Therefore, institutions must decide whether to seek to end the violence by encouraging victim reporting and by otherwise openly acknowledging the problem, thereby risking developing a reputation as a dangerous campus, or to ignore the problem, thus discouraging victim reporting either passively or actively and appearing to be less dangerous. Moreover, if the campus next door or across town or one step below or above in the rankings chooses to ignore the problem, its choice could translate into a competitive disadvantage for the institution seeking to increase reporting. All schools conducting the same survey removes this competitive advantage and, with it, any incentives created by it to discourage victim reporting (Cantalupo, 2011, pp. 219–23).

The second method by which to decriminalize reporting, which ideally would be combined with the survey discussed above, is to require institutions to create certain programs related to peer sexual violence and then to funnel reporting through those programs. For instance, one of the most effective ways of addressing the myriad challenges related to campus peer sexual violence is to create a visible (yet confidential) and centralized victims' services office, a method which has received increasing recognition as a best practice for responding to campus peer sexual violence (Karjane, 2002, p. 132; Office on Violence Against Women, 2012).

A victims' services office can help with reporting by acting as a central location for both services and reports. Such offices are generally more trusted by survivors than traditional law enforcement or other school officials, because of their experience working with survivors and their ability to provide survivors with a "one-stop shop" for the various academic, medical, counseling and advocacy needs of victims. One can picture a campus student services system for sexual violence victims as a metaphorical wheel, with a victims' services office at the hub of the wheel and the various places where a student might initially report at the ends of the wheel spokes. These places could include the medical center, campus police, counseling services, residence life, individual faculty, the student conduct office, etc. This wheel-like structure allows the offices where a student initially reports immediately to refer the student to the victims' services office. That office could likewise refer students out to the different offices from which they can get needed services, thus alleviating the need for a victim to go from office to office trying to figure out the system on her own.

The victims' services office can also provide a source of expertise in an area where schools need a lot more information and training, especially in light of the training requirements and education recommendations contained in the April 2011 "Dear Colleague Letter" (Ali, 2011, pp. 4, 7, 12, 14–15), which will be strengthened further by the *Campus SaVE Act,* should it be enacted into law. Office staff would have the background and knowledge to implement such training and education programs and could provide deeper expertise in active cases. Faculty and staff could be minimally trained in how to handle reports, mainly by referring them to the victims' services office as the campus expert, which usually is a relief to the majority of faculty and staff members who do not feel prepared to deal with such reports. Survivors would also be more likely to report to a confidential advocate and all-around resource, and such an office could provide raw numbers without breaching confidentiality. Centralizing reports with a victims' services office is one of the most effective ways of both getting survivors to report and making sure an institution's response is effective once a report occurs (see also Cantalupo, 2009, pp. 681–82).

In light of the benefits of such offices, the most effective way for the *Clery Act* to both capture reports and ensure that sexual violence survivors' rights are protected (as required by the CSAVBR portion of the *Clery Act*) may very well be to mandate that every school create and professionally staff such an office. Such an approach would not only increase reporting, but would also provide an on-campus expert who would facilitate creation of the right policies and procedures, as well as preventive educational programming. A legal regime that truly wants to end the campus peer sexual violence problem could not do better than mandating such an office at every school.

Neither the survey nor victims' services office necessarily need to replace the *Clery Act's* current reporting structure, although it is worth considering whether the resources that schools and other entities put toward meeting the *Clery Act's* current requirements would be more efficiently and effectively utilized to fund one of these methods. In addition, any amendments to the *Clery Act* should appropriate money for ED to design the survey and compile and analyze the data, giving schools the less resource intensive role of administering the survey and collecting the data, which might be made quite easy if, for instance, ED were to design a survey method that was electronic and automated. The design might also include questions, like the voluntary American College Health Association survey currently does, that deal with other important topics about which schools want to assess their students' experiences. Moreover, with the majority of the expenses of designing and administering the survey removed from the institution itself, schools could put the resources formerly used for campus crime reporting towards the victims' services office.

Adopting both of these methods is ultimately in the interests of schools, given the potentially very expensive liability that schools face, particularly under *Title IX.* The *Title IX* liability scheme gives schools a clear incentive to get their institutional responses to campus peer sexual violence right. Although schools could keep their current "criminalized" approaches in place and continue to avoid knowledge of the problem generally and individual cases specifically, they would do so at their own – and at significant – risk. In addition, proper institutional responses present the best hope for schools to address the problem and prevent it from happening in the first place, by breaking the cycle of nonreporting and violence, gathering enough campus-specific information about the problem to create other forms of prevention, and bringing in expert victims' services professionals to inform and implement best prevention and response practices. Aside from wanting to do the right thing and prevent the violence from an altruistic standpoint, violence prevention and effective institutional responses also save schools from many of the difficulties and resource expenditures that specific cases can involve when schools are unprepared to deal with them. Finally, with institutional reporting and information gathering approaches made applicable to all schools, schools seeking to address the violence problem would not be faced with the competitive disadvantage dilemma created by the high rate of violence but low rate of victim reporting.

Conclusion

If colleges and universities are ever going to end, or even significantly diminish, the distressingly high and persistent incidence of peer sexual violence on their campuses, they must decriminalize their institutional responses to the violence. While *Title IX,* the *Clery Act* and case law regarding the due process rights of students accused of misconduct warranting suspension or expulsion make it clear that schools should not be treating student disciplinary proceedings like criminal trials, they assume a traditional policing, criminal justice approach to victim-reporting. This assumption significantly diminishes the effectiveness of both these laws and an institution's responses to sexual violence because they perpetuate a high victim nonreporting rate that is likely caused in large part by survivors' documented fear and distrust of law enforcement's and other school officials' attitudes towards survivors. Therefore, institutions should be seeking not only to decriminalize their disciplinary procedures on the back end of a student's progress through a school response system, but also to decriminalize their reporting mechanisms on the front end. Amending the *Clery Act* or passing new regulations under *Title IX* or *Clery* could provide two ways to decriminalize reporting: first by mandating that all institutions conduct a regular, national survey on sexual violence among their students and second by requiring institutions to create victims' services offices in which to centralize reporting and service provision as well as to serve as an expert for training and education purposes.

NOTES

1. This article updates and unifies more extensive discussions regarding specific aspects of how institutions of higher education should respond to campus peer sexual violence as both a legal and policy matter. Those more extensive discussions may be found in Cantalupo (2009, 2011) .

2. Other than when I am discussing studies or other sources that use terms such as "sexual assault" or "rape," I use "sexual violence" instead of terms such as "sexual assault" or "rape" because in my view "sexual violence" is a broader, more descriptive term that is not a term of art, and which I regard to include a wider range of actions that may not fit certain legal or readers' definitions of "sexual assault" or "rape." The term therefore includes "sexual assault" or "rape," as well as other actions involving physical contact of a sexual nature (while I acknowledge that non-physical actions can constitute violence, including those forms of violence here is beyond the scope of this chapter). When I am discussing studies or other sources that use terms such as "sexual assault" or "rape," I retain use of those terms as the original researchers and authors used them. Similarly, my definition of "report" and "reporting" is not a technical one. I regard a report as any time a victim discloses the violence to any professional with any role or authority to help victims, including but not limited to medical, counseling, security or conduct-related, residential life or other student affairs personnel, as well as faculty and community or campus advocates. In addition, I use "victim" and "survivor" interchangeably to refer to people who say that they have been victims of sexual violence. Therefore, "victim" is again not a term of art used to indicate a finding of responsibility for sexual violence. I use "perpetrator" or "assailant" when someone accused of sexual violence has been found responsible or in discussions where it can be assumed the person perpetrated the sexual violence, such as statistical analyses. I use "accused" or "alleged" to indicate when I am referring to those who have been charged but not found responsible for committing sexual violence and "accuser" when discussing the role of the victim/survivor in a disciplinary proceeding. Because studies confirm that the majority of victims are women and the majority of perpetrators and accused students are men, I use female pronouns to refer to victims and male pronouns to refer to perpetrators and accused students. Finally, I use "school" and "institution" to identify either K–12 schools or higher education institutions, although I also use "college," "university," "campus," or "higher education" to refer to the latter category of schools.

3. Note that although some of the studies that are cited here are somewhat old, they are included because the findings of the older studies are quite consistent with the most recent ones, even when the studies have been conducted in different decades. This indicates that the findings of older studies are still valid in terms of what we see today.

4. Note that some studies find that college students are less likely to be the victim of sexual assault than nonstudents (Baum & Klaus, 2005, p. 3). The discrepancy in these two findings is due to the wording of questions asked during data collection. The conclusions of Baum and Klaus are based on the National Crime Victimization Survey, which gathers information on sexual assault by asking category-centered

questions, such as "Has anyone attacked or threatened you in [this way]: rape, attempted rape or other type of sexual attack" (Baum & Klaus, 2005, p. 3). The conclusions that Sampson (2003) cites are based on studies such as the National College Women Sexual Victimization study, which use behavior-oriented questions, such as "Has anyone made you have sexual intercourse by using force or threatening to harm you or someone close to you?" (Fisher et al., 2000, pp. 6, 13). Other than the wording of the questions, the basic methodology of the two studies was identical, yet behavior-oriented questions have been found to produce 11 times the number of reported rapes (Fisher et al., 2000, p. 11).

5. Note that a fair number of cases decided under *Title IX* are against school districts, not colleges and universities. However, while factors like the age of the students and level of close supervision by teachers and other school officials can influence the outcome of a case, there is significant commonality among the kinds of institutional responses that schools at all levels of education use, as well as significant commonality in how courts judge those responses. Moreover, because *Title IX* applies to all levels of education, as long as the school accepts federal funds (Office for Civil Rights, 2001, pp. 2–3), while the factual similarities (such as school type, student age, etc.) are always helpful in comparing cases, legal questions decided in a case involving one kind of school are still applicable to other types of schools, including colleges and universities. How "mandatory" a particular court decision is for another court deciding a similar case depends on factors such as the court's jurisdiction, not the school's characteristics.

6. The number of district courts that insist upon actual knowledge of harassment of a specific victim is doubly surprising because it suggests a certain acceptance of victim-blaming attitudes by some courts. A belief that the identity of the victim of harassing behavior is relevant to whether the school is obligated to respond to the harassment focuses the school or court on the victim's and not the perpetrator's behavior, suggesting that some victims must do something that invites the harassment, whereas other victims are "blameless." Indeed, if a perpetrator is known to have harassed or assaulted multiple victims, this should suggest that the victim's identity and behavior are *not* relevant, because the perpetrator himself does not find the identity of the victim relevant.

REFERENCES

Abbariao v. Hamline Univ. Sch. of Law, 258 N.W.2d 108 (Minn. 1977).

Ahlum v. Administrators of Tulane Educ. Fund, 617 So. 2d 96 (La. Ct. App. 1993).

Albiez v. Kaminski, 2010 U.S. Dist. LEXIS 59373 (E.D. Wisc. June 14, 2010).

Ali, R. (2011, Apr. 4). Letter to "Dear Colleague." Retrieved from http://www2.ed.gov/about/offices/list/ocr/letters/colleague-201104.pdf.

American College Health Association. (n.d.). National College Health Assessment II. Retrieved from http://www.acha-ncha.org/docs/ACHA-NCHAII_sample.pdf.

American College Health Association. (n.d.). Participation History. Retrieved from http://www.acha-ncha.org/partic_history.html.

American College Health Association. (n.d.). Publications and Reports. Retrieved from http://www.acha-ncha.org/reports_ACHA-NCHAII.html.

Babler v. Arizona Bd. of Regents, Case 2:10-cv-01459-RRB (D. Ariz. 2010).

Baum, K., & Klaus, P. (2005). Violent Victimization of College Students, 1995–2002. Retrieved from http://bjs.ojp.usdoj.gov/content/pub/pdf/vvcs02.pdf.

Benson, B. J., Gohm, C. L., & Gross, A. M. (2007). College women and sexual assault: The role of sex-related alcohol expectancies. *Journal of Family Violence, 22,* 341–51.

Bohmer, C., & Parrot, A. (1993). *Sexual assault on campus: The problem and the solution.* Lanham, MD: Lexington Books.

Brands v. Sheldon Cmty. Sch., 671 F. Supp. 627 (N.D. Iowa 1987).

B. S. v. Bd. of Sch. Trs., 255 F. Supp. 2d 891 (N.D. Ind. 2003).

Burlington Indus., Inc. v. Ellerth, 524 U.S. 742 (1998).

Cannon v. Univ. of Chicago, 441 U.S. 677 (1979).

Cantalupo, N. C. (2011). Burying our heads in the sand: Lack of knowledge, knowledge avoidance, and the persistent problem of campus peer sexual violence. *Loyola University Chicago Law Journal, 43,* 205–66.

Cantalupo, N. C. (2009). Campus violence: Understanding the extraordinary through the ordinary. *Journal of College and University Law, 35,* 613–90.

Carter, S. D. (2004, Oct. 7). Letter to Douglas Parrott (on file with author).

Cass, A. I. (2007). Routine activities and sexual assault: An analysis of individual- and school-level factors. *Violence and Victims, 22,* 350.

Center for Public Integrity. (2009–2010). Sexual assault on campus. Retrieved from http://www.publicintegrity.org/investigations/campus_assault/.

Centre Coll. v. Trzop, 127 S.W.3d 562 (Ky. 2004).

Cloud v. Trs. of Boston Univ., 720 F.2d 721 (1st Cir. Mass. 1983).

Cohen, L. E., & Felson, M. (1979). Social changes and crime rate trends: A routine activities approach. *American Sociological Review, 44,* 588–608.

Coleman, M. (2007, June 4). Letter to Valerie I. Harrison, Esq., in Temple University, OCR Case No. 03062060 (on file with author).

Coplin v. Conejo Valley Unified Sch. Dist., 903 F. Supp. 1377 (C.D. Cal. 1995).

Coveney v. President & Tr. of Holy Cross Coll., 445 N.E.2d 136 (Mass. 1983).

Covington County v. G.W., 767 So. 2d 187 (Miss. 2000).

Criswell, C. D. (2010, Sept. 24). Letter to Dave L. Armstrong, Esq., in Notre Dame College, OCR Case No: 15-09-6001. Retrieved from http://www2.ed.gov/about/offices/list/ocr/docs/investigations/15096001.html.

Davis v. Monroe County Bd. of Educ., 526 U.S. 629 (1999).

Dixon v. Alabama State Bd. of Educ., 294 F.2d 150 (1961).

Doe ex rel Doe v. Coventry Bd. of Educ., 630 F. Supp. 2d 22 (D. Conn. 2009).

Doe v. Erskine Coll., 2006 U.S. Dist. LEXIS 35780 (D.S.C. 2006).

Doe v. North Allegheny Sch. Dist., 2011 U.S. Dist. LEXIS 93551 (W.D. Pa. Aug. 22, 2011).

Doe v. Univ. of the South, 2011 U.S. Dist. LEXIS 35166 (E.D. Tenn. 2011).

Faragher v. City of Boca Raton, 524 U.S. 775 (1998).

Federal Bureau of Investigation. (2004). Uniform Crime Reporting Handbook. Retrieved from http://www.fbi.gov/about-us/cjis/ucr/additional-ucr-publications/ ucr_handbook.pdf.

Fellheimer v. Middlebury Coll., 869 F. Supp. 238 (D. Vt. 1994).

Fisher, B., & Cullen, F. (2000). Measuring the sexual victimization of women: Evolution, current controversies, and future research. Retrieved from https://www. ncjrs.gov/criminal_justice2000/vol_4/04g.pdf.

Fisher B., Cullen, F., & Turner, M. (2000). The sexual victimization of college women. Retrieved from http://www.ncjrs.gov/pdffiles1/nij/182369.pdf.

Flint v. St. Augustine High Sch., 323 So. 2d 229 (La. 1975).

Franklin v. Gwinnett County Public Sch., 503 U.S. 60 (1992).

Gebser v. Lago Vista Indep. Sch. Dist., 524 U.S. 274 (1998).

Goldbecker, S. (2004, May 5). Letter to John J. DeGioia, in Georgetown University, OCR Case No. 11-03-2017 (on file with author).

Gomes v. Univ. of Maine Sys., 365 F. Supp. 2d 6 (D. Me. 2005).

Gooding, Rep. H.R. REP. NO. H11499-01, at 1 (1990) (Conf. Rep.).

Goss v. Lopez, 419 U.S. 565 (1975).

Granowitz v. Redlands Unified Sch. Dist., 105 Cal. App. 4th 349 (Cal. App. 4th Dist. 2003).

Grossman, J. L. (2003) The culture of compliance: The final triumph of form over substance in sexual harassment law. *Harvard Women's Law Journal, 26,* 4–75.

Halvorson v. Indep. Sch. Dist. No. I-007, 2008 U.S. Dist. LEXIS 96445 (W.D. Okla. 2008).

Hibino, T. J. (2012, June 15). Letter to Dorothy K. Robinson, in Yale University, OCR Case No. 01-11-2024. Retrieved from http://www2.ed.gov/documents/press-releases/yale-letter.pdf.

Howard-Kurent, L. (2001, Aug. 17). Letter to Norman Cohen, in Utah College of Massage Therapy, OCR Case No. 08012022-B (on file with author).

Jackson, G. D. (1995, Apr. 4). Letter to Jane Jervis, in The Evergreen State College, OCR Case No. 10922064 (on file with author).

James v. Indep. Sch. Dist. No. 1-007, 2008 U.S. Dist. LEXIS 82199 (W.D. Okla. 2008).

Jeanne Clery Disclosure of Campus Security Policy and Campus Crime Statistics Act, 20 USC § 1092 (f)(8) (2008).

Jensen v. Reeves, 45 F. Supp. 2d 1265 (D. Utah 1999).

J. K. v. Ariz. Bd. of Regents, 2008 U.S. Dist. LEXIS 83855 (D. Ariz. 2008).

Jones, K. (2010, Feb. 25). Lax enforcement of Title IX in campus sexual assault cases: feeble watchdog leaves students at risk, critics say. Retrieved from http:// www.publicintegrity.org/investigations/campus_assault/articles/entry/1946/.

Jones v. Ind. Area Sch. Dist., 397 F. Supp. 2d 628 (W.D. Pa. 2005).

J. S. v. Isle of Wight County Sch. Bd., 362 F. Supp. 2d 675 (E.D. Va. 2005).

Kallem, H. (2004, Mar. 26). Letter to Stephen W. Vescovo, in Christian Brothers University, OCR Case No. 04-03-2043 (on file with author).

Karjane, H., Fisher, B., & Cullen, F. (2002). Campus sexual assault: How America's institutions of higher education respond. Retrieved from https://www.ncjrs.gov/ pdffiles1/nij/grants/ 196676.pdf.

Kelly v. Yale Univ., 2003 U.S. Dist. LEXIS 4543 (D. Conn. 2003).

Kimmel, M. (2010, October 17). The men, and women, of Yale. *Ms. Magazine Blog*. Retrieved from http://msmagazine.com/blog/blog/2010/10/17/the-men-and-women-of-yale/.

Krebs, C. P., Lindquist, C. H., Warner, T. D., Fisher, B. S., & Martin, S. L. (2007). *The Campus Sexual Assault Study: Final report*. Retrieved from http://www.ncjrs.gov/pdffiles1/nij/grants/221153.pdf.

Larcom, G. (2008, June 6). Eastern Michigan University to pay $350,000 in federal fines over Laura Dickinson case. *The Ann Arbor News*. Retrieved from http://blog.mlive.com/annarbornews/2008/06/eastern_michigan_university_to_ html.

Leinwand, D. (2000, October 4). Campus crime underreported. *USA Today*.

Lisak, D., & Miller, P. M. (2002). Repeat rape and multiple offending among undetected rapists. *Violence and Victims, 17*, 73–84.

Loreng, J. (2001, Dec. 17). Letter to Fred Zook (on file with author).

M. v. Stamford Bd. of Educ., 2008 U.S. Dist. LEXIS 51933 (D.Conn. 2008).

Marshall v. Maguire, 102 Misc. 2d 697 (N.Y. Sup. Ct. 1980).

McGrath v. Dominican Coll., 672 F. Supp. 2d 477 (S.D.N.Y. Nov. 25, 2009).

Menard, J. (2007, May 10). EMU slaying probe reopens wounds. *The Detroit News*.

Morrissey v. Brewer, 405 U.S. 951 (1972).

Muggeridge, T. (2009, February 3). ASU settlement ends in $850,000 payoff. *State Press*. Retrieved from http://www.statepress.com/archive/node/4020.

Mustaine, E. E., & Tewksbury, R. (2002). Sexual assault of college women: A feminist interpretation of a routine activities analysis. *Criminal Justice Review, 27*, 89–123.

Noble v. Branch Intermediate Sch. Dist., 2002 U.S. Dist. LEXIS 19600 (W.D. Mich. 2002).

Office for Civil Rights. (2001). *Revised Sexual Harassment Guidance: Harassment of Student by School Employees, Other Students, or Third Parties*. Retrieved from http://www.ed.gov/offices/OCR/archives/pdf/shguide.pdf.

Office of Postsecondary Education. (2005). T*he Handbook for Campus Crime Reporting*. Retrieved from http://www.ed.gov/admins/lead/safety/handbook.pdf.

Office of Postsecondary Education. (2011). *The Handbook for Campus Safety and Security Reporting 73 (2011)*. Retrieved from http://www2.ed. gov/admins/lead/safety/handbook-2.pdf.

Office on Violence Against Women. (2012). *OVW Fiscal Year 2012 Grants to Reduce Sexual Assault, Domestic Violence, Dating Violence, and Stalking on Campus Program*. Retrieved from http://www.ovw.usdoj.gov/docs/campus-solicitation.pdf.

Osgood, D. (2011, June 30). Letter to The Reverend John I. Jenkins, C.S.C., President, in University of Notre Dame, OCR Case No. 05072011. Retrieved from http://www2.ed.gov/about/offices/list/ocr/docs/investigations/05072011.html.

Ostrander v. Duggan, 341 F.3d 745 (8th Cir. Mo. 2003).

Pahssen v. Merrill Cmty. Sch. Dist., 668 F.3d 356 (6th Cir. 2012).

Palomino, J. E. (1994, Apr. 29). Letter to Ruben Armiñana, in Sonoma State University, OCR Case No. 09-93-2131 (on file with author).

Palomino, J. E. (1994, Jun. 15). Letter to Karl Pister, in University of California, Santa Cruz, OCR Case No. 09-93-2141 (on file with author).

Patterson v. Hudson Area Sch., 2009 U.S. App. LEXIS 25 (6th Cir. 2009).

Rape, Abuse and Incest National Network. (2009). The offenders. Retrieved from http://www. rainn.org/get-information/statistics/sexual-assault-offenders.

Ray v. Wilmington Coll., 106 Ohio App. 3d 707 (Ohio Ct. App. 1995).

Remer v. Burlington Area Sch. Dist., 286 F.3d 1007 (7th Cir. 2002).

Rinsky v. Boston Univ., 2010 U.S. Dist. LEXIS 136876 (D. Mass. 2010).

Rollins v. Cardinal Stritch Univ., 626 N.W.2d 464 (Minn. Ct. App. 2001).

Rosenfeld, D. L. (2008). Changing social norms? Title IX and legal activism: Concluding remarks. *Harvard Journal of Law & Gender, 31,* 407–22.

Ross v. Mercer Univ., 506 F. Supp. 2d 1325 (M.D.Ga. 2007).

Sampson, R. (2003). Acquaintance rape of college students. Retrieved from http://www.cops.usdoj.gov/pdf/e03021472.pdf.

Schaer v. Brandeis Univ., 735 N.E.2d 373 (Mass. 2000).

Schultz, M. (2007, October 15). EMU murder trial begins today. *The Detroit News.*

Schwartz, M. D., DeKeseredy, W. S., Tait, D., & Alvi, S. (2001). Male peer support and a feminist routine activities theory: Understanding sexual assault on the college campus. *Justice Quarterly, 18,* 623–649.

Siebin, L. (2011, Apr. 15). Education Dept. issues new guidance for colleges' sexual-assault investigations. Retrieved from http://chronicle.com/article/Education-Dept-Issues-New/127004/.

Siewert v. Spencer-Owen Cmty. Sch. Corp., 497 F. Supp. 2d 942 (S.D. Ind. 2007).

Simpson v. Univ. of Colorado Boulder, 500 F.3d 1170 (10th Cir. 2007).

Stephens, S. W. (2004, June 10). Letter to David Schmidly, in Oklahoma State University, OCR Case No. 06032054 (on file with author).

Soriano ex rel. Garcia v. Bd. of Educ. of N.Y.C., 2004 WL 2397610 (E.D.N.Y. 2004).

South, T. (2011, Sept. 3). Jury finds Sewanee and student at fault; awards student $26,500. Retrieved from http://timesfreepress.com/news/2011/sep/03/jury-finds-sewanee-and-student-fault-awards-50000/.

S. S. v. Alexander, 177 P.3d 724 (Wash. App. Div. 1 2008).

Staehling v. Metro. Gov't of Nashville & Davidson County, 2008 U.S. Dist. LEXIS 91519 (M.D.Tenn. 2008).

Stoner II, E. N. (2000). Reviewing your student discipline policy: A project worth the investment. Retrieved from http://www.eric.ed.gov/PDFS/ED444074.pdf.

Susman, F., & Sikora, G. (1997, Sept. 11). Letter to James Garland (on file with author).

Terrell v. Del. State Univ., 2010 U.S. Dist. LEXIS 74841 (D. Del. 2010).

Theriault v. Univ. of S. Me., 353 F. Supp. 2d 1 (D. Me. 2004).

U.S. Department of Education. (n.d.), How to File a Discrimination Complaint with the Office for Civil Rights, Retrieved from http://www2.ed.gov/about/offices/list/ocr/docs/howto.html?src=rt.

U.S. Department of Education. (n.d.). How the Office for Civil Rights handles complaints. Retrieved from http://www.ed.gov/about/offices/list/ocr/complaints-how.html.

U.S. Department of Education. (n.d). Recent Resolutions. Retrieved from http://www2.ed.gov/about/offices/list/ocr/docs/investigations/index.html.

Vance v. Spencer County Pub. Sch. Dist., 231 F.3d 253 (6th Cir. 2000).

Warshaw, R. (1988). *I never called it rape.* New York: Harper & Row.

Williams, C. (2008, May 8). EMU killer denies guilt, gets life. *The Detroit News.*

Williams v. Bd. of Regents, 477 F.3d 1282 (11th Cir. Ga. 2007).

Chapter 6

STATE-LEVEL *CLERY ACT* INITIATIVES: SYMBOLIC POLITICS OR SUBSTANTIVE POLICY?

JENNIFER M. BURKE AND JOHN J. SLOAN, III

Those who would treat politics and morality apart will never understand the one or the other.

– Rousseau

INTRODUCTION

In 1990, Congress passed the *Student Right-to-Know and Campus Security Act* (20 U.S.C. 1092[f]), now known as the *Jeanne Clery Disclosure of Campus Security Policy and Campus Crime Statistics Act* (hereafter, *Clery*).[1] The legislation requires postsecondary institutions participating in federal financial programs to annually report to the U.S. Department of Education (ED) and make available for public inspection, a comprehensive campus security report, annual statistics covering multiple prior years for crimes and drug/alcohol-related offenses known to campus police, and other information The legislation also allows the ED to levy fines and other sanctions on institutions for noncompliance. By passing this legislation, Congress appeared to signal that the federal government was both concerned about and willing to address campus crime/ security issues, by requiring colleges and universities to "come clean" with their crime statistics and security policies, and sanctioning institutions which failed to comply.

With Congress taking such a step, one might assume state legislatures would follow suit and pass their own legislation, if for no other reason than to show constituents that they, too, were concerned about campus crime. In the case of campus crime and security information, Griffaton (1995, p. 67) has argued:

> While the passage of the federal Crime Awareness and Campus Security Act
> ensures minimum disclosure and security standards . . . *states remain in the*
> *best position to require their public and private colleges to adopt specific policies and*
> *procedures* (emphasis added).

Griffaton (1995) argued that the states, were they inclined to do so, could ensure that current and prospective students, among others, have access to campus crime and security facts by withholding state-level aid or accreditation from both public colleges and universities as well as private schools.

Indeed, there are numerous examples of states passing legislation that parallels federal law in such areas as welfare reform, immigration, and illegal drug possession. In some instances, state laws may create entirely new classes of offenses and may impose even more serious sanctions on offenders that their federal counterparts. In most cases, however, state statutes do little more than "echo the sentiments" of federal legislation and become examples of what political scientists have termed *symbolic politics* (see Edelman, 1964; 1977; 1988). When engaging in symbolic politics, legislators introduce legislation intended to notify targeted constituents they are concerned about an issue in the hope of rallying political capital, but ultimately do not actually pass laws creating new duties or obligations. Thus, in some instances state legislators pass new laws that will parallel federal statutes and have a substantive effect, while in others, the legislation involves little more than symbolic politics. The question we explore in this chapter is whether state-level *Clery* legislation falls into the former or the latter category.

As discussed more fully below, despite the states possibly being in the best position to make campus crime and security information available to students, their parents, and postsecondary institutional employees, as of February 2012, only 16 states have actually passed what we classify as *Clery*-style legislation. Also as discussed below, the provisions found in these statutes evidence wide variation. For example, some states' *Clery*-type legislation focuses only on policies relating to on-campus sexual assaults occurring at public, postsecondary institutions. In other states, the statutes focus on institutional compiling of, and creating public access to, campus security reports. Still others simply indicate that schools "should report" their crime statistics to the state agency responsible for compiling statistics received from state, county, and local police agencies for inclusion in the FBI's annual Uniform Crime Reports program.[2] Since passage of the original version of *Clery* in 1990, a handful of states have passed "campus crime" legislation but, as discussed below, almost none of this legislation actually mirrors the provisions found in *Clery* and some of the legislation is so narrowly tailored it barely fits the label as "campus crime" legislation.

We have divided the chapter into several sections, beginning with a brief discussion of the key provisions of *Clery*. Following this, we discuss the methods we used to identify state-level *Clery* statutes and regulations. Next, we examine the extent that state-level legislation possesses one or more key *Clery* provisions, including whether that statute prescribes penalties for institutional noncompliance. We end the chapter by describing how state-level *Clery* legislation constitutes symbolic public policy, rather than genuine efforts by the states to address crime and security issues at postsecondary institutions.

A Brief Overview of *Clery*

After their daughter was brutally raped and murdered while sleeping in her dorm room at Lehigh University in 1986, Jeanne Ann Clery's parents mounted a grass-roots campaign to try to prevent other students from experiencing the same fate (Sloan & Fisher, 2011). They spearheaded this movement by lobbying the Pennsylvania legislature, and later Congress, to pass legislation requiring colleges and universities to "come clean" with their crime statistics and security policies. Their efforts culminated first with Pennsylvania passing "campus crime" legislation, and later Congress passing the *Student Right-to-Know and Campus Security Act of 1990* (20 U.S.C. 1092[f]). Subsequent amendments over the next 15 years included renaming the legislation as the *Jeanne Clery Disclosure of Campus Security Policy and Campus Crime Statistics Act*.

Considered part of the *Higher Education Act of 1965* (PL89-329, 79 STAT 1219), *Clery* requires that colleges and universities participating in federal student aid programs annually disclose timely information about campus crime statistics and security policies, including those relating to on-campus sexual assault and the power/authority of campus police/security. The ED, charged with enforcing *Clery* and the agency with which citizens are supposed to file complaints of alleged *Clery* violations, is authorized by the legislation to levy civil fines on violators of up to $25,000 per violation or take other enforcement action, including suspending federal aid to the school.[3]

Key Clery Provisions[4]

ANNUAL REPORT. The first key *Clery* provision is that postsecondary institutions must publish by September 1 each year, an annual "security report" containing the following information about current security policies at the school: a description of the procedures students may use to report criminal activity or emergencies; a description of policies regarding the security of and access to campus facilities; and the location where students should go to report crimes. The report is supposed to be automatically distributed to all current students and employees and made available to prospective students upon request. Schools are also required to provide the report and all statistical information to the ED each year.

CRIME STATISTICS. A second *Clery* provision is that each school must also disclose three years' worth of statistics about crime occurring on its campus, as well as crimes occurring in noncampus and public properties near the campus. The school must gather the statistics from reports to campus police/security, local police, and student judicial affairs officials. Institutions are supposed to compile data for eight categories and sub-categories of crime including murder; manslaughter; sex offenses (broken down by forcible (including rape) and nonforcible); robbery; aggravated assault; burglary; motor vehicle theft; and arson. Schools are also required to report three types of incidents if they resulted in either an arrest or a disciplinary referral: liquor law violations, drug law violations, and illegal weapons possessions.

TIMELY INFORMATION AND CRIME LOGS. *Clery* further requires schools to provide "timely reports" or "timely warnings" to the campus community about crimes that are occurring and that campus officials consider a threat to the community. Schools must also maintain and make publicly available, daily logs of crimes known to campus police/security. The timely warning requirement is triggered when the school considers a crime to pose an "ongoing threat to students and employees." Timely warnings are limited to the eight categories of crimes listed above.

Logs, on the other hand, are records of *all* crime incidents reported to campus police or security and include all crimes – not just those listed above – such as theft. State-level crime definitions may be used for classification purposes in the logs.[5] Schools that maintain police or security departments are required to disclose in the log any reported crime occurring within the patrol jurisdiction of the campus police/security department. The log must include the nature, date, time, and general location of each crime, as well as its disposition, if known, and be publicly available and accessible by students, employees, and the public, including parents or the local press. Logs remain open for 60 days and after that time, must be made available within two business days of a request.

EMERGENCY NOTIFICATIONS. In addition to timely warnings and crime logs, *Clery* was amended in 2008 to require school officials to issue "emergency notifications" after confirming that a significant emergency was occurring on campus that posed an immediate threat to the health or safety of students on campus. This amendment came about because family members of victims in the 2007 Virginia Tech shootings vociferously lobbied Congress for laws requiring schools to warn students about dangerous situations. "Emergency warnings" differ from "timely warnings" in that they apply to a broader range of issues in more localized spaces. For example, an "emergency warning" may be required if a fire is detected on a campus. In contrast, a "timely warning" is issued under narrower circumstances, including the presence of any of the eight categories of crimes listed above and may cover a larger geographic area, including not only the campus but adjacent areas as well. Some situations, like an armed, active shooter loose on campus would trigger both warnings. To comply with this provision of the statute, schools must describe in their annual security report both their emergency notification mechanism (e.g., mass email or text messages) and their emergency evacuation procedure(s).

CAMPUS POLICE/SECURITY. Yet another key *Clery* provision is that postsecondary institutions with campus police or security departments are required to disseminate information about the power and authority of these agencies in the annual security report. Information about these agencies that is supposed to appear in the report includes a description of the arrest powers of campus police officers; the jurisdictional limits of the agency; and other information relating to department operations and administration.

SEXUAL ASSAULT INFORMATION AND POLICIES. *Clery* further requires institutions to describe in the annual security report their policies concerning campus sexual assault prevention programs and procedures followed after a sex offense occurs. An institution is also supposed to list its policies concerning on-campus disciplinary action in cases of alleged sexual assault, including a clear statement that the accuser and accused are entitled to the same opportunities to have others present during a disciplinary proceeding and have the board inform both parties of the outcome of the disciplinary proceeding.

SANCTIONS FOR INSTITUTIONAL NONCOMPLIANCE. Finally, one of the most important provisions of *Clery* is the stipulation that the ED may impose sanctions on institutions failing to comply with *Clery's* provisions. Congress granted the ED the power to investigate allegations of noncompliance and to impose civil penalties involving fines of up to $25,000 per violation of *Clery's* provisions. Additional sanctions are possible, including loss of federal financial aid funds. Implicit in the provision is the prospect of public censure due to adverse publicity arising from institutional noncompliance: no college or university wants to endure negative press for failing to provide required information to current or prospective members of the campus community. Thus, Congress gave "teeth" to the legislation by allowing the ED to impose sanctions for institutional noncompliance.

In summary, *Clery's* drafters apparently intended the legislation to force campus officials to be forthcoming with their crime statistics and security policies, and quickly disseminate to the campus community information about threats posed by a "crime in progress" or other emergency. Theoretically, current and prospective students and their parents, employees, and the media would then use this information to assess a particular campus' level of safety and see to it that schools implement reasonable security policies. In turn, these actions would presumably reduce on-campus victimization by raising the awareness of students, employees, and the public about campus crime.

Supporters of these goals could argue that enactment of *Clery*-style legislation by the states would assist the goal of raising awareness by exerting additional pressure on campus authorities to report their crime data and security policies. States could also exert even more pressure by imposing additional duties and sanctions on institutions failing to comply with state law. Critics, on the other hand, might argue: (1) there is no need for state-level legislation when the federal *Clery Act* applies to *all* postsecondary institutions (public and private) participating in federal student aid programs and (2) state-level campus crime legislation, like its federal counterpart, is an example of symbolic policy (Edelman, 1964). Forcing schools to *report* their crime statistics and security policies is not the same as *requiring them to actually develop and implement programs and policies that effectively reduce crime and enhance security on campus.* This chapter sheds light on these issues by identifying and examining state-level *Clery* type legislation and examining whether such laws are examples of symbolic politics.

Identifying and Analyzing State-Level *Clery*-Style Legislation and Regulations

To identify state-level *Clery* legislation and regulations, during the period December 1, 2011 through February 6, 2012, we conducted computerized searches of the *LexisNexis*™ "state codes and regulations" database. We conducted these searches in several steps.

First, to identify state codes relating to higher education, we used the search terms "postsecondary institution" or "higher education" to find state legislation specifically relating to colleges and universities. Next, we searched within each state's results using the terms "campus crime," "campus security," "*Clery Act*," "campus police," and "campus sexual assault" to identify legislation one could reasonably construe as *Clery*-type statutes. Finally, we ran the same sets of searches in the administrative code database for each state. Of note, we did not include Pennsylvania in this set of searches. As previously mentioned, Pennsylvania passed legislation containing almost all of the key *Clery* provisions, but did so before Congress passed *Clery*. Thus, Pennsylvania did not follow Congress – it led the way and therefore should not be included when determining how many states followed the lead of Congress, and whether the legislation that followed was of substance, or merely symbolic.

In deciding whether a particular state statute constituted *Clery*-type legislation, we focused on the whether the legislation contained the above discussed key provisions of *Clery*, including whether the law required institutions to: (1)

distribute an annual report on crime and security issues to students; (2) make annual reports about their crime statistics to state authorities; (3) maintain publicly accessible daily crime logs; (4) provide "timely warnings" of crimes that posed threats to the campus community; (5) describe to students the power and authority of campus police/security officials; (6) describe to students policies relating to on-campus sexual assaults; (7) issue emergency notifications; and (8) prescribed sanctions for noncompliance. Using these parameters, our search uncovered 16 states possessing what we consider *Clery*-type legislation.

Analyzing State-Level Clery Legislation

Table 6.1 presents the results of our search, organized as follows. The first column in the table contains the name of the state that had passed the legislation. The second column identifies the specific statute we analyzed. The next eight columns present the key provisions of *Clery* and indicate whether the state's legislation contained each particular provision (Yes/No). The final column of the table presents a count of the number of key *Clery*-type provisions (of the seven listed) the legislation contained. The final row of the table contains the number of states whose statute contained the individual provision listed in the column.

Results

Since 1990, a total of 16 states passed what we characterize as *Clery*-type legislation, including California, Connecticut, Delaware, Iowa, Kentucky, Louisiana, Maryland, Massachusetts, Minnesota, New York, South Carolina, Tennessee, Virginia, Washington, West Virginia, and Wisconsin. As discussed below, however, most of these states' legislation includes only a few key *Clery* provisions. In addition, none of these states have passed regulations that could be characterized as imposing *Clery*-like requirements on post-secondary schools.

KEY PROVISIONS. After determining which states have passed *Clery*-like legislation, we next analyzed the extent to which the provisions of the state statutes mirrored those found in *Clery*. As shown in Table 6.1, only three states – Connecticut, Delaware, and Tennessee – came closest to containing all the key requirements of *Clery*, with each state's legislation containing five of the eight provisions. Among the remaining states, four of them, including California, Kentucky, Massachusetts, and New York, passed legislation that contained three provisions, while two states' (Louisiana and Washington) legislation contained two provisions. The remaining seven states passed legislation containing only one key *Clery* provision.

Table 6.1

Key Requirements: State-Level *Clery* Laws and Regulations

State	Relevant Statutes or Regulations	Requires Institutions to Disseminate Annual Security Report	Requires Institutions to Annually Report Campus Crime Statistics	Requires Institutions to Compile Daily Crime Logs	Requires Institutions to Provide "Timely Warning" Regarding On-Campus Crimes in Progress	Requires Institutions to Distribute Description of Campus Po-lice or Security Personnel	Requires Institutions to Publish Policy on Institutional Handling of On-Campus Sexual Assault Cases	Requires Institutions to Provide Emergency Warnings of Confirmed On-Campus Emergencies	Penalty Stipulated for Institutional Noncompliance	Total Number of Clery Requirements Present
CA[a]	Cal Ed Code §67382 §67385 §67385.7	Yes	Yes	No	No	No	Yes	No	No	3/8
CT[b]	Conn. Gen. Stat. §10a-55a §10a-55c	Yes	Yes	No	No	Yes	Yes	Yes	No	5/8
DE	14 Del. C. §9003 §9004 §9006	Yes	Yes	No	No	Yes	Yes	No	Yes	5/8
IA	Iowa Code §260C.14 §261.9 §262.9	No	No	No	No	No	Yes	No	No	1/8
KY	KRS §164.9481 §164.9485	No	Yes	Yes	Yes	No	No	No	No	3/8
LA	La. R.S. 17: 3351	No	Yes	No	No	Yes	No	No	No	2/8
MA	ALM GL Ch. 6 §168C	Yes	Yes	No	No	Yes	No	No	No	3/8
MD[c]	Md. Educ. Code Ann. §13-601	No	No	No	No	No	No	No	No	0/8
MN	Minn. Stat. §135A.15	No	No	No	No	No	Yes	No	No	1/8

Table 6.1 *(Continued)*

Key Requirements: State-Level *Clery* Laws and Regulations

State	Relevant Statutes or Regulations	Requires Institutions to Disseminate Annual Security Report	Requires Institutions to Annually Report Campus Crime Statistics	Requires Institutions to Compile Daily Crime Logs	Requires Institutions to Provide "Timely" Warning Regarding On-Campus Crimes in Progress	Requires Institutions to Distribute Description of Power/Authority of Campus Police or Security Personnel	Requires Institutions to Publish Policy on Institutional Handling of On-Campus Sexual Assault Cases	Requires Institutions to Provide Emergency Warnings of Confirmed On-Campus Emergencies	Penalty Stipulated for Institutional Noncompliance	Total Number of Clery Requirements Present
NY	NY CLS Educ. §6432–§6433	Yes	Yes	No	No	No	Yes	No	No	3/8
SC	S.C. Code Ann. §59-105-40 §59-105-50	No	No	No	No	No	Yes	No	No	1/8
TN	Tenn. Code Ann. §49-7-129 §49-7-2203 through 2206	Yes	Yes	Yes	No	Yes	No	No	Yes	5/8
VA	VA Code 23-9.2:11	No	No	No	No	No	No	Yes	No	1/8
WA[b]	Rev. Code Wash. §28B.10.569	Yes	Yes	No	No	No	No	Yes	No	3/8
WV[d,e]	W. Va. Code §18B-4-5a	No	Yes	No	No	No	No	No	No	1/8
WI	Wis. Stat. §36.11	No	No	No	No	No	Yes	No	No	1/8
Number of states possessing the provision		**7/16 (44%)**	**10/16 (63%)**	**2/16 (13%)**	**1/16 (6%)**	**5/16 (31%)**	**8/16 (50%)**	**3/16 (19%)**	**2/16 (13%)**	

[a] The statute(s) may also have specific requirements concerning institutional responses to allegations of sexual assaults occurring on campus.
[b] Connecticut and Washington require schools to develop an emergency response plans but this requirement falls short of *Clery* requirements.
[c] Maryland requires schools to develop a plan to report campus-based "hate crimes" that is consistent with *Clery* requirements concerning these crimes.
[d] The statute also requires that post-secondary institutions implement an "anti-hazing" policy.
[e] West Virginia requires institutions to report crime statistics on a "regular and timely" basis but does not mandate annual reporting.

BREADTH OF CLERY PROVISIONS. Having identified how many of the key provisions states' legislation possessed, we next examined which states' legislation contained specific key provisions of *Clery*. As shown in the table, the most commonly occurring *Clery* provision was that relating to institutions having to publish their annual crime statistics. A total of 10 states (63%) with *Clery*-style legislation have this requirement. The next most commonly occurring provisions in the states' legislation involved publication of policies regarding handling of on-campus sexual assault (50%), followed by dissemination of the annual security report (44%) and describing the power and authority of campus security (31%) in the report.

Only three (19%) states (Virginia, Connecticut, and Washington) have laws that require schools to issue emergency warnings. Interestingly, Virginia passed its law requiring an emergency response plan and notifications in 2008, the same year that *Clery* was amended and in the aftermath of the Virginia Tech shootings. As a result, it is not clear if Virginia's law is like *Clery* or if the *Clery* amendment mirrors Virginia's law. Regardless, Connecticut's and Washington's requirements fall far short of the emergency warnings required by *Clery*. Specifically, although Virginia requires a full emergency response notification system, Connecticut and Washington merely require schools to develop a written safety plan, but such plans do not specifically require warnings to be issued. Similarly lacking were provisions about timely warnings of crimes in progress. Only one state, Kentucky, required timely warnings of crimes in progress. Only two states (12%), Tennessee and Kentucky, required daily crime logs.

Finally, we found that only two states' legislation, Delaware and Tennessee, contained a provision for sanctioning institutions that failed to follow legislative dictates. While some states' legislation directed institutions to submit their statistical or other information to a specific state-level agency such as the attorney general's office, even when the legislation listed *mandatory requirements* (regardless of breadth) for institutions to follow, we could find only *two instances* where legislation listed possible sanction(s) for institutional noncompliance. Thus, among the key provisions of *Clery*, crime logs, "timely warnings," and sanctions for noncompliance were the least commonly occurring provisions found in states' campus crime legislation.

Discussion

The patterns emerging from our analyses lead us to conclude that state-level *Clery* initiatives are examples of symbolic public policy (Edelman 1964, 1977, 1988), where legislators drafted, supported, and then passed *Clery*-style initiatives to promote personal and/or public policy goals, to protect themselves electorally, and theoretically to "represent their constituents" (see Bell

& Scott, 2006). In effect, when legislators drafted *Clery*-style statutes, they used certain language in the provisions. This language helped target certain constituent groups and to gain their support for not only the legislation but for those legislators who drafted and supported it. U.S. presidents have also used symbolic language in directives that have little substantive impact, but which constituents greet with much political support (Oliver, 2001; Marion, 1994; Stolz, 1992). According to Oliver (2001, p. 1) in symbolic politics ". . . [T]he words themselves 'become the action,'" and thus in both the legislative and executive arenas, "symbols derive their meaning not from content, but from the values people attach to them" (p. 3). We believe the evidence presented below strongly suggests state-level *Clery* statutes fit into this framework.

First, among the 49 states (again, Pennsylvania is not included) and the District of Columbia, just one-third of them have *Clery*-style legislation relating to campus crime and security. This figure is disappointing given that states may be in a better position to regulate schools in their borders and are typically charged with controlling local issues like education (Griffaton, 1995). Closer analysis reveals an even more dismal picture. Only a handful of states that have passed legislation have included a substantial number of the key provisions found in *Clery*. And, only two of them impose a penalty for noncompliance. If Congress gave *Clery* teeth, state legislation largely remains toothless as most states' statutes fall short of providing the kind of coverage intended by the *Clery* drafters.

That so few states would pass comprehensive versions of *Clery* speaks volumes. Were "campus crime" a legislatively significant issue, states would either have (1) pre-empted Congress and passed their own legislation (Pennsylvania actually did this, but was the only state that did, as far as we know), or (2) quickly followed on the heels of *Clery* and passed their own laws to increase political pressure on schools to "come clean." Neither occurred, which could indicate state legislatures have not felt pressed to pass their own versions of *Clery*. The states thus missed an opportunity to "get the jump" on federal legislation by: (1) passing their own statutes first; (2) bolstering existing law; or (3) creating additional more stringent provisions (such as requiring institutions to report additional offenses not required by *Clery,* such as larceny-theft and simple assault, which research consistently shows as the most common offenses occurring on campus) (e.g., Fisher, Sloan, Cullen, & Lu, 1998). Instead, most state legislators did nothing or, at best, drafted and passed quasi *Clery*-type statutes to gain political support by showing they "cared" about campus crime and security issues.

Second, beyond the limited number of states passing *Clery*-type legislation, the provisions contained in the legislation that have passed hardly mirror those found in *Clery*. Only three states – Connecticut, Delaware, and Tennessee – have legislation containing a majority of *Clery's* key provisions. Of the remaining states with *Clery*-style legislation, most have provisions that mirror only one or two of those found in *Clery,* primarily in the area of publishing policies regarding campus sexual assaults, disseminating campus security reports, and reporting annual campus crime figures. Apparently, the "public reporting" aspects of *Clery* struck something of a chord with at least some state legislatures. One could argue, however, that the public reporting provisions that are included in the legislation allow postsecondary institutions to "kill two birds with one stone" – by fulfilling the requirements of *Clery,* they also fulfill the requirements of the state statutes. Thus, even when states *did* pass *Clery*-type legislation, more often than not, its scope has been far narrower than that of its federal counterpart. Thus, it seems that that limiting the scope of state-level provisions represents the legislature symbolically "doing something" about campus crime without really placing any burden on colleges and universities beyond those already imposed by *Clery.* In effect, the provisions allow postsecondary institutions to address both state and federal requirements simultaneously. Moreover, almost none of the states' statutes include either a "timely warning" or "emergency warning" provision, both of which would alert students to a need to take precautionary measures. In the wake of incidents involving shootings on campus, which are rare but deadly, this seems to be a real flaw in the state statutes.

Our final but perhaps most important finding is that almost none of the provisions found in state-level *Clery* legislation include any mention of institutional sanctions for noncompliance.[6] This fact, perhaps more than any other, provides strong evidence that state-level *Clery* legislation is symbolic at best.[7] If state legislatures were serious about creating additional pressure on postsecondary institutions to publicly disseminate their crime and security information; create policies to better address campus sexual assault; and do more to keep the campus community informed of serious situations via emergency and timely warnings, those same legislatures would surely have provided either civil or criminal (or both) sanctions for institutional noncompliance.

Based on our analyses of state-level *Clery*-type legislation, we agree with scholars who suggest that in both the legislative and the executive arenas, symbolic politics represents a reasonable explanation for "loud support" followed by little chance of substantive impact (see Fisher et al., 2002 for elaboration). When state legislators (or members of Congress) support legislation allegedly designed to address key crime and security-related issues affecting postsecondary institutions, yet the legislation largely omits most (if not all) key provisions of *Clery,* generally does not require postsecondary institutions to expend any effort beyond that needed to comply with *Clery,* and contains no provision for sanctions for institutional noncompliance, one can hardly expect such legislation to have much impact.

Conclusion

Since 1990, when Congress passed the *Student Right-to-Know and Campus Security Act of 1990,* now referred to as the *Clery Act,* a number of states passed their own legislation designed to address crime and security issues at postsecondary institutions. However, when we closely scrutinized these statutes, we found most of this legislation, at best, could be considered "symbolic politics" at work rather than substantive legislative efforts to pressure postsecondary institutions to "come clean" with their crime data and security policies. Importantly, even among the handful of states that apparently tried to either mirror *Clery* or even enhance some or all of its provisions, because, aside from two instances, the legislation makes no provision for sanctioning offending institutions, one could reasonably assume a less than stellar level of compliance (although this is an empirical question that future research could address).

In the state-level policy arena, legislation allegedly addressing concerns over crime and related issues on postsecondary institutions seemingly reflect efforts by legislators to generate support for their political futures rather than policies that pressure colleges and universities to "come clean" with their crime and security information. Perhaps the future holds a day when state legislatures will develop substantive policies to address campus crime. Until then, symbolic politics better describes state-level efforts to address campus crime.

NOTES

1. See Carter & Bath (2007) for a complete review and analysis of the original *Clery Act.*

2. The FBI developed the UCR program in the 1930s and has administered it ever since. Each year, the Bureau solicits data from thousands of state, county, and municipal law enforcement agencies about crimes known to, and arrests made by, the agencies representing jurisdictions in which over 95 percent of the U.S. population lives. The FBI then analyzes and compiles this information into an annual report, *Crime in the United States.* The report can be downloaded from http://www.fbi.gov/ucr/ucr.htm#cius.

3. To date, however, the ED has sanctioned only a few post-secondary institutions for failing to comply with the statute's provisions. For analysis of postsecondary institutional compliance with *Clery,* see Sloan, Fisher, & Cullen (1997), Karjane, Fisher & Cullen (2002), and Fisher, Karjane, Cullen, Blevins, Santana, and Daigle (2007).

4. Information for this section was retrieved December 14, 2011 from the Security on Campus, Inc. website, http://www.securityoncampus.org.

5. This is a key problem with the logs. Because state-by-state definitions of crimes vary (a situation remedied by the UCR reporting program that provides "standard-

ized definitions" of offenses which makes interstate comparisons of crime rates possible), it becomes next to impossible to compare the logs of schools in one state with those in another since UCR guidelines for classifying offenses are not followed for the logs. A classic example would be for burglary (one of the offenses for which *Clery* includes in its crime reporting provision), where some states (e.g., Maryland) still use the common law definition of burglary while others (e.g., California and Arkansas) have modified this definition.

6. To be fair, some states (e.g., California) have provisions in their codes of civil procedure that allow individuals to bring civil actions against postsecondary institutions for failing to provide the requestor with campus crime information. Still other states (e.g., Wisconsin) have legislation allowing for the imposing of criminal sanctions on administrators who fail to comply with a school's general obligation to follow state law. But these still fall short of imposing specific sanctions for noncompliance with the state *Clery* legislation.

7. One could make a convincing argument that *Clery* is also symbolic policy. *Clery's* provision of a maximum civil penalty of $25,000 for noncompliance, combined with the fact the ED has sanctioned so few schools for noncompliance, does little to foster a belief that through *Clery*, Congress sought to genuinely pressure postsecondary institutions to do more to address campus crime and security issues (see Fisher, Hartman, Cullen, & Turner, 2002).

REFERENCES

Bell, L. C., & Scott, K. (2006). Policy statements or symbolic politics? Explaining Congressional court limiting attempts. *Judicature, 89,* 196–201.

Carter, S. D., & Bath, C. (2007). The Evolution and Components of the *Jeanne Clery Act:* Implications for Higher Education. In B. Fisher & J. Sloan (Eds.), *Campus crime: Legal, social, and policy perspectives* (2nd ed.) (pp. 27–44). Springfield, IL: Charles C Thomas.

Edelman, M. (1964). *The symbolic uses of politics.* Urbana, IL: University of Illinois Press.

Edelman, M. (1977). *Political language: Words that succeed and policies that fail.* Chicago: Academic Press.

Edelman, M. (1988). *Constructing the political spectacle.* Chicago: University of Chicago Press.

Fisher, B. S., Hartman, J. L., Cullen, F. T., & Turner, M. G. (2002). Making campuses safer for students: The *Clery Act* as symbolic legal reform. *Stetson Law Review, 31,* 61–91.

Fisher, B. S., Karjane, H. M., Cullen, F. T., Blevins, K. R., Santanna, S. A., & Daigle, L. E. (2007). Reporting sexual assault and the *Clery Act:* Situating findings from the National Campus Sexual Assault Policy Study within college women's experiences. In B. Fisher & J. Sloan (Eds.), *Campus crime: Legal, social, and policy perspectives* (2nd ed.) (pp. 65–86). Springfield, IL: Charles C Thomas.

Fisher, B. S., Sloan, J. J., Cullen, F., & Lu, C. (1998). Crime in the 'Ivory Tower': The level and sources of student victimization. *Criminology, 33,* 671–711.

Griffaton, M. C. (1995). State-level initiatives and campus crime. In B. Fisher & J. Sloan (Eds.), *Campus crime: Legal, social, and policy perspectives* (pp. 53–73). Springfield, IL: Charles C. Thomas.

Karjane, H. M., Fisher, B. S., & Cullen, F. T. (2002). *Campus sexual assault: How America's institutions of higher education respond.* Final Report, National Institute of Justice Grant No. 99-WA-VX-0008. Retrieved from http://www.ncjrs.org/pdffiles1/nij/grants/196676. pdf.

Marion, N. E. (1994). Symbolism and federal crime control legislation, 1960–1990. *Journal of Crime & Justice, 17,* 69–91.

Oliver, W. M. (2001). Executive orders, symbolic politics, criminal justice policy, and the American presidency. *American Journal of Criminal Justice, 26,* 1–20.

Sloan, J. J., & Fisher, B. S. (2011). *The dark side of the ivory tower: Campus crime as a social problem.* New York: Cambridge University Press.

Sloan, J. J., Fisher B. S., & Cullen, F. T. (1997). Assessing the *Student Right-to-Know and Campus Security Act of 1990:* An analysis of the victim reporting practices of college and university students. *Crime and Delinquency, 43,* 168–185.

Stolz, B. A. (1992). Congress and the war on drugs: An exercise in symbolic politics. *Journal of Crime and Justice, 15,* 119–136.

Part II

THE SOCIAL CONTEXT
OF CAMPUS CRIME

Part II

THE SOCIAL CONTEXT OF CAMPUS CRIME

INTRODUCTION

Since the 1980s, social scientists have studied the social context of campus crime from a variety of disciplines and theoretical perspectives. Questions that were raised and − in some cases − answered by these studies revolved around issues involving the *extent* of criminal victimization suffered by students. These researchers focused their attention on developing better definitions and measures of students' criminal victimizations. Other researchers focused their attention on the *nature* of student victimization through testing different theories and using advanced quantitative methods and causal modeling to understand *how and why* students are victims. Still other researchers, using rapidly advancing information technology, including crime mapping and global positioning systems (GPS), examined the *spatial* and *temporal distribution* of crime on campus, or analyzed the *clustering* of crime in specific physical locations on college campuses in an effort to understand the dynamics of such clusters. Cumulatively, these efforts have produced a sizable body of research that has contributed to a fuller understanding of college student victimization patterns. Importantly, much of this research goes well beyond mere attempts to describe or explain, but also offers policy and program recommendations that postsecondary institutions can undertake to address the on-campus victimization of college students and evaluate their effectiveness so they can make improvement that are tailored to the unique crime problems faced by their respective campus. Part II of the book explores each of these issues.

In Chapter 7, "The Violent Victimization of College Students: Findings from the National Crime Victimization Survey," Timothy Hart uses data from the National Crime Victimization Survey, an annual, national-level victimization survey of several thousand adults to answer questions asked by researchers concerning the extent and nature of victimizations suffered by college students. Hart's focus is on serious violence experienced by students, and by comparing violent victimization patterns of students and nonstudents Hart shows significant differences between the groups. He also profiles other aspects of the violent victimization of college students, including characteristics of incidents and offenders. Answers to basic questions about the extent and nature of violent victimization of college students are clearly important, particularly since the *Clery Act* focuses on institutional reporting of such offenses and mandates that schools undertake efforts to both prevent crime and provide services to victims of certain forms of violence (e.g., sexual assault).

Elizabeth Mustaine and Richard Tewksbury, in Chapter, 8 provide a comprehensive overview of the current state of theoretically-based victimization research of college students. As the title of their chapter, "The Routine Activities and Criminal Victimization of Students: Lifestyle and Related Factors," implies, they frame their discussion of research findings by focusing on how motivated offenders, suitable targets, and lack of guardianship impact college students' risk for criminal victimization. Their summary of how students' lifestyles and routine activities heightens or reduces victimization risk provides postsecondary administrators with excellent ideas for crime prevention strategies including self-protection, integrating alcohol and drug use/abuse education into new student orientation, and developing better ways to enhance guardianship. Mustaine and Tewksbury suggest that postsecondary schools consider ways to increase students' use of currently available programs and services and "thereby effectively lower their risk."

In Chapter 9, George Dowdall explores "The Role of Alcohol Abuse in College Student Victimization" by discussing the complex relationship between alcohol use and student victimization risk. Drawing largely from public health-oriented research, Dowdall describes students' drinking behavior, including so-called "binge drinking" and how such activities enhance victimization risk. He also discusses the factors known to shape college drinking patterns and presents empirical evidence suggesting that alcohol abuse is associated with a wide range of problematic outcomes, including interpersonal violence. Dowdall presents a balanced assessment of whether a causal link exists between alcohol use/abuse and violence and then closes the chapter by discussing what the current research shows about preventing college student abuse of alcohol.

Chapter 10, "Violence Against Women on College Campuses: Rape, Intimate Partner Abuse, and Sexual Harassment," by Joanne Belknap and Edna Erez, synthesizes several decades' worth of published victimization research that focuses on the violent victimization of college women. Belknap and Erez describe what research has uncovered about the incidence and characteristics of aggression against college women, along with institutional and attitudinal factors that facilitate such violence. They also outline actions campus administrators can take to address the reality of sexual victimization on college and university campuses and provide services to survivors.

Chapter 11, "Vulnerabilities and Opportunities 101: The Extent, Nature, and Impact of Stalking and Cyberstalking Among College Students and Implications for Campus Policy and Programs," by Megan Stewart and Bonnie Fisher, examines the extent and nature of stalking and cyberstalking among college students. In the chapter, Stewart and Fisher discuss how the socio-demographic characteristics of students, their lifestyles, and the characteristics of college campuses combine to make students vulnerable stalking targets, while simultaneously providing perpetrators with ample stalking opportunities. Drawing from existing literature on campus stalking victims and perpetrators, Stewart and Fisher present a range of pertinent issues designed to provide the reader a detailed picture of who is stalked, why they are stalked, for how long they are typically stalked, and the tactics used by stalkers. These researchers also highlight the emerging problem of cyberstalking, detail coping strategies students have used to stop the stalking, and describe the emotional and psychological toll stalking takes on targets. They present evidence-based policies and programs that postsecondary administrators can adopt to help prevent stalking and cyberstalking behaviors among college students.

Part II concludes with Chapter 12 by Matthew Robinson and Sunghoon Roh that is titled "Crime on Campus: Spatial Aspects of Campus Crime at a Regional Comprehensive University." Robinson and Roh use crime mapping technology to explore the spatial and temporal distribution of crime at a regional university campus and present a place-specific approach to understanding not only the spatial distribution of student victimization, but how crime prevention efforts can be developed using such an approach. Their explanation for the patterns of "hot spots" of crime on campus provides postsecondary administrators and campus police with results that should inform place-based or situational crime prevention strategies that campus administrators may wish to implement.

The chapters comprising Part II address a range of issues to help readers understand the social context of campus crime. Each chapter either presents a review of results from published social scientific research studies that describe or explain the extent and nature of student victimization or presents original research. Chapter authors show that many questions concerning the social context of student victimization have been addressed over the past two decades and their answers have crime prevention policy and program, and victim service implications. Most important, each chapter lays the foundation for *future* theoretically and empirically-driven research on the social context of campus crime.

Chapter 7

THE VIOLENT VICTIMIZATION OF COLLEGE STUDENTS: FINDINGS FROM THE NATIONAL CRIME VICTIMIZATION SURVEY

Timothy C. Hart

INTRODUCTION

Research examining the extent and nature of campus crime, its impact on students, and the response to it by administrators and security officials has improved our understanding of this important social issue. A growing body of campus crime research suggests that victimization is a rare occurrence, consisting mostly of nonviolent incidents such as personal thefts and property crimes (Bromley, 1992, 1995a; Fisher, Sloan, Cullen, & Lu, 1998; Hart, 2007; Hart & Miethe, 2011; Sellers & Bromley, 1996; Sigler & Koehlor, 1993; Sloan, 1992, 1994). In spite of relatively low campus crime rates, however, college students often express a high level of fear about becoming crime victims (Fisher, 1995; McCreedy & Dennis, 1996; Meijer, 1995). Campus administrators and security officials have responded to crime and concerns of victimization among students, parents, and surrounding communities by addressing environmental design and contextual factors believed to be associated with campus crime, such as improving lighting, implementing residence hall restrictions, and developing educational crime prevention programs (Bromley, 1994; 1995b; Fisher & Nasar, 1992; Fisher & Sloan, 1993).

Although research into the predictors of campus crime rates and college student victimization are enlightening, many are based on a convenience sample at a single or limited number of schools or on anecdotal evidence (Gross, Winslett, Roberts, & Gohm, 2006; Henson & Stone, 1999; Nicholson, Maney, Blair, Wamboldt, Mahoney, & Yaun, 1998; Robinson & Mullen,

2001). Indeed, few national-level studies of college student victimization exist (Barberet, Fisher, & Taylor, 2004; Fisher & Cullen, 1999; Fisher, Cullen, & Turner, 2000; Fisher et al., 1998; Hart, 2007). As a result, our understanding of college student victimization – especially incident-level characteristics of violent victimization – is limited (see Fisher, Cullen, & Turner, 2000). Yet, improving our knowledge and understanding of college student victimization is vital. Doing so will enable campus administrators and security officials to refine prevention efforts so that they are specifically tailored to the situation. Data collected by the National Crime Victimization Survey (NCVS) is well suited for this task.

This chapter uses NCVS data collected from 2001 through 2010 to provide estimates of nonfatal violent victimization of college students. Comparisons between levels of violence experienced by college students and similarly aged nonstudents are also provided. Incident characteristics, such as where (i.e., on campus or off campus) and when (i.e., during the day or at night) college students are more likely to be victimized are then examined. Next, victim characteristics such as gender, race, and Hispanic origin are reported. Finally, offender characteristics – such as relationship to the victim and whether they were perceived to be under the influence of drugs and/or alcohol at the time of an incident – are offered. Collectively, the findings provide a new and informative perspective on the social context of campus crime. Before findings are presented, however, a brief overview of the NCVS is provided.

The National Crime Victimization Survey

The NCVS has been collecting information on crime incidents, victims, and trends for over three decades. The NCVS is a stratified, multistage, cluster sample, employing a rotating panel design. Interviews are conducted every six months with members of sampled households, for a period of three years. Household members eligible for interview are individuals age 12 or older residing in the sampled household at the time of the survey. Interviews with respondents are gathered both in person and over the telephone.

The NCVS contains a basic screening interview in which demographic information such as age, gender, race, and Hispanic origin for each eligible household member is collected. Some of this information (i.e., age and marital status) is updated during subsequent interviews if necessary. When a criminal incident is identified during the screening process, detailed, incident-based data are then collected for each incident identified.

A subset of NCVS data is used for the analyses that follow. With the exception of comparisons made between students and nonstudents, data are limited to only college students defined as a respondent who identified him- or herself as between the ages of 18 and 24 and was enrolled in a college or university at least part-time at some point during the six months prior to their most recent NCVS interview.

Although violent, property, and personal theft crimes are identified by the survey, only nonfatal *violent* victimizations are included in the current analyses. Violent crimes include threatened, attempted, or completed rape or sexual assault; robbery; aggravated assault; and simple assault. Rape or sexual assault consists of those incidents involving forced sexual intercourse that includes psychological coercion and physical force. Robbery is defined as property or cash taken directly from a person by use or threat of force, with or without a weapon, and with or without injury. Aggravated assault is defined as an attack or attempted attack with a weapon, regardless of whether or not it resulted in an injury, or an attack or attempted attack without a weapon when serious injury results. Finally, simple assault is defined as an attack without a weapon which results in no injury or a minor injury such as a bruise, cut, scrape, or scratch.

Violent Victimization of College Students

Past research suggests that college students face high risk for criminal victimization (Fisher & Cullen, 1999; Fisher et al., 2000; Fisher et al., 1998). One way to assess these claims is to compare victimization rates between students and nonstudents using data produced from the NCVS. To do so, Table 7.1 presents average annual rates of violent victimization experienced by both college students and nonstudents, between 2001 and 2010. Results show that college students experienced overall nonfatal violence at an average annual rate of 34.4 per 1,000 students and serious violent crime at a rate of 14.2 per 1,000 students. Not only are these rates far below the levels measured in previous studies (Fisher et al., 1998; Hart, 2007), but also they are well below the levels reported by nonstudents.

The rate of violent crime among college students (34.4 per 1,000 students) is much less than the rate of similarly aged nonstudents (47.3 per 1,000 nonstudents). College students also reported experiencing robbery, aggravated assault, simple assault, and overall serious violent crime at significantly lower rates than their nonstudent counterparts: 3.9 per 1,000 students versus 5.8 per 1,000 nonstudents; 7.7 per 1,000 students versus 11.0 per 1,000 nonstudents; 20.3 per 1,000 students versus 28.3 per 1,000 nonstudents; and 14.2 per 1,000 students versus 19.0 per 1,000 nonstudents, respectively.

Both students and nonstudents experienced a significant decrease in overall rates of violent crime between 2001 and 2010. For example, the rate of violence against college students declined by about 20 percent and by about 16 percent among similarly aged nonstudents. For both students and nonstudents, the decline in overall violence is attributable to the significant drop in

Table 7.1

Nonfatal Violent Victimization of College Students and Nonstudents, 2001–2010

Victims age 18–24	Violent crime	Rape/ sexual assault	Robbery	Aggravated assault	Simple assault	Serious violent crime[a]
College students						
Average annual rate	34.4[b]	2.6	3.9[b]	7.7[b]	20.3[b]	14.2[b]
Percent change, '01–'10	-46.9[c]	-74.4[d]	-43.5	-31.5	-47.6[c]	-45.7[c]
Nonstudents						
Average annual rate	47.3	2.2	5.8	11.0	28.3	19.0
Percent change, '01–'10	-31.6[c]	-44.0	6.5	-31.3[d]	-38.4[c]	-22.7

Note: On average, from 2001 through 2010, the estimated student population was 9,647,780. For nonstudents, the estimated population during that period was 18,887,190.

a Serious violent crime includes rape/sexual assault, robbery, and aggravated assault.

b The difference between the college students' rate and nonstudents' rate is at the 95%-significance level.

c The difference from 2001 to 2010 is at the 95%-significance level.

d The difference from 2001 to 2010 is at the 90%-significance level. No difference between the decline in rates among college students and nonstudents from 2001 to 2010 was observed at either the 90% or 95%-significance level for any of the crime measures.

simple assaults observed during this period. Since simple assaults account for more of the overall violent crime total than any other specific type of violent crime, a decline in the rate of simple assault has a greater impact on the overall violent crime rate.

Although both students and nonstudents experienced significant declines in violence between 2001 and 2010, no difference between the decreased rates among college students and their nonstudent counterparts for any type of violence was observed. Said differently, between 2001 and 2010, college students experienced a rate of decline for all types of violence that was statistically similar to the rate of decline experienced by similarly aged nonstudents.

Using NCVS data to estimate levels of violent victimization among college students helps add to our understanding of the nature and extent of campus crime, and provides a foundation upon which other comparisons can be made – such as comparing violence among students and nonstudents as well as comparing changes in the levels of violence among college students and nonstudents over time. But NCVS data can provide even greater insight into the issue of campus crime. For example, NCVS data contain meaningful information associated with the characteristics of incidents, which is often unavailable in data collected and reported by colleges and universities in accordance with the *Jeanne Clery Act* (2000).

Incident-level Characteristics

The following section presents analysis of event-specific data for both on-campus and off-campus college student victimization to broaden our understanding of violence committed against college students.

Location of Incidents

A perennial question is whether college students are more likely to be victimized on or off campus. Figure 7.1 illustrates trends in on-campus and off-campus violence experienced by college students. Findings indicate that most violent crimes experienced by college students occur *off* campus. For example, between 2001 and 2010, the average annual rate of *off-campus* victimization of college students (32.3 per 1,000 students) was about *16 times greater* than the average annual rate of *on-campus* victimization of college students (2.1 per 1,000 students). While this finding reveals the magnitude of the difference between on-campus and off-campus violent victimization of college students is much greater than has been demonstrated in past studies (e.g., Fisher et al., 1998), it is consistent with previous research that indicates violence against college students is more likely to occur away from campus (Fisher et al., 1998;

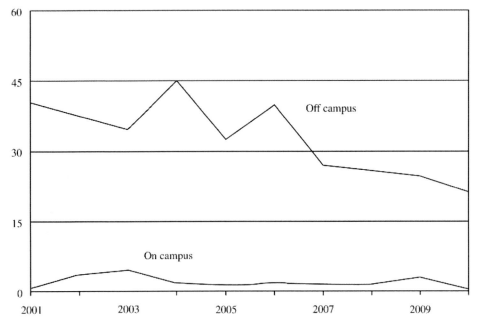

Figure 7.1. Rate per 1,000 students age 18–24 of nonfatal violent victimization by location: 2001–10.

Hart, 2003, 2007; Hart & Miethe, 2011; Sellers & Bromley, 1996; Sigler & Koehlor, 1993).

NCVS findings also reveal an interesting pattern with respect to the rates of decline in both on-campus and off-campus violence. Specifically, from 2001 through 2010, there was a significant decline in the rate of off-campus violence against college students (from 40.4 to 21.4 per 1,000), but the decline in on-campus violence (from 1.0 to 0.6 per 1,000) was not as significant. Thus, findings from the NCVS not only demonstrate that the risk of violent victimization among college students is far greater off campus, but also that similar trends in on-campus and off-campus victimization have not been observed over the past several years.

Metropolitan Statistical Area (MSA)

In addition to producing information on *where* college student victimization occurs, NCVS data also provide insight into *when* college student violence is likely to take place. That is, NCVS data can be used to answer the question: When are college student most likely to become victims of violent crime?

Table 7.2 presents information on incident characteristics of college student violence that occurred both on campus and off campus. Results show that college students living in urban areas are at somewhat greater risk of violent victimization while off campus than while on campus. Conversely, students living in rural areas are at slightly greater risk of being violently victimized while on campus than while off campus. These results demonstrate regional differences in college student victimization by where violence occurs (i.e., on campus versus off campus). Current findings also suggest temporal differences in college student victimization and where these incidents are likely to occur.

Time of Incidents

Results show that college students experience about 2.5 times more violence at night (between the hours of 6 p.m. and 6 a.m.) than during the day. However, a different pattern emerges for violence that occurs on campus; that is, when location is considered *in conjunction* with time. On-campus violence is more likely to take place during the day (52%) than at night (26%). On the other hand, violence experienced by college students off campus occurs more frequently during nighttime hours (70%) than during the daytime (42%). This is likely the result of the kinds of activities in which students tend to be involved while on campus during the day and off campus at night. During the day, students tend to be in class, at the library, or in the dorms – engaging in activities that usually do not lead to violence. Conversely, college students fre-

Table 7.2
Nonfatal Violent Victimization of College Students by Location
and Incident Characteristics, 2001–2010

Incident characteristics	Average annual number		Percent of all violence	
	On campus	Off campus	On campus	Off campus
MSA				
Urban	6,570	147,548	32.7	47.3
Suburban	8,263	124,396	41.2	39.9
Rural	5,236[a]	40,077	26.1[a]	12.8
Time of incident				
Day (6 a.m. – 6 p.m.)	10,353	80,361	51.6	25.8
Night (6 p.m. – 6 a.m.)	8,498	217,280	42.3	69.6
Don't know	1,218[a]	13,532	6.1[a]	4.3
Injuries				
No	16,410	215,392	81.8	69.0
Yes	3,659[a]	96,628	18.2[a]	31.0
Reported to the police				
No	11,131	178,950	55.5	57.4
Yes	8,469	127,419	42.2	40.8
Don't know	470[a]	5,375	2.3[a]	1.7
Victim's assistance				
No	18,787[a]	292,654	93.6[a]	93.8
Yes	1,282	17,602	6.4	5.6
Don't know	0[a]	862[a]	0.0[a]	0.3[a]

Note: Detail may not add to 100% due to rounding or missing data.
a Based on 10 or fewer sample cases.

quently spend their evenings, especially weekend nights, at parties, drinking, and blowing off steam – engaging in behavior that is more likely to lead to violence.

Injuries Incurred by Student Victims

Incident-level characteristics can also be used to answer the question: To what extent does injury result when college students are violently victimized? Results in Table 7.2 reveal that about seven out of ten violent crimes committed against college students result in injurious harm. These findings are consistent with past research that suggests college student victims of violence sustain injuries infrequently (Baum & Klaus, 2005; Hart, 2003, 2007; Hart & Miethe, 2011).

Since nearly 14 out of every 15 crimes against college students occur off campus, the extent to which violence resulting in injury among college students *on campus* can be overshadowed if not examined separately. Indeed, a different pattern emerges when injurious college student victimization is viewed in light of where violence occurs than when location of the crime is not taken into consideration. The amount of off-campus violence that results in injury (31%) is slightly higher than the amount of on-campus violence that results in injury (18%). These findings suggest that not only are college students safer from violence while on campus, but also that the violence they experience on campus is less severe than off-campus violence.

Incidents Reported to Police

Another event-specific characteristic related to campus crime that can be examined using NCVS data is the extent to which violence against college students is reported to police. For the general population, about one-half of all violent crime is reported to police (see Truman, 2011; Hart & Rennison, 2003). And although patterns of reporting violence experienced by college students vary from that which is observed in the general population, the reasons why college students report violence to the police are much the same (Hart & Rennison, 2003).

Findings presented in Table 7.2 show that about two-fifths of all violent victimizations experienced by college students are reported to the police. In other words, police are *unaware* of most of the violence experienced by college students. Although other incident-related characteristics of college student victimization vary based on where the incident takes place, location of the incident has little influence on whether it is reported to police. That is, the amount of on-campus violence reported to police (42%) is statistically similar to the amount of off campus violence reported to police (41%). These findings paint a complex picture of campus crime. Namely, while college students are far less likely to experience violence on our nation's campuses, when it does occur, it is not likely to be reported to police. The logical question then becomes why?

College students *do not* report violence to the police for many reasons. Table 7.3 contains information on the specific reasons why college students say they do not report it. Results show that an estimated 35 percent of victimizations experienced by college students on campus were not reported to police because they were considered a "private or personal matter." Moreover, while 17 percent of on-campus violence is not reported to police because it was reported to another official, fewer incidents of off-campus violence were not reported to police for the same reason (6%). Conversely, a greater percentage of off-campus crime than on-campus crime was not reported to police because the victim indicated they lacked sufficient proof (26% versus 6%, respectively).

From 2001 through 2010, about 10 percent of on-campus violence against college students was not reported to police because reporting the crime was

Table 7.3

**Nonfatal Violent Victimization of College Students by Location
and Reasons for Not Reporting Violence to Police, 2001–2010**

Reasons for not reporting	Percent of reasons	
	On campus	Off campus
Private or personal matter	34.6	31.4
Reported to another official	17.4	6.3
Small/no loss	10.7	5.6
Inconvenient	10.3	2.0
Lack of proof	6.4	25.9
Not important to police	3.1	3.0
Not clear a crime occurred	0.0	4.2
Protect offender	0.0	3.9
Police ineffective	5.7	3.8
Fear of reprisal	0.0	0.5
Other	11.8	13.5

Note: Detail may not add to 100% due to rounding or missing data.

"inconvenient," while about 6 percent of on-campus crime was not reported to police because the victim felt the police would be "ineffective." Although about 4 percent of off-campus student-victimization was *not* reported to police in order to either protect the offender or because the victim was unclear a crime had occurred, none of the students who experienced *on-campus* violence indicated these were the reasons for *not* reporting an incident to police.

Victims' Use of Assistance Agencies or Organizations

Recently, colleges and universities have attempted to develop or expand programs geared towards assisting the victims of campus crime, with most providing group presentations on awareness and prevention or publishing crime-safety bulletins or announcements (Bromley & Fisher, 2002; Karjane, Fisher, & Cullen, 2005). With few exceptions, however, little is known about the extent to which college-student victims of violence utilize these services (Hart, 2007).

Findings presented in Table 7.2 reveal that very few college students seek assistance after being victimized. An estimated nine out of ten incidents of violence committed against students result in the students *not* seeking help from a victim's assistance agency or organization. This pattern holds true regardless of whether an incident occurs on campus or off campus. In other words, college students victimized *on* campus are no more likely to seek help from victim assistance agencies or organizations (6%) than students victimized *off* campus (6%).

In summary, analysis of incident-specific characteristics associated with college-student victimization reveals patterns associated with (1) where and when campus violence occurs, (2) the extent to which campus violence results in injury, (3) the extent to which it is reported to police, and (4) whether college-student victims of violence reportedly seek assistance from organizations or programs designed to aid victims of violence. NCVS data also contain information specific to crime-victim characteristics.

Characteristics of College Student Victims of Violence

One of the hallmarks of NCVS data is they provide detailed information about victims, unlike official crime statistics gathered and produced by colleges and universities. Student-victim characteristics such as gender, race, and ethnic origin are examined below to identify whether individual-level characteristics of college students are linked to increased risk of violent campus crime such as those identified in the general population (see Sampson & Lauritsen, 1994).

Gender

In 2010, although males age 12 or older experienced overall violent crime at similar rates as females, males experienced robbery and aggravated assault at much higher rates than females (Truman, 2011). A somewhat different pattern emerges among college students, as shown in Table 7.4, which provides demographic information on these victims of violence. Results show, for example, the overall rate of on-campus violence is more than twice as high among male students (3.1 per 1,000 students) than for female students (1.2 per 1,000) and the on-campus rate of simple assault is more than four times higher for males than females (2.5 versus 0.6 per 1,000 students). Among students victimized off campus, the overall violent crime rate, robbery rate, aggravated assault rate, and the simple assault rate (37.2, 5.2, 9.7, and 21.7 per 1,000 students, respectively), is significantly higher for male students than their female counterparts (28.0, 2.3, 5.3, and 16.1 per 1,000 students, respectively). Female college students are victims of off-campus rape and sexual assault at rates that are significantly higher than male students (4.2 versus 0.7 per 1,000 students). For all crime types measured, the on-campus victimization rates for both male and female students were significantly lower than the off-campus victimization rates.

Table 7.4
Nonfatal Violent Victimization of College Students by Location and Demographic Information, 2001–2010

Victims of violence	Population	Violent crime	Rape/sexual assault	Robbery	Aggravated assault	Simple assault	Serious violent crime
			Average annual rates per 1,000 students age 18–24				
College students	9,647,780	34.4	2.6	3.9	7.7	20.3	14.2
On campus							
Gender							
Male	4,540,450	3.1	0.0[a]	0.1[a]	0.4[a]	2.5	0.6
Female	5,107,330	1.2	0.1[a]	0.2[a]	0.3[a]	0.6[a]	0.6[a]
Race/ethnicity[b]							
White	6,330,640	2.3	0.1[a]	0.1[a]	0.2[a]	1.9	0.4[a]
Black	1,116,850	2.7[a]	0.0[a]	0.9[a]	0.9[a]	1.0[a]	1.7[a]
Other	906,960	1.3[a]	0.0[a]	0.0[a]	0.0	1.3[a]	0.0[a]
Hispanic, any race	1,293,330	1.0[a]	0.0[a]	0.0[a]	0.8[a]	0.3[a]	0.8[a]
Off campus							
Gender							
Male	4,540,450	37.2	0.7[a]	5.2	9.7	21.7	15.6
Female	5,107,330	28.0	4.2	2.3	5.3	16.1	11.8
Race/ethnicity[b]							
White	6,330,640	34.4	3.2	3.0	7.7	20.5	13.9
Black	1,116,850	37.9	1.6[a]	7.5	10.9	17.8	20.1
Other	906,960	16.1	1.2[a]	2.9[a]	3.2[a]	8.8	7.3
Hispanic, any race	1,293,330	29.1	1.1[a]	4.1	5.8	18.1	11.0

a Based on 10 or fewer sample cases.
b All racial categories do not include Hispanics. "Other" category includes Asians, Native Hawaiians, Pacific Islanders, Alaska Natives, and American Indians combined.

Race and Ethnicity

Results presented in Table 7.4 also demonstrate that regardless of the race or ethnic origin of college students, rates of overall violence, serious violence, and simple assault are greater off campus than on campus. For example, white college students experience overall violence off campus at levels that are about 15 times greater than the rate of violence that white students experience on campus (34.4 versus 2.3 per 1,000 students); black college students are victims of off-campus violence at about 14 times the rate of black college students that are victims of on-campus violence (37.9 versus 2.7 per 1,000 students); and off-campus violence is experienced by Hispanic students at rates that are estimated to about 29 times greater than the rate of on-campus violence experienced by this group (29.1 versus 1.0 per 1,000 students). These findings are consistent with recent analysis of Hispanic college student victimization, which shows that about 96 percent of all violence experienced by these students occurs off campus (Hart & Rennison, 2011).

In addition to characteristics of campus-crime events and victim-based characteristics associated with campus crime, NCVS data include information related to criminal offenders. For each incident identified during an interview, a respondent is asked to recall specific characteristics associated with the person (or persons) by whom they were victimized. For example, victims are asked whether the offender was someone they knew, whether the offender was believed to be under the influence of drugs or alcohol, and whether the offender had a weapon. Like event- and victim-specific information associated with campus crime, offender-based information aids in developing a more robust understanding of the nature and extent of campus crime.

Offender Characteristics

Victim-Offender Relationship

Is the violence experienced by college students committed by offenders known to the victim or by strangers? Table 7.5 presents information on offender characteristics for both on-campus and off-campus violence. Findings show that about one-half of all college-student violence is committed by someone the student does *not* know. In addition, college students experience on-campus and off-campus violence by non-strangers (i.e., a spouse, ex-spouse, boyfriend, girlfriend, parent, child, other relative or a victim's friend or acquaintance) at similar rates. Moreover, there is significant difference between the levels of on-campus violence committed by an offender that is known to the victim (32%) than by someone the victim reportedly does not know (55%). Off-campus victimization follows a similar pattern. A greater percentage of off-campus violence among college students is committed by a stranger (52%) than by someone the victim knows (42%).

Table 7.5

Nonfatal Violent Victimization of College Students by Location and Offender Characteristics, 2000–2010

Offender characteristics	Average annual number		Percent of all violence	
	On campus	Off campus	On campus	Off campus
Relationship to victim				
Known	6,382	132,322	31.8	42.4
Stranger [b]	11,121	160,688	55.4	51.5
Don't know	2,567 [a]	19,010	12.8 [a]	6.1
Perceived alcohol/drug use [c]				
Using	4,476 [a]	129,579	22.3 [a]	41.5
Not Using	6,933	50,874	34.5	16.3
Don't know	7,691	113,831	38.3	36.5
Presence of weapon				
No	12,726	209,339	63.4	67.1
Yes	4,460	80,742	22.2	25.9
Don't know	2,883 [a]	21,939	14.4	7.0

Note: Detail may not add to 100% due to rounding or missing data.

a Based on 10 or fewer sample cases.

b A spouse, ex-spouse, boyfriend, girlfriend, parent, child, other relative or a victim's friend or acquaintance.

c Alcohol/drug use based on whether the victim believed offender(s) was under the influence at the time of incident.

Perceived Drug/Alcohol Use by the Offender

During the NCVS interview, crime victims are asked if they believe that the offender(s) was under the influence of either drugs or alcohol at the time of the incident. Responses to this question are used to understand the extent to which drugs and alcohol use play a role in the violent victimization.

Findings presented in Table 7.5 indicate that according to college-student victims of violence, more on-campus incidents are committed by an offender who the victim believes was *not* under the influence of drugs or alcohol (35%) than by an offender whom the victim believes *was* under the influence (22%). The opposite pattern emerges when off-campus violence is considered. Specifically, more off-campus incidents are committed by an offender whom the victim believed was under the influence of drugs or alcohol (42%) than by an offender whom the victim believed was not (16%).

Use of Weapon by the Offender

Finally, findings from past research suggest a growing number of students carry weapons on college campuses; and that as weapon carrying among students increases, so does the risk of weapon use in crimes against students (Summers & Hoffman, 1998). However, based on information derived from NCVS data, most violence experienced by college-student does not reportedly involve a weapon.

Specifically, results in Table 7.5 show that an estimated 63 percent of non-fatal violence experienced by college students on campus and about 67 percent of college-student victimization occurring off campus do *not* involve a weapon. In short, regardless of whether college students are victimized on campus or off, most of the time, weapons are not involved.

Conclusion

Self-report victim-survey data produced from the NCVS offer several note-worthy results as to the extent and nature of violence experienced by college students. First, college students experience violent crime at rates that are lower than similarly aged non-students. Second, the rate of violent victimization among college students has declined significantly over the past decade; but the rate of decline is no different than similarly aged nonstudents. Third, violence against college students is most likely to occur off campus. Indeed, on-campus violence among students is a rare event, occurring about 16 times less often than off-campus crime. Fourth, college students tend not report their victimization to police – regardless of whether it occurs off campus or on campus. More on-campus violence than off-campus violence is not reported to police because it is reported to another official. Fifth, most college-student victims of violence do not seek help from organizations designed to provide victim assistance. Sixth, while male students are more likely than female students to experience campus violence, no measurable differences in on-campus violence were observed between race/ethnic groups. And finally, most violence on college campuses reportedly does *not* involve a weapon, does *not* result in an injury, and is committed by an offender who is *not* believed to be under the influence of drugs or alcohol at the time of the incident.

Patterns and trends identified above provide useful insight into violence against college students. Results contained herein suggest ways administrators and security officials can improve responses to college-student violence. For example, current findings show that the college-student victims of violence rarely seek support from organizations designed to help them. Simply establishing victim assistance programs is apparently not an adequate response to student victimization. University officials must constantly remind students – especially victims of violence – that assistance programs are not just available, but must be utilized.

In some instances, current findings challenge past research in ways that offer new guidance to the research community. Prior studies suggest that college women are at increased risk for sexual victimization on college campuses (Belknap & Erez, 1995; Brantingham & Brantingham, 1999; Fisher, Cullen, & Turner, 2000), and reveal certain lifestyle factors that play a role in female students' increased risk of campus crime such as rape/sexual assault (see Fisher et al., 1998; see also Mustaine & Tewksbury, 2002; Schwartz & Pitts, 1995). Current findings indicate, however, that neither the average annual rate of rape/sexual assault nor the decline in the rate of rape/sexual assault experienced by college students is measurably different from that which is experienced by similarly aged nonstudents. Although estimates of sexual victimization of college students produced from the current analyses are seemingly at odds with past research, differences could be due to the methodological approaches to the way studies measure victimization (see Rand & Rennison, 2004a, 2004b). Nevertheless, these findings add to the scientific dialog associated with the violent victimization of college students. Indeed, analyzing patterns and trends in the violent victimization of college students – using data produced from the NCVS – broadens our overall understanding of the nature and extent of campus crime and college-student victimization beyond that which can be gleaned from official statistics such as those required by the *Jeanne Clery Act* (2000).

REFERENCE

Baum, K., & Klaus, P. (2005). *Violent victimization of college students, 1995–2002.* Washington, DC: Bureau of Justice Statistics. Government Printing Office. (NCJ 206836).

Barberet, R., Fisher, B. S., & Taylor, H. (2004). *University student safety in East Midlands.* London: Home Office.

Belknap, J., & Erez, E. (1995). The victimization of women on college campuses: Courtship violence, date rape and sexual harassment. In B. S. Fisher & J. J. Sloan (Eds.), *Campus crime: Legal, social, and policy perspectives* (pp. 126–178). Springfield, IL: Charles C Thomas.

Brantingham, P. L., & Brantingham, P. J. (1999). A theoretical model of crime hot spot generation. *Studies on Crime and Crime Prevention, 8,* 7–26.

Bromley, M. L. (1992). Campus and community crime rate comparisons: A statewide study. *Journal of Security Administration, 15,* 49–64.

Bromley, M. L. (1994). Correlates of campus crime: A nationwide exploratory study of large universities. *Journal of Security Administration, 17,* 37–52.

Bromley, M. L. (1995a). Comparing campus and city crime rates: A descriptive study. *American Journal of Police, 14,* 131–148.

Bromley, M. L. (1995b). Factors associated with college crimes: Implications for campus police. *Journal of Police and Criminal Psychology, 10,* 13–19.

Bromley, M. L., & Fisher, B. S. (2002). Campus policing and victim services. In L. J. Moriarty (Ed.), *Policing and victims* (pp. 133–158). Upper Saddle River, NJ: Prentice-Hall.

Fisher, B. S. (1995). Crime and fear on campus. *Annals of the American Academy of Political and Social Science, 539,* 85–101.

Fisher, B. S., & Cullen, F. T. (1999). *The extent and nature of violence against college women: Results from a national-level study.* Final report submitted to the Bureau of Justice Statistics. (NCJ 179977).

Fisher, B. S., Cullen, F. T., & Turner, M. G. (2000). *Sexual victimization of college women.* Washington, DC: National Institute of Justice. Government Printing Office. (NCJ 182369).

Fisher, B. S., & Nasar, J. L. (1992). Students' fear of crime and its relation to physical features of the campus. *Journal of Security Administration, 15,* 65–75.

Fisher, B. S., & Sloan, J. J. (1993). University response to the Campus Security Act of 1990: Evaluating programs designed to reduce campus crime. *Journal of Security Administration, 16,* 67–80.

Fisher, B. S., Sloan, J. J., Cullen, F. T., & Lu, C. (1998). Crime in the ivory tower: The level and sources of student victimization. *Criminology, 36,* 671–710.

Gross, A. M., Winslett, A., Roberts, M., & Gohm, C. L. (2006). Examination of sexual violence against college women. *Violence against women, 12,* 288–300.

Hart, T. C. (2003). *Violent victimization of college students.* Washington, DC: Bureau of Justice Statistics. Government Printing Office. (NCJ 196143).

Hart, T. C. (2007). Violent victimization of college students: Findings from the National Crime Victimization Survey. In B. S. Fisher & J. J. Sloan (Eds.), *Campus crime: Legal, social, and policy perspectives* (2nd ed.) (pp. 129–146). Springfield, IL: Charles C Thomas.

Hart, T. C., & Miethe, T. D. (2011). Violence against college students and its situational contexts: Prevalence, patterns, and policy implications. *Victims and Offenders, 6,* 157–180.

Hart, T. C., & Rennison, C. M. (2003). *Reporting crime to the police, 1992–2001.* Washington, DC: Bureau of Justice Statistics. Government Printing Office. (NCJ 195710).

Hart, T. C., & Rennison, C. M. (2011). Violent victimization of Hispanic college students: Findings from the National Crime Victimization Survey. *Race and Justice, 1,* 362–385.

Henson, V. A., & Stone, W. E. (1999). Campus crime: A victimization study. *Journal of Criminal Justice, 27,* 295–307.

Jeanne Clery Act. (2000). Pub. L. 101-542, 20 U.S.C. §1092(f).

Karjane, H., Fisher, B. S., & Cullen, F. T. (2005). *Sexual assault on campus: What colleges and universities are doing about it.* Washington, DC: National Institute of Justice. Government Printing Office. (NCJ 205521).

McCreedy, K. R., & Dennis, B. G. (1996). Sex-related offenses and fear of crime on campus. *Journal of Contemporary Criminal Justice, 12,* 69–80.

Meijer, J. (1995). Surveying campus crime: What can be done to reduce crime and fear? *Campus Law Enforcement Journal, 25,* 2, 4, 6, 15.

Mustaine, E. E., & Tewksbury, R. (2002). Sexual assault of college women: A feminist interpretation of a routine activities analysis. *Criminal Justice Review, 27,* 89–123.

Nicholson, M. E., Maney, D. W., Blair, K., Wamboldt, P. M., Mahoney, B. S., & Yaun, J. (1998). Trends in alcohol-related campus violence: Implications for prevention. *Journal of Alcohol and Drug Education, 43,* 34–52.

Rand, M. R., & Rennison, C. M. (2004a). How much violence against women is there? In B. S. Fisher (Ed.), *Violence against women and family violence: Developments in research, practice, and policy.* Washington, DC: Government Printing Office.

Rand, M. R., & Rennison, C. M. (2004b). Bigger is not necessarily better: An analysis of violence against women estimates from the National Crime Victimization Survey and the National Violence Against Women Survey. *Journal of Quantitative Criminology, 21,* 267–291.

Robinson, M. B., & Mullen, K. L. (2001). Crime on campus: A survey of space users. *Crime Prevention and Community Safety: An International Journal, 3,* 33–46.

Sampson, R. J., & Lauritsen, J. L. (1994). Violent victimization and offending: Individual-, situational-, and community-level risk factors. In A. J. Reiss & J. A. Roth (Eds.), *Understanding and preventing violence: Social influences on violence, vol. 3.* (pp. 1–114). Washington, DC: National Research Council. National Academy Press.

Schwartz, M. D., & Pitts, V. L. (1995). Exploring a feminist routine activities approach to explaining sexual assault. *Justice Quarterly, 12,* 9–31.

Sellers, C. S., & Bromley, M. L. (1996). Violent behavior in college student dating relationships: Implications for campus service providers. *Journal of Contemporary Criminal Justice, 12,* 2–27.

Sigler, R. T., & Koehlor, N. (1993). Victimization and crime on campus. *International Review of Victimology, 2,* 331–343.

Sloan, J. J. (1992). Campus crime and campus communities: An analysis of crimes known to campus police and security. *Journal of Security Administration, 15,* 31–47.

Sloan, J. J. (1994). Correlates of campus crime: An analysis of reported crimes on college and university campuses. *Journal of Criminal Justice, 22,* 51–61.

Summers, R. W., & Hoffman, A. M. (1998). Weapon carrying on campus. In A. M. Hoffman, J. H. Schuh, & R. H. Fenske (Eds.), *Violence on campus: Defining the problems, strategies for action* (pp. 53–68). Fredrick, MD: Aspen.

Truman, J. L. (2011). *Criminal victimization, 2010.* (NCJ-235508). Washington, DC: Bureau of Justice Statistics. Government Printing Office.

Chapter 8

THE ROUTINE ACTIVITIES AND CRIMINAL VICTIMIZATION OF STUDENTS: LIFESTYLE AND RELATED FACTORS

Elizabeth Ehrhardt Mustaine and Richard Tewksbury

INTRODUCTION

The last few decades have seen significant advances in understandings of students' victimization experiences. Studies exploring student victimization on campus have included discussions of the dynamics of criminal incidents, the participation and interaction of students in these criminal incidents as victims and offenders, and the role guardianship can play in the thwarting (or not) of criminal events in progress or the warding off (or not) of criminal attempts before they begin. Routine activities theory has been the driving perspective in much of this research, utilizing two central propositions – that daily routine activities, or lifestyles, create criminal opportunities by increasing (or decreasing) the frequency of contact between individuals who are potential offenders and those who are potential victimization targets. Second, the suitability of a target, along with its level of guardianship determines victim selection. Routine activities theory – originally proposed by Cohen and Felson (1979) – incorporates both structural aspects of the environment as well as issues of physical environments and free will (e.g., choice) in explaining criminal victimization (Meithe & Meier, 1990). In this way, research inspired by routine activities theory has consistently shown that criminal victimization risks are not randomly distributed in society but are related to the lifestyles and routine activities of victims and offenders. Particularly those lifestyles and routines that increase the likelihood of victims and offenders coming together in the same space and time outside of the prevue of effective and willing guardians are critical to the occurrence of criminal events.

Theoretically, college students have above average risks for criminal victimization because they tend to have daily routines that put them into situations and locations where there are a greater number of potential offenders (Maxfield, 1987). Additionally, college students have routines whereby at these more dangerous or risky locations they are more vulnerable as targets due to a lack of capable guardianship, or an inability to recognize the danger(s) involved in their circumstances. For example, college students are more likely to go out to bars or other public places to drink alcohol, they attend parties where alcohol and drugs may be present, and, while they may start their evenings out in groups, these groups do not necessarily stay together throughout the course of the night. Additionally, many students live in off-campus apartments. These residential locations are typically full of transient students who do not know each other, and cannot effectively guard each other's person or property since they do not know who should be present or not.

In this way, then, routine activities theory is well suited to serve as a framework for understanding the criminal victimization patterns of college students. Below, we discuss and highlight the common conclusions of routine activities scholars with regard to how potential offenders, suitable targets, and guardianship efforts (or lack thereof) impact the victimization risks of college students. To do so, we first turn to a discussion of potential offenders, their characteristics, proximity to college student potential victims, and daily activities of those who may be motivated to take advantage of presented criminal opportunities. This is followed by a discussion of how the lifestyles of college students can heighten or reduce their chances for criminal victimization. This discussion highlights the types of activities, interaction contexts, and lifestyles that college students have that place them into closer proximity to potential offenders, as well as those routines that decrease their self-protective behaviors or fail to utilize effective guardianship practices. Next, we turn to a discussion of those specific self-protective behaviors and guardianship practices that may be effective in reducing one's chances for criminal victimization while a college student. Finally, we summarize these common conclusions and consider how they are policy relevant for university administrators and other personnel who are concerned with reducing the victimization experiences of students.

Potential Offenders

Co-Presence with Potential Offenders

Central to routine activities theory is the idea that victimization is contingent upon the presence of potential offenders. Suitable targets can and only will become victims when others seeking opportunities to offend encounter them in situations and settings that lack capable guardianship. Therefore, presence in settings, at times, and in ways of presenting oneself to others are all critical issues for predicting victimization, especially when potential offenders are present.

The persons that one spends time with are important for understanding students' exposure to potential offenders. This may be especially important for college students, as the most common perpetrators of crimes against students are other students (Fisher & Sloan, 1995; Siegel & Raymond, 1992). For example, students on campuses with a greater proportion of minority students experience generally increased rates of officially reported campus crime (Sloan, 1992; 1994). Conversely, and certainly not unexpectedly, students who spend more of their weekdays and weekends alone have decreased risks of violent victimization (Mustaine & Tewksbury, 2000). However, so too do those who spend more time with strangers (as opposed to friends, family and acquaintances) have decreased risks of being assaulted (again, this is not surprising). Yet, for some specific offenses – such as stalking – women who were married or cohabitating (and presumably spending more time with their partners) report lower odds of being stalked (Fisher, Cullen, & Turner, 2002).

Where and with whom students spend their social time are important for determining proximity to potential offenders, and hence, chances of being a victim. Perhaps best established in the literature regarding campus locations is the evidence that fraternity houses may be especially risky for victimization. Women who are affiliated with sororities (Franklin, 2010) and those who spend more time in fraternity houses have significantly increased risks for sexual assault (Stombler, 1994) and other illegal victimizations (Franklin, 2010). Theoretically, this is because fraternity members are overrepresented among college campus sexual assault perpetrators (Copenhaver & Grauerholz, 1991; Frintner & Rubinson, 1993; Martin & Hummer, 1989). To elaborate, fully 24 percent of sorority women report having experienced an attempted, and 17 percent report a completed sexual assault (Copenhaver & Grauerholtz, 1991); many of these victimizations occurred in fraternity houses. These facts contribute to the beliefs of some that fraternities maintain and perpetuate a rape culture (Martin & Hummer, 1989; Sanday, 1990; Tyler, Hoyt, & Whitbeck, 1998). Evidence, then, suggests that these increased risks are due to women being in close proximity to fraternity men who have higher levels of acceptance for rape myths (Schaeffer & Nelson, 1993). This is also likely to be the case as fraternity men may be more likely to adhere to masculine identities, thereby having greater frequencies of binge drinking (Peralta, Steele, Nofziger, & Rickles, 2010).

Proximity to potential offenders may also be a function of time. As stated above, those who spend time away from home, especially in the evening are at increased risks for victimization. Sexual assaults of female college students may be especially likely in the evenings or late at night, as the majority of unwanted sexual experiences for women occur at or after parties (Banyard, Ward, Cohn, Plante, Moorhead, & Walsh, 2007; Barberet, Fisher, & Taylor, 2004; Ward, Chapman, Cohn, White, & Williams, 1991). Also related to time, for theft victimization, afternoons appear to be the most risky time (Barberet et al., 2004; Seng, 1996).

The most influential of predictors related to proximity to potential offenders are the activities in which one's friends, acquaintances, and associates participate. When spending more time on campus "partying," victimization risks increase (Fisher, Sloan, Cullen, & Lu, 1998). And, the younger the people are with whom one drinks, the higher are the chances of victimization (Mustaine & Tewksbury, 1998c). Similarly, students who are present when others are using drugs experience increased vandalism victimization risks (Tewksbury & Mustaine, 2000).

Other locations in which one spends time and the type of persons with whom one spends time are important predictors of college student victimization. Simply being on campus more often increases risks for victimization (Clodfelter, Turner, Hartman, & Kuhns, 2010). Mustaine and Tewksbury (1998c) have shown that the number of evenings students spend away from home for leisure purposes, and the later one returns home from leisure activities are strong predictors of violent crime victimization for students. When victimized, college students are more likely to be engaged in leisure activities than noncollege students who were more likely to be doing something other than leisure (Baum & Klaus, 2005). Additionally, near campus bars appear to be riskier places to drink (Pino & Johnson-Johns, 2009). However, at least for violent victimizations, most of them happen off campus (Barberet et al., 2004; Sigler & Koehlor, 1993; Baum & Klaus, 2005). Fully 72 percent of violent victimizations of students happen away from campus (Baum & Klaus, 2005). It is not only leisure activities, however, that take students into public domains. So too do many students leave home for purposes of studying. As the amount of time students go away from their homes to study increases, so too do their risks of property crime victimization increase (Mustaine & Tewksbury, 1998a).

Another form of immersion with potential offenders can be seen when students engage in recreational activities. Simple endeavors such as going to a shopping mall frequently, eating out frequently, and going to the gym or playing organized sports (for men) have all be shown to be related to violent crime victimization risks (Mustaine & Tewksbury, 1998c). Also, regularly spending time in bars can increase risks for sexual assault (Mustaine & Tewksbury, 1998b; Tewksbury and Mustaine, 2001), "uncomfortable" sexual advances (Schwartz & Pitts, 1995) and stalking (Mustaine & Tewksbury, 1999). Similarly, simply "hanging out" and doing nothing in particular is related to increased sexual assault risks for women (Mustaine & Tewksbury, 2002). Also, women who have friends who get women drunk for purposes of gaining sexual access to women are more likely to be sexually victimized (Banyard et al, 2007; Schwartz & Pitts, 1995). Here, the relationship may be as simple as men being more sexually aggressive in drinking settings (Thompson & Cracco, 2008).

All of these activities are presumed to increase the risks of victimization not because of anything inherent in the activities, but rather because of the types of persons such activities bring one in contact with. Conversely, other common forms of recreational activities have been shown to predict reduced levels of victimization risks, presumably because these activities are less likely to immerse students with potential offenders. These activities include going to the movies (Mustaine & Tewksbury, 2002), playing basketball or tennis in a public setting (Mustaine & Tewksbury, 1998a), attending community festivals/events (Mustaine & Tewksbury, 2000), and attending church services (Mynatt & Allgeier, 1990).

Finally, the role of athletic activities and their relationship to victimization risks can be seen in the experiences of college athletes. Simply being a college athlete can increase risks for both physical assault (Bausell, Bausell & Siegel, 1991) and sexual victimization, for both females (Mustaine & Tewksbury, 2002) and males (Tewksbury & Mustaine, 2001). Here, the relationship may be that as with fraternity men, male college athletes may be more supportive of rape myths (Benedict, 1997; Benedict & Klein, 1997) or heavier drinkers (Peralta et al, 2010; McMahon, 2007; Tewksbury, Higgins, & Mustaine, 2008). Additionally, aggressiveness in sports may translate into greater psychological, physical, and sexual aggression (Forbes, Adams-Curtis, Pakalka, & White, 2006). Property crime likelihood is also higher for members of university athletic teams – athletes have higher rates of theft victimization (Fisher et al., 1998). Again, risks are considered to be greater not because of anything about athletic activities themselves, but because of the types of persons with whom athletic activities may bring one in contact.

Being with and near others who may be motivated to offend is critically important to understanding the victimization risks of college students. Being away from one's "safe zone" of home, and out and about with others – especially while engaged in leisure activities and/or committing criminal offenses one's self are especially important predictors of victimization risks. The types of locations where college students are likely to encounter and be exposed to potential offenders are many, but those most dangerous are those away from where students actually live. While both on- and off-campus locations are known to increase/decrease risks for different types of activities, it is recreational settings that appear to be the most risky.

Similarities Between Offenders and Victims

In addition to the locations where individuals spend their time, routine activities theory scholars also argue that it is important to assess the general characteristics of potential offenders and victims. Typically this is done by employing demographic characteristics as proxy indicators of lifestyle. The thinking here is based on the idea that a number of demographic variables (e.g., lifestyles) are shared by persons found in similar locations; or, said differently, lifestyle variables are theoretically linked to characteristics based on the patterns people with these similarities establish. For example, nonwhites, younger students, and students of lower socioeconomic classes are more likely to be victimized because of their similarity to offenders (and the connection that criminal offenders victimize those who are similar to themselves). Similarly, some characteristics are inferred to have certain lifestyles. For example, married persons have lower risks for victimization than single persons, since married persons do not go out as often for leisure activities (Laub, 1990).

While demographic characteristics are occasionally found to be significant indicators of heightened (or lowered) victimization risks, more recent routine activities theory scholars have found that their effects are attenuated when other, more specific lifestyles are examined concurrently (see Mustaine & Tewksbury, 1997). Two such factors, however, have regularly shown to influence the victimization risks of college students, despite controls for lifestyle behaviors. Students who are from a lower socioeconomic background have a higher risk for larceny victimization (Mustaine & Tewksbury, 1998a). And, those students who are unemployed are more likely to be victims of property offenses (Tewksbury & Mustaine, 2000). This plays out for crimes of violence also. Porter and Williams (2011) showed that members of minority groups (e.g., race, ethnicity, and sexual orientation) are more likely to be raped.

In short, lifestyles that are similar to those of "typical" criminal offenders are also the lifestyles that are associated with increased victimization risks. Because many settings are largely (although not universally) homogenous in regards to the characteristics of persons in the setting, it is only logical that potential offenders are going to have the most frequent and easy access to individuals with whom they share lifestyles and characteristics. The characteristics of college students that are associated with increased likelihood of victimization is where we turn next.

Also important here are lifestyles that are criminal, as those who commit crimes are also more likely to be victims (Jennings, Higgins, Tewksbury, Gover, & Piquero, 2010; Klevens, Duque, & Ramirez, 2002; Mustaine & Tewksbury, 2000; Schreck, Stuart, & Osgood, 2008). Again, the theoretical relationship here is that those who commit crimes are more likely to be in proximity to other criminals. To elaborate, students who engage in behaviors that victimize others (typically in a group setting) are themselves more likely to be victimized (Tewksbury & Mustaine, 2000). The simple act of intending to engage in a variety of risk taking behaviors may increase one's risk for sexual assault (Combs-Lane & Smith, 2002). Similarly, participating in a physical fight or theft of money also is related to increased risks of victimization (Tewksbury & Mustaine, 2000). Students who are aggressive and threaten others – whether with a weapon or not – are also more likely to be theft victims (Mustaine & Tewksbury, 1998a).

Suitable Targets

Another element in the examination of the lifestyle and related risks for college student victimization is the presence of suitable targets. Routine activities theory generally acknowledges that suitable targets could be either persons or property items that are viewed by offenders as easily or safely victimizable or valuable. In this way, persons or property could be either acceptably vulnerable or worth the risks of getting caught. It is also possible that persons and property could be suitable simply because of the opportunity each presents to a potential offender.

Although routine activities theory was originally proposed as a macro-level theory (Cohen & Felson, 1979), more recent scholars working with the theory have moved to examinations of suitable targets on the micro-sociological level. In this way the focus has moved away from looking at patterns and trends across social institutions and instead looks at specific lifestyle behaviors or statuses that make someone (or something) more likely to be targeted for victimization. This also means that routine activities theory suggests that victimization is most likely for people (and things) who are less able to put up any effective resistance, more desirable or valuable, more often in circumstances that inhibit self-protective concerns or help seeking behaviors, are in circumstances that are risky, dangerous, or otherwise crime prone, and/or are frequently in exposed circumstances with those who are potential offenders.

Research assessing college students and their behaviors and statuses that are associated with higher risks for criminal victimization (due to increased suitability as a target) looks at both risky behaviors found to be associated with victimization in the general populace and behaviors specifically found among college students. Such scholars find a number of lifestyles or other risk factors to be important sources.

Location of College Student Residences

One aspect of college students' lifestyles that is often unique to their circumstances is the location of college student residences. For example, students who live in all-male dorms have been shown to have higher theft risks, especially when residing in small dorms (Fisher et al., 1998). Typically, college students live in either dorms on campus, or off-campus apartments, often in more transient or less-well physically maintained neighborhoods. Some research has also shown that most violence happens in students' residences (Fisher, Sloan, Cullen, & Lu, 1997). Students who spend many nights on campus per week have increased victimization risks, especially for crimes of theft (Fisher et al., 1998). And, for the crime of stalking, college women were most likely to be stalked either on campus or both on and off campus, with most being stalked at their residences (Fisher et al. 2002).

Theoretically, the living situation of the on-campus dorm should protect students from criminal victimization because students in dorms know each other, they know who lives in their dorm and who does not, and most on-campus dorms have resident assistants, who are older and more experienced students, who reside on each floor and function to help, advise, and offer a certain amount of protection for students.

Conversely, living in an apartment or complex in a more socially disorganized neighborhood is more likely to be associated with increased criminal victimization because of the anonymous nature of apartment living (Zito, 1974). Students in apartments often move from year to year, change roommates, spend a great deal of time away from their residence, and as a result, may be leaving their residence and possessions unguarded (Robinson, 1997). These neighborhoods are also less able to utilize effective crime prevention efforts because residents do not know each other or who should be hanging around the complex and who should not (Zito, 1974; Robinson, 1997). As such, routine activities theory would posit that students living in dorms on campus should experience an insulated effect with crime, while students living off campus would encounter more crime and criminal victimization.

A final theoretical relationship between location or residence and criminal victimization risks is whether or not students live near other community structures or conditions that are crime-prone locations (e.g., places that are not well guarded, places where unsupervised youth hang out, etc.). As discussed below, research on these relationships between residential location and criminal victimization risks has some contrary findings but more often than not supports these assertions.

Regarding on-campus or off-campus residential location, research has found that women who live on campus have lower risks for stalking victimization (Mustaine & Tewksbury, 1999). However, female students who live on campus have increased risks for sexual victimization (Fisher et al., 2000). This relationship persists across location of university, as campuses in rural communities have comparable rates of sexual coercion and violence as those reported by females at urban universities (Vanderwoerd, 2009) as well as size of study body, as students on smaller campuses report as much victimization as those on larger campuses (Bryden & Fletcher, 2007). Although geographically smaller campuses may have fewer sexual assaults because there are fewer convergence locations and guardians can cover more space proportionally (Cass, 2007).

It is interesting and important to point out that research examining this relationship with data other than self-reports of victimization provide contradictory findings. For instance, Sloan (1992) reported that when a greater proportion of students lived on campus the crime rates reported in the Uniform Crime Reports (e.g., those offenses reported to law enforcement agencies) increased. But, others have found that based on self-reports of victimization, when there is a greater proportion of students who live on campus, the campus theft rate decreases (Fisher et al, 1998).

Among certain college students, living in the dorm does not insulate them from criminal behavior. Research has found that victimization risks are increased when students are in authority positions or possess items desirable to steal. Palmer (1993) has shown that dormitory resident assistants are the most likely targets of violence, vandalism, and verbal harassment in dormitories. Additionally, students living in dorm suites (Cross, Zimmerman, & O'Grady, 2009), residence halls (O'Hare, 1990), fraternity and sorority housing (Capone, Wood, Borsari, & Laird, 2007), and co-ed housing (Harford, Wechsler, & Muthen, 2003) drink more frequently and more heavily, thereby increasing their vulnerability and proximity to potential offenders. And, students who spend large sums of money on nonessential items are more likely than other students to be victims of theft (Fisher et al., 1998). Finally, research shows that students who live in all-male dorms have been shown to have higher theft risks, especially when residing in small dorms (Fisher et al., 1998).

Proximity to crime prone locations is also related to criminal victimization risks, thus supporting routine activities theory assertions. To elaborate, living near a park produces higher risks for victimization in general (Mustaine & Tewksbury, 1998c), as well as for vandalism specifically (Tewksbury & Mustaine, 2000). Not surprisingly, when students perceive their neighborhood as having too much crime and/or being too noisy their risks for victimization in general (Tewksbury & Mustaine, 2000), as well as theft in particular, are increased (Mustaine & Tewksbury, 1998a). Further, students who perceive their neighborhoods as having disruptive neighbors have higher assault victimization risks (Mustaine & Tewksbury, 2000). Interestingly, using a macro perspective, Grossman and Markowitz (1999) found that communities with lower priced beer had higher rates of sexual victimization.

Relatedly, with whom one lives is an important aspect of victimization risk. To specify, female college students who live with their parents have lower rates of sexual victimization than women living not with parents (Buddie & Testa, 2005). And, women living alone have higher risks for being victims of stalkers (Fisher et al 2002).

In sum, college students who live in settings characterized by transience and low levels of social cohesion (and hence, higher levels of social disorganization) are at increased risks for victimization. The effects on victimization are not from only the actual residence of students, but also from the structures (and hence people and activities) that are in the immediate vicinity of the student's residence. Additionally, students' activities may also be important for understanding their risks of victimization.

Alcohol Use

Student lifestyles that frequently are found to be associated with criminal victimization are those where students use or frequently use alcohol. Important measures for explaining why some college students have higher risks of criminal victimization than other college students also include the quantities of alcohol consumed and the locations of alcohol consumption.

Initially, researchers showed that simply the use of alcohol is a predictor of sexual victimization for women (Combs-Lane & Smith, 2002; Schwartz & Pitts, 1995). But, more recently, routine activities theory scholars have examined the specifics of alcohol consumption. For example, assessments of the amount of drinking in which students engage, rather than simply whether or not they drink alcohol. The number of times a college student drinks alcohol in a particular time period is strongly related not only to that individual's risks for criminal victimization in general (Franklin, 2010), but particularly violent victimization (Fagan, McCormick, Konto, Venable, & Anderson, 2011; Franklin, 2010; Krebs, Lindquist, Warner, Fisher, & Martin, 2009a; Harford et al., 2003; Mohler-Kuo, Dowdall, Koss, & Wechsler, 2004; Palmer, McMahon, Rounsaville, & Ball, 2010; Wechsler, Davenport, Dowdall, Moeykems, & Castillo, 1994). Theoretically, when a person drinks alcohol, his/her responses are dulled and s/he is less able not only to identify potentially dangerous situations but to resist victimization attempts after they begin. To specify, research has found that students who consume alcohol a greater number of days per week experience higher risks for victimization (Mustaine & Tewksbury, 1998c) and specifically, violent victimization (Mustaine & Tewksbury, 1998b), such as sexual assault (Fagan et al., 2011; Franklin, 2010; Krebs et al., 2009a; Palmer et al., 2010). Additionally, students who are victims of violence multiple times use significantly more alcohol and drugs than students who are victimized only once (or never) (Bausell et al., 1991). Not surprisingly, female students who have a higher frequency of alcohol consumption, both in conjunction with sexual activities and in general, have higher sexual assault victimization risks (Schwartz & Pitts, 1995; Testa & Durmen, 1999).

Not only is the frequent use of alcohol important in specifying students' risks for victimization, but so too is the quantity of alcohol consumed when drinking occurs. Routine activities theory suggests that persons who are drunk, specifically those who are drunk in dangerous places are particularly vulnerable to criminal attack. Students who are intoxicated would be severely hampered from being aware of the goings on around them, taking any necessary evasive action, or putting up effective resistance efforts. Research tends to validate this theoretical assertion. For example, male students who perceived themselves as being more masculine were also more likely to binge drink more frequently, thereby increasing their risks for both crime and victimization (Peralta et al., 2010). Also, students who got drunk frequently during the week had increased assault victimization risks (Mustaine & Tewksbury, 2000), and college females who had been drunk in public recently had increased risks for violent victimization (Fagan et al., 2011; Fisher et al., 2000; Mustaine & Tewksbury, 1998b, 1999; Palmer et al., 2010; Parks & Miller, 1997; Schwartz & Pitts, 1995; Tanioka, 1986; Testa & Durmen, 1999; Testa & Livingston, 2000; Tewksbury & Mustaine, 2001; Ullman, Karabatsos, & Koss, 1999). More specifically, Mustaine and Tewksbury (1998c) found that the number of days a student was intoxicated was associated with higher risks for victimization. And, research has found frequent binge drinkers were more likely to be sexually assaulted (Fagan et al., 2011; Palmer et al., 2010; McCauley, Calhoun, & Gidycz, 2010).

Others have also found a similar relationship between the frequent consumption of large quantities of alcohol and higher victimization risks. Higher weekly consumption of alcohol was related to higher sexual assault victimization risks for females (Testa & Durmen, 1999). And, women who drank, consumed greater quantities of alcohol, and/or got drunk in public places had increased risks for sexual assault (Fisher et al., 2000; Parks & Miller, 1997; Schwartz & Pitts, 1995; Tanioka, 1986; Testa & Livingston, 2000; Ullman, Karabatsos, & Koss, 1999; Tewksbury & Mustaine, 2001). This relationship appears to be particularly strong with freshman and sophomore women who are just beginning to drink heavily (Littleton, Grills-Taquechel, & Axsom, 2009) or who are more vulnerable for victimization because they have only recently arrived on campus (Warshaw, 1988 refers to this time period as the 'red-zone').Researchers have also found this relationship to be present at a more macro level, as students who attend schools with high rates of binge drinking are more likely to be victims of violence or sexual violence than students at schools with lower rates of binge drinking (Wechsler et al., 1994). Unfortunately, this relationship between alcohol use and sexual assault victimization of college women should not be surprising, however, as in one study, one in four male undergrads admitted to purposely getting a woman drunk in order to have sex with her (Tyler et al., 1998).

Some researchers have also considered location of alcohol consumption and its association with victimization risks. Specifically, female students who, when they drink alcohol, drink at home have increased risks for stalking victimization (Mustaine & Tewksbury, 2002), although the authors did note that drinking alcohol at home could be a response to stalking victimization rather than a source. Additionally, just because a student drinks at home does not mean that the student is immune from victimization risks. Indeed, fully 81 percent of violent acts in residence halls are alcohol related (Rickgarn, 1989). However, drinking in public settings may be the most risky. College student women who go to bars have higher risks for sexual assault, and amongst those in bars, women with the highest risks are those who are younger, have a history of victimization, and spend a greater amount of time in bars (Parks & Zettes-Zanatta, 1999). Even though scholars have used a variety of measures to capture the use, extent, frequency, and location of alcohol consumption among college students, clearly there is a strong and consistent relationship between their alcohol consumption and higher student victimization risks.

The research regarding college students' alcohol consumption and victimization risks is clear: students who drink have increased risks. The more one drinks, the higher the risk. The more one drinks away from one's home, and the more one drinks away from home among others who may either have a "reason" to see one get intoxicated or that the individual does not know well, the greater are the risks of victimization. Alcohol, while perhaps the most common intoxicating substance used by college students is not the only such substance; so too may illicit drug use be related to victimization risks.

Drug Use

Related to alcohol use is illegal drug use. This lifestyle has a similar relationship to increased risks for criminal victimization as alcohol, in that it typically lowers one's ability to recognize dangerous or risky situations, or to respond appropriately, effectively, or timely enough to threats or attempts to victimize one. Drug use, however, also has the element of illegality, and as such, can be used as an assessment of a student's proximity to potential offenders. In this way, people who use, buy, or sell drugs, are already in the proximity of offenders (not those who are still potential offenders), and may suffer victimization as a result. For example, drug use is associated with greater sexual aggression, particularly over time. Thus, students who are in contact with drug users may have elevated sexual assault risks (Swartout &

White, 2010). To specify, students who use recreational drugs are more likely to be victimized than students who do not (Fisher et al., 1998; Fisher & Wilkes, 2003; Tewksbury & Mustaine, 1998b). Additionally, even smoking tobacco increases risks for violent crime victimization in general (Tanioka, 1986). College students who use marijuana have higher risks for larceny victimization (Mustaine & Tewksbury, 1998a) and sexual assault (Tewksbury & Mustaine, 2001), including incapacitating sexual assault (Krebs et al., 2009b), as well as for any type of personal victimization whenever they are participating in "leisure activities" (Mustaine & Tewksbury, 1998b). Scholars have also found that the use of two drugs in particular – marijuana and depressants – significantly increase the likelihood of violence in relationships but only for females (Nabors, 2010).

Beyond an examination of the risks for victimization due to simple illegal drug use, researchers have also examined students who are involved with illegal drugs in other ways. For example, female college students who have bought drugs recently have higher risks for violent victimization (Mustaine & Tewksbury, 1998b), stalking victimization (Mustaine & Tewksbury, 1999), and sexual assault (Mustaine & Tewksbury, 2002). Relatedly, men who grow marijuana are more likely to be victims of violence (Mustaine & Tewksbury, 1998b).

Similar to alcohol, one's location of drug use is also an important predictor of victimization risks for college students. One's risks for sexual assault increase when the greater proportion of one's drug use is either at parties or in other public settings (Mustaine & Tewksbury, 2002; Tewksbury & Mustaine, 2001).

One methodological issue that arises when examining the relationship between drug (and alcohol) use and crime victimization is that of causal ordering; or which comes first: is the drug use the cause of increased victimization or is it the consequence? Messman-Moore, Ward, and Brown (2009) addressed this issue with a sample of college women. They found that women who had been sexually assaulted and responded to this trauma by using substances had a significantly increased risk for rape.

In sum, scholars have examined various aspects of illegal drug use with regard to a variety of types of criminal victimization, and consistently have shown a strong relationship between higher or more serious drug use and higher rates of victimization. As is the case with alcohol, drug use may bring one into contact with motivated offenders and reduces one's ability to protect oneself from victimization. Alcohol and drug use are clearly related to increased risks of victimization.

Memberships in Student Clubs and Organizations

Other lifestyle behaviors that are specific to college students and are related to their risks for criminal victimization include membership in a variety of student organizations. Theoretically, membership in student organizations could have the effect of spending more time with others who may be criminally inclined or simply having student be absent from home more frequently (and therefore leaving their homes unguarded). Or, such memberships and participation could serve as safe, organized activities that would lessen one's exposure to criminally motivated others. Previous research tends to support the assertion that membership in clubs, organizations, or Greek social groups has the effect of increasing one's exposure to potential offenders. For example, researchers have found that students who are members of a larger number of groups, clubs, or organizations have increased risks for theft (Mustaine & Tewksbury, 1998a). Further, women who are members of a larger number of groups, clubs, or organizations also have increased risks for sexual assault in particular (Mustaine & Tewksbury, 2002).

Greek social organizations, in particular, are seen as dangerous and risky groups to which one may belong. Previous research has found that similar to the situation for collegiate athletes (Benedict, 1997; Benedict & Klein, 1997, to mention a few), fraternities are places where men have attitudes that promote the use of forced sex against women who frequent their houses, either at parties or for other purposes. To elaborate, Siegel and Raymond (1992) concluded that membership in a fraternity or sorority was important in constructing an at-risk model for college students. Specifically, sorority women are more likely than nonsorority women to have been forced to have sexual intercourse (Kalof, 1993; Johnson & Sigler, 1996; Minow & Einolf, 2009; Tyler et al., 1998). Further, in terms of theft victimization, fraternity and sorority members were more likely to have their purses or wallets stolen (Sigler & Koehlor, 1993), but less likely to be victims of theft in general (Fisher et al., 1998). And, when using a macro-perspective, Sloan (1992, 1994) found that colleges and universities with a greater number of national Greek organizations had higher rates of officially reported crimes on campus.

Exposure to large numbers of other persons through organization and club membership is also exposure to increasing numbers of potential offenders. As such, students who are involved in more organizations and organized activities have a greater likelihood of being victimized. Interpersonal and close relationships, however, may have a different effect on victimization risks.

Relationships and Sexual Activity

Another lifestyle highly studied among college students is sexual activity and relationship statuses. Theoretically, routine activities theory would suggest that students who are in relationships may be more likely to be victims of intimate partner crimes (e.g., sexual assault, stalking, physical abuse), but would be less likely to be victims of theft or other property crimes because they may not go out as frequently for leisure as single, unpartnered college students. Specifically, regarding crimes for which women are the most likely victims, routine activities theory would predict that those women who are sexually active would be more likely to be victims of sexual assault, given their closer exposure to others who may be willing to use criminal means to gain access to sex.

Previous research tends to bear out these theoretical assertions. Specifically, sexually active women are more likely to be sexually assaulted (Fisher et al., 2002; Franklin, 2010; Johnson & Sigler, 1996; Mynatt & Allgeier, 1990). Similarly, women who have had a greater number of casual sexual encounters and partners are more likely to be sexual assault victims (Franklin, 2010; Testa & Dermen, 1999). Number of sexual partners is also related to risks for victimization, as Johnson and Sigler found that women with a greater number of sexual partners in the previous year were more likely to be sexually assaulted (1996, also see Koss & Dinero, 1989). Relatedly, Porter and Williams (2011) found that heterosexual women were more likely to be victims of attempted rape. If one examines dating violence in particular, these relationships persist. Dating violence is more likely in relationships with greater degrees of intimacy and commitment (Banyard et al., 2007; Sellers & Bromley, 1996) as well as women who date fraternity men because Greek men are more likely to have an expectation of sex after a date, especially when they have been drinking (Nurius, Norris, Dimeff, & Graham, 1996).

Dating, with or without sexual intimacy, is a lifestyle that is related to college students' (particularly women) risks for victimization. For example, college women who are dating, especially those who have been dating someone for less than a year, have higher odds of being stalked (Fisher et al., 2002). Additionally, those female college students who had a greater number of dating partners, dated more often, and/or had more sexual experience were more likely to be victims of sexual assault (Abbey, Ross, McDuffie, & McAuslan, 1996; Combs-Lane & Smith, 2002).

Finally, college students (particularly females) who have a prior sexual victimization also have increased odds of another sexual victimization (Fisher et al., 2000; Gidycz, Coble, Latham, & Layman, 1993; Krebs et al., 2009a; Stets & Pirog-Good, 1989;), including incapacitating sexual assault (Krebs et al., 2009b). Relatedly, college men who report having used sexually coercive strategies with female partners are also more likely to be sexually victimized (Russell & Oswald, 2002).

Although not a great deal is known about the effects of relationships and sexual activities on the victimization risks of men, it is clear that women who date more often and who are sexually active (especially with multiple partners) have significantly higher risks of victimization than other college women. These risks are especially keen for risk of sexual assault.

Guardianship

The third of the routine activities theory concepts necessary for a criminal event (e.g., victimization) to occur is that a setting and meeting between a potential offender and suitable target must occur in the absence of a capable guardian. This means that the potential target is neither equipped nor capable of avoiding or fending off a victimization attempt, and that no outside guardian is present to intervene or deter a criminal event. Unfortunately, there has been relatively little research done to assess the efficacy, forms, frequency of use, or any other issues related to the guardianship concept and how they impact the criminal event. This applies not only to research on the victimization of college students, but in fact to all forms of victimization, for all types of persons and property.

Generally speaking, college students do not employ guardianship tools or activities in their daily routines (Barberet et al., 2004; Fisher et al., 1997; Sloan, Fisher, & Wilkins, 1995; Tewksbury & Mustaine, 2003). Especially for crimes of theft, students routinely fail to engage in simple guardianship which could reduce their risks for theft (Fisher et al., 1997; Sloan et al., 1995).

Even so, some college students do utilize measures of self-protection. Among college students, those who are employed are less likely to use guardianship measures (Tewksbury & Mustaine, 2003). Students who spend more time with strangers are also seemingly more trusting, and show lower rates of guardianship utilization (Tewksbury & Mustaine, 2003). Also, students who report higher alcohol consumption are less likely to employ self-protective strategies (Herzog & Yeilding, 2009; Palmer et al., 2010). Some students, however, do actively seek to protect themselves from victimization; Miller, Hemenway, and Wechsler (2002) report that 4.3 percent of a national sample of students report owning and carrying a gun. Those most likely to do so are those who have previously been threatened by someone else with a gun. Similarly, students who live near police stations, those who are in social settings with strangers on weekends, and those who use "hard drugs" are all more likely than their counterparts to engage in self-protective activities (Tewksbury & Mustaine, 2003). Additionally, college students whose main form of transportation in the evening is to walk are more likely than other students to employ at least one means of attempting to protect themselves (Tewksbury & Mustaine, 2003). Finally students who carry pepper spray and are more frequently escorted to their cars have lower rates of sexual harassment (Clodfelter et al., 2010).

Data regarding the presence of formal agents of guardianship (e.g., law enforcement on campuses) is not clear on the deterrent effect of such a presence. However, as the ratio of students to full-time police on a campus increases so does the official crime rate (Sloan, 1992). And, campuses that have higher levels of police enforcement also report higher crime rates (Fox & Hellman, 1985). However, this may be an issue of enforcement activities being a reaction to crime on campus). Another view on this is that if potential offenders believe they will not be caught, their likelihood to offend (including to sexually assault) increases (Schwartz & Pitts, 1995). Nevertheless, overall, the research suggests that formal guardianship agents/efforts may not significantly affect victimization risks.

The types of effective self-protective behaviors that college students engage in to lower their risks of victimization – at least for property crimes – includes installing extra locks on doors and window, and having a dog in the residence (Mustaine & Tewksbury, 1998a). Other activities such as simply asking another person to keep a watch on one's property (Fisher et al., 1998) or attending a crime prevention educational workshop (Fisher et al., 1998) can also effectively reduce college students' victimization risks. Regarding sexual assault revictimization, the use of self-protective actions during a sexual assault reduced the risks of another sexual assault (Fisher, Daigle, & Cullen, 2010).

The research on the effects of guardianship activities on college students' victimization risks is not especially well developed to date. However, what is known is that many students do take steps to attempt to protect themselves and their property, but the efficacy of such efforts are largely unknown. Formal agents of guardianship, while common and sometimes highly visible on college campuses, also may or may not be effective. The issue of guardianship in routine activities theory is by far the least developed of the three central concepts, and one that clearly calls for more research.

Online Victimization

Recently, scholars of routine activity theory and victimization risks have begun looking at the virtual world and the risks associated with criminal victimization online. Here, too, researchers have considered the types of "behaviors" and routine activities that increase (or decrease) the chances of being victims of cybercrimes. This initial research indicates that rates of cyber victimization are high. For example, Melander (2010) found that 75 percent of her sample was victimized by at least one aggressive cyber behavior during the past 12 months, although Taylor (2009) found that verbal harassment, incessant unwanted behaviors, and sexual harassment were more common and serious online victimizations were rare. Additionally, Beebe (2010) found that nearly 51 percent of her sample reported being victims of cyberbullying. Although, Snyder and Sickmund (2006) stated only 20 percent of adolescents on the internet received at least one unwanted sexual solicitation in the last year. Thus far, researchers have found that variables measuring online exposure to risk, online proximity to motivated offenders, online guardianship, online target attractiveness, and online deviance were significant predictors of online victimization (Reyns, Henson, & Fisher, 2011; Holt & Bossler, 2008), albeit the literature provides some inconsistent results. Nonetheless, many findings echo those for more traditional (person-to-person) victimization.

To elaborate, the literature indicates that students who have greater online exposure (or proximity to online offenders) have heightened victimization risks. Specifically, those who engaged in more frequent online behaviors such as spending more time on the computer (for work, school, or play), using more social networking sites, updating their statuses more often, posting more pictures online, and using instant messaging more frequently had correspondingly greater risks for online victimization (Beebe, 2010; Reyns et al., 2011; Melander, 2010) as well as communicating with strangers or people one has only met online and sharing personal information with them over the Internet were strongly related to online victimization (Mitchell, Wolak, & Finkelhor, 2008; Marcum, 2009). Although Holt and Bossler (2008) found that measures of routine computer use and physical guardianship had little influence on likelihood of being harassed while chatting on-line.

Online guardianship is also related to victimization risks (as it typically is with more traditional victimization). To specify, students who have set their online profiles to private and use profile trackers are less likely to experience online victimization (Reyns et al., 2011), although the use of other guardianship behaviors may not provide significant protection (Marcum, 2009). Although Melander (2010) found that more online guardianship was associated with greater cyber aggression victimization.

Regarding target attractiveness, females were more likely to be cyber victimized than males (Beebe, 2010; Holt & Bossler, 2008; although see Reyns, Henson, & Fisher, 2011). And, similarly to traditional victimization, those who engage in cybercrime are also more likely to be victimized. For example, those committing computer-based deviance themselves (downloading pornography; using pirated copies of music, software, and other media; guessing others' passwords, and hacking into others' accounts) had increased risks for online victimization (Holt & Bossler, 2008) as did those who engaged in both online and offline misbehavior (Selwyn, 2008).

Conclusion

In sum, it is safe to say that the risks for criminal victimization of college students are related to their daily routines and lifestyles. These lifestyles encompass many types of behaviors, locations, and associations. And, while some of these behaviors are common among the general population, some are unique to college students. Research has found that college students who engage in activities that bring them in close proximity to potential offenders have higher risks for many types of criminal victimization. Further, college students who engage in behaviors that make them more vulnerable or desirable have higher odds for victimization. Additionally, since most college students do not use even the most simple of items or strategies for guardianship, their risks for victimization are increased. Finally, the lifestyles of college students frequently encompass all of the above relationships: they engage in behavior that lessens their abilities to recognize or resist danger, while going to events or gatherings that are likely to have many potential offenders in attendance, while at the same time, neglecting to utilize self-protection. All in all, this makes college students, in general, and many in particular, experience high risks for criminal victimization.

These findings have policy implications for university administrators, law enforcement personnel, and victim advocates, among others (e.g., Greek affairs directors, residence hall directors, student success coordinators). Obvious suggestions are to increase student programming and services related to self-protection and reduction of alcohol and drug use. However, most universities have plenty of programs and services to offer students already. Further, as noted by Barberet et al. (2004), only a small proportion of students are aware of such programming and services, and of those who are aware (in most cases, less than one-half), only a small proportion utilize such benefits (often less than one-third).

So, the most important question may be how to convince students that they are, in fact, vulnerable to crime, and worse, that they have an above average risk of being crime victims. If students believe that they have heightened risks for being victims, they may utilize the already present programs and services and thereby effectively lower their risks.

REFERENCES

Abbey, A., Ross, L. T., McDuffie, D., & McAuslan, P. (1996). Alcohol and dating risk factors for sexual assault among college women. *Psychology of Women Quarterly, 20,* 147–169.

Banyard, V. L., Ward, S., Cohn, E. S., Plante, E. G., Moorhead, C., & Walsh, W. (2007). Unwanted sexual contact on campus: A comparison of women's and men's experiences. *Violence and Victims, 22,* 52–70.

Barberet, R., Fisher, B. S., & Taylor, H. (2004). *University student safety in the East Midlands.* London: Home Office.

Bartolli, A. M., & Clark, M. D. (2006). The dating game: Similarities and differences in dating scripts among college students. *Sexuality & Culture, 10,* 54–80.

Baum, K., & Klaus, P. (2005). *Violent victimization of college students, 1995–2002.* Washington, DC: Bureau of Justice Statistics.

Bausell, R. B., Bausell, C. R., & Siegel, D. G. (1991). *The links among alcohol, drugs and crime on American college campuses: A national followup study.* Towson, MD: Towson State University.

Beebe, J. E. (2010). *The prevalence of cyber bullying victimization and its relationship to academic, social and emotional adjustment among college students.* Unpublished doctoral dissertation, University of Northern Colorado.

Benedict, J. (1997). *Public heroes, private felons: Athletes and crimes against women.* Boston: Northeastern University Press.

Benedict, J., & Klein, A. (1997). Arrest and conviction rates for athletes accused of sexual assault. *Sociology of Sport, 14,* 86–94.

Bryden, P. J., & Fletcher, P. C. (2007). Personal safety practices, beliefs and attitudes of academic faculty on a small university campus: Comparison of males and females (part 1). *College Student Journal, 41,* 613–622.

Buddie, A. M., & Testa, M. (2005). Rates and predictors of sexual aggression among students and non-students. *Journal of Interpersonal Violence, 20,* 713–724.

Capone, C., Wood, M. D., Borsari, B., & Laird, R. D. (2007). Fraternity and sorority involvement, social influences, and alcohol use among college students: A prospective examination. *Psychology of Addictive Behaviors, 21,* 316–327.

Cass, A. I. (2007). Routine activities and sexual assault: An analysis of individual- and school-level factors. *Violence and Victims, 22,* 350–366.

Clodfelter, T. A., Turner, M. G., Hartman, J. L., & Kuhns, J. B. (2010). Sexual harassment victimization during emerging adulthood. *Crime & Delinquency, 56,* 455–481.

Cohen, L. E., & Felson, M. (1979). Social changes and crime rate trends: A routine activities approach. *American Sociological Review, 44,* 588–608.

Combs-Lane, A. M., & Smith, D. W. (2002). Risk of sexual victimization in college women: The role of behavioral intentions and risk-taking behaviors. *Journal of Interpersonal Violence, 17,* 165–183.

Copenhaver, S., & Grauerholtz, E. (1991). Sexual victimization among sorority women: Exploring the link between sexual violence and institutional practices. *Sex Roles, 24,* 31–41.

Cross, J. E., Zimmerman, D., & O'Grady, M. A. (2009). Residence hall room type and alcohol use among college students living on campus. *Environment and Behavior, 41,* 583–603.

Fagan, J., McCormick, L. J., Konto, A., Venable, R. H., & Anderson, P. B. (2011). The influence of gender and race on sexual assault among high risk drinkers. *Race, Gender and Class, 18,* 215–229.

Fisher, B. S., Cullen, F. T., & Turner, M. G. (2002). Being pursued: Stalking victimization in a national study of college women. *Criminology and Public Policy, 1,* 257–308.

Fisher, B. S., Cullen, F. T., & Turner, M. G. (2000). *The sexual victimization of college women.* Washington, DC: U.S. Bureau of Justice Statistics.

Fisher, B. S., Daigle, L. E., & Cullen, F. T. (2010). What distinguishes single from recurrent sexual victims? The role of lifestyle-routine activities and first incident characteristics. *Justice Quarterly, 27,* 2010.

Fisher, B. S., & Sloan, J. J. (1995). *Campus crime: Legal, social, and policy perspectives.* Springfield, IL: Charles C Thomas.

Fisher, B. S., Sloan, J. J., Cullen, F. T., & Lu, C. (1998). Crime in the ivory tower: The level and sources of student victimization. *Criminology, 36,* 671–710.

Fisher, B. S., Sloan, J. J., Cullen, F. T., & Lu, C. (1997). The on campus victimization patterns of students: Implications for crime prevention by students and post-secondary institutions. In S. P. Lab (Ed.), *Crime prevention at a crossroads.* Cincinnati, OH: Anderson.

Fisher, B. S., & Wilkes, A. R. P. (2003). A tale of two ivory towers: A comparative analysis of victimization rates and risks between university students in the United States and England. *British Journal of Criminology, 43,* 526–545.

Forbes, G. B., Adams-Curtis, L. E., Pakalka, A. H., & White, K. B. (2006). Dating aggression, sexual coercion and aggression-supporting attitudes among college men as a function of participation in aggressive high school sports. *Violence Against Women, 12,* 441–455.

Fox, J. A., & Hellman, D. A. (1985). Location and other correlates of campus crime. *Journal of Criminal Justice, 13,* 429–444.

Franklin, C. A. (2010). *Sorority affiliation and rape-supportive environments: The institutionalization of sexual assault victimization through vulnerability-enhancing attitudes and behaviors.* Unpublished doctoral dissertation, Washington State University.

Frintner, M. P., & Rubinson, L. (1993). Acquaintance Rape: The influence of alcohol, fraternity membership, and sports team membership. *Journal of Sex Education and Therapy, 19,* 272–284.

Gidycz, C. A., Coble, C. N., Latham, L., & Layman, M. J. (1993). Sexual assault experience in adulthood and prior victimization experience: A prospective analysis. *Psychology of Women Quarterly, 17,* 151–168.

Grossman, M., & Markowitz, S. (1999). *Alcohol regulation and violence on college campuses.* Cambridge, MA: National Bureau of Economic Research.

Harford, T. C., Wechsler, H., & Muthen, B. O. (2003). Alcohol-related aggression and drinking at off-campus parties and bars: A national study of current drinkers in college. *Journal of Studies on Alcohol, 64,* 704–711.

Hertzog, J., & Yeilding, R. (2009). College women's rape awareness and use of commonly advocated risk reduction strategies. *College Student Journal, 43,* 59–73.

Holt, T. J., & Bossler, A. M. (2008). Examining the applicability of lifestyle-routine activities theory for cybercrime victimization. *Deviant Behavior, 30,* 1–25.

Jennings, W. G., Higgins, G. E., Tewksbury, R., Gover, A. R., & Piquero, A. R. (2010). A longitudinal assessment of the victim-offender overlap. *Journal of Interpersonal Violence, 25,* 2147–2174.

Johnson, I. M., & Sigler, R. T. (1996). Forced sexual intercourse on campus: Crime or offensive behavior? *Journal of Contemporary Criminal Justice, 12,* 54–68.

Kalof, L. (1993). Rape supportive attitudes and sexual victimization experiences of sorority and non-sorority women. *Sex Roles, 29,* 767–780.

Koss, M. P., & Dinero, T. E. (1989). Discriminant analysis of risk factors for sexual victimization among a national sample of college women. *Journal of Consulting and Clinical Psychology, 57,* 242–250.

Klevens, J., Duque, L. F., & Ramirez, C. (2002). The victim-offender overlap and routine activities: Results from a cross-sectional study in Bogota, Columbia. *Journal of Interpersonal Violence, 17,* 206–216.

Krebs, C. P., Lindquist, C. H., Warner, T. D., Fisher, B. S., & Martin, S. L. (2009a). College women's experiences with physically forced, alcohol- or other drug-enabled, and drug-facilitated sexual assault before and since entering college. *Journal of American College Health, 57,* 639–649.

Krebs, C. P., Lindquist, C. H., Warner, T. D., Fisher, B. S., & Martin, S. L. (2009b). The differential risk factors of physically forced and alcohol- or other drug-enabled sexual assault among university women. *Violence and Victims, 24,* 302–321.

Laub, J. H. (1990). Patterns of criminal victimization in the United States. In A. J. Lurigio, W. G. Skogan & R. C. Davis (Eds.), *Victims of crime: Problems, policies, and programs* (pp. 23–49). Newberry Park, CA: Sage.

Littleton, H., Grills-Taquechel, A., & Axsom, D. (2009). Impaired and incapacitated rape victims: Assault characteristics and post-assault experiences. *Violence and Victims, 24,* 439–457.

Marcum, C. D. (2009). *Adolescent online victimization: A test of routine activities theory.* Unpublished doctoral dissertation, Indiana University of Pennsylvania.

Martin, P. Y., & Hummer, R. A. (1989). Fraternities and rape on campus. *Gender & Society, 3,* 457–473.

Maxfield, M. G. (1987). Household composition, routine activity, and victimization: A comparative analysis. *Journal of Quantitative Criminology, 3,* 301–320.

McCauley, J. L., Calhoun, K. S., & Gidycz, C. A.. (2010). Binge drinking and rape: A prospective examination of college women with a history of previous sexual victimization. *Journal of Interpersonal Violence, 25,* 1655–1668.

McMahon, S. (2007). Understanding community-specific rape myths: Exploring student-athlete culture. *Affilia, 22,* 357–370.

Meithe, T. D., & Meier, R. F. (1990). Opportunity, choice, and criminal victimization: A test of a theoretical model. *Journal of Research in Crime and Delinquency, 27*(3), 243–266.

Melander, L. A. (2010). *Explaining college partner violence in the digital age: An instrumental design mixed methods study.* Unpublished doctoral dissertation, University of Nebraska.

Messman-Moore, T. L., Ward, R. M., & Brown, A. L. (2009). Substance use and PTSD symptoms impact the likelihood of rape and revictimization in college women. *Journal of Interpersonal Violence, 24,* 499–521.

Miller, M., Hemenway, D., & Wechsler, H. (2002). Guns and gun threats at college. *Journal of American College Health, 51,* 57–65.

Minow, J. C., & Einolf, C. J. (2009). Sorority participation and sexual risk. *Violence Against Women, 15,* 835–851.

Mitchell, K. J., Wolak, J., & Finkelhor, D. (2008). Are blogs putting youth at risk for online sexual solicitation or harassment? *Child Abuse & Neglect, 32,* 277–294.

Mohler-Kuo, M., Dowdall, G. W., Koss, M. P., & Wechsler, H. (2004). Correlates of rape while intoxicated in a national sample of college women. *Journal of Studies on Alcohol, 65,* 37–45.

Mustaine, E. E., & Tewksbury, R. (1997). Obstacles in the assessment of routine activities theory. *Social Pathology, 3,* 177–194.

Mustaine, E. E., & Tewksbury, R. (1998a). Predicting risks of larceny theft victimization: A routine activity analysis using refined lifestyle measures. *Criminology, 36,* 829–857.

Mustaine, E. E., & Tewksbury, R. (1998b). Specifying the role of alcohol in predatory victimization. *Deviant Behavior, 19,* 173–199.

Mustaine, E. E., & Tewksbury, R. (1998c). Victimization risks at leisure: A gender-specific analysis. *Violence and Victims, 13,* 231–249.

Mustaine, E. E., & Tewksbury, R. (1999). A routine activity theory explanation of women's stalking victimizations. *Violence Against Women, 5,* 43–62.

Mustaine, E. E., & Tewksbury, R. (2000). Comparing the lifestyles of victims, offenders and victim-offenders: A routine activity theory assessment of similarities and differences for criminal incident participants. *Sociological Focus, 33,* 339–362.

Mustaine, E. E., & Tewksbury, R. (2002). Sexual assault of college women: A feminist interpretation of a routine activities analysis. *Criminal Justice Review, 27,* 89–123.

Mynatt, C. R., & Allgeier, E. R. (1990). Risk factors, self-attributions, and adjustment problems among victims of sexual coercion. *Journal of Applied Social Psychology, 20,* 130–153.

Nabors, E. L. (2010). Drug use and intimate partner violence among college students: An in-depth exploration. *Journal of Interpersonal Violence, 25,* 1043–1063.

Nurius, P. S., Norris, J., Dimeff, R., & Graham, T. L. (1996). Expectations regarding acquaintance sexual aggression among sorority and fraternity members. *Sex Roles, 35,* 427–444.

O'Hare, T. M. (1990). Drinking in college: Consumption patterns, problems, sex-differences and legal drinking age. *Journal of Studies on Alcohol, 51,* 536–541.

Palmer, C. J. (1993). *Violent Crimes and Other Forms of Victimization in Residence Halls.* Ashville, NC: College Administration Publications.

Palmer, R. S., McMahon, T. J., Rounsaville, B. J., & Ball, S. A.. (2010). Coercive sexual experiences, protective behavioral strategies, alcohol expectancies and consumption among male and female college students. *Journal of Interpersonal Violence, 25,* 1563–1578.

Parks, K. A., & Miller, B. A. (1997). Bar victimization of women. *Psychology of Women Quarterly, 21,* 509–526.

Parks, K. A., & Zettes-Zanatta, L. M. (1999). Women's bar-related victimization: Refining and testing a conceptual model. *Aggressive Behavior, 25,* 349–364.

Peralta, R. L., Steele, J. L., Nofziger, S., & Rickles, M. (2010). The impact of gender on binge drinking behavior among U.S. college students attending a Midwestern university: An analysis of two gender measures. *Feminist Criminology, 5,* 355–379.

Pino, N. W., & Johnson-Johns, A. M. (2009). College women and the occurrence of unwanted sexual advances in public drinking settings. *The Social Science Journal, 46,* 252–267.

Porter, J., & Williams, L. M. (2011). Intimate violence among underrepresented groups in a college campus. *Journal of Interpersonal Violence, 26,* 321–324.

Reynes, B. W., Henson, B., & Fisher, B. S. (2011). Being pursued online: Applying cyberlifestyle-routine activities theory to cyberstalking victimization. *Criminal Justice and Behavior, 38,* 1149–1169.

Rickgarn, R. L. (1989). Violence in the residence halls: Campus domestic violence. In J. M. Sherrill & D. G. Siegel (Eds.), *Responding to violence on campus.* San Francisco: Jossey-Bass.

Robinson, M. B. (1997). Environmental characteristics associated with residential burglaries of student apartment complexes. *Environment and Behavior, 29,* 657–675.

Russell, B. L., & Oswald, D. L. (2002). Sexual coercion and victimization of college men: The role of love styles. *Journal of Interpersonal Violence, 17,* 273–285.

Sanday, P. R. (1990). *Fraternity gang rape: Sex, brotherhood, and privilege on campus.* New York: New York University Press.

Schaeffer, A., & Nelson, E. (1993). Rape supportive attitudes: Effects of on campus residence and education. *Journal of College Student Development, 34,* 175–179.

Schreck, C. J., Stewart, E. A., & Osgood, D. W. (2008). A reappraisal of the overlap of violent offenders and victims. *Criminology, 46,* 871–906.

Schwartz, M. D., & Pitts, V. L. (1995). Exploring a feminist routine activities approach to explaining sexual assault. *Justice Quarterly, 12,* 9–31.

Sellers, C. S., & Bromley, M. L. (1996). Violent behavior in college student dating relationships: Implications for campus service providers. *Journal of Contemporary Criminal Justice, 12,* 1–27.

Selwyn, N. (2008). A safe haven for misbehaving? An investigation of online misbehavior among university students. *Social Science Computer Review, 26,* 446–465.

Seng, M. (1996). Theft on campus: An analysis of larceny-theft at an urban university. *Journal of Crime and Justice, 19,* 33–44.

Siegel, D. G., & Raymond, C. H. (1992). An ecological approach to violent crime on campus. *Journal of Security Administration, 15,* 19–27.

Sigler, R. T., & Koehlor, N. (1993). Victimization and crime on campus. *International Review of Victimology, 2,* 331–343.

Sloan, J. J. (1994). The correlates of campus crime: An analysis of reported crimes on college and university campuses. *Journal of Criminal Justice, 22,* 51–61.

Sloan. J. J. (1992). Campus crime and campus communities: An analysis of crimes known to campus police and security. *Journal of Security Administration, 15,* 31–46.

Sloan, J. J., Fisher, B. S., & Wilkins, D. L. (1995). *Crime, fear of crime, and related issues on the U.A.B. campus: Final report.* Birmingham, AL: University of Alabama at Birmingham.

Snyder, H. N., & Sickmund, M. (2006). *Juvenile offenders and victims: 2006 national report.* Washington, DC: Office of Juvenile Justice and Delinquency Prevention.

Stets, J. E., & Pirog-Good, M. A. (1989). Patterns of physical and sexual abuse for men and women in dating relationships: A descriptive analysis. *Journal of Family Violence, 4,* 63–77.

Stombler, M. (1994). 'Buddies' or 'Slutties': The collective sexual reputation of fraternity little sisters. *Gender & Society, 8,* 297–323.

Swartout, K. M., & White, J. W. (2010). The relationship between drug use and sexual aggression in men across time. *Journal of Interpersonal Violence, 25,* 1716–35.

Tanioka, I. (1986). Evidence links smoking to violent crime victimization. *Sociology and Social Research, 71,* 58.

Taylor, M. A. (2009). *Victimization and social networking sites.* Unpublished thesis, University of Nevada, Las Vegas.

Testa, M., & Durmen, K. H. (1999). The differential correlates of sexual coercion and rape. *Journal of Interpersonal Violence, 14,* 548–561.

Testa, M., & Livingston, J. A. (2000). Alcohol and sexual aggression: Reciprocal relationships over time in a sample of high risk women. *Journal of Interpersonal Violence, 15,* 413–427.

Tewksbury, R., Higgins, G. E., & Mustaine E. E. (2008). Binge drinking among college athletes and non-athletes. *Deviant Behavior, 29,* 275–293.

Tewksbury, R., & Mustaine, E. E. (2003). College students' lifestyles and self-protective behaviors: Further considerations of the guardianship concept in routine activity theory. *Criminal Justice and Behavior, 30,* 302–327.

Tewksbury, R., & Mustaine, E. E. (2001). Lifestyle factors associated with the sexual assault of men: A routine activity theory analysis. *Journal of Men's Studies, 9,* 153–182.

Tewksbury, R., & Mustaine, E. E. (2000). Routine activities and vandalism: A theoretical and empirical study. *Journal of Crime and Justice, 23,* 81–110.

Thompson, E. H., & Cracco, E. J. (2008). Sexual aggression in bars: What college men can normalize. *Journal of Men's Studies, 16,* 82–96.

Tyler, K. A., Hoyt, D. R., & Whitbeck, L. B. (1998). Coercive sexual strategies. *Violence and Victims, 13,* 47–61.

Ullman, S. E., Karabatsos, G., & Koss, M. P. (1999). Alcohol and sexual assault in a national sample of college women. *Journal of Interpersonal Violence, 14,* 603–625.

Vanderwoerd, J. R. (2009). Experiences of sexual coercion, awareness of services, and acceptance of rape myths among students in rural colleges. *Rural Social Work and Community Practice, 14,* 17–28.

Ward, S. K., Chapman, K., Cohn, E., White, S., & Williams, K. (1991). Acquaintance rape and the college social scene. *Family Relations, 40,* 65–71.

Warshaw, R. (1988). *I never called it rape: Report on recognizing, fighting and surviving date and acquaintance rape.* New York: Harper Perennial.

Wechsler, H., Davenport, A., Dowdall, G., Moeykems, B., & Castillo, S. (1994). Health and behavioral consequences of binge drinking in college: A national survey of students at 140 campuses. *Journal of the American Medical Association, 272,* 1672–1677.

Zito, J. M. (1974). Anonymity and neighboring in an urban high-rise complex. *Urban Life and Culture, 3,* 243–263.

Chapter 9

THE ROLE OF ALCOHOL ABUSE IN COLLEGE STUDENT VICTIMIZATION[1]

GEORGE W. DOWDALL

INTRODUCTION

Alcohol plays a very important, complex, but often unrecognized or poorly understood role in campus crime. Many of the college crime incidents reported to the police are alcohol related, and many if not most of the serious crimes on college campuses involve alcohol. Students who abuse alcohol are more likely to be victims of crime than nonusers or nonbingeing users, and are more likely to experience health, behavioral, and academic problems. That many college students use or abuse alcohol is well known, but alcohol's impact on other aspects of college life is more controversial. The role that alcohol plays in campus crime, particularly victimization, deserves reexamination. Is student use of alcohol the engine that drives most of campus crime or is it merely one of a number of factors, and perhaps a minor one at that, that play very limited roles? Should colleges and universities focus on preventing alcohol abuse as a way to prevent campus crime? Alternatively, can efforts to prevent campus crimes such as sexual assault and rape ignore the role of alcohol? Given the recent changes in policy surrounding *Title IX* that prohibits sexual harassment in college, what must colleges do about excessive student drinking?

This chapter describes the nature and extent of alcohol use and alcohol-related crime victimization among college students. The beginning section discusses alcohol and campus crime, noting that most violations reported by campus police involve alcohol and that alcohol violations have increased recently, a time when crime in the broader society was falling. The chapter discusses the extent of college drinking in detail, including the nature of binge drinking, followed by a section that examines the factors that shape college drinking. We then examine the consequences of college drinking by looking at the kinds of alcohol-related problems associated with it, among the most serious of which are sexual assault and rape. The following section explores whether alcohol is a cause of violence, given the very powerful correlation between alcohol and violence. The chapter then turns to an examination of what research shows about preventing college alcohol abuse, ranging from programs that focus on individuals to public policies that affect everyone. A conclusion offers a summary of the chapter and some implications for those trying to understand or contain campus crime. We begin by exploring the relationship between alcohol and campus crime.

Alcohol and Campus Crime

Studying this issue is complex (Dowdall & Wechsler, 2002). The term "college student" seems clear enough, until we begin to realize that it covers over 17 million undergraduates studying at over four thousand colleges, universities, and other higher education institutions (for a snapshot of students and their institutions: Chronicle of Higher Education, 2011). These students have all kinds of living arrangements (their own apartments, university dorms, parental homes, etc.); may be taking only a course or two or dozens of credits at once; may live in "dry" communities or in "wet" places filled with bars, liquor stores, and other alcohol outlets. They may live in states with fairly tight enforcement of liquor control laws or in states with little control over alcohol sales or consumption. Their behavior may be relatively constant or vary greatly by day of the week or season of the year. The regular tools of social science and public health research – observing behavior directly, running experiments, using existing data including crime reports, or taking surveys – may yield incomplete and inconsistent findings (Dowdall & Wechsler, 2002), making it very difficult to generalize about student conduct.

But the public media are filled with dramatic images of a few hardly random episodes of student alcohol use. The public's attention usually falls on the extremes. A seemingly unending series of sensational student deaths, sexual assaults, and rapes has made urgent the task of examining the relationship between alcohol and campus crime. In this section, we explore that relationship, given that alcohol-related incidents have become the most common kind of crime activity on American college campuses.

Like all other Americans, college students are at risk of crime victimization, ranging from larceny to violent events such as rape (Fisher, Cullen, & Turner, 2000; Fisher & Sloan, 2007; Sloan & Fisher, 2011). For example, during the period 1995–2002, rates of violent victimization of Americans ages 18 to 24 fell for both college students (a decrease of 54%) and for nonstudents (a decrease of 45%), part of a broad decline in violent crime experienced for most Americans during these years (Baum & Klaus, 2005; Hart, 2003). The same data show that college students ages 18–24 experience lower rates of violent crime such as robbery, aggravated assault, and simple assault (except for rape/assault) than do nonstudents; the glaring exception is rape, experienced by both students and nonstudents at the same rate.

For college students, studying or living on a college campus brings a unique set of both risk and protective factors (Fisher et al., 2000; Fisher & Sloan, 1995, 2005; Sloan & Fisher, 2011). Arguably highest among the risks is the greater use of alcohol and other drugs than among noncollege youth in the broader society. National Crime Victimization Survey (NCVS) data on violent victimizations of college students show that roughly 40 percent of offenders were perceived to be using alcohol or drugs, whether the crime was any violence (41%), rape/sexual assault (40%), aggravated assault (44%), or simple assault (42%). Only robbery (25%) had lower rates of perceived drug and alcohol use by the perpetrator (Baum & Klaus, 2005; Hart, 2003). Observers widely suspect substance use plays an important role in crime, especially violence, in the broader society and that it is involved in much, if not most, campus crime. An extensive study of college student victimization found that recreational drug use and a lifestyle with high levels of partying were the main predictors of a college student being the victim of a violent crime (Fisher, Sloan, Cullen, & Lu, 1998). An analysis of 32 universities found a positive correlation between the number of alcohol outlets near campus and the rate of sexual assault and rape (Scribner et al., 2010).

Alcohol and other drug use (AOD) is a particularly strategic issue for those concerned with college crime prevention for three reasons. First, "recreational" drugs like marijuana and cocaine are illegal for *all* students and alcohol for those undergraduates under 21, so substance use is of immediate importance to campus police and other college administrative personnel, placing AOD high on the list of problems with which they must deal with, if not at the top. Second, researchers believe substance use increases the overall risk of criminal victimization on campus, as it does in the broader society, suggesting that campus police and security should play a crucial role in restricting access to AOD. Published reports of such phenomena as date or acquaintance rape present widely different and even contradictory pictures of whether college students are at very low or very high risk of victimization, and the role of alcohol and other drug use in victimization of all forms is even more unclear. Third, the U.S. Department of Education mandated in 2011 that colleges and universities receiving federal funds enforce *Title IX* of the Education Act. *Title IX* coordinators must become informed about the alcohol-violence connection, a subject discussed later in this chapter.

Crimes associated with alcohol and drug use are arguably the most prevalent crimes on college campuses today. Since alcohol is overwhelmingly the substance of choice on college campuses, we will focus most of our attention on alcohol use and abuse. But it is important to remember that other substances are used by college students with serious consequences as well. Some of these are illicit substances like marijuana and other illegal drugs. One large survey of college students reported that in 2009, 68 percent had used alcohol in the past 30 days, while 26 percent used tobacco, and 17 percent used marijuana, 3 percent used amphetamines, and less than 2 percent used one of the other illegal substances (SIUC/Core Institute 2011). Other substances are licit but are abused by college students, such as the nonmedical use of prescription drugs (McCabe, Knight, Teter, & Wechsler, 2005). To make matters more complex, alcohol is often used by college students who are under the legal drinking age. Licit and illicit drug use and the use of alcohol by those under age 21 are not only correlated, but are also used together or sequentially by some college students.

Occasional use of alcohol by young Americans is widespread, but on college campuses as in the broader society, heavy episodic or binge drinking poses a particular danger of serious safety, health and other consequences for both the abuser of alcohol and others in the immediate environment. Binge drinking has been defined as a male consuming more than five drinks in a row or a female drinking four in a row in a short period of time (Wechsler, Dowdall, Davenport, & Rimm, 1995). Binge drinking was first described as a behavior pattern among college students; binge drinking has now been recognized as a problem for many adults, especially young adults (Wechsler, Davenport, Dowdall, & Castillo, 1994; Naimi et al., 2003). The U.S. Centers for Disease Control and Prevention has described it as "a dangerous and costly public health problem" (Centers for Disease Control and Prevention, 2012, p. 1).

New estimates show that binge drinking is a bigger problem than previously thought. More than 38 million U.S. adults binge drink, about four times a month, and the largest number of drinks per binge is on average eight. This behavior greatly increases the chances of getting hurt or hurting others due to car crashes, violence, and suicide. Drinking too much, including binge drinking, causes 80,000 deaths in the U.S. each year and, in 2006, cost the economy $223.5 billion. Binge drinking is a problem in all states, even in states with fewer binge drinkers, because they are bingeing more often and in larger amounts (Centers for Disease Control and Prevention, 2012).

Research has confirmed that binge drinking poses a major challenge to the criminal justice system and to college and university administrators, with one estimate that alcohol is involved in two-thirds of college student suicides, in 90 percent of campus rapes, and 95 percent of violent crime on campus

(Commission on Substance Abuse at Colleges and Universities, 1994). Alcohol contributes to the leading causes of accidental death, such as motor vehicle crashes and falls, and is the third-leading cause of preventable death in the United States. Alcohol abuse contributes to almost half of motor vehicle fatalities, the most important cause of death among young Americans (Robert Wood Johnson Foundation, 2001). On college campuses, alcohol-related crime involves underage drinking, driving under the influence, public intoxication, and a variety of criminal acts ranging from theft to violence (Engs & Hanson, 1994; Perkins, 2002).

Hoover (2005) reported on data about campus crime gathered as part of the requirements of the *Clery Act* by the United States Department of Education.[2] Alcohol arrests had increased at American colleges for 12 years running; liquor law violations rose from 108,846 reported in 1999 to 161, 974 in 2003.[3] In the period from 2008 to 2010, on campus disciplinary actions at all American institutions of higher education had risen to 185,005 in 2008, 185,590 in 2009, and 186,487 in 2010 (United States Department of Education, 2012). These figures may reflect both rising amounts of alcohol-related crime and increased attention to alcohol issues by college security officials. In any case, the numbers of alcohol arrests are far more numerous than other kinds of reported crime. For the period 2001 to 2003, the U.S. Department of Education data on campus crime listed 84 murders and/or manslaughters, 7,941 forcible/nonforcible sex offenses as being reported to campus authorizes, and 514,568 liquor law arrests and/or cases involving disciplinary proceedings occurring (Security on Campus, Inc., 2006). For 2008 to 2010, the data showed 53 murders and/or manslaughters, 8,217 forcible/nonforcible sex offenses, and 557,082 liquor law violations reported on college campuses nationwide.

In summary, alcohol and crime involving college students are powerfully connected. There is little doubt that alcohol plays some kind of role in much of the crime and even violence on college campuses, and that alcohol use is a major risk factor for college student victimization. We now turn to a closer look at alcohol consumption by college students. In the next section, we examine the extent and nature of alcohol consumption among college students.

The Extent of Drinking Among College Students

In this section, we assess the extent of drinking among American college students with particular attention paid to the amount of binge or heavy episodic drinking. Over the past two decades, several published studies of college drinking included large-scale surveys produced by the Harvard School of Public Health College Alcohol Study (CAS) (e.g., Wechsler & Wuetrich, 2002; Wechsler & Nelson, 2008). CAS results have been very consistent with other large-scale efforts, but the CAS uses scientific sampling techniques to produce a representative national sample of colleges and students, and so we will mostly refer to its findings here. For its original survey, the CAS chose 195 four-year colleges and universities using probability proportionate to size sampling. A total of 140 colleges participated in the initial study. Because the CAS promised confidentiality to each participating institution, it is not possible to identify individual schools but to simply note that the sample is representative of four-year American colleges and universities with full-time students. Each college provided the researchers with a random sample of full-time students, with roughly 60 percent completing a very detailed 20-page questionnaire about their alcohol and drug use as well as behaviors and values. The CAS conducted surveys of large samples of roughly 15,000 to 17,000 students in 1993, 1995, 1997, and 2001. A later study of 32 CAS universities, including 18 schools with heavy drinking rates among students (above 50%), was conducted in 2005 (Nelson, Xuan, Lee, Weitzman, & Wechsler, 2009).

Almost all college students drink occasionally, but roughly two out of every five four-year fulltime college students are binge drinkers (Wechsler et al., 1994). Binge drinking has been operationalized in these studies by the "5/4" definition: male binge drinkers consume five or more drinks in a row in the two weeks prior to completing the questionnaire, while female bingers consume four or more drinks in a row in the same time period (Dowdall & Wechsler 2002; Wechsler et al., 1995). Note that the "5/4" definition includes the phrase "or more," since many bingers do not just stop at the cutoff. Table 9.1 presents data from the 1993–2001 CAS surveys about college drinking at a representative sample of four-year colleges, along with data from 2005 at 18 of the colleges with heavy levels of student drinking. Clearly, attending a heavy drinking college is linked to higher levels of drinking.

Table 9.1
Self-Reported Drinking Behavior of American College Students (2001)
and Students at Heavy Drinking Colleges (2005)

Type of Behavior	2001 (All Colleges) Percent	2005 (Heavy Drinking Colleges) Percent
Abstained	19.3	13.8
Drank in Past Year	80.7	86.2
Binge Drinking	44.4	55.8
Frequent Binge Drinking	22.8	32.0
Drank on 10 or More Occasions in the Past 30 Days	22.6	27.6
Was Drunk 3+ Times in the Past Month	29.4	39.7

Sources: Pastore & Maguire 2003; Nelson, Xuan, & Weitzman 2009.

Any discussion of college drinking should of course highlight the fact that most college students do not binge drink. But this is hardly cause for celebration, since Table 9.1 shows that a substantial minority do binge; even more troubling, one out of five college students is a frequent binge drinker (bingeing at least three times in the two-week period), and almost a third of all college students were drunk three or more times in the past month. Almost half of all students drink to get drunk. Many of the undergraduates at U.S. colleges are under the minimum drinking age, guaranteeing that many episodes of drinking by college students violate various state laws (Wechsler, Kuo, Lee, & Dowdall, 2000).

Trends in college drinking over the past few decades show relatively little change, though there have been small increases in binge drinking (from 41.7% to 44.7%) in the period from 1998–2005. During the same period, college students continued to binge drink more than do their noncollege peers, and, probably reflecting the impact of the minimum drinking age laws, those students and nonstudents aged 19–20 binge drink at significantly lower rates than those 21–24 (Hingson, Zha, & Weitzman, 2009).

Most college students only drink occasionally throughout the year, but four in ten binge drink, and roughly one in five frequently binge drinks. Considerable evidence exists about the amount and form of college drinking, and the risks and consequences of that drinking. The next section reviews the evidence about college drinking by exploring the factors that shape college drinking, including how much colleges vary in rates of bingeing.

Factors That Shape College Student Drinking

What are the causes of college drinking? While no definitive answer exists, we know an increasing amount about the factors that shape drinking behavior.[4] Figure 9.1 suggests some of the most important issues, grouped into those that precede college and those that occur during college (Dowdall & Wechsler, 2002; Dowdall 2009).

Of those factors preceding college, some research has examined genetic issues, with one study suggesting that college students who binge may have different genetic components than those who do not (Herman, Philbeck, Vasilopoulos, & Depetrillo, 2003). Parental drinking, religion, race, and social class are all correlated with higher rates of college drinking by students. High school students who plan to attend college have lower rates of binge drinking than those who do not plan to pursue higher education.

But it is not just genes, parents, or the past that shape college alcohol use. A central insight of the path breaking Harvard School of Public Health studies was that college drinking is a product of the physical and social environment in which students live their lives (Wechsler & Nelson, 2008; Wechsler &

Before College	College
Family Factors: • Genetics • Parental drinking behavior • Social class • Race or ethnicity • Religion	Individual Factors: • Age of drinking onset • High school drinking • Drug or tobacco use • Gender • Race
Public Policy: • National laws • State laws • Enforcement of minimum drinking age • Local community ordinances	College Environment: • Peer norms • Residential system • Greek life • Athletics • Academics • Community Service • Religious involvement
Alcohol Environment: • Price of alcohol • Advertising • Marketing practices • Outlet density • Hours of sale	Alcohol Environment On Campus: • Dry or wet campus • Availability • Price • Alcohol policy
Social/Institutional Structures: • Neighborhood • Middle and high school • Church, synagogue, mosque • Subcultures	Alcohol Environment Off Campus: • Retail price • Outlet density and proximity • Advertising • Marketing

Source: Adapted from Dowdall & Wechsler (2002).

Figure 9.1. Antecedents to Alcohol Abuse.

Wuetrich, 2002). Access to alcohol or other substances is a potent factor, joining many others in shaping use. Access is in turn shaped by college characteristics, the local environment, and public policy. Many colleges have little drinking or drug abuse, while in others a majority of students participates in those practices. Public policy shapes college drinking, including the minimum legal drinking age of 21 and its enforcement, and students who live in states with effective alcohol control policies or who attend schools with few alcohol outlets nearby drink less than their peers (Dowdall, 2009; Nelson et al., 2005). Although alcohol may play a more significant role in crimes of violence than illegal drugs, public policy stretching back almost a century makes alcohol a legal substance for those over 21 (Parker & Rebhun, 1995; Wagenaar & Toomey, 2002). The overall alcohol environment shapes the level of drinking in a community, with the cost of alcohol, its promotion through advertising and marketing, and its availability all playing a role (Dowdall, 2009). Finally, subcultures of drug and alcohol use within high schools or neighborhoods exert some influence as well.

Figure 9.1 includes college factors that shape college drinking. For the individual student, researchers have identified age of drinking onset as an important factor in alcohol abuse and dependence; the earlier the onset, the higher the risk of later problems with alcohol (National Institute on Alcohol Abuse and Alcoholism, 2000). Other personal factors include gender (with men still drinking more than women), high school bingeing, current drug or alcohol use, and attaching little importance to religion in college all raising the likelihood of college binge drinking (Wechsler, Dowdall, Davenport, & Castillo, 1995). Other factors are components of the college environment. Students who misperceive the amount of drinking on a campus may drink more than those who accurately perceive the norms. Students who are part of the social worlds of athletics or fraternities and sororities drink more, while students who think religion should be an important part of their college lives or who regularly perform community service drink less. The alcohol environment on and off campus plays an important role, with the cost, availability, and promotion of alcohol products also play an important role in shaping how much drinking takes place (Wechsler & Nelson 2008)

Figure 9.1 hardly exhausts the factors that shape college drinking, but it does support the important argument that what may seem like a purely individual choice – to drink, or to binge drink – is shaped by many factors including some that are part of a larger context. Research about college drinking and interventions to change college drinking need to take into account this broader view by "widening the lens and sharpening the focus" on all of these precollege and college factors, not merely the traits of the individual student (Dowdall & Wechsler, 2002).

Binge drinking varies greatly from college to college. Figure 9.2 presents the percent binge drinking among students at the 140 colleges in the original CAS study, but a very similar pattern has marked each of the CAS surveys. At one college, almost no students binge, while more than 70 percent do so at the top campus. About one-third of the schools had more than 50 percent of their students defined as binge drinkers. Figure 9.2 helps make the important point that there is no single pattern of binge drinking that describes college students in general, with each campus having its unique configuration.

Many factors, ranging from personal traits and values to campus characteristics and public policy, shape college drinking. Moreover, colleges vary greatly in how much binge drinking occurs among their students, with some having virtually no binge drinkers and others having a significant majority of binge drinking. Having described patterns of drinking among college students, we now turn to the crucial question of what are the health and behavioral consequences of college drinking.

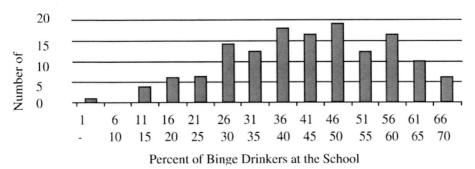

Figure 9.2. Distribution of Colleges by Percent of Binge Drinkers.
Source: Adapted from Wechsler, Davenport, Dowdall, Moeykens, & Castillo, 1994.

Consequences of College Student Drinking

Many adults view binge drinking as a harmless rite of passage, but the CAS and other studies point to a darker reality. The National Institute on Alcohol Abuse and Alcoholism's (NIAAA) *Task Force on College Drinking* (NIAAA, 2002a) commissioned extensive studies of the issue, which in turn have been updated (e.g., Hingson, Heeren, Winter, & Wechsler, 2005; Hingson et al., 2009).[5] The NIAAA (2012) published a snapshot of the impact of college drinking on student health, wellness, and academic success. The consequences of excessive and underage drinking affect virtually all college campuses, college communities, and college students, whether they choose to drink or not:

- **Death:** 1,825 college students between the ages of 18 and 24 die from alcohol-related unintentional injuries, including motor vehicle crashes (Hingson et al., 2009).
- **Injury:** 599,000 students between the ages of 18 and 24 are unintentionally injured under the influence of alcohol (Hingson et al., 2009).
- **Assault:** 696,000 students between the ages of 18 and 24 are assaulted by another student who has been drinking (Hingson et al., 2009).
- **Sexual Abuse:** 97,000 students between the ages of 18 and 24 are victims of alcohol-related sexual assault or date rape (Hingson et al., 2009).
- **Unsafe Sex:** 400,000 students between the ages of 18 and 24 had unprotected sex and more than 100,000 students between the ages of 18 and 24 report having been too intoxicated to know if they consented to having sex (Hingson et al., 2009).
- **Academic Problems:** About 25 percent of college students report academic consequences of their drinking including missing class, falling behind, doing poorly on exams or papers, and receiving lower grades overall (Engs et al., 1996; Presley, Meilman, & Cashin, 1996a; Presley,

Meilman, Cashin, & Lyerla, 1996b; Wechsler et al., 2002).

- **Health Problems/Suicide Attempts:** More than 150,000 students develop an alcohol-related health problem (Hingson et al., 2009), and between 1.2 and 1.5 percent of students indicate that they tried to commit suicide within the past year due to drinking or drug use (Presley, Meilman, & Cashin, 1996a; Presley, Meilman, Cashin, & Lyerla, 1996b).
- **Drunk Driving:** 3,360,000 students between the ages of 18 and 24 drive under the influence of alcohol (Hingson et al., 2009).
- **Vandalism:** About 11 percent of college student drinkers report that they have damaged property while under the influence of alcohol (Wechsler et al., 2002).
- **Property Damage:** More than 25 percent of administrators from schools with relatively low drinking levels and over 50 percent from schools with high drinking levels say their campuses have a "moderate" or "major" problem with alcohol-related property damage (Wechsler et al., 1995).
- **Police Involvement:** About 5 percent of four-year college students are involved with the police or campus security as a result of their drinking (Wechsler et al., 2002), and 110,000 students between the ages of 18 and 24 are arrested for an alcohol-related violation such as public drunkenness or driving under the influence (Hingson et al., 2009).
- **Alcohol Abuse and Dependence:** 31 percent of college students met criteria for a diagnosis of alcohol abuse and 6 percent for a diagnosis of alcohol dependence in the past 12 months, according to questionnaire-based self-reports about their drinking (Knight et al., 2002).

Table 9.2 presents CAS data on alcohol related problems, including ties between alcohol abuse and campus crime victimization. A significant minority of American college students report very troubling alcohol-related problems. From 1998 to 2005, the proportion of students who drove under the influence of alcohol during the past year rose from 26.5 percent to 28.9 percent (Hingson et al., 2009). One in ten report damaging property and the same proportion are hurt or injured because of their own drinking. Over 6 percent say that they have gotten into trouble with campus or local police because of their drinking. Each one of these outcomes is very strongly associated with the level of alcohol consumption, with those who are frequent binge drinkers much more likely to report victimization than are infrequent binge drinkers; non-binge drinkers are least likely to report being crime victims.

Another large survey of college students sheds additional light on the question of alcohol-related victimization. Unlike the Harvard CAS data cited earlier, data collected by the American College Health Association in its National College Health Assessment (NACHA) are not based on a representative sample of colleges and universities, but only those institutions who are mem-

Table 9.2

College Students who Drank Alcohol who Reported the Following Consequences Occurring in the Last 12 Months as a Result of their Drinking, Spring 2010

Consequences	Male Percent	Female Percent	Total Percent
Did something you later regretted	35.3	34.2	34.6
Forgot where you were or what you did	33.1	29	30.4
Got in trouble with the police	5.4	2.6	3.6
Had sex with someone without giving your consent	1.6	2.4	2.1
Had sex with someone without getting their consent	0.7	0.3	0.5
Had unprotected sex	18.7	15.2	16.5
Physically injured yourself	16.4	13.9	14.9
Physically injured another person	3.8	1.5	2.3
Seriously considered suicide	1.9	1.5	1.7
Reported one or more of the above	52.8	48.7	50.1

Note: Students responding "N/A, don't drink" were excluded from this analysis.
Source: http://www.acha-ncha.org/pubs_rpts.html, accessed 9/27/11.

bers of ACHA and who chose to participate in the survey and were part of the reference group assembled by ACHA researchers.[6] Frequently the survey is not given to a representative sample of students at each school but is distributed in classes whose instructors choose to do so. Nonetheless, the NACHA data are collected at 39 institutions (both public and private, and both two- and four-year colleges) across the country with a large number of student participants. In the Fall 2010 reference group, for example, the NACHA survey had 30,093 undergraduate respondents with an overall response rate of 31 percent. Table 9.2 presents NACHA survey data for Spring of 2010. Trend data on NACHA are not presented here because in Fall 2008 the survey's design was changed and comparing data points before and after this point might be misleading

Another data set (Table 9.3), the CORE surveys for 1993 to 2002, show that many students experienced threats of physical violence (9.6%), ethnic or racial harassment (5.7%), actual physical violence (4.7%), forced sexual touching or fondling (5.0%), or theft involving force or threat of force (47.9%). Many students reported that they had consumed alcohol or drugs before the incident. Except for ethnic or racial harassment, prior alcohol use by the victim powerfully links to risk of victimization. To be sure, no one but the perpetrator of a crime is responsible for that crime, and these data should not be used to "blame the victim." Nevertheless, the data clearly suggest how alcohol use is associated with a higher likelihood of victimization as well as other consequences (Perkins, 2002).

Alcohol is associated with a wide range of problematic outcomes among college students. More than 1,800 students die each year because of drinking. Hundreds of thousands of other students are affected either because of their

Table 9.3
Students Self-Reporting Criminal Victimization
and Substance Use Prior to Victimization

Type of Victimization	Reported Being a Victim (Percent)	Consumed Drugs or Alcohol Prior to Victimization (Percent)
Threat of Physical Violence	9.6	34.2
Ethnic or Racial Harassment	5.7	13.5
Actual Physical Violence	4.7	67.3
Forced Sexual Touching or Fondling	5.0	74.0
Theft Involving Force or Threat of Force (Robbery)	1.9	47.9

Source: Pastore & Maguire 2003. (http://www.albany.edu/sourcebook, accessed 3/3/06).

own drinking or because of the secondhand effects of others' drinking. The next section examines one of the most serious consequences of alcohol abuse, rape, and sexual assault among college women.

Alcohol Use/Abuse and Rape Among College Women

Arguably one of the most serious forms of alcohol-related crime on campus is rape, so this section presents data on the extent of rape, including rape when a woman is too drunk to give consent to sex, termed "intoxicated rape" (Mohler-Kuo, Dowdall, Koss, & Wechsler, 2004). Like other forms of violence against women, research has implicated rape as an outcome of alcohol consumption in many settings (Abbey, 2002, 2011; Bachar & Koss, 2001; Renzetti, Edleson, & Bergen, 2011). The number of reports of rape on college campuses is clearly the small tip of a large iceberg. For a number of reasons, women rape victims do not usually report their victimizations to the campus or community police, especially when alcohol is involved (Koss, Gidycz, & Wisniewski, 1987; Wolitzky-Taylor et al., 2011).

A Department of Justice-sponsored study (Fisher et al., 2000) estimated that the chances of a woman experiencing a rape during her undergraduate studies were between one in four and one in five. Koss and colleagues (Koss et al., 1987) found that more than 15 percent of college women had experienced a completed rape, and another 12 percent an attempted rape, since age 14. Abbey (2002, 2011) reviewed research reporting similar prevalence rates, and noted that alcohol-related sexual assault was a common problem, with alcohol associated with more than half of college sexual assaults on women. After reviewing the alcohol-sexual assault research, Abbey (2002, p. 125) argued that alcohol increased the likelihood of sexual assault through several related pathways, including ". . . beliefs about alcohol, deficits in higher order cognitive processing and motor impairments induced by alcohol and peer group norms that encourage heavy drinking and forced sex."

Using data from the 1997, 1999, and 2001 CAS surveys of students attending 119 colleges and universities, Mohler-Kuo, Dowdall, Koss, & Wechsler (2004) assessed the correlates of rape while intoxicated among a large national cross-section of over 25,000 women students at four-year schools. Questions that conformed to the legal definition of rape in many states were included to indicate forced rape ("Since the beginning of the school year, have you ever had sexual intercourse against your wishes because someone used force?"); rape while threatened ("Apart from question 1, since the beginning of the school year, have you had sexual intercourse against your wishes because someone threatened to harm you?"); and rape while intoxicated ("Apart from questions 1 and 2, since the beginning of the school year, have you had sexual intercourse when you were so intoxicated that you were unable to consent?"). The CAS surveys' possible responses ("0 times, 1 time, 2 times, 3 or more times") were dichotomized into "yes" or "no."

Table 9.4
Prevalence of Rape Since the Beginning of the School Year

	Year			
Type of Rape	*All years (%)* *(n=23,980)*	*1997 (%)* *(n=8,567)*	*1999 (%)* *(n=8,425)*	*2001 (%)* *(n=6,988)*
Any Type	4.7	5.1	4.5	4.3
While Intoxicated	3.4	3.6	3.4	3.2
Forced	1.9	2.1	1.8	1.7
Threatened	0.4	0.5	0.3	0.3

Source: Mohler-Kuo, Dowdall, Koss, & Wechsler (2004).

Table 9.4 presents the prevalence of these types of rape based on asking women during the spring semester whether they had sex without consent "since the beginning of the school year," a period on average of about seven months. Roughly, one in 20 college women have been raped in that short time period, with 72 percent of those raped experiencing rape while intoxicated, the most frequent form of rape. Except for rape by threat, there were no significant differences across the three surveys.

Women who went to colleges with medium and high binge-drinking rates had more than a 150 percent increased chance of being raped while intoxicated than did women from institutions with lower binge drinking rates. Other factors that raised the risk of rape included being under the age of 21, being white, residing in sorority houses, using illicit drugs, and having binge drank in college. According to Mohler-Kuo et al. (2004, p. 43), these findings have important implications for prevention programs:

College prevention programs must give increased attention to educating male students that one of the first questions they must ask themselves before initiating sex with a woman is whether she is capable of giving consent . . . College men must be educated for their own protection that intoxication is a stop sign for sex. College women need to be warned not only about the vulnerability created by heavy drinking, but also about the extra dangers imposed in situations where many other people are drinking heavily. The person who commits rape is, of course, responsible in both the legal and the moral sense, and we must view rape from that perspective. For purposes of prevention, however, identifying the factors that place women at increased vulnerability to rape is also important.

The reporting of campus crime remains a major challenge, even after the passage of the *Clery Act* in 1990 (Fisher & Sloan, 2007; Sloan & Fisher 2011). This is particularly problematic in the case or rape and sexual assault. A telephone survey of 2,000 women at four-year colleges found that 230 had experienced rape (Wolitzky-Taylor et al., 2011). But only 16 percent of forcible rape victims had filed a formal report with law enforcement. Less than 3 percent of women who had experienced incapacitated rape or drug or alcohol-facilitated rape had made formal reports. The most common form of nonconsensual sex among college women is also virtually never reported to the authorities and college women are less likely to report rape than noncollege women.

Alcohol is clearly present in many of the crimes of violence among college students, and in more than seven of ten rapes that occur among college women. The powerful correlation of alcohol abuse and rape victimization is one of the most robust findings about the consequences of college drinking. However, does its presence indicate that it is a cause of violence? The next section examines this controversial question.

Is Alcohol a Cause of College Student Violence?

The data presented so far make a strong case for a powerful correlation between alcohol and crime among individual college students and among campuses. However, is there a *causal* link between alcohol and crime? The question is not merely of academic concern. If the two are causally linked, then there would be strong evidence supporting the thesis that preventing crime on campus depends in part on somehow lowering the rate of alcohol abuse. If no causal link exists, reigning in binge drinking might have no effect on crime rates.

The question of whether alcohol is a *cause* of violence provokes considerable controversy, at least in part because it may inadvertently shift attention away from the issue of the criminal responsibility of the perpetrator. It is also controversial because of the difficulty of establishing causality in the social sciences. Some observers (e.g., Abbey, 2002, 2011) claim alcohol and drug use and criminal events are closely, even causally, linked, while others argue that there is almost no relationship or "less than meets the eye" (e.g., Collins, 1989; Giancola, 2002; Martin, 1992, 1993).

To establish causality, a researcher needs to provide three pieces of evidence. First, time order (temporal priority) needs to be established: changes in alcohol use must precede changes in crime. Second, the researcher must demonstrate that alcohol and crime co-occur. Finally, the researcher must eliminate other possible causal factors; in other words, the researcher has to remove the possibility that some third factor brings about both alcohol use and crime.

While the data presented earlier make a powerful case for correlation, no research has yet proved definitively a causal link between alcohol use and crime on college campuses or among college students. However, the fact that research has found this same correlation among noncollege populations strengthens the case for the causal link at the college level (Fagan, 1993; Greenfield, 1998). Abbey (2011) has explored how alcohol might be associated with sexual assault among college students. Establishing time order would help understand this relationship. For example, instead of alcohol consumption causing sexual assault, the reverse could be true: men consumed alcohol before perpetrating assault to provide an excuse for their criminal behavior. Finally, eliminating rival causal hypotheses would increase confidence in the alcohol-rape connection. For example, some third factor such as peer group norms that promote heavy drinking and the perpetration of sexual assault might explain the correlation and therefore negate a possible causal link. Research cannot yet present a definitive answer to these questions, given methodological limitations in the studies of sexual assault reviewed by Abbey (2011). For similar reasons, considerable controversy exists in the broader scientific literature about whether a causal link exists between alcohol use/abuse and violence (National Institute on Alcohol Abuse and Alcoholism, 2000). Evidence that at least part of the relationship between alcohol and physical and sexual assault and alcohol and delinquent behavior is nonspurious and is in fact causal has been presented with both American and European data (Felson & Burchfield 2004; Felson, Savolainen, Aaltonen, & Moustgaard, 2008). Recent collections of research about alcohol and violence are also consistent with the argument that alcohol plays a causal role.[7]

If alcohol plays a causal role in much, if not most, of the violence among college students then preventing alcohol abuse *must* become part of the effort to lower crime among students. Put another way, without dealing with the high rates of alcohol abuse among college students, can institutions make progress to lower campus crime? How can colleges reduce rates of alcohol abuse and thus lower the risk of crime? The next section examines what research shows about preventing college student abuse of alcohol.

Preventing Binge Drinking and Alcohol-Related Crime

Studying the link between college alcohol use and campus crime is important in its own right, but the hope is that researchers can use that knowledge to figure out ways of reducing the amount of college crime.

This section examines how to prevent college alcohol abuse. A reasonable working assumption is that high rates of alcohol abuse among college students relate to substantial amounts of college crime. Put another way, it will be difficult to make much progress against certain kinds of college crime – particularly violence against women and vandalism on campus – unless something is first done to lower the rates of alcohol abuse. Research shows that purely educational efforts against both violence and alcohol abuse fail (Bachar & Koss, 2001; NIAAA, 2002a, 2002b). What researchers need is a fresh line of thought that explores linking them. On a more theoretical level, Abbey (2011) has presented some important ideas about how alcohol and sexual violence might be connected. On a practical level, Langford (2005, 2006) offers suggestions about how administrators and activists can attack the roots of much campus crime, in part, by reducing abusive drinking. A particularly important set of findings from the NIAAA task force report concerns what works, or shows promise of working, in lowering the risk of college drinking. The NIAAA report divides strategies into four tiers, based on how much evidence supports their efficacy, according to a review by a panel of experts of published studies about prevention. The following discussion highlights the main findings from the original NIAAA Report (2002a) and its more recent update (NIAAA, 2007).

Different Strategies

Tier one comprises strategies with evidence of effectiveness among college students who are problem, at-risk, or alcohol-dependent drinkers. This tier includes several strategies:

- Combining cognitive-behavioral skills training with norms clarification and motivational enhancement interventions.
- Offering brief motivational enhancement interventions.
- Challenging alcohol expectancies.

One of the best known of these programs is called BASICS (Brief Alcohol Screening and Intervention for College Students):

BASICS is administered in the form of two individual sessions in which students are provided feedback about their drinking behavior and given the opportunity to negotiate a plan for change based on the principles of motivational interviewing. High-risk drinkers who participated in the BASICS program significantly reduced both drinking problems and alcohol consumption rates, compared to control group participants, at both the 2-year follow-up . . . and 4-year outcome assessment periods. BASICS has also been found to be clinically significant in an analysis of individual student drinking changes over time . . . (National Institute on Alcohol Abuse and Alcoholism, 2002a, p. 17)

Tier two strategies consist of those for which there is evidence of success with general populations and that could be applied to college environments. This tier includes strategies such as:

- Increased enforcement of minimum legal drinking age laws.
- Implementation, increased publicity, and enforcement of other laws to reduce alcohol-impaired driving.
- Restrictions on alcohol retail outlet density.
- Increased price and excise taxes on alcoholic beverages.
- Responsible beverage service policies in social and commercial settings.
- The formation of a campus and community coalition involving all major stakeholders.

These strategies seek to change the broader environment, with many affecting not only college students, but also underage persons who are not in college.

A primary example of a Tier two strategy is increasing the minimum legal drinking age (MLDA). An examination of 241 empirical analyses of changes in MLDA that were published between 1960 and 2000 shows powerful evidence of an inverse relationship between the MLDA and both alcohol consumption and traffic accidents (Wagenaar & Toomey, 2002). The MLDA is effective in spite of minimal enforcement – public policies of this type have an impact on problematic drinking and alcohol-related problems among college students; considerable evidence backs the contention that a lowering of the drinking age would likely result in increased harm (Wechsler & Nelson, 2010).

Tier three strategies include those showing evidence of logical and theoretical promise, but which require comprehensive evaluations to establish their effectiveness. Among these strategies are:

- Campus-based policies and practices that appear to be capable of reducing high-risk alcohol use, including eliminating keg parties, banning alcohol on campus, and expanding alcohol-free events.
- Increased enforcement at campus-based events that promote excessive drinking.

- Increased publicity about and enforcement of underage drinking laws on campus and eliminating "mixed messages."
- Conducting marketing campaigns to correct student misperception about alcohol use.

Among the strategies listed in this tier are attempts to change the social norms about drinking that students perceive to be prevalent on a campus, usually via a marketing campaign that contrasts actual drinking behavior with perceived drinking behavior. Proponents of this approach claim to have had success in lowering drinking, but evidence published so far remains below the level necessary to label the approach a proven, as opposed to a promising strategy. One major study found that the approach was particularly ineffective at campuses where alcohol consumption is high and alcohol is available at many outlets (Scribner et al., 2008).

Tier four lists strategies shown to be ineffective when used alone include:

- Informational, knowledge-based, or values clarification interventions about alcohol and the problems related to its excessive use, when used along.
- Providing blood alcohol content feedback to students.

Purely informational programs assume that students lack the knowledge of the effects of alcohol, and that providing them with more information will change their behavior; by contrast, moving toward broader changes in the environment does change behavior (DeJong & Langford, 2002). Yet purely informational programs remain perhaps the most popular response to college drinking problems.

A decade ago, the NIAAA *Task Force Report* (NIAAA, 2002a,2002b; see also Goldman, Boyd, & Faden, 2002) provided support for moving from purely educational interventions (with limited or no evidence of effectiveness) to environmental strategies that have been proven effective (e.g., DeJong & Langford, 2002). NIAAA has updated evidence about successful interventions (2007; DeJong, Larimer, Wood, & Hartman, 2009). One significant research finding was the demonstration that comprehensive environmental interventions (like the American Medical Association's "A Matter of Degree" or AMOD Program) can be effective in lowering the health and behavioral consequences of excessive college drinking (Weitzman, Nelson, Lee, & Wechsler, 2004). Comparison of those campuses that implemented the AMOD environmental interventions most fully showed small but statistically significant decreases in alcohol consumption and in alcohol-related harms, including criminal victimization, when compared with those institutions that had not properly implemented the AMOD program. Interventions funded by NIAAA were shown to add effective new ways of dealing with excessive alcohol consumption (DeJong et al., 2009). A popular online program called Alcohol.edu was shown to have small but significant effects in tempering student drinking in the early months of attending college. Research at public universities in California confirmed that effective community interventions could bring down problematic behavior associated with heavy alcohol consumption off campus (Saltz, Paschall, McGaffigan, & Nygaard, 2010).

This section has summarized the NIAAA Task Force Report's findings about the effectiveness of different college prevention strategies. A critical issue concerns the validity of the general assumption that broad environmental management strategies (that might include combinations of Tiers one through three) will probably have the best effects on college populations (DeJong & Langford, 2002).[8] A mixture of countermeasures will probably work better than one single prevention approach.

In addition to efforts to intervene with individual college students, research began to suggest an even broader public health approach that targets environmental change and public policy might be effective. Additional recent research shows that "the state sets the rate," that across the U.S. states (constitutionally charged with alcohol policy development, for the most part) public policies and effective enforcement play an important role in lowering the rate of binge drinking; whether such policies change alcohol-related crime remains to be tested (Nelson, Naimi, Brewer, & Wechsler, 2005). An international research team developed a powerful argument that public alcohol policy could shape alcohol consumption, recognizing that alcohol was "no ordinary commodity" (Babor, 2010). Research suggested that national alcohol policy accounted for significant differences in youth alcohol consumption (Paschall, Grube, & Kypri, 2009).

Conclusion

There is a powerful link between alcohol use/abuse and crime. Data consistently show that individual college students who report binge drinking are much more likely to be either the victims or the perpetrators of crime. Campuses with high rates of binge drinking and surrounded by many alcohol outlets also experience relatively higher rates of criminal victimization. At a time when societal-wide rates of crime have fallen significantly, campus alcohol related crimes such as rape appear stable, probably reflecting the largely unchanged rate of alcohol abuse among college students.

A great deal has been learned about college drinking and its health and behavioral consequences, including evidence consistent with a causal link between alcohol and crime victimization (Dowdall, 2013). Interventions have been demonstrated to work with individual college students and general populations. But colleges have lagged behind the science, either continuing to use ineffective programs or failing to adopt evidence-based ones (Nelson et al., 2009).

In the case of rape and sexual assault, and particularly when alcohol is involved, few victims report incidents. Rape prevention programs often ignore or downplay the role of alcohol, (Bachar & Koss, 2001).One higher education newspaper published a story whose title points to the problem:"Rape-prevention programs proliferate, but 'it's hard to know' whether they work." (Fogg, 2009). A plausible reason for this failure is ignoring the powerful role of alcohol in affecting the aggression of perpetrators, the vulnerability of victims, the reporting of crime, and the exoneration of perpetrators including serial rapists (Lisak & Miller, 2002).

A decade has now elapsed since the path breaking NIAAA Task Force Study on College Drinking. Clearly, its influential framework for establishing tiers needs updating. Social norms programs may be ineffective (and not promising, as ranked in 2002) at precisely those types of institutions, high binge colleges, where they were most needed. Looking solely at individual campuses and their cultures ignores the role that state policy and policy enforcement play (Nelson et al., 2005).

One of the first tangible products of U.S. health care reform, the *Affordable Care Act of 2010,* was a new National Prevention Strategy, which identifies drug abuse and excessive alcohol use as one of the top targets for prevention (National Prevention Council, 2011). Particularly noteworthy are the clear emphasis on college drinking as an issue and the shift toward a broad environmental approach (including public policy changes).

The recent "Dear Colleague" letter from the Department of Education to all higher education institutions underscores how much work needs to be done to guarantee student safety and security (Ali, 2011). The letter notes that *Title IX* of the Education Acts of 1972 prohibits discrimination on the basis of sex in educational programs receiving federal funds, and then argues that sexual harassment and sexual violence (including sex against a person's will or when incapacitated by drugs or alcohol) falls under this prohibition. The letter suggests that each institution's *Title IX* coordinator be trained on the "link between alcohol and drug abuse and sexual harassment and violence and best practices to address that link." As they work to implement this new mandate, colleges can draw on a growing body of evidence about how to prevent campus crime and lower substance abuse (Sloan & Fisher, 2011; Dowdall, 2013).

Changing the culture of alcohol use on college campuses will be neither easy nor simple, and commitment to change should be realistic and assume the necessity of long-term efforts. A major obstacle remains how differently perceived and organizationally situated issues like campus crime, sexual assault and rape, and binge drinking are in the contemporary university (Sloan & Fisher, 2011). Progress will also depend on changes in policy and policy enforcement at the county, community, and state level. But there is a glimmer of hope. By better understanding the alcohol-crime connection, we can begin to field interventions that will lower both the rates of binge drinking and the rates of crime. Some crime on campus has little to do with binge drinking, so one should not cast alcohol abuse reduction in the role of panacea. Nonetheless, environmental interventions offer evidence of successfully reducing both alcohol abuse and its primary and secondary consequences, including college student victimization (Langford, 2006). College administrators who specialize in addressing crime, sexual assault, or alcohol abuse should forge partnerships to address more effectively, the alcohol-crime connection.

NOTES

1. I wish to thank the following people for their help or suggestions: Antonia Abbey, Catherine Bath, Kathleen Bogle, Amber Chase, Fred Donodeo, Bonnie Fisher, Alison Kiss, Mary Koss, Linda Langford, Maureen Rush, John Sloan, and Henry Wechsler. Any errors that remain are entirely mine.

2. The Department of Education website http://www.ope.ed.gov/security/, presents data on reported campus crime and alcohol and drug violations at thousands of institutions of higher learning across the country. Dowdall (2013) presents data on alcohol and crime for almost 400 individual U.S. colleges and universities.

3. It is difficult to compare *Clery Act* data over time because of changes in *Clery*-related crime definitions and requirements. *Clery Act*-related alcohol violations do *not* include public drunkenness, underage drinking, or driving under the influence and thus represent only some of the alcohol-related crime. The data on liquor law violations were taken from http://www.securityoncampus. org/crimestats/index htm (retrieved 6/01/06).

4. For a review of natural and social science research about alcohol use and abuse, see the National Institute on Alcohol Abuse and Alcoholism (2000). For comprehensive review of the literature about college student drinking, see Goldman, Boyd, and Faden (2002) and Dowdall (2013).

5. Readers interested in an extensive discussion should go to its website, http://www.collegedrinking prevention.gov, which contains its final report, a special supplement of the *Journal of Studies on Alcohol;* a series of reports about the question, and updates.

6. For a full discussion of the Core Survey and its basic findings, see http://www.siu.edu/departments/coreinst/public_html/.

7. See *Contemporary Drug Problems,* vol. 38, no. 2, Summer 2011 and *Drug and Alcohol Review,* vol. 30, no. 5, Sept. 2011.

8. Readers interested in more detailed examination of the alcohol – crime link on college campuses might want to explore the website of the Higher Education Center (http://www.edc.org/hec) which is funded by the U.S. Department of Education. Its website provides many documents about the scope of alcohol and other drug use as

well as summaries and a searchable database of recent research. Another helpful website is provided by the campus watchdog Security on Campus, which recently changed its name to the *Clery Center on Campus Safety* (http://www.securityoncampus.org/). See Dowdall (2013) for a comprehensive listing of websites about college drinking.

REFERENCES

Abbey, A. (2002). Alcohol-related sexual assault: A common problem among college students. *Journal of Studies on Alcohol Supplement No. 14,* 118–128.

Abbey, A. (2011). Alcohol's role in sexual violence perpetration: Theoretical explanations, existing evidence and future directions. *Drug and Alcohol Review, 30,* 481–489.

Ali, R. (2011). *"Dear Colleague" letter on Title IX compliance.* Washington, DC: United States Department of Education.

Bachar, K., & Koss, M. P. (2001). From prevalence to prevention: Closing the gap between what we know about rape and what we do. In C. M. Renzetti, J. L. Edelson & R. K. Bergen (Eds.), *Sourcebook of violence against women* (pp. 117–142). Thousand Oaks, CA: Sage.

Baum, K., & Klaus, P. (2005). *Violent victimization of college students: 1995–2002.* Washington, DC: United States Department of Justice, Office of Justice Programs.

Babor, T. (2010). *Alcohol: No ordinary commodity* (revised edition). Oxford: Oxford University Press.

Centers for Disease Control and Prevention. (2012). Binge drinking. *CDC Vital Signs.* Atlanta, GA: Centers for Disease Control and Prevention.

Chronicle of Higher Education (2011). *Annual Almanac.* August 26, 2011.

Collins, J. (1989). Alcohol and interpersonal violence: Less than meets the eye. In N. A. Weiner & M. E. Wolfgang (Eds.), *Pathways to criminal violence* (pp. 49–67). Newbury Park, CA: Sage.

Commission on Substance Abuse at Colleges and Universities. (1994). *Rethinking rites of passage: Substance abuse on America's campuses.* New York: Columbia University.

DeJong, W., Larimer, M. E., Wood, M. D., & Hartman, R. (2009). NIAAA's rapid response to college drinking problems initiative: Reinforcing the use of evidence-based approaches in college alcohol prevention. *Journal of Studies on Alcohol and Drugs, Supplement No. 16,* 5–11.

DeJong, W., & Langford, L. M. (2002). A typology for campus-based alcohol prevention: Moving toward environmental management strategies. *Journal of Studies on Alcohol, Supplement No. 14,* 140–147.

Dowdall, G. W. (2013). *College drinking: Reframing a social problem / Changing the culture.* Sterling, VA: Stylus.

Dowdall, G. W. (2006). How public alcohol policy shapes prevention. In R. J. Chapman (Ed.), *When they drink: Practitioner views and lessons learned on preventing high-risk collegiate drinking* (p. 80–96). Glassboro, NJ: Rowan University.

Dowdall, G. W., & Wechsler, H. (2002). Studying college alcohol use: Widening the lens, sharpening the focus. *Journal of Studies on Alcohol, Supplement No. 14,* 14–22.

Engs, R. C., & Hanson, D. J. (1994). Boozing and brawling on campus: A national study of violent problems associated with drinking over the past decade. *Journal of Criminal Justice, 22,* 171–180.

Engs, R. C., Diebold, B. A., & Hansen, D. J. (1996). The drinking patterns and problems of a national sample of college students, 1994. *Journal of Alcohol and Drug Education, 41,* 13–33.

Fagan, J. (1993). Interactions among drugs, alcohol, and violence. *Health Affairs, 12,* 65–79.

Felson, R. B., & Burchfield, K. B. (2004). Alcohol and the risk of physical and sexual assault victimization. *Criminology, 42,* 837–860.

Felson, R., Savolainen, J., Aaltonen, M., & Moustgaard, H. (2008). Is the association between alcohol use and delinquency causal or spurious? *Criminology, 46,* 785–808.

Fisher, B. S., Cullen, F. T., & Turner, M. G. (2000). *The sexual victimization of college women.* (NCJ 182369). Washington, DC: National Institute of Justice.

Fisher, B. S., & Sloan III, J. J. (Eds.). (1995). *Campus crime: Legal, social, and policy perspectives.* Springfield, IL: Charles C Thomas.

Fisher, B. S., & Sloan III, J. J. (Eds.). (2005). *Campus crime: Legal, social, and policy perspectives* (2nd ed.). Springfield, IL: Charles C Thomas.

Fisher, B. S., Sloan III, J. J., Cullen, F. T., & Lu, C. (1998). Crime in the ivory tower: The level and sources of student victimization. *Criminology, 36,* 671–710.

Fogg, P. (2009). Rape-prevention programs proliferate, but "It's hard to know" whether they work. *Chronicle of Higher Education,* November 15, 2009.

Giancola, P. R. (2002). Alcohol-related aggression during the college years: Theories, risk factors and policy implications. *Journal of Studies on Alcohol, Supplement No. 14,* 129–139.

Goldman, M. S., Boyd, G. M., & Faden, V. (2002). College drinking, what it is, and what to do about it: A review of the state of the science. *Journal of Studies on Alcohol, Supplement No. 14,* 23–37.

Greenfield, L. A. (1998). *Alcohol and crime: An analysis of national data on the prevalence of alcohol involvement in crime.* Washington, DC: United States Department of Justice.

Hart, T. C. (2003). *Violent victimization of college students.* Washington, DC: United States Department of Justice.

Herman, A. I., Philbeck, J. W., Vasilopoulos, N. L., & Depetrillo, P. B. (2003). Serotonin transporter promoter polymorphism and differences in alcohol consumption behaviour in a college student population. *Alcohol & Alcoholism, 38,* 446–449.

Hingson, R. W., Zha, W., & Weitzman, E. R. (2009). Magnitude of and trends in alcohol-related mortality and morbidity among U.S. college students ages 18–24, 1998–2005. *Journal of Studies on Alcohol and Drugs, Supplement No. 16,* 12–20.

Hingson, R., Heeren, T., Winter, M., & Wechsler, H. (2005). Magnitude of alcohol-related mortality and morbidity among U.S. college students ages 18–24: Changes from 1998 to 2001. *Annual Review of Public Health, 26,* 259–279.

Hoover, E. (2005). For the 12th straight year, arrests for alcohol rise on college campuses. *The Chronicle of Higher Education, 51,* June 24, 2005.

Knight, J. R., Wechsler, H., Kuo, M. C., Seibring, M., Weitzman, E. R., & Schuckit, M. A. (2002). Alcohol abuse and dependence among US college students. *Journal of Studies on Alcohol, 63,* 263–270.

Koss, M. P., Gidycz, C. A., & Wisniewski, N. (1987). The scope of rape. *Journal of Consulting and Clinical Psychology, 55,* 162–170.

Langford, L. (2005). *Preventing violence and promoting safety in higher education settings: Overview of a comprehensive approach.* Newton, MA: The Higher Education Center for Alcohol and Other Drug Abuse and Violence Prevention.

Langford, L. (2006). The role of alcohol and other drugs in campus violence prevention. *Catalyst, 7,* 206.

Lisak, D., & Miller, P. M. (2002). Repeat rape and multiple offending among undetected rapists. *Violence and victims, 17,* 73–84.

Martin, S. (Ed.) (1993). *Alcohol and interpersonal violence: Fostering multidisciplinary perspectives.* Rockville, MD: National Institute on Alcohol Abuse and Alcoholism.

Martin, S. (1992). The epidemiology of alcohol-related interpersonal violence. *Alcohol Health & Research World, 16,* 230–237.

McCabe, S. E., Knight, J. R., Teter, C. J., & Wechsler, H. (2005). Non-medical use of prescription stimulants among US college students: Prevalence and correlates from a national survey. *Addiction, 99,* 96–106.

Mohler-Kuo, M., Dowdall, G. W., Koss, M. P., & Wechsler, H. (2004). Correlates of rape while intoxicated in a national sample of college women. *Journal of Studies on Alcohol, 65,* 37–45.

Naimi, T. S., Brewer, R. D., Mokdad, A., Denny, C., Serdula, M. K., & Marks, J. S. (2003). Binge drinking among US adults. *Journal of the American Medical Association, 289,* 70–75.

National Institute on Alcohol Abuse and Alcoholism. (2000). *10th special report to the U.S. Congress on alcohol and health.* Rockville, MD: National Institute on Alcohol Abuse and Alcoholism.

National Institute on Alcohol Abuse and Alcoholism. (2002a). *A call to action: Changing the culture of drinking at U.S. colleges.* Rockville, MD: National Institute on Alcohol Abuse and Alcoholism.

National Institute on Alcohol Abuse and Alcoholism. (2002b). *Task force on college drinking: Final report of the panel on prevention and treatment – How to reduce high-risk college drinking.* Rockville, MD: National Institute on Alcohol Abuse and Alcoholism.

National Institute on Alcohol Abuse and Alcoholism. (2007). *What colleges need to know now: An update on college drinking research.* Rockville, MD: National Institute on Alcohol Abuse and Alcoholism.

National Institute on Alcohol Abuse and Alcoholism. (2012). *College drinking.* Rockville, MD: National Institute on Alcohol Abuse and Alcoholism.

National Prevention Council. (2011). *National prevention strategy.* Washington, DC: U.S. Department of Health and Human Services, Office of the Surgeon General.

Nelson, T. F., Naimi, T. S., Brewer, R. D., & Wechsler, H. (2005). The state sets the rate: The relationship among state-specific college binge drinking, state binge drinking rates, and selected state alcohol control policies. *American Journal of Public Health, 95,* 441–446.

Nelson, T. F., Xuan, Z., Lee, H., Weitzman, E. R., & Wechsler, H. (2009). Persistence of heavy drinking and ensuing consequences at heavy drinking colleges. *Journal of Studies on Alcohol and Drugs, 70,* 726–734.

Paschall, M. J., Grube, J. W., & Kypri, K. (2009). Alcohol control policies and alcohol consumption by youth: A multi-national study. *Addiction, 10,* 1849–1855.

Pastore, A. L., & Maguire, K. (Eds.) (2003). *Sourcebook of criminal justice statistics* [Online]. Retrieved from http://www.albany.edu/sourcebook.

Parker, R. N., & Rebhun, L. (1995). *Alcohol and homicide.* Albany, NY: State University of New York Press.

Perkins, H. W. (2002). Surveying the damage: A review of research on consequences of alcohol misuse in college populations. *Journal of Studies on Alcohol, Supplement No. 14,* 91–100.

Presley, C. A., Meilman, P. W., & Cashin, J. R. (1996a). *Alcohol and drugs on American college campuses: Use, consequences, and perceptions of the campus environment, Vol. IV: 1992–1994.* Carbondale, IL: Core Institute, Southern Illinois University.

Presley, C. A., Meilman, P. W., Cashin, J. R., & Lyerla, R. (1996b). *Alcohol and drugs on American college campuses: Use, consequences, and perceptions of the campus environment, Vol. III: 1991–1993.* Carbondale, IL: Core Institute, Southern Illinois University.

Renzetti, C. M., Edleson, J. L., & Bergen, R. K. (2011). *Sourcebook on violence against women* (2nd ed.). Los Angeles: Sage.

Robert Wood Johnson Foundation. (2001). *Substance abuse: The nation's number one health problem.* Princeton, NJ: Robert Wood Johnson Foundation.

Saltz, R. F., Paschall, M. J., McGaffigan, R. P., & Nygaard, P. M. O. (2010). Alcohol risk management in college settings: The Safer California Universities randomized trial. *American Journal of Preventive Medicine, 39,* 491–499.

Schwartz, M. D., & DeKeseredy, W. S. (1997). *Sexual assault on the college campus: The role of male peer support.* Thousand Oaks, CA: Sage.

Scribner, R., Mason, K. E., Simonsen, N. R., Theall, K., Chotalia, J., Johnson, S., Schneider, S. K., & DeJong, W. (2010). An ecological analysis of alcohol-outlet density and campus-reported violence at 32 U.S. colleges. *Journal of Studies on Alcohol and Drugs, 71,* 184–191.

Scribner, R., Mason, K., Theall, K., Simonsen, N., Schneider, S. K., Towvim, L. G., & DeJong, W. (2008). The contextual role of alcohol outlet density in college drinking. *Journal of Studies on Alcohol and Drugs, 69,* 112–120.

Security on Campus. (2006). *Campus Watch, 12,* 7.

SIUC/Core Institute. (2011). *Executive summary: Core alcohol and drug survey – Long form.* Carbondale, IL: SIUC/Core Institute.

Sloan, III, J. J., & Fisher, B. S. (2011). *The dark side of the ivory tower: Campus crime as a social problem.* New York: Cambridge University Press.

United States Department of Education, Office of Postsecondary Education. (2005). *The handbook for campus crime reporting.* Washington, DC: United States Department of Education.

United States Department of Education, Office of Postecondary Education. (2012). The campus safety and security data analysis cutting tool. Retrieved from http://ope.ed.gov/security/index.aspx.

Wagenaar, A. C., & Toomey, T. L. (2002). Effects of minimum drinking age laws: Review and analyses of the literature from 1960 to 2000. *Journal of Studies on Alcohol, Supplement No. 14,* 206–225.

Wechsler, H., Davenport, A., Dowdall, G., Moeykens, B., & Castillo, S. (1994). Health and behavioral consequences of binge drinking in college: A national survey of students at 140 colleges. *Journal of the American Medical Association, 272,* 1672–1677.

Wechsler, H., Dowdall, G., Davenport, A., & Rimm, E. (1995). A gender-specific measure of binge drinking among college students. *American Journal of Public Health, 85,* 982–985.

Wechsler, H., Dowdall, G., Davenport, A., & Castillo, S. (1995). Correlates of college student binge drinking. *American Journal of Public Health, 85,* 921–926.

Wechsler, H., Kuo, M., Lee, H., & Dowdall, G. W. (2000). Environmental correlates of underage alcohol use and related problems of college students. *American Journal of Preventive Medicine, 19,* 24–29.

Wechsler, H., Lee, J. E., Kuo, M., Seibring, M., Nelson, T. F., & Lee, H. P. (2002). Trends in college binge drinking during a period of increased prevention efforts: Findings from four Harvard School of Public Health study surveys, 1993–2001. *Journal of American College Health, 50,* 203–217.

Wechsler, H., & Nelson, T. F. (2008). What we have learned from the Harvard School of Public Health College Alcohol Study: Focusing attention on college student alcohol consumption and the environmental conditions that promote it. *Journal of Studies on Alcohol and Drugs, 69,* 481–90.

Wechsler, H., & Nelson, T. F. (2010). Will increasing alcohol availability by lowering the minimum legal drinking age decrease drinking and related consequences among youths? *American Journal of Public Health, 100,* 986–992.

Wechsler, H., & Wuetrich, B. (2002). *Dying to drink: Confronting binge drinking on college campuses.* Emmaus, PA: Rodale.

Weitzman, E. R., Nelson, T. F., Lee, H., & Wechsler, H. (2004). Reducing drinking and related harms in college: Evaluation of the A Matter of Degree Program. *American Journal of Preventive Medicine, 27,* 187–196.

Wolitzky-Taylor, K. B., Resnick, H. S., Armstadter, A. B., McCauley, J. L., Ruggiero, K. J., & Kilpatrick, D. G. (2011). Reporting rape in a national sample of college women. *Journal of American College Health, 59,* 582–587.

Chapter 10

VIOLENCE AGAINST WOMEN ON COLLEGE CAMPUSES: RAPE, INTIMATE PARTNER ABUSE, AND SEXUAL HARASSMENT

Joanne Belknap and Edna Erez

INTRODUCTION

Until the 1980s, most people assumed that college campuses were a safe environment for women. The little concern that existed for women's safety on campus was limited to stranger rapes, though these assaults are relatively rare compared to women's victimizations by men they know (Aizenman & Kelly, 1988; Lott, Reilly, & Howard, 1982; Reilly, Lott, Caldwell, & DeLuca, 1992; Roark, 1987; Warshaw, 1988).

Although intimate partner abuse (domestic violence), stranger rape, and sexual harassment were recognized as social problems at the beginning of the 1970s, it was not until the late 1970s and early 1980s that intimate partner abuse in dating relationships, acquaintance rapes (including "date rapes"), and the sexual harassment of college students began to receive attention (e.g., Aizenman & Kelly, 1988; Belknap & Erez, 1997; Koss, Gidycz, & Wisniewski, 1987; Makepeace, 1981; Project on the Status and Education of Women, 1978; Warshaw, 1988).

Victimizations of college women include various expressions of coercive sexuality in the social and institutional aspects of campus life: physical and sexual abuse in dating relationships, in student parties, and unethical sexual advances by professors and staff (Leidig, 1992). This chapter explores these phenomena. It presents the definitions and characteristics of aggression against college women, and addresses explanations for the frequency and persistence of these violations. It then reviews the dynamics of intimate partner abuse, acquaintance rape, and sexual harassment and their consequences for offenders and victims. Finally, the chapter discusses policy recommendations to deter and better respond to aggression against college women.

Defining the Concepts

Sexual harassment, rape, and intimate partner abuse are distinctively feminist issues. First, the victims of these offenses are predominantly women and the offenders are predominantly men. Furthermore, when females use physical aggression in intimate and dating relationships, it is rarely sexual, it is usually in self-defense (to fight back against male-initiated aggression), and the violence is generally far less extreme, injurious, and fear-inducing than the violence men direct against women (Belknap & Melton, 2005; Das Dasgupta, 2001; Lane & Gwartney-Gibbs, 1985; Makepeace, 1983, 1986; Molidor & Tolman, 1998; O'Keefe & Treister, 1998; Warner, 2010). Stated alternatively, when women are "violent" in dating and martial relationships, it is typically to resist abuse initiated by their male dates or partners. A recent study on college students' intimate partner abuse found men tend to initiate it, while women are more likely to be reacting to men's perpetrated intimate partner abuse (Allen, Swan, & Raghavan, 2009). Thus, the perspective guiding our analysis of women's sexual victimization on campus reflects the reality of the phenomenon, namely, that men commit the overwhelming majority of rapes, intimate partner abuses, and sexual harassments against women.

Historical Context and Concept Development

The phrases "sexual harassment" and "battered woman" did not exist until the 1970s, while the term "date rape" was not coined until the early 1980s. Although not named until the second wave of the women's movement, such behavior has been prevalent for centuries. For example, what we currently call acquaintance and date rape occurred with alarming frequency in England during the eighteenth and nineteenth centuries (Clark, 1987). Similarly, research from the 1950s (e.g., Kanin, 1957) reported the same rate of unwanted sexual contact (including rapes) on dates as research from the 1980s and 1990s. Early sexual harassment research in the 1970s focused on its occurrence in the workplace and only later was it extended to academic settings (Project on the Status and Education of Women, 1978). The lack of labels for violence and violations against women has resulted in their prolonged invisibility (Belknap, 2007). Persistent beliefs that sexual harassment is just "good fun" added to the behavior going unnoticed, as did the notion that sexual assault by one's date is not "real rape" but merely miscommunication or women changing their mind after the fact.

Since the 1970s, feminist activism on behalf of women helped reverse the invisibility of these phenomena, and revealed misconceptions about men's aggression toward women. Once social scientists and activists identified and labeled the behavior, they helped institute education programs and policies to deter and respond to these violations. However, one of the problems in identifying and responding to violence against women has been the ambiguity of definitions used for aggression and harassment including those used for intimate partner abuse or domestic abuse, sexual assaults, rape, and sexual harassment (see Fitzgerald, 1990; Rivera & Regoli, 1987). Are date rapes a form of acquaintance rape? Are sexual assaults during college parties instances of rape? Research, for instance, has documented that college women are most at risk of unwanted sexual contact (including rape) perpetrated by male acquaintances or friends, followed by boyfriends, and strangers (e.g., Banyard, Plante, Cohn, Moorhead, Ward, & Walsh, 2005; Ward, Chapman, White, & Williams, 1991). Additionally, research shows that many rapes and other types of sexual abuse that college women experience occurs during fraternity, dormitory, house, and apartment parties, and not necessarily on a date (Banyard et al., 2005; Black, Belknap, & Ginsberg, 2012; Boswell & Spade, 1996; Ehrhart & Sandler, 1985; Gwartney-Gibbs & Stockard, 1989; Martin & Hummer, 1989; Sanday, 1990; Schwartz & Nogrady, 1996; Ward et al., 1991; Warshaw, 1988).

For the purposes of this chapter, it is useful to make distinctions between sexual harassment, rape, and intimate partner abuse, at the same time that it is vital to understand the overlap among them. A professor's or a boss's sexual harassment of a student or employee can include inappropriate touching, sexual inquiries and comments, but it can also include a violent rape. A boyfriend, date, or husband can slap or hit a woman, but *he* can also rape her. Thus, while we make the distinctions between these types of abuses, it is important to remember that they are not always distinct.

Sexual harassment is a violation of *Title VII* of the *Civil Rights Act*, or in an educational context (a violation of the *Title IX* of the *Civil Rights Act*) (see Belknap & Erez, 1997). Brandenburg (1982) defined *sexual harassment* as "any attempt to coerce an unwilling person into a sexual relationship, or to subject a person to unwanted sexual attention, or to punish a refusal to comply." These behaviors range from "leering" and telling off color sexual jokes or making offensive sexual comments or inquiries, to violently forcing sex. Most commonly, however, both socially and legally, sexual harassment comprises inappropriate sexual behavior that occurs at work or in educational settings. It is useful to recognize that sexual harassment definitions in more recent years recognize that such behavior can be perpetrated not just by those with power over the victim (e.g., a professor or boss), but can also be perpetrated by peers (e.g., co-workers or "fellow" students).

This chapter refers to *rape* as nonconsensual oral, anal, or vaginal penetration or nonconsensual oral sex performed on another's genitals. Although such activities are typically thought of as "forceful" (see Estrich, 1987), it is important to remember that these sexual violations are often more "exploitative" and "coercive" than "forceful" (see Russell, 1984). For example, Estrich (1987) reports that the general public views "real rape" in terms of strangers jumping out of alleys and bushes and forcing penile-vaginal intercourse. While that is most certainly rape, so is having sex with someone too intoxicated from alcohol and/or debilitated by drugs (be they prescription, illegal recreational, or "date rape" drugs) to be able to consent to sexual activity. Research has identified a significant increase in recent years of what they labeled DFSA, or "drug facilitated sexual assaults" (McGregor, Lipowska, Shah, Du Mont, & De Siato, 2003). So-called "date rape drugs" such as rohypnol (commonly referred to as "roofies") and gamma hydroxyl-butyrate ("GHB") are often slipped into women's drinks by sexual predators (often known to the women, or men they meet at bars or parties) with the precise goal of causing unconsciousness and loss of memory so that they can be sexually abused (McGregor et al., 2003). While these sexual acts (rapes) are not always *per se* violent, they are most certainly *violating, coercive, and illegal.*

The final victimization of college women covered in this chapter is that of *intimate partner abuse:* the physical, sexual and/or emotional/psychological abuse committed by a current or former date, lover, boy/girlfriend, or spouse (see Belknap & Potter, 2006). While the public often minimize emotional/psychological abuse of partners, it can devastate victims. Examples of this type of abuse include a boyfriend who physically assaults his girlfriend, but threatens to harm himself if she breaks up with him or flirts with another man; a male student who does not physically assault his girlfriend, but calls her "ugly," "stupid," "fat," and disparage her when he is alone with her or around others.

Different forms of violence against women – whether sexual harassment or abuse – can be physical and/or verbal as well as emotional and/or psychological in nature. For example, a professor could grab a student's breast during his office hours (physical abuse), shove her against a wall and force a kiss (physical abuse), promise to give her an A if she performs a sexual act (psychological abuse), or threaten to fail her if she will *not* perform a sexual act (psychological abuse). All of these examples legally constitute sexual harassment and are violations of *Title IX* of the *Civil Rights Act.* Similarly, a boyfriend can push his girlfriend out of a moving car (physical violence), punch her in the face and knock out a tooth (physical violence), steal her keys and lock her out of her own apartment to "punish" her for his belief that she flirted with someone else (psychological abuse), threaten to kill himself if she breaks up with him (psychological abuse), or drive in a threatening way while she is a passenger to scare her (psychological abuse).

The Continuum of Sexual Victimization

To understand behaviors constituting sexual victimizations (including sexual harassment), it is useful to present these victimizations as occurring along a continuum from coercion to force, as seen in Figure 10.1.

Coercion		Force
psychological coercion	verbal threats	physical force

Figure 10.1. The continuum of sexual victimization.

It is important to understand and distinguish *force* from *coercion* (as well physical abuse from psychological/emotional abuse) when explaining the dynamics of the victimization of college women. Examples of *coercion* include a professor telling a student he will not pass her in the course if she does not perform a sexual favor for him, or a man who tells his date that he will not drive her home unless she has sex with him. Other forms of coercion include sexually victimizing someone in an altered state from alcohol or drug use. *Force,* on the other hand, includes physically pushing a woman down or using a weapon and the perpetrator actually making the victim have sex with him. Clearly, this is physical as well as sexual violence. Between coercion and force lay behaviors like *verbal threats* of violence, for example, "If you don't comply and have sex with me, then I will physically force you to do so."

To assess the various forms of coercion and force in sexual victimizations, researchers have devised distinct categories of behaviors that one can position on the continuum of coercion to force. Figure 10.2 presents examples of researchers' categorizations of sexually victimizing behaviors and identify where those behaviors fit on the coercion to force continuum.

Koss et al. (1987) developed four categories of male dating behavior: (1) *sexually non-aggressive* males participated only in mutually desired, noncoercive, and nonabusive sex; (2) *sexually coercive* males used extreme verbal pressure such as false promises and threats to end the relationship if the woman would not have sexual intercourse; (3) *sexually abusive* males obtained sexual contact or attempted intercourse (where penetration did not occur) through force or threat of force; and (4) males used the threat of harm or actual force to obtain oral, anal, or vaginal intercourse. DeKeseredy and Kelly (1993) developed a similar continuum of behavior (see Figure 10.2); other research on college students also supports such a continuum in the levels of sexual aggression in date rapes (Banyard et al., 2005; Gross, Winslett, Roberts, & Gohm, 2006; Koss & Oros, 1982; Rivera & Regoli, 1987; Ward et al., 1991).

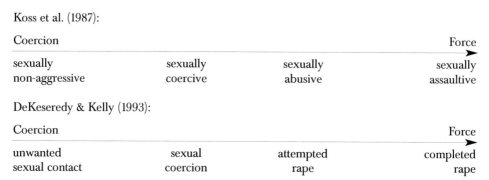

Figure 10.2. Research examples of different continuums of date rape.

Following the path of distinguishing coercive rapes (often using verbal pressure and threats), more recent rape research, primarily on college women, identifies what is often called "incapacitated rape" (IR) or "alcohol-related sexual assault" (e.g., Brown, Testa, & Messman-Moore, 2009; Lawyer et al., 2010; Nguyen, Kaysen, Dillworth, Brajchich, & Larimer, 2010). For example, Brown (2009) and her colleagues identify *incapacitated rapes* as sex with someone "who is unable to consent or resist sexual intercourse owing to alcohol or drug intoxication" (p. 898); to distinguish it from *forcible rapes* (where actual or threatened physical force are used to obtain sex) and *verbally coercive rapes* (sex against the victim's will where the perpetrator does not use any actual or threat of force against the victim, and the victim is not incapacitated by drugs or alcohol). In their study of 265 college women who reported experiencing unwanted sexual intercourse since their 17th birthdays, 47 percent were verbal coercion rapes, 42 percent as incapacitated rapes, and 11 percent were forcible rapes (Brown et al., 2009, p. 905). A similar study found alcohol- and drug-related sexual assaults on college campuses are more frequent than forcible assaults and are typically preceded by voluntary alcohol consumption by the victims (Lawyer et al., 2010).

Researchers have undertaken similar efforts to describe the continuum of sexual harassment, again ranging from coercion to force. Figure 10.3 presents two representative examples of such work. Adams and Abarbanel (1988), for example, suggest that categories of sexual harassment in an educational context (e.g., perpetrated by professors or instructors at students) could include: (1) *undue attention,* like being too eager to please or help; (2) *body language,* including leering or standing too close; (3) *verbal sexual advances,* like expressions of sexual attraction; (4) *invitation for dates;* (5) *physical advances,* including kissing, touching, and fondling breasts; and (6) *sexual bribery,* involving pressure to sexually comply to receive a good grade (see also Benson & Thomson, 1982), which capture the range from coercion to force.

Fitzgerald, Weitzman, Gold, and Ormerod (1988) suggest a similar continuum exists for sexual harassment, which comprises the categories of: (1) *gender harassment,* including general sexist remarks and behavior; (2) *seductive behavior,* like sanction-free sexual advances; (3) *sexual bribery,* soliciting sex by promise of reward; (4) *sexual coercion,* coercing sex through threat of punishment; and finally, (5) outright *sexual assault.* In one study, female college seniors reported experiencing harassing behaviors perpetrated by their instructors ranging from "vague to blatant," from invitations to dinner, to invitations to a weekend at a mountain resort. Many students reported instructors would not accept "no" for an answer and would call repeatedly after being firmly rejected (Benson & Thomas, 1982).

Adams & Abarbanel (1988):

Coercion   Force

sexist comments	undue attention	body language	verbal advances	invitations for dates	physical advances	explicit propositions	sexual bribery

Fitzgerald et al. (1988):

Coercion   Force

gender harassment	seductive behavior	sexual bribery	sexual coercion	sexual assault

Figure 10.3. Research examples of continuums in sexual harassment.

The varying degrees of coercion in sexual harassment make specific scenarios difficult to define both legally and personally (Paludi et al., 1990). While categories along the continuum involving force and punishment for failure to comply are severe, victims of harassment find less extreme categories of behavior very confusing and extremely disturbing. It is thus necessary to understand that coercion – as much as force – is a serious violation of a person's self-determination. Further, understanding the continuum of sexually exploitive behaviors acknowledges that sexual aggression, even by men known to victims, can involve both coercive violations as well as extreme violence. Viewing violence against women on a continuum facilitates an understanding of the wide spectrum of violations, recognizes the objectification of women underlies these victimizations, and increases appreciation of the impact these offenses have on students' lives (Leidig, 1992).

Finally, it is important to mention the potentially damaging ramifications of consensual sexual relationships between students and faculty members, or fellow students who are teaching assistants in a course. Research has well documented the occurrence of intimate relationships between faculty members and students on college campuses (see Fitzgerald et al., 1988; Glaser & Thorpe, 1986; Skeen & Nielson, 1983), and many universities have debated whether there should be policies against these relationships. Proponents of policies prohibiting such relationships argue that a relationship between a faculty member and a student is *always* asymmetric in nature and that students have as much to lose by participating in them as by refusing to do so. Moreover, it is sometimes difficult to determine whether student-faculty relationships are inherently coercive (or whether such is true in specific cases). The situation with teaching assistants may be even more difficult to sort out. Women students who experienced consensual sexual relationships with male faculty members reported they later felt the actions of the professor were coercive, and the relationship had resulted in negative consequences for the students (see Glaser & Thorpe, 1986). Because academic opportunities (and work in general) are characterized by vertical stratification and asymmetrical relations between teachers and students and supervisors and subordinates, individuals in positions of power can use their positions to receive sexual compliance from students or subordinates. The interaction of gender and organizational power in an institutional structure increases the likelihood resistance will be minimal or nonexistent.

The Incidence and Characteristics of Aggression Perpetrated Against College Women

Studies of intimate partner abuse have found that about three of every five students in college know someone involved in a violent dating relationship, and about one in five has actually experienced violence in a dating relationship (Bogal-Allbritten & Allbritten, 1985; Cate, Henton, Koval, Christopher, & Lloyd, 1982; Knutson & Mehm, 1986; Makepeace, 1981; Matthews, 1984; Stets & Pirog-Good, 1987). One recent survey study of women at two U.S. universities, however, found that almost half (48%) reported experiencing dating violence (Amar & Gennaro, 2005). Another study comparing battering in intimate relationships as documented in police reports found that physical violence and weapon use was more common in unmarried (boyfriend/girlfriend and ex-marital relationships) than married couples (Erez, 1986). Similarly, studies of college students found that cohabiting couples (unmarried heterosexual couples living together) report more violence and physical injury than heterosexual couples who date but do not live together or are married (Makepeace, 1989; Stets & Straus, 1989).

The most frequent reasons given for intimate partner abuse are jealousy, disagreements over drinking behaviors, and anger over sexual denial (Lane & Gwartney-Gibbs, 1985; Makepeace, 1981, 1986; Matthews, 1984). Thus, sexuality and jealousy are associated with nonsexual physical violence in intimate partner abuse.

It should not be surprising, then, that many relationships in which intimate partner abuse occurs will include sexual violence. For example, a study of unmarried college students found that injury was most common in rapes where the victim and offender were an estranged couple, "suggesting that some men use rape and violence during a rape to punish the victim for some grievance" (Felson & Krohn, 1990). Other research confirmed that acquaintance rapes could be quite violent. In fact, one study on acquaintance rapes found that the better known the acquaintance, the more likely (1) the victim suffers injuries and (2) attempts at rape will be completed (Belknap, 1989).

In the U.S., date rape is largely invisible because such rapes have not been viewed as "real rape" (Estrich, 1987). Self-report victimization studies of women suggest that between 8 percent and 15 percent of women experienced *forced* intercourse, mostly as college students (Amick & Calhoun, 1987; Berger, Searles, Salem, & Pierce, 1986; DeKeseredy & Kelly, 1993; Gross et al., 2006; Korman & Leslie, 1982; Koss et al., 1987; Koss & Oros, 1982; Lane & Gwartney-Gibbs, 1985; Lott et al., 1982; Muehlenhard & Linton, 1987; Reilly et al., 1992; Rivera & Regoli, 1987; Ward et al., 1991; Warshaw, 1988). Rates of self-reported coerced intercourse are much higher (Miller & Marshall, 1987). The *National College Women Sexual Victimization* Study (NCWSV) (see Fisher, Cullen, & Turner, 2000) estimated that 2.8 percent of their national sample of college women had experienced either a completed rape (1.7%) or an attempted rape incident (1.1%). These percentages translate to a victimization rate of 27.7 rapes per 1,000 female students. Of those incidents, 12.8 percent of completed rapes, 35.0 percent of attempted rapes, and 22.9 percent of threatened rapes took place on a date. One study found that, using the same survey in 1988 and in 2000, unwanted sexual contact of women decreased but rates of unwanted intercourse remained the same (Banyard et al., 2005).

One recent study (Gross et al., 2006) found that over one-quarter (27%) of college women reported an unwanted sexual experience that ranged from kissing and petting to oral, anal, or vaginal intercourse, with African American women reporting a higher rate (36%) than white women (26%). One-third of these sexually victimized women reported multiple forced sexual experiences and one-fifth (19%) of this sample of college women reported experiencing forced anal, oral, or vaginal intercourse. Notably, in this study, the most frequently reported victim-offender-relationship was boyfriend (41% of the rapes), followed by friends (29%), and acquaintances (21%), emphasizing that college women are most at risk of rape by known and sometimes well-trusted males. Notably, the research on self-reported sexual assaults by college males, while confirming the frequency of date rape, generally suggests that such victimizations are less common than women report (DeKeseredy & Kelly, 1999; Miller & Marshall, 1987; Ward et al., 1991). This might be due to few men committing rapes against many women and/or because male offenders are less likely than are female victims to report a behavior as rape or force. However, a recent study of young, single men from a large metropolitan area found that "43 percent reported that they made a woman have sex against her wishes," and this was done primarily through verbal coercion or impairing the victim with alcohol (Abbey & Jacques-Tiura, 2011, p. 2881).

Sexual harassment is also prevalent on college campuses. As noted previously, the behavior most commonly researched is harassment perpetrated by male faculty members or instructors against female students. Studies of sexual harassment among college women estimate that between 30 percent and 53 percent of all female students (graduate and undergraduate) experience sexual harassment by at least one faculty member over the course of their education (Benson & Thomson, 1982; Cortina, Swan, Fitzgerald, & Waldo, 1998; Dziech & Weiner, 1984; Kalof, Eby, Matheson, & Kroska, 2001; McKinney, Olsen, & Satterfield, 1988), and over one half (56%) when peers (other students), staff, and administrators were included (Huerta, Cortina, Pang, Torges, & Magley, 2006). When definitions of sexual harassment include sexist remarks and other forms of "gender harassment," the incidence in undergraduate populations nears 70 percent (Lott et al., 1982) or even 92 percent when peers are included as potential sexual harassers (Huerta et al., 2006).

Studies have also found little variation across departments in sexual harassment victimizations occurring in academic settings (Benson & Thomson, 1982; Fitzgerald et al., 1988). College women students report that sexual harassment often interferes with their education, makes them uncomfortable, threatens their self-confidence and commitment to academic pursuits, and causes them to wonder about their true classroom abilities (Benson & Thomson, 1982; McKinney et al., 1988). Victims may be reluctant to go to a professor's office to receive academic guidance or request a letter of recommendation, and victims find themselves in a situation where they must adopt strategies to minimize interactions with the potential for further harassment (Benson & Thomson, 1982; Dziech & Weiner, 1984). Sexual harassment thus not only impedes victims' opportunities, but also can deter fellow women students from pursuing additional classes with the harasser. Indeed, students report they avoid working with, or taking classes from, faculty members with a reputation for making sexual advances at students (McKinney et al., 1988). Such outcomes led researchers to conclude that "sexual harassment may be particularly stressful during college years when young women are at a critical stage of their personal and professional development" (Huerta et al., 2006).

Finally, it is important to note that the research on campus violence against women sometimes treats college students, including college women, as a monolithic group. It is often useful to examine differences across groups. For example, DeFour (1990) is concerned that sexual harassment research routinely omitted the students' race in analyses of this problem, and thus failed to account for the role and dynamic of race in exploring harassment. She believes that it is likely that women of color are sexually harassed more often than are their white counterparts because of the interaction of racism and sexism (DeFour, 1990). For example, attitudes that African-American women are "sexually free," Asian women are "docile and submissive," Hispanic women are "hot-blooded," and so on, greatly impact women of color's vulnerability to sexual harassment (DeFour, 1990).

Some research on college sexual harassment has explored variations in likelihood to commit or be victimized by sexual harassment across various groups. A study conducting gender comparisons of college students found men were twice as likely as women to sexually harass and three times as likely to be sexually coercive as women (Ménard, Hall, Phung, Ghebrial, & Martin, 2003). Regarding race/ethnicity, one study found sexual harassment was even more prevalent among African American (62%) and Latinas (60%), than white (56%) and Asian/East Indian (46%) college women (Cortina et al., 1998). Another study found students of color are more likely than white students to report sexual abuse by intimate partners (Porter & Williams, 2011). Research on lesbian/gay/bisexual or other sexual minority status (SMS) students finds that they are more at risk than their heterosexual counterparts on college campuses for sexual harassment (Cortina et al., 1998), sexual assaults (Martin, Fisher, Warner, Krebs, & Lindquist, 2011), and both physical and psychological intimate partner abuse (Porter & Williams, 2011). A study examining deaf and hard of hearing college students found that they were significantly more likely than their hearing counterparts to report sexual abuse by their intimate partners (Porter & Williams, 2011). Taken together, these findings indicate that the more a student is marginalized by gender, race/ethnicity, sexual identity, and disability, the more at risk she (or he) is of victimizations such as sexual harassment, sexual assault, and intimate partner abuse.

Factors Related to Sexual Aggression Against Women on Campus

The Climate

Campus climate and prevailing attitudes toward violence against women affect the level of sexual aggression perpetrated by students. Campus fraternity practices and values, in particular, are conducive to coercive and violent sex and aggression against women. Generally, about one-third of college males have reported that they would rape women under some circumstances if they knew that they would not get caught (Check & Malamuth, 1985; Malamuth, 1981; Reilly et al., 1992; Tieger, 1981). Additionally, compared to women, men view sexually related behavior on the job and at school as more natural, less serious, and something to be expected (Lott et al., 1982).

Fraternities, which overemphasize a macho conception of men and masculinity, and a narrow and stereotyped conception of women and femininity, use activities associated with these conceptions to commodity women. These include using them for "bait" to attract new members or to "take care of the guys," and provide sexual access to them as a presumed "benefit" of fraternity membership. Excessive alcohol use, competitiveness between fraternities, and normative support for secrecy within fraternities further facilitates coercive sex and the treatment of rape as an intrafraternity sport or contest. Women thus become the prey in the intrafraternity rivalry games (Black et al., 2012; Martin & Hummer, 1989).

Research found that the risk of rape relates to the culture of a particular fraternity on a given campus (Black et al., 2012; Martin & Hummer, 1989). More specifically, rape is unheard of in some fraternities, happens occasionally in others, and there is a high-risk of rape in still others. This variation in fraternities' level of sexual violence explains why some people who hear or read about fraternity rapes claim they do not believe it because the fraternity with which they have been associated is not one where rape occurs.

Research also identified racial differences between fraternities in the extent of sexual aggression. Black et al. (2012) compared African American and white fraternities and found that nonsexual male-on-male physical aggression was far more common in African American than in white fraternities, but sexual violence against women was almost unheard of in the African American fraternities but very common in some white fraternities. They speculated that structural differences related to race and class between white and African American fraternities explained the differences. White fraternities typically had their own "houses" where there was no security overseeing parties. On the other hand, the African American fraternities did not have their own houses, so they had to reserve various halls to hold parties and dances, had to pay security officers to oversee the party, and were not allowed to consume alcohol or drugs. Thus, the black fraternity members who wanted to get "high" would arrive at the party already having consumed drugs and/or alcohol, whereas at the white fraternities, members would typically consume increasing amounts of alcohol and drugs as the night wore on. The white fraternities also had private rooms to take women where they could be raped.

Reports also note that date or fraternity rapists, sexual harassers, or men who physically abuse their girlfriends are rarely sanctioned (DeKeseredy & Kelly, 1993; Lopez, 1992; Sanday, 1990; Warshaw, 1988). This failure to sanction violators is partly due to victims' unwillingness to report the incident, but also to university authorities' and the criminal justice system's reluctance to take action against such offenders. Men may trivialize these victimizations and joke about them as the "sporting parts" of men's lives (Leidig, 1992).

One answer, then, as to why some men rape, abuse, and sexually harass women on campus is because they can. Recent research confirms that men who abuse women rarely receive negative consequences and their male peers seldom shun them (Gamache, 1991; Martin & Hummer, 1989; Siegel & Raymond, 1992). In fact, some research has found that men who participate in intimate partner abuse and date rape often receive peer support from their male friends, who may even encourage the abuse (DeKeseredy, 1988; Gwartney-Gibbs & Stockard, 1989; Martin & Hummer, 1989). Other studies find that although couples in physically abusive relationships most frequently attach anger and confusion as the reason for the abuse; about one-quarter believe abuse signifies "love" by the abuser (Cate et al., 1982; Matthews, 1984).

Gender Differences and Stereotypes

Much of the rape myth adherence research focuses on characteristics of the egalitarian nature of dating, yet research suggests that heterosexual dating has not become much more gender egalitarian in the last 35 years (Eaton & Rose, 2011). As expected, men in general, and particularly men who report being abusive, are more likely than are women to believe rape myths, such as that a woman should expect to have intercourse if a man spent a lot of money on her and consequently support sexual aggression (Basow & Minieri, 2011; Gilmartin-Zena, 1988; Malamuth, 1989; Muehlenhard & Linton, 1987; Reilly et al., 1992; Warshaw, 1988; Wilson, Raison, & Britton, 1983). However, there is significant evidence that many *women* also express hostility towards rape and sexual harassment victims and blame them for their experiences (Gowan, 2000, Ullman, 2010). One study found that college men are more likely to blame women for their sexual victimizations if the women consented to a certain level of sexual activity, and then wanted to stop (Yescavage, 1999). One recent self-report study of college men found that men who participated in aggressive high school sports were more likely than were counterparts not in these sports to report psychological, physical, and sexual aggression against their dating partners, and causing injuries to their dates. Former aggressive high school athletes were also more likely to adhere to rape myths and were more homophobic than are non-athletes (Forbes, Adams-Curtis, Pakalka, & White, 2006).

Male Entitlement

Male entitlement is a common theme throughout the analysis of the causes of intimate partner abuse, date rape, and sexual harassment. Whether it is the professor who believes he has the right to date or harass his students, the fraternity member who believes all women who attend parties are "fair game," or the boyfriend who "justifies" hitting his girlfriend because she talked with another man, perceptions of male entitlement are common in the victimization of women. Perhaps nowhere is this more evident than women students physically and sexually victimized by male athletes (Bohmer & Parrot, 1993; Eskenazi, 1990; Warshaw, 1988; Yescavage, 1999). Athletes often view these victims as "groupies" who got what they "asked for" and women who changed their minds after the "consensual" sex are "gold diggers" trying to make money off athletes. Yescavage's (1999) study of the self-reported behaviors of college men viewed male entitlement as a significant risk factor for these men victimizing women. These men held patriarchal views that women are the property of men, and thus women have no right to deny men sex, can be treated as men want, and sometimes deserve to be "taught a lesson" when they are too independent.

Altered States: The Effect of Alcohol and Drugs

Research on date rape and fraternity gang rape finds strong links between alcohol/drug consumption and unwanted sexual experiences, including intimate partner abuse (Abbey, Zawacki, Buck, Clinton, & McAuslan 2001; Bogal-Allbritten & Allbritten, 1985; Fair & Vanyur, 2011; Fisher, Cullen, & Turner, 2000; Lott et al., 1982; Martin & Hummer; 1989; Muehlenhard & Linton, 1987; Pritchard, 1988; Testa, Vanzile-Tamsen, & Livingston, 2004; Ward et al., 1991; Warshaw, 1988). Moreover, there is considerable evidence that these rapists often *plan* before the date or party how to debilitate their victims through drugs and alcohol (Abbey & Jacques-Tirua, 2011; Ehrhart & Sandler, 1985; Kanin, 1985; Martin & Hummer, 1989; Sanday, 1990) and that many college men self-report alcohol-related sexual coercion and hold "many rape-supportive attitudes and beliefs" (Carr & VanDeusen, 2004). A potential victim placed in an altered state increases her inability to resist the attacker, particularly if she is unconscious. Additionally, while the public and criminal justice decision makers view the rapist as *less* responsible for raping if *he* was drunk, they view the rape *victim* as *more* responsible for being raped if she was drunk (Bromley & Territo, 1990; Ehrhart & Sandler, 1985; Lundberg-Love & Geffner, 1989; Warshaw, 1988).

Recent research on college students found alcohol use was linked to higher incidents of dating and sexual coercion and aggression among intimate partners, while decreasing the likelihood of condom use (Fair & Vanyur, 2011). Another study found the association between problem drinking and perpetrating intimate partner abuse was much stronger among college men than women, suggesting gendered (sexist) beliefs about alcohol consumption and effects (Fossos et al., 2007). This is compounded when considering the findings from another study on college men that found the men with the riskiest attitudes regarding sexual aggression might also be those most likely to use alcohol, creating something of a perfect storm for their victims (Hoyt & Yeater, 2011).

The Dynamics and the Consequences of Victimization

Given that women are blamed for their sexual and intimate partner victimizations (see Estrich, 1987; Warshaw, 1988; Yescavage, 1999), it is hardly surprising that many victims internalize that blame and fail to define themselves as victims (Fisher et al., 2000; Koss, 1990; Rabinowitz, 1990; Ullman, 2010). First, there is a cultural stigma attached to being a victim of these crimes. Victims often trivialize their experiences to protect their senses of vulnerability and integrity (Koss, 1990). Second, along with society, victims often blame themselves for their own battering, rape, or sexual harassment victimization (Berger et al., 1986; Koss, 1990). They often feel ashamed of their victimizations, particularly if they were attracted to their dates or professors before being raped, battered, or sexually harassed. A long period usually passes before a victim acknowledges her victimization. One exception to this generalization involves women who resist and respond immediately: "Often the woman who speaks out is a person with a strong sense of integrity who can no longer ignore injustice" (Koss, 1990).

Recent research found that a history of child sexual abuse victimization placed a college woman at significantly greater risk of sexual victimization during their first semester of college, than women without such a history (Reese-Weber & Smith, 2011). Similarly, another study found women entering college who had a "nonconsensual sexual experience" (NSE) were more likely to report more drinking (including binge drinking), and more negative drinking consequences, which would likely include the greater risk of sexual victimization (Ross et al., 2011). A study comparing Asian American and white women college students, found the Asian American students who experience incapacitated rapes (IRs) appear to be at more risk for negative alcohol outcomes, such as significant increase in alcohol consumption to self-medicate the pain of the rape aftermath (Nguyen et al., 2010).

Not surprisingly, college women who report dating violence have significantly higher levels of depression, anxiety, hostility, and other mental health dysfunction than do their nonabused counterparts (Amar & Gennaro, 2004).

Unfortunately, fewer than 3 percent of those experiencing college dating violence visited a mental health professional (Amar & Gennaro, 2004). Similarly, college women reporting sexual harassment evidence increased levels of psychological distress, lower academic satisfaction, greater physical illness, and higher rates of eating disorders than do college women who have not experienced sexual harassment (Huerta et al., 2006). When higher status individuals, such as faculty, staff, and administrators, perpetrated the sexual harassment, academic satisfaction among victims was lower than among nonvictims. However, sexual harassment was equally detrimental to the victims' mental health, regardless of the status of the perpetrator (e.g., student, faculty, staff, or administrator) (Huerta et al., 2006).

Women often do not report sexual harassment, date rape, or intimate partner abuse to formal authorities (e.g., university personnel or the police) and often not even to informal support persons – friends, family, and counselors (Belknap, 1989; Benson et al., 1992; DeKeseredy & Kelly, 1993; Fisher et al., 2000; Miller & Marshall, 1987; Stets & Pirog-Good, 1987; Ward et al., 1991). Many victims fear the authorities will not take them seriously (Berger et al., 1986; U.S. Merit Systems Protection Board, 1981), believe the authorities will hold them responsible for the victimization, or doubt the authorities will take any corrective action (Brandenburg, 1982). At least some of these fears are realistic – offenders frequently go unpunished, whereas victims are negatively sanctioned in the media, on the campus, or at the work site (Sanday, 1990; U.S. Merit Systems Protection Board, 1981). In fact, many victims of date and fraternity rapes, and sexual harassment, drop out of school while their offenders continue at the university (Sanday, 1990; Warshaw, 1988).

The extent of violence against women on college campuses and the harmful short- and long-term effects such victimization has on female students, have prompted universities and colleges to institute rules, regulations and procedures to address sexual victimization of women. Educational institutions around the country initiated awareness programs and established disciplinary measures to respond to those engaged in sexual aggression. Colleges and universities also launched support services and assistance programs, including resistance training (e.g., Senn, 2011) to help actual and potential victims. These programs and services are continuously examined, refined and improved in light of the accumulated knowledge about the reasons and motivation behind sexual aggression on campus and the harmful effects it has on college women (see review in Vladutin, Martin, & Macy, 2011).

Policy Implications and Conclusion

In the last decade, activists have made great headway in raising awareness about the various kinds of victimizations of women on college campuses. Yet there is still denial about the magnitude of the problem, and considerable ignorance of the harm these actions inflict on victims. Furthermore, students, faculty, and staff are often unsure about resources available for the victims, as well as the policies and procedures regarding acquaintance victimizations (Metha & Nigg, 1982; Sullivan & Bybee, 1987). For too long, the focus in many universities has been preventing stranger rape, for example, by improving campus lighting and providing extra security locks, ignoring the far more common victimizations involving acquaintances (Miller & Marshall, 1987; Steenbarger & Zimmer, 1992).

To deter and prevent violence against college women, certain steps need to be taken. The first and most important action that college or university administration can take is to acknowledge that sexual harassment, date rape, and intimate partner abuse continue to be realities on campuses (Benson et al., 1992; Roark, 1987). The second step is prevention. Enforcing policies and laws regarding acquaintance victimizations often results in accepting one person's word (and credibility) against another's, making prevention particularly important. Institutions can best serve prevention by promoting education and awareness of the dynamics of sexual harassment, date rape, and intimate partner abuse to students, faculty members, and staff (Amick & Calhoun, 1987; Benson et al., 1992; Bohmer & Parrot, 1993; Leidig, 1992; Roark, 1987; Steenbarger & Zimmer, 1992; Ward et al., 1991; Warshaw, 1988). Awareness may prevent potential offenders from committing these offenses and keep potential victims from experiencing them. Moreover, such knowledge will help those in the academic community to better understand, and thus respond appropriately to victims who approach them.

Third, it is important that institutions continue to examine and refine existing policy statements about sexual harassment, date rape, and intimate partner abuse (or institute such statements if they have not been established) These policy statements should clearly identify: (1) definitions of sexual harassment, date rape, and intimate partner abuse; (2) who is responsible for handling charges regarding victimizations on campus, both formally (e.g., the police or a grievance board) and informally (e.g., mediation through a counselor or ombudsman's office); and (3) the consequences for offenders of violating the policies (Benson et al., 1992; Bohmer & Parrot, 1993; The State Council of Higher Education for Virginia, 1992).

Fourth, the grievance boards or administrators in charge of processing the charges should ensure that institutions take action quickly, efficiently, confidentially, and as carefully as possible. Key to this step is providing a safe place on campus and "safe people" where and to whom victims report their experiences (Grauerholz, Gottfried, Stohl, & Gabin, 1999).

Fifth, the university needs to disseminate the policies so everyone in the academic community (students, faculty members, and staff) has access to them (Amar & Gennaro, 2005; Bohmer & Parrot, 1993; Benson et al., 1992; Brandenburg, 1982; Metha & Nigg, 1982). Use of handbooks, and postings to university websites, on including policy statements in student orientations and semester course schedules are examples of how these policies can be communicated.

Sixth, there needs to be an ongoing evaluation of the effectiveness of the policies to ensure that those responsible for enforcement take these violations seriously (Bohmer & Parrot, 1993; Brandenburg, 1982; Metha & Nigg, 1982). Surveys of victims, workers involved with delivering victim services, and counselors could be used to collect data on the extent policies and procedures are followed and satisfaction with them. Academic research on the effectiveness of programs and approaches should also be encouraged and conducted (e.g., Potter, Moynihan, & Stapleton, 2011)

Seventh, there must be on-campus victim advocate services available to respond to the short- and long-term emotional, medical, and logistical needs associated with filing complaints by victims/survivors (Amar & Gennaro, 2005; Benson et al., 1992; Bohmer & Parrot, 1993; Leidig, 1992; Roark, 1989). These services are necessary to address the needs of victim/survivors so that they can move successfully forward with their lives.

Eighth, it is useful to remember that violence against women is not simply a "woman's problem" – most men have women who are close to them in life (e.g., mothers, sisters, girlfriends, friends, etc.) *and* men are usually the perpetrators (Scully, 1990). Given that men are the ones who commit most of the abuse of women, men can be key in stopping male-perpetrated abuse and violence of women. DeKeseredy, Schwartz, and Alvi (2000) point out that "profeminist men can begin to tilt the balance against male aggression. This can include shaming or working with bullies or those who are abusive, protesting pornography, and involving oneself with education programs and/or support groups."

Ninth, campus policies and strategies to combat abuse and victimization of women must take into account racial and ethnic differences among women (Koikari & Hippensteele, 2000). Treating such sexual victimizations as a "white woman's issue" or as race/ethnicity-neutral poses the threat of splintering those groups which are advocating for equality and better treatment on campus.

Finally, student victims need to know that they may take a sexual harassment grievance directly to the Office of Civil Rights in the U.S. Department of Education or press charges in a private lawsuit against offenders perpetrating sexual harassment, date rape, and intimate partner abuse, regardless of whether a grievance procedure exists on their campus (Brandenburg, 1982). Such an option should convince university administrators that if they fail to adequately work toward prevention and inadequately respond once victimizations occur, victims can appeal to the legal system and move the issue outside the academic community.

The *Higher Education Amendment Act of 1992* is not only landmark in recognizing campus sexual victimization, but it is well thought out and provides funding for its stated goals of developing rape education/awareness, disciplinary boards, victim counseling and medical services, and dissemination of legal information and assistance to victims (The State Council of Higher Education for Virginia, 1992). Such federal recognition of one of the victimizations that college women frequently encounter is an important step in legitimizing the seriousness of campus rapes. We hope that similar state-level legislation will help combat sexual harassment and intimate partner abuse on college campuses.

REFERENCES

Abbey, A., & Jacques-Tiura, A. J. (2011). Sexual assault perpetrators' tactics: Associations with their personal characteristics and aspects of the incident. *Journal of Interpersonal Violence, 26,* 2866–2889.

Abbey, A., Zawacki, T., Buck, P. O., Clinton A. M., & McAuslan, P. (2001). Alcohol and sexual assault. *Alcohol Research and Health, 25,* 43–51.

Adams, A., & Abarbanel, G. (1988). *Sexual assault on campus: What colleges can do.* Santa Monica, CA: Rape Treatment Center.

Aizenman, M., & Kelly, G. (1988). Incidence of violence and acquaintance rape in dating relationships among college men and women. *Journal of College Student Development, 29,* 305–311.

Allen, C. T., Swan, S. C., & Raghavan, C. (2009). Gender symmetry, sexism, and intimate partner violence. *Journal of Interpersonal Violence, 24,* 1816–1834.

Amar, A. F., & Gennaro, S. (2005). Dating violence in college women: Associated physical injury, healthcare usage, and mental health symptoms. *Nursing Research, 54,* 235–242.

Amick, A. E., & Calhoun, K. S. (1987). Resistance to sexual aggression. *Archives of Sexual Behavior, 16,* 153–163.

Banyard, V. L., Plante, E. G., Cohn, E. S., Moorhead, C., Ward, S., & Walsh, W. (2005). Revisiting unwanted sexual experiences on campus. *Violence Against Women, 11,* 426–446.

Basow, S. A., & Minieri, A. (2011). "You owe me": Effects of date cost, who pays, participant gender, and rape myth beliefs on perceptions of rape. *Journal of Interpersonal Violence, 26,* 479–497.

Belknap, J. 1989. The sexual victimization of unmarried women by nonrelative acquaintances. In M. Pirog Good & J. Stets (Eds.), *Violence in dating relationships: Emerging social issues* (pp. 205–218). New York: Praeger.

Belknap, J. (2007). *The invisible woman: Gender, crime, and justice* (3rd ed.). Belmont, CA: Wadsworth.

Belknap, J., & Erez, E. (1997). Redefining sexual harassment: Confronting sexism in the 21st century. *Justice Professional, 10,* 143–159.

Belknap, J., & Melton, H. (2005, March). *Are heterosexual men also victims of intimate partner abuse?* Retrieved from, http://www.vawnet.org/DomesticViolence/Research/VAWnetDocs/AR_MaleVictims.pdf.

Belknap, J., & Potter, H. (2006). Intimate partner abuse. In C. Renzetti, L. Goodstein, & S. Miller (Eds.), *Women, crime, and criminal Justice* (2nd ed.) (pp. 168–184). Los Angeles: Roxbury.

Benson, D., Charleton, C., & Goodhart, F. (1992). Acquaintance rape on campus. *Journal of American College Health, 40,* 157–65.

Benson, D. J., & Thomson, G. E. (1982). Sexual harassment on a university campus: The confluence of authority relations, sexual interest, and gender stratification. *Social Problems, 29,* 236–251.

Berger, R. J., Searles, P., Salem, R. G., & Pierce, B. A. (1986) Sexual assault in a college community. *Sociological Focus, 19,* 1–26.

Black, T., Belknap J., & Ginsburg J. (2012). Racism, sexism and aggression: A study of black and white fraternities. In T. L. Brown, G. S. Parks, & C. M. Phillips (Eds.), *African American fraternities and sororities: The legacy and the vision* (2nd ed.) (pp. 363–392). Lexington, KY: The University Press of Kentucky.

Bogal-Allbritten, R., & Allbritten, W. L. (1985). The hidden victims: Courtship violence among college students. *Journal of College Student Personnel, 26,* 201–204.

Bohmer, C., & Parrot, A. (1993). *Sexual assault on campus.* New York: Lexington.

Boswell, A. A., & Spade, J. D. (1996). Fraternities and collegiate rape culture: Why are some fraternities more dangerous places for women? *Gender & Society, 10,* 133–147.

Brandenburg, J. B. (1982). Sexual harassment in the university: Guidelines for establishing a grievance procedure. *Signs, 8,* 320–336.

Bromley, M. L., & Territo, L. (1990). *College prevention and personal safety awareness.* Springfield, IL: Charles C Thomas.

Brown, A. L., Testa, M., & Messman-Moore, T. L. (2009). Psychological consequences of sexual victimization resulting from force, incapacitation, or verbal coercion. *Violence Against Women, 15,* 898–919.

Carr, J. L., & VanDeusen, K. M. (2004). Risk factors for male sexual aggression on college campuses. *Journal of Family Violence, 19,* 279–289.

Cate, R. M., Henton, J. M., Koval, J., Christopher, F. S., & Lloyd, S. (1982). Premarital abuse: A social psychological perspective. *Journal of Family Issues, 3,* 79–90.

Check, J., & Malamuth, N. (1985). An empirical assessment of some feminist hypotheses about rape. *International Journal of Women's Studies, 8,* 414–423.

Clark, A. (1987). *Women's silence, men's violence: Sexual assault in England, 1770–1845.* London: Pandora Press.

Cortina, L. M., Swan, S. C., Fitzgerald, L. F., & Waldo, C. (1998). Sexual harassment and assault: Chilling the climate for women in academia. *Psychology of Women Quarterly, 22,* 419–441.

Das Dasgupta, S. (2001). *Towards an understanding of women's use of non-lethal violence in intimate heterosexual relationships.* Retrieved from http://www.vawnet.org/DomesticViolence/Research/VAWnetDocs/AR_womviol.php.

DeFour, D. C. (1990). The interface of racism and sexism on college campuses. In M. A. Paludi (Ed.), *Ivory power: Sexual harassment on campus* (pp. 45–52). Albany, NY: State University of New York Press.

DeKeseredy, W. S. (1988). Women abuse in dating relationships: The relevance of social support theory. *Journal of Family Violence, 3,* 1–13.

DeKeseredy, W. S., & Kelly, K. (1993). The incidence and prevalence of woman abuse in Canadian university and college dating relationships. *Canadian Journal of Sociology, 18,* 137–159.

DeKeseredy, W. S., Schwartz, M. D., & Alvi, S. (2000). The role of pro-feminist men in dealing with woman abuse on the Canadian college campus. *Violence Against Women, 6,* 918–935.

Dziech, B. W., & Weiner, L. (1984). *The lecherous professor: Sexual harassment on campus.* Boston: Beacon Press.

Eaton, A. A., & Rose, S. (2011). Has dating become more egalitarian? A 35 year review using sex roles. *Sex Roles, 64,* 843–862.

Ehrhart, J. K., & Sandler, B. R. (1985). Campus gang rape: Party games? In Project on the Status of Education and Women (Eds.), *Sexual harassment: Hidden issue.* Washington, DC: National Association of Colleges.

Erez, E. (1986). Intimacy, violence, and the police. *Human Relations, 39,* 265–281.

Eskenazi, G. (1990). The male athlete and sexual assault. *The New York Times,* June 30, p. 27.

Estrich, S. (1987). *Real rape.* Cambridge, MA: Harvard University Press.

Fair, C. D., & Vanyur, J. (2011). Sexual coercion, verbal aggression, and condom use consistency among college students. *Journal of American College Health, 59,* 273–280.

Felson, R. B., & Krohn, M. (1990). Motives for rape. *Journal of Research in Crime & Delinquency, 27,* 222–242.

Fisher, B. S., Cullen, F. T., & Turner, M. G. (2000, December). *The sexual victimization of college women* (NCJ 182369). Washington DC: National Institute of Justice.

Fitzgerald, L. F. (1990). Sexual harassment: The definition and measurement of a construct. In M. A. Paludi (Ed.), *Ivory power: Sexual harassment on campus* (pp. 21–44). Albany, NY: State University of New York Press.

Fitzgerald, L. F., Weitzman, L. M., Gold, Y., & Ormerod, M. (1988). Academic harassment. *Psychology of Women Quarterly, 12,* 329–340.

Forbes, G. B., Adams-Curtis, L. E., Pakalka, A. H., & White, K. B. (2006). Dating aggression, sexual coercion, and aggression-supporting attitudes among college men as a function of participation in aggressive high school sports. *Violence Against Women, 12,* 441–455.

Fossos, N., Neighbors, C., Kaysen, D., & Hove, M. C. (2007). Intimate partner violence perpetration and problem drinking among college students: The roles of expectancies and subjective evaluations of alcohol aggression. *Journal of Studies on Alcohol and Drugs, 68,* 706–713.

Gamache, D. (1991). Domination and control: The social context of dating violence. In B. Levy (Ed.), *Dating violence: Young women in danger* (pp. 69–83). Seattle, WA: Seal.

Gilmartin-Zena, P. (1988). Gender differences in students' attitudes toward rape. *Sociological Focus, 21,* 279–292.

Glaser, R. D., & Thorpe, J. S. (1986). Unethical intimacy. A survey of sexual contact and advances between psychology educators and female graduate students. *American Psychology, 41,* 43–51.

Gowan, G. (2000). Women's hostility toward women and rape and sexual harassment myths. *Violence Against Women, 6,* 238–246.

Grauerholz, L., Gottfried, H., Stohl, C., & Gabin, N. (1999). There's safety in numbers: Creating a campus advisers' network to help complainants of sexual harassment and complaint receivers. *Violence Against Women, 5,* 950–977.

Gross, A. M., Winslett, A., Roberts, M., & Gohm, C. L. (2006). An examination of sexual violence against college women. *Violence Against Women, 12,* 288–300.

Gwartney-Gibbs, P., & Stockard, J. (1989). Courtship aggression and mixed-sex peer groups. In M. Pirog-Good & J. E. Stets (Eds.), *Violence in dating relationships* (pp. 185–204). New York: Praeger.

Hoyt, T., & Yeater, E. A. (2011). Individual and situational influences on men's responses to dating and social situations. *Journal of Interpersonal Violence, 26,* 1723–1740.

Huerta, M., Cortina, L. M., Pang, J. S., Torges, C. M., & Magley, V. J. (2006). Sex and power in the academy: Modeling sexual harassment in the lives of college women. *Personality and Social Psychology Bulletin, 32,* 616–628.

Kalof, L., Eby, K. K., Matheson, J. L., & Kroska, R. J. (2001). The influence of race and gender on student self-reports of sexual harassment by college professors. *Gender & Society, 15,* 282–302.

Kanin, E. J. (1957). Male aggression in dating courtship relations. *American Journal of Sociology, 63,* 197–204.

Kanin, E. J. (1985). Date rapists: Differential sexual socialization and relative deprivation. *Archives of Sexual Behavior, 14,* 219–31.

Knutson, J. F., & Mehm J. G. (1986). Transgenerational patterns of coercion in families and intimate relationships. In G. Russell (Ed.), *Violence in intimate relationships.* New York: PMA.

Koikari, M., & Hippensteele, S. K. (2000). Negotiating feminist survival: Gender, race, and power in academe. *Violence Against Women, 6,* 1269–1296.

Korman, S. K., & Leslie, G. R. (1982). The relationship of feminist ideology and date expense sharing to perceptions of sexual aggression in dating. *Journal of Sex Research, 18,* 114–129.

Koss, M. P. (1990). Changed lives: The Psychological Impact of Sexual Harassment. In M. A. Paludi (Ed.), *Ivory power: Sex and gender harassment in the academy* (pp. 73–92). Albany, NY: State University of New York Press.

Koss, M. P., & Oros, C. J. (1982). Sexual experiences survey: A research instrument investigating sexual aggression and victimization. *Journal of Consulting and Clinical Psychology, 50,* 455–457.

Koss, M. P., Gidyz, C. A., & Wisniewski, N. (1987). The scope of rape: Incidence and prevalence of sexual aggression and victimization in a national sample of higher education students. *Journal of Consulting and Clinical Psychology, 55,* 162–170.

Lane, K. E., & Gwartney-Gibbs, P. A. (1985). Violence in the context of dating and sex. *Journal of Family Issues, 6,* 45–59.

Lawyer, S., Resnick, H., Bakanic, V., Burkett, T., & Kilpatrick, D. (2010). Forcible, drug-facilitated, and incapacitated rape and sexual assault among undergraduate women. *Journal of American College Health, 58,* 453–460.

Leidig, M. W. (1992). The continuum of violence against women: psychological and physical consequences. *Journal of American College Health, 40,* 149–55.

Lopez, P. (1992). He said . . . she said . . . An overview of date rape from commission through prosecution through verdict. *Journal of Criminal Justice, 13,* 275–302.

Lott, B., Reilly, M. E., & Howard, D. R. (1982). Sexual assault and harassment: A campus community case study. *Signs, 8,* 296–319.

Lundberg-Love, P., & Geffner, R. (1989). Date rape: Prevalence, risk factors, and a proposed model. In M. A. Pirog-Good & J. E. Stets (Eds.), *Violence and dating relationships: Emerging social issues* (pp. 169–184). New York: Praeger.

Makepeace, J. M. (1981). Courtship violence among college students. *Family Relations, 30,* 97–102.

Makepeace, J. M. (1983). Life events, stress and courtship violence. *Family Relations, 32,* 101–109.

Makepeace, J. M. (1986). Gender differences in courtship violence victimization. *Family Relations, 35,* 383–388.

Makepeace, J. (1989). Dating, living together and courtship violence. In M. A. Pirog-Good & J. E. Stets (Eds.), *Violence in dating relationships.* New York: Praeger.

Malamuth, N. (1981). Rape proclivity among males. *Journal of Social Issues, 37,* 138–157.

Martin, P. Y., & Hummer, R. A. (1989). Fraternities and rape on campus. *Gender & Society, 3,* 457–73.

Martin, S. L., Fisher, B. S., Warner, T. D., Krebs, C. P., & Lindquist, C. H. (2011). Women's sexual orientations and their experiences of sexual assault before and during university. *Women's Health Issues, 21,* 199–205.

Matthews, W. J. (1984). Violence in college couples. *College Student Journal, 18,* 150–158.

McGregor, M. J., Lipowska, M., Shah, S., Du Mont, J., & De Siato, C. (2003). An exploratory analysis of suspected drug-facilitated sexual assault seen in a hospital emergency department. *Women & Health, 37,* 71–80.

McKinney, K., Olson, C., & Satterfield, A. (1988). Graduate students' experiences with and responses to sexual harassment. *Journal of Interpersonal Violence, 3,* 319–325.

Ménard, K. S., Hall, G. C. N., Phung, A. H., Ghebrial, M. F. E., & Martin, L. (2003). Gender differences in sexual harassment and coercion in college students: Developmental, individual, and situational determinants. *Journal of Interpersonal Violence, 18,* 1222–1239.

Metha, A., & Nigg, J. (1982). Sexual harassment: Implications of a study at Arizona State University. *Women's Studies Quarterly, 10,* 24–26.

Miller, B., & Marshall, J. C. (1987). Coercive sex on the university campus. *Journal of College Student Personnel, 28,* 38–47.

Molidor, C., & Tolman, R. (1998). Gender and contextual factors in adolescent dating violence. *Violence Against Women, 4,* 180–194.

Muehlenhard, C. L., & Linton, M. A. (1987). Date rape and sexual aggression in dating situations: Incidence and risk factors. *Journal of Counseling Psychology, 34,* 186–196.

Nguyen, H. V., Kaysen, D., Dillworth, T. M., Brajchich, M., & Larimer, M. E. (2010). Incapacitated rape and alcohol use in white and Asian American college women. *Violence Against Women, 16,* 919–933.

O'Keefe, M., & Treister, L. (1998). Victims of dating violence among high school students: Are predictors different for males and females? *Violence Against Women, 4,* 195–223.

Paludi, M. A., Grossman, M., Scott, C. A., Kindermann, J., Matula, S., Oswald, J., Dovan, J., & Mulcahy, D. (1990). Myths and realities: Sexual harassment on campus. In M. A. Paludi (Ed.), *Ivory power: Sexual harassment on campus* (pp. 1–14). Albany, NY: State University of New York Press.

Porter, J., & Williams, L. M. (2011). Intimate violence among underrepresented groups on a college campus. *Journal of Interpersonal Violence, 26,* 3210–3224.

Potter, S. J., Moynihan, M. M., & Stapleton, J. G. (2011). Using social and self-identification in social marketing materials aimed at reducing violence against women on campus. *Journal of Interpersonal Violence, 26,* 971–990.

Pritchard, C. (1988). *Avoiding rape on and off campus.* Wenonah, NJ: State College.

Project on the Status and Education of Women. (1978). *Sexual harassment: A hidden issue.* Association of American Colleges, Washington, DC.

Rabinowitz, V. C. (1990). Coping with sexual harassment. In M. A. Paludi (Ed.), *Ivory power: Sexual harassment on campus* (pp. 103–118). Albany, NY: State University of New York Press.

Reese-Weber, M., & Smith, D. M. (2011). Outcomes of child sexual abuse as predictors of later sexual victimization. *Journal of Interpersonal Violence, 26,* 1884–1905.

Reilly, M. E., Lott, B., Caldwell, D., & DeLuca, L. (1992). Tolerance for sexual harassment related to self-reported sexual victimization. *Gender & Society, 6,* 122–138.

Rivera, G. F., Jr., & Regoli, R. M. (1987). Sexual victimization experiences of sorority women. *Sociology and Social Research, 72,* 39–42.

Roark, M. L. (1987). Preventing violence on college campuses. *Journal of Counseling and Development, 65,* 367–370.

Ross, L. T., Kolars, C. L. K., Krahn, D. D., Gomberg, E. S. L., Clark, G., & Niehaus, A. (2011). Nonconsensual sexual experiences and alcohol consumption among women entering college. *Journal of Interpersonal Violence, 26,* 399–413.

Russell, D. E. H. (1984). *Sexual exploitation: Rape, child sexual abuse, and workplace harassment.* Beverly Hills, CA: Sage.

Sanday, P. R. (1990). *Fraternity gang rape: Sex, brotherhood, and privilege on campus.* New York: New York University Press.

Schwartz, M. D., & Nogrady, C. A. (1996). Fraternity membership, rape myths, and sexual aggression on a college campus. *Violence Against Women, 2,* 163–179.

Scully, D. (1990). *Understanding sexual violence.* Boston: Unwin Hyman.

Senn, C. Y. (2011) An imperfect feminist journey: Reflections on the process to develop an effective sexual assault resistance program for university women. *Feminism & Psychology, 21,* 121–137.

Siegel, D. G., & Raymond, C. H. (1992). An ecological approach to violent crime on campus. *Journal of Security Administration, 15,* 21.

Skeen, R., & Nielson, J. M. (1983). Student-faculty sexual relationships: An empirical test of two explanatory models. *Qualitative Sociology, 6,* 99–117.

Steenbarger, B. N., & Zimmer, C. G. (1992). Violence on campus. *Journal of American College Health, 40,* 147–148.

Stets, J. E., & Pirog-Good, M. A. (1987). Violence in dating relationships. *Social Psychology Quarterly, 50,* 237–246.

Stets, J. E., & Straus, M. A. (1989). The marriage license as a hitting license. In M. A. Pirog-Good & J. E. Stets (Eds.), *Violence in dating relationships* (pp. 33–52). New York: Praeger.

Sullivan, C. M., & Bybee, D. (1987). Female students and sexual harassment. *Journal of the National Association for Women Deans, Administrators, and Counselors, 50,* 11–16.

Testa, M, Vanzile-Tamsen, C., & Livingston, J. A. (2004). The role of victim and perpetrator intoxication on sexual assault outcomes. *Journal of Studies on Alcohol, 65,* 320–329.

Tieger, T. (1981). Self-rated likelihood of raping and the social perception of rape. *Journal of Research in Personality, 15,* 147–158.

Ullman, S. E. (2010). *Talking about sexual assault: Society's response to survivors.* Washington, DC: American Psychological Association.

United States Merit Systems Protection Board. (1981). *Sexual harassment in the federal workplace: Is it a problem?* Office of Merit Systems Review and Studies. Washington, DC: United States Government Printing Office.

The State Council of Higher Education for Virginia. (1992). *Sexual assault on Virginia's campuses.* (Senate Document No. 17). Richmond, VA: Commonwealth of Virginia.

Vladutiu, C. J., Martin, S. L., & Macy, R. J. (2011) College- or university-based sexual assault prevention programs: A review of program outcomes, characteristics, and recommendations. *Trauma, Violence & Abuse, 12,* 67–86.

Ward, S. K., Chapman, K., White, S., & Williams, K. (1991). Acquaintance rape and the college social scene. *Family Relations, 40,* 65–71.

Warner, T. D. (2010). Violent acts and injurious consequences. *Journal of Family Violence, 25,* 183–193.

Warshaw, R. (1988). *I never called it rape.* New York: Sarah Lazin Books.

Wilson, K., Raison, R., & Britton, G. M. (1983). Cultural aspects of male sex aggression. *Deviant Behavior, 4,* 241–255.

Yescavage, K. (1999). Teaching women a lesson: Sexually aggressive and sexually nonaggressive men's perceptions of acquaintance and date rape. *Violence Against Women, 5,* 796–812.

Chapter 11

VULNERABILITIES AND OPPORTUNITIES 101: THE EXTENT, NATURE, AND IMPACT OF STALKING AND CYBERSTALKING AMONG COLLEGE STUDENTS AND IMPLICATIONS FOR CAMPUS POLICIES AND PROGRAMS

MEGAN C. STEWART AND BONNIE S. FISHER

See your face every place that I walk in
Hear your voice every time that I'm talking
You will believe in me
And I will never be ignored . . .

Violate all the love that I'm missing
Throw away all the pain that I'm living
You will believe in me
And I can never be ignored . . .

I would die for you
I would kill for you
I will steal for you
I'd do time for you
I will wait for you
I'd make room for you
I'd sail ships for you
To be close to you
To be part of you
Cause I believe in you
I believe in you
I would die for you

– Garbage, 1996, "#1 Crush," *William Shakespeare's*
Romeo + Juliet Music from the Motion Picture

INTRODUCTION

The above lyrics are not from a song about having a romantic crush on someone, as many individuals believe. Quite the contrary, these lyrics are about a stalker – someone who is not "quite right" (Simpson, 1995). This song is one of many contemporary pop songs (e.g., The Police's *Every Breath You Take,* Sarah McLachlan's *Possession*) that have been linked to stalking. Unfortunately being stalked – repeatedly pursued in a manner that causes a reasonable person fear for his or her safety – is much more serious than lyrics to a modern pop song. In the United States, stalking is a criminal act in all 50 states, the District of Columbia, and at the federal level (Fox, Nobles, & Fisher, 2011).

Stalking also is a grim reality for a large proportion of women and men (see Black, Basile, Brieding, Smith, Walters, Merrick, Chen, & Stevens, 2011; Cupach & Spitzberg, 2004; Davis & Frieze, 2000; Tjaden & Thoennes, 1998). Over a decade ago, the National Violence Against Women Survey (NVAWS), the first national study of stalking among the general population, estimated that between 8 percent–12 percent of women and between 2 percent–4 percent of men in the United States have been stalked at some point in their lives.[1] Annual estimates from the NVAWS reported that 1 percent–6 percent of women were stalked and 0.4 percent–1.5 percent of men were stalked (Tjaden & Thoennes, 1998). More recently, the National Intimate Partner and Sexual Violence Survey (NISVS), a national-level study of stalking among the general population, released a report (Black et al., 2011). NISVS estimated that one in six women (16.2%) and one in 19 men (5.2%) in the United States have experienced a stalking victimization in which they felt very fearful or believed that someone close to them would be harmed or killed as a result. Annual estimates from the NISVS reported that 4 percent of women and 1.3 percent of men were stalked.

There is overwhelming evidence that stalking is common among young adults, especially those 25 years old and under (Baum, Catalano, Rand, & Rose, 2009; Black et al., 2011; Tjaden & Thoennes, 1998). National studies also have consistently shown that women are the primary targets of stalkers (Baum et al., 2009; Black et al., 2011; Tjaden & Thoennes, 1998). Furthermore, stalkers are most likely to be a male known to the victim. In all likelihood, the stalker is some type of intimate partner – such as a current or former spouse or boyfriend, or a date – or an acquaintance (Black et al., 2011). Stalking victims adopt coping strategies but even so, researchers have consistently reported that being stalked takes a negative psychological and physical toll on the victims (see Davis, Frieze, & Maiuro, 2002; Ravensberg & Miller, 2003). Among the most unfortunate effect is the infrequent fatal outcome that is often oversensationalized by the media (Cupach & Spitzberg, 2004).

The purpose of this chapter is to provide an overview of the stalking re-search that has focused on the experiences of college students in the United States (see also Fisher, 2001).[2] First, we discuss the socio-demographic char-acteristics, lifestyle and routine activities of college students that may make them vulnerable stalking targets while simultaneously providing opportunities to stalk someone. We also highlight the characteristics of campuses that pro-vide ample opportunities for stalking to occur. Second, we review studies of college students that examined the extent of stalking victimization and per-petration. Our discussion also includes a description of characteristics of stalk-ing victims and stalkers. Third, we highlight what researchers know about the nature of pursuit behaviors stalkers use, the frequency and duration of stalk-ing, and its role in dating and intimate relationships. We also present results that provide insights into the known characteristics of stalking victims and stalkers. Fourth, we summarize strategies student victims have used to cope with their stalking victimization. Included in this section are discussions of the personal, reporting, and legal strategies students use to stop the stalker's pur-suit. Fifth, we examine the emotional and psychological toll stalking has on its targets. Last, we provide evidence-based policy and program implications that campus administrators will hopefully find helpful for addressing stalking victimization and perpetration on their respective campuses.

Vulnerabilities of Being Stalked and Opportunities for Stalking

Two sizable bodies of research informed by a variety of disciplines suggest that certain types of individuals are more vulnerable to criminal victimization and certain types of individuals are more likely to commit deviant or crimi-nal acts. Research consistently shows that particular demographic character-istics, as well as lifestyle and routine activities among the public, significantly predict who is at a high risk of experiencing predatory victimization (Cohen, Kluegel, & Land; 1981; Hindelang, Gottfredson, & Garofalo, 1978; Miethe & Meier, 1994). Similarly, research shows certain demographic characteristics and lifestyles and routine activities, some of which overlap with high-risk fac-tors for victimization, are common among predatory offenders in the general population (Lauritsen, Sampson, & Laub, 1991). Interestingly, specific char-acteristics of college students' demographics and their lifestyle and routine ac-tivities are similar to those found to create vulnerabilities for stalking victim-ization and opportunities to stalk in the general population research (Fisher, 2001; Mustaine & Tewksbury, 2013). Below, we discuss the socio-demograph-ic characteristics of college students, and the lifestyle and routine activities that make them vulnerable to being stalked and create opportunities for them to easily stalk their targets.

Socio-Demographic Characteristics of Stalking Victims and Stalkers

Over the past decade, researchers developed a better understanding of the demographic characteristics of both stalking victims and stalkers. For example, Baum et al. (2009) reported the risk of being stalked decreased with age, supported by the NVAWS which revealed over one-half of stalking victims were between the ages of 18 and 29. The NISVS reported that over half of females and a third of males were stalked prior to the age of 25 (Black et al., 2011). While Tjaden and Thoennes (1998; p. 5) refer to stalking as "a gender-neutral crime" and research shows both females and males are stalked, females at a much greater risk of being stalked (see also Baum et al., 2009). The NVAWS reported, for example, that 78 percent of stalking victims were female. Many definitions of stalking require a degree of fear, and the NISVS found that 16.2 percent of women who had experienced stalking sometime in their lifetime reported either being very fearful for herself or that someone close to her would be hurt or killed (Black et al., 2011).

Research has also shown that stalking perpetrators look much like stalking victims. Cupach and Spitzberg (2004) calculated national estimates of stalking perpetration prevalence across eight studies and found, on average, nearly 15 percent of males and almost 9 percent of females reported they had engaged in stalking behavior. According to the NCVS SVS, stalking victims are most likely to be stalked by someone who is the same age and race. For example, 41.6 percent of those victims age 18 to 20, and 48.2 percent of those 21 to 29, were stalked by someone of the same age (Baum et al., 2009).

The college population possesses many of the noted characteristics that research suggests make those in the general population vulnerable to being a stalking target (young and female) or perpetrator (young and male). According to the U.S. Department of Commerce (2011), of those in the general population, 51.7 percent of those ages 20–21, 30.4 percent of those 22–24, and 13.5 percent of those 25–29 were enrolled in school in 2009. Of all undergraduate students attending degree-granting postsecondary institutions, 56.8 percent were female (Aud et al., 2011). The sheer number of unmarried young women and men who routinely converge in classes and social settings over several years provides a sizeable pool of both potential stalking victims and perpetrators. Finally, the chance of becoming a stalking target or of stalking someone may be enhanced by consumption of alcohol (including binge drinking) and experimentation with illegal substances that occurs among a substantial portion of college students at parties and social events (see Dowdall, 2013).

The Campus Setting:
Providing Ample Opportunities for Stalking

A necessary element of criminal stalking is that the pursuit behavior must be a repeated course of conduct (Fox et al., 2011; Tjaden & Thoennes, 1998). Therefore, a stalker must have access – physical or electronic – to the target, as well as have the time to engage in repeated pursuit behavior.

From the stalker's perspective, access to the campus and its buildings, including dormitories and parking areas is relatively easy, especially if he or she is also a student. The ease of access onto a college campus is evident in its park-like setting with seemingly no physical boundaries other than a public thoroughfare or a sizable body of water (e.g., lake, ocean) that is contiguous. Campuses typically are "open" 24 hours, seven days a week, 365 days of the year to house, educate, employ, and entertain not only students, faculty, and staff but also daily visitors.

This eclectic campus population can easily flow legitimately from building to building or dorm to dorm anytime during the day or night. Many buildings are not routinely locked during the school year, especially during when classes are scheduled. Even those buildings, such as dormitories, whose doors are supposed to be routinely secured, can be jimmied to remain open unnoticed. On-campus parking garages and lots are also relatively easy to access. Because of the daily fluidity of the campus population, many parking areas have unrestricted admission and any patron can park and pay a fee, or freely walk through parking areas unnoticed by an attendant or closed circuit TV.

Given students' academic, employment, and social schedules, they are typically easy to locate on campus or communicate with for several reasons. First, their classes are scheduled at the same day and time and, most likely, in the same classroom over the course of a 10- or 15-week term. Even though their classes change from term to term, their schedules are very predictable for a set time. Their class schedule coupled with the ease of access to classroom buildings and to the larger campus provides an endless number of opportunities for watching someone, waiting for someone outside or inside a building, or leaving written notes or objects.

Second, many students live in university-owned or affiliated housing and park their vehicles on campus in assigned areas. Students' campus residential addresses, telephone numbers, and email addresses are found easily in printed or electronic directories available directly from the school. For would-be stalkers, getting this information is as easy as getting on the Internet and searching for a specific person at a specific school and waiting a few seconds for the directory results to appear on the screen. Many schools assign all their students name-based email accounts, so it is not too difficult to figure out a student's email address even without a web-based directory. Finding where a student parks his or her car on campus is just as easy, as most schools have designated student-parking areas. Stalkers can use this contact and location information to approach the victim by following him or her to class, waiting outside a classroom or motor vehicle, communicating via email, texting, social networking website, or postal service, sending gifts, or damaging the target's property.

Third, students spend much time on campus – a physical space easily monitored by a stalker. For example, a large proportion of students are employed on campus, such as in the library or as a parking attendant or lab assistant for their work study requirement. Students' routine work schedules could make them easy prey for a stalker at his or her place of employment. Students also frequently participate in regularly scheduled recreational activities on campus which can provide another setting for stalking. Finally, technology has made it relatively easy for a stalker to locate a particular person when they are just about anywhere, including on campus. For example, students frequently identify where they are going to be on particular days and times via websites like Facebook (www.facebook.com), or cell phone applications such as foursquare (www.foursquare.com).

Students' Lifestyle and Routine Activities: Stalking Vulnerabilities and Opportunities Abound

The lifestyles and routine activities that are characteristic of "average" college students can provide many opportunities for stalking victimization and perpetration. First, stalking not only involves having access to the victim but also having the time during the day or night to engage in pursuit behaviors. While at college, students have fairly unrestricted access to campus facilities around the clock, seven days a week during the academic term. Couple this ease of access with the large amounts of flexible and unsupervised time most students have and what arises are ample opportunities to stalk someone, especially another student.

Second, researchers have shown that stalking happens throughout the dating continuum from the absence of a relationship (but wanting one to develop), to during the relationship, to after the relationship ends (Williams & Frieze, 2005). Stalking research has well established that in over a majority of incidents, some type of prior relationship – spouse/former spouse, intimate partner (including current/former cohabiting partner, date, girl/boyfriend), or acquaintance – existed between the victim and pursuer (see Davis & Frieze, 2000). The most likely perpetrator of female stalking victims is a current or former intimate partner (marriage, cohabitation, or dating) whereas men are most likely to be stalked by a stranger or an acquaintance (Tjaden & Thoennes, 1998).

Third, college students widely use technology – the Internet and cell phones – that provide opportunities for a would-be stalker to easily and repeatedly access them day and night. A recent poll of Generation 2001 conducted by Harris Interactive (2001) reported that 100 percent of the sampled college students use the Internet, with only two-thirds of the general population accessing the Internet. The students' Internet usage averaged from six to 11 hours a week, with nine out of ten of them sending and receiving emails on a daily or frequent basis. Social networking sites (e.g., Facebook, Twitter, Myspace, Friendster) have also become exceedingly popular (Henson, Reyns, & Fisher, 2011). Many recent studies have revealed that nearly all college students have a cell phone. Hakoama and Hakoyama (2011) found that 99 percent of students in their survey reported having a cell phone, and Hanley reported that 99.8 percent of students in his study had a cell phone (Hernandez, 2010). Furthermore, Salaway, Caruso, and Nelson (2007) reported that in their large-scale study encompassing multiple college campuses, that 100 percent of students used e-mail, 84 percent used Instant Messenger, and 80 percent used social networking websites. Similarly, Junco and Mastrodicasa (2007) revealed that in a study of students at seven schools, 75.5 percent of students used Instant Messenger and two-thirds of students had Facebook accounts. Marketers are not the only interested parties to recognize the potential of opportunities created by a large proportion of college students frequently using technology. Stalkers also may take advantage of new technology to easily and quickly monitor their prey's phone calls or computer use, track their prey using hidden cameras or global positioning systems, or pursue their prey via email or cell phones (Spitzberg & Hoobler, 2002).

Fourth, the college years provide many opportunities for routinely encountering a variety of individuals, including other students and their friends, professors, staff, and visitors. Making acquaintances, developing friendships, initiating and maintaining dating relationships, and experiencing sexual intimacy are popular social activities for most college-aged populations, especially undergraduates who are typically single. Each of these experiences, however, may also be a stalking opportunity waiting to happen. Furthermore, Spitzberg and Rhea (1999) claimed that relational mobility (which also suggests relationship termination) may be highest during the college years. In their study of a single campus using a convenience sample of students enrolled in a basic communication course at a large public university in Texas, Spitzberg and Rhea (1999) reported that students had dated an average of five persons since high school. Other studies show a large proportion of stalking occurs among college students within the context of dating and relationship continuums (see Cupach & Spitzberg, 2004).

In sum, a range of characteristics from youthfulness and lifestyles to the campus setting provides ample opportunities for a stalker to easily and repeatedly pursue his or her prey. As we will discuss shortly, for a substantial proportion of students being a stalking victim or stalking someone is a reality. In the next section, we review the studies that have examined the extent and nature of stalking within the college student population.

Stalking Victimization and Perpetration Among College Students

The Extent of Stalking Victimization

Estimates of the proportion of college students who have been stalked are based on one national-level study of a large representative sample of 4,000 college women at 233 two- and four-year postsecondary institutions, the National College Women Sexual Victimization (NCWSV) study (Fisher, Cullen, & Turner, 2000, 2002) and numerous single-campus studies using nonprobability, primarily convenience, samples of students (see Cupach & Spitzberg, 2004; Ravensberg & Miller, 2003). Results from these studies show that compared to lifetime stalking estimates compiled by the NVAWS, college students are at a higher risk of experiencing stalking than are members of the general population. Lifetime prevalence estimates of stalking for female college students range from 12.2 percent (LeBlanc, Levesque, Richardson, & Ladislav, 2001) to 40.4 percent (Jordan, Wilcox, & Pritchard, 2007), with an average across eight studies of 24.5 percent (95% CI = 7.2%–41.8%) (Amar, 2006, 25.0%; Bjerregaard, 2000, 24.7%; Del Ben & Fremouw, 2002, 27.3%; Fremouw, Westrup, & Pennypacker, 1997, 30.7%; Nobles, Fox, Piquero, & Piquero, 2009, 20.5%; Westrup, Fremouw, Thompson, & Lewis, 1999; 15.5%). Lifetime prevalence stalking estimates for males range from 1.7 percent (LeBlanc et al., 2001) to 16.7 percent (Fremouw et al., 1997, with an average across four studies of 8.9 percent (95% CI = 0%–21.4%) (Bjerregaard, 2000, 10.9%; Nobles et al., 2009, 6.4%).

Research that examined stalking victimization during the school year reveals a substantial proportion of students are stalked during this relatively short time period. The NCWSV reported that 13 percent of college women had been stalked (Fisher et al., 2000, 2002). Noteworthy is that similar to the NVAWS results, the NCWSV study reported that a much larger proportion of college women are stalked during an academic term than are raped (3%) (see Tjaden & Thoennes, 1998). Mustaine and Tewksbury (1999), using a convenience sample of female college students enrolled in nine schools, found 11 percent of the women in their sample reported they had been stalked over a six-month period. Jordan et al. (2007) similarly found 11.3 percent of women in their sample had reported being stalked in the past 12 months.

Three studies have focused on stalking behaviors after the break-up of a heterosexual dating or marital relationship. From this limited research, it appears that college students, like those in the general population, are not immune from experiencing stalking after a relationship ends. Estimates range from between 9 percent and 34 percent of college women who recently ended a romantic relationship report their former romantic partner had stalked them (see Coleman, 1997; Logan, Leukefeld, & Walker, 2000; Roberts, 2002). Jordan, Wilcox, & Pritchard (2007) reported that of those college students stalked by an intimate partner, 85.2 percent experienced the stalking victimization following the end of the relationship. What is still unknown among college students is whether the stalking began *before* the relationship ended and why some stalking behaviors cease.

The Extent of Cyberstalking Victimization

Cyberstalking has received little attention in the research, as compared to the research on stalking. Most of the existing studies that have examined the cyberstalking of college students are plagued methodologically, mainly relying on convenience samples of college students (Reyns, Henson, & Fisher, 2012). Only one national-level study has been located that asked female college students about cyberstalking (via email), and that study found that 24.7 percent of women who were stalked reported being "repeatedly emailed in a way that seemed obsessive or resulted in feelings of fear" (Fisher et al., 2002). In their college student sample, Reyns, Henson, and Fisher (2012) reported that 40.8 percent of students experienced some form of cyberstalking during their lifetime. Spitzberg and Hoobler (2002) found that 14.5 percent of students self-identified themselves as victims of cyberstalking. The lowest estimate of cyberstalking was reported by Alexy, Burgess, Baker, and Smoyak (2005), who found that 3.7 percent of the college students in their sample had been cyberstalked. Holt and Bossler (2009) examined online harassment, and reported that 18.9 percent of their college student sample had experienced such victimization. Similarly, Finn (2004) looked at online harassment and found 10 percent of students were victims of cyberstalking by nonstrangers, and 15 percent were victims of stranger cyberstalking. As technology advances with cell phones and computers, and social networking sites like Facebook and Twitter grow in popularity, it is clear more research will contribute to better understanding the extent of cyberstalking on college campuses.

Characteristics of College Student Victims of Stalking

Overwhelmingly, studies of stalking among college students indicate that demographic characteristics do not differentiate victims from nonvictims (see

Bjerregaard, 2000; Coleman, 1997; Kraft & Wang, 2010; Mustaine & Tewksbury, 1999; Roberts, 2002). This lack of differentiation among stalking victims and nonvictims is most likely due to the fact that college students are a relatively homogeneous group, especially with respect to age (18–25 years old) and marital status (single or never married). However, the NCWSV (Fisher et al. 2000) did identify distinguishing characteristics among females that were significantly related to being a stalking victim. Compared to Caucasians and non-Hispanic/Latina college students, Native Americans or Alaska Natives were significantly more likely to be victimized, while Asians or Pacific Islanders were significantly less likely to be victimized. Family class was significantly related to being stalked: those from higher-class families were more likely to be stalking victims. Also, undergraduates were more likely to have been stalked than graduate students. Fisher and her colleagues speculated that undergraduates may be more likely to be stalked because they place themselves in a wider diversity of social situations that increase their exposure to the types of people who prey on young adults, especially women.

Research has also shown that lifestyle and routine activities of college women are significant risk factors for stalking. Mustaine and Tewksbury (1999) found that females who: (1) frequently go to the mall for shopping, (2) live off campus, (3) are employed, and (4) who participate in some drinking and drug use behaviors had an increased risk of experiencing stalking. Turning to a lifestyle perspective, they suggested that frequently going to the mall exposes females to more perpetrators, or that stalking victims may go to the mall because it is a public place and potentially offers a safer atmosphere than while at home. Employment, they argued, increases exposure to potential perpetrators and living off campus decreased the guardianship provided by living on campus. Finally, Mustaine and Tewksbury argued that female students who engage in some drinking and drug use behaviors may make themselves more vulnerable to stalkers.

Fisher et al.'s NCWSV study (2000) reported results that support the characteristics of college women stalking victims found by Mustaine and Tewksbury. Fisher and her colleagues found that living alone, dating or being in the early stages of a relationship, having a propensity to be in places with alcohol, and having experienced a prior victimization were significant predictors of female stalking victimization. It is also plausible that individuals who live alone are more suitable targets than those who live with other individuals. Those who date or were in the early stages of a relationship were more likely to be victims of stalking, quite possibly because they were being stalked by former partners, as previous research has shown. Finally, similar to Mustaine and Tewksbury's (1999) findings, Fisher et al.'s NCWSV results support the finding that those who frequent places with alcohol present may be more vulnerable and have greater exposure to stalking perpetrators.

Very little research exists that compares victims of cyberstalking to nonvictims. In one study, Kraft and Wang (2010) found that victims did not differ significantly from nonvictims in regards to age, race, whether or not they lived on campus, or whether or not they had a social networking account. However, the authors also reported that victims and nonvictims were different in regards to how much they visited a social networking account. Victims were more likely to visit their social networking account 14 or more times a week (49%) than nonvictims (23%).

Stalking Perpetration Among College Students

How Many Stalkers?

A handful of studies using small convenience samples of students have reported estimates of the extent of stalking perpetration in the college student population. Among the first studies to study student stalkers, Fremouw et al. (1997) reported that a very small proportion of students at West Virginia University – 2 percent of males and 0 percent of the females – had stalked someone in their lifetime. Lewis, Fremouw, Del Ben, and Farr (2001) reported slightly higher proportions – just over 4 percent of males and 5 percent of females – met their behavioral criteria for having stalked someone within the last 18 months while a student at West Virginia University. Asked if they had even been a stalker, nearly 3 percent of LeBlanc et al.'s (2001) sample of undergraduates at the Worcester Polytechnic Institute admitted to ever doing so. None of the females in their sample reported that they had stalked anyone. In more recent studies, Nobles et al. (2009) reported that in their sample of college students, 3.8 percent of females and 2 percent of males had admitted to stalking someone during their lifetime while Reyns et al. (2012) revealed that 4.9 percent of their sample of college students reported that they had perpetrated at least one cyberstalking victimization.

Characteristics of Student Stalkers

Research has shown that stalkers have identifying socio-demographic characteristics. In their summary of published stalker studies, Westrup and Fremouw (1998) concluded that a majority of stalkers are (1) single and never had been married, and (2) better educated, and (3) "smarter," that is, have a higher IQ than comparable nonstalking criminal populations.

Lewis et al. (2001) found that male stalkers, when compared to nonstalker controls, had considerably less developed problem-solving skills and cognitive flexibility. This study also found that stalkers (both male and female) reported increased difficulty with dependency, trust, abandonment, and security issues. Several studies have also found that stalkers lack social skills or are socially incompetent (Meloy, 1996; Mullen, Pathé, Purcell, & Stuart, 1999).

Differences between male and female stalking perpetrators also have been documented. For men, stalking perpetration was associated with heavy drinking and the use of alcohol or drugs during sex. For women, only the use of alcohol and drugs during sex was significantly related to stalking perpetration (Logan et al., 2000).

Research suggests that individuals who are known to the victim, at least on some level, perpetrate most stalking incidents. In the NCWSV study, Fisher et al. (2002) found that 80.3 percent of the victims reported that they knew or had seen their stalker before (53% of which reported they knew the stalker well), and that only 17.7 percent of the victims identified the stalker as a complete stranger. Similarly, in a sample of students enrolled at a large southeastern public university, Bjerregaard (2000) found that most of the victims had some former relationship to their stalker (e.g., former partner, acquaintance, or friend). To elaborate, 38.5 percent of females and 40.7 percent of males reported that they had been stalked by an ex-boyfriend/girlfriend, and only 18 percent of females and 11.1 percent of males reported that they had been stalked by a stranger. Fremouw et al. (1997) showed that over 80 percent of male and female victims reported that they knew their stalker, and 16.1 percent of females and 17.1 percent of males reported that the stalker was a stranger. Amar (2006) reported more than two-thirds of the female college students were stalked by someone interested in them (39%) or a former boyfriend (32%). Jordan et al. (2007) found 15.7 percent of students were stalked by an intimate partner, 43.6 percent by an acquaintance, and 40.7 percent by a stranger. In their sample of college women, Buhi, Clayton, and Surrency (2009) revealed that stalkers were most commonly acquaintances (48.7%), classmates (37.2%), or boyfriends/ex-boyfriends (34.6%). Overall, the large majority of stalking incidents are perpetrated by someone that is known to the victim. Of those incidents where the stalker is known to the victim, it is commonly a former romantic partner or someone known very well.

Unlike with stalking victimization, not much is known about the perpetrators of cyberstalking. However, one recent study by Reyns and his colleagues (2012) revealed that unlike with stalking, cyberstalking perpetrators typically were strangers to the victim (44.1%). When specifically examining perpetrators who are known to the victim, the most common victim-offender relationships were friends/former friends (25.4%), boyfriends/ex-boyfriends (12.1%) and acquaintances (8.7%). It is evident that more research needs to be completed on cyberstalking perpetrators to achieve a better understanding of the characteristics of these types of perpetrator.

A small number of studies have also looked at perpetrators of stalking and found a wide array of characteristics differentiating stalkers from nonstalkers. Roberts (2002) examined characteristics of stalking former partners. He found relative to nonstalkers, such individuals were more likely to: (1) frequently use alcohol and nonprescription drugs, (2) have mental health problems, (3) have criminal convictions, (4) have a history of violence, (5) have difficulty forming relationships, (6) frequently react with inappropriate emotion, (7) be jealous of relationships with others, and (8) be suspicious of relationship with others.

Del Ben and Fremouw (2002) also reported female victims' perceived differences between male stalkers and nonstalkers. Specifically, they found victims rated stalkers as controlling, hostile, and jealous while in the relationship, and tended to have an insecure attachment style. Victims in the "serious relationship" group also reported that they experienced a greater number of stalking behaviors than those females who were in the "casual relationship" group.

Collective results from these studies suggest that stalking perpetrators commonly have mental health problems, social-skill deficits and emotional problems, histories of violence, insecure attachments, and substance abuse issues. A majority of victims also report that former partners who stalk also had problems in relationships, usually involving reacting inappropriately with feelings of anger, jealousy, and suspiciousness. There has been no published study that has focused on the mental health status of college-student stalking perpetrators. Such a study is much needed because only then can we really begin to effectively prevent stalking.

The Nature of Stalking Behaviors

State and federal anti-stalking laws define a variety of repeat pursuit behaviors as illegal. Researchers have examined not only these illegal behaviors but also those behaviors not specifically defined as illegal but used to pursue someone (see Cupach & Spitzberg, 2004). Below, we provide an overview of what researchers who have studied college student stalking know about the pursuit behaviors perpetrators have commonly used to prey on targets.

Types of Stalking Behaviors

Overall, research suggests that the two most common types of stalking behaviors involve *approaching* (e.g., some form of contact via mail, face-to-face, email) and *surveillance* (e.g., spying, watching from afar). For example, Fisher and her colleagues (2000, 2002) reported that 77.7 percent of female victims were telephoned by their stalkers, 47.9 percent were waited for outside or inside of places, 44 percent were watched from afar, 42 percent were followed,

30.7 percent were sent letters, and 24.7 percent were emailed. Amar (2006) found that the most commonly reported stalking behaviors in her sample of female college students were communication against the respondents will (72%), being followed or spied on (72%), and receiving unsolicited calls (70%).

In studies comparing stalking behaviors experienced by female and male students, the most common type of behavior students experienced was being called on the telephone (see Black et al., 2011; Logan et al., 2000). Bjerregaard (2000), for example, found that 76.2 percent of female stalking victims were telephoned by their stalker, 74.6 percent reported that their stalker attempted face-to-face contact, and 27.9 percent were sent mail. Over 82 percent of victims reported that the stalker was successful in contacting them. For male victims, 72.4 percent were telephoned by their stalker, 69 percent reported that their stalker attempted face-to-face contact, and 24.1 percent were sent mail. Over 84 percent reported that the stalker successfully contacted them. Interestingly, the average number of telephone calls made to female victims was 43.7, whereas for male victims the average number of calls was, 89.2 – more than double the average for females.

Stalkers commonly used surveillance behaviors, especially after the termination of a romantic relationship. A substantial proportion of students report that the stalker would unexpectedly show up at places. For example, in Logan et al.'s (2000) study, 62.5 percent of the females who were stalked by their former partner were called at home while nearly 21 percent of the former partners stalked these women by driving by the victim's house. For male victims who were stalked by a former partner, 54.5 percent were called at home by their stalker and 36.4 percent of the stalkers came to the victim's house. A similar percentage of stalkers came to the victim's work or school.

Duration and Frequency of Stalking

Stalking victims have indicated that the duration and frequency that the stalker pursues them is not a trivial amount of time. The duration of the stalking behaviors is not brief but rather persists for some time. Fisher et al. (2000) reported that for college women the mean duration for stalking victimization, which is skewed by outliers, was 147 days. In contrast, the median duration was 60 days. Roberts (2002) reported a much higher average among female undergraduates: 19.5 months (approximately 585 days). This is also a much higher estimate than Bjerregaard (2000) reported. She found that men reported being stalked, on average, 182 days. Female students reported being stalked, on average, many less days – 83.4 days – than the male students.

While very little is known about the duration of cyberstalking, one study (Reyns et al., 2012) looked at the number of cyberstalking incidents that victims experienced. Reyns et al. (2012) reported that the overall average number of cyberstalking incidents in their college student sample was 2.95 incidents per victim, with females experiencing a higher average of 3.17 incidents per victim.

Stalking as a Stage in the Cycle of Intimate Partner Violence and Dating

The occurrence of abusive and aggressive behavior during an intimate or dating relationship appears to be related to the occurrence of stalking after the relationship ends. Davis, Frieze, and Maiuro (2002, p. 482) pointed out that "Kurt (1995) reminds us that stalking is part of the constellations of behaviors associated with domestic violence." Results from Logan et al.'s (2000) study of stalking among college students after a difficult breakup are supportive of Kurt's claim that stalking is another stage in an abusive relationship (see Cupach & Spitzberg, 2004; Davis & Frieze, 2000). Logan and her colleagues reported that students who reported being stalked after the breakup experienced significantly more physical and psychological victimization during the relationship than those who reported no stalking after the breakup. They also reported differences among females and males. Stalking was significantly associated with physical and psychological abuse for women victims. For male victims, stalking was associated with psychological abuse. Given their results, Logan et al. (2000) concluded that "stalking is a continuation of intimate partner violence toward a partner after the relationship ends" (p. 102).

Length of the relationship also has been shown to be significantly related to stalking by former partners. Roberts (2002) found that the duration of the former relationship for stalking victims was significantly longer than for harassed students and nonharassed students. Stalking victims, on average, were in the former relationship for 34.7 months compared to harassed victims who averaged 21.5 months and non-harassed victims who averaged 20.7 months.

Coping Strategies Used to Stop Stalking

The duration and frequency of stalking and its unpredictable timing and uncertain potential to become problematic for the victims raise an important issue: how victims respond to and cope with their experience. Studies have shown that a large proportion of students who are stalked take action. Bjerregaard (2000) found that 77.9 percent of females and 55.2 percent of males specifically requested the person stop the behavior. Fisher et al. (2002) found that 72.5 percent of female victims reported taking some action because of the stalking incident.

Students use a variety of strategies, many in conjunction with each other, in an attempt to cope with, and eventually stop the stalking (Cupach & Spitzberg, 1998). Fremouw et al. (1997) examined coping behaviors for both male and female stalking victims. They found that students most frequently chose to change their social environment or ignore their stalker. Female victims commonly: (1) ignored/hung up on their stalker, (2) confronted their stalker, (3) changed their schedule, and/or (4) carried a weapon (repellent spray). Male victims responded with similar strategies. They commonly: (1) confronted their stalker, and/or (2) ignored/hung up on their stalker. Unlike females, males were more likely to reconcile with their stalker. In Bjerregaard's (2000) study, the most common action females took was to change their phone number (22.1%) or to change their residence (22.1%). She also found that female victims were more fearful than male victims. Females were also more likely to call the police. This fear was substantiated by findings that showed females were more likely to be threatened and/or harmed, as compared to males. In Amar's (2006) study, female students most commonly reported that they: (1) avoided contact with the perpetrator (47%), (2) took extra precautions (38%), and (3) received help from family and friends (33%).

Finally, Fisher and her colleagues (2000, 2002) reported that the most common types of action taken among their sample of college women included: (1) avoiding or trying to avoid the stalker (43.2%), (2) confronting the stalker (16.3%), (3) not acknowledging messages or email (8.8%), (4) becoming less trustful or more cynical of others (5.6%), (5) installing caller ID (4.9%), (6) improving the security system of their residence (4.1%), and (7) traveling with a companion (3.9%). A large percentage of victims, 21.8 percent, adopted an unspecified form of action.

Although stalking is illegal, most students do not report their experience to the police or initiate the court's authority for relief. Among college women, Fisher et al. (2002) found that 83.1 percent of respondents did not report their stalking victimization to the police. These women cited numerous reasons for not reporting that included thinking the incident was not serious enough (72%), not knowing that the incident was a crime or that there was intent to harm (44.6%), and believing that the police would think the incident was not serious enough (33.6%). In a more recent study, Cass and Rosay's (2012) results indicated that college students did not believe that the criminal justice system would be as responsive if the stalking perpetrator was an ex-intimate, as opposed to a stranger. This belief among college students also might help to explain why many stalking victims do not report to police.

College women were also not likely to use the courts to address the stalker's pursuit behaviors. Fisher et al. (2002) reported that in less than 4 percent of the stalking incidents did a respondent seek a restraining order from the court and in only 1.9 percent of the incidents did the women file criminal charges against suspected perpetrators. Civil charges were filed in a little over one percent of the incidents. Supportive of these results, Fremouw et al. (1997) found that very few students resorted to legal interventions – either reporting to the police or having a restraint/warrant issued against the stalker. Bjerre-gaard (2000) reported that female victims are more likely than male victims to go to court regarding their stalking incident. To illustrate, nine percent of females went to court whereas none of the males did so. One possible expla-nation may be due to the Cass and Rosay's (2012) finding that men do not view the criminal justice system as being as responsive to female perpetrators who stalked males as it does to male perpetrators who stalked females.

No published study, to our knowledge, has evaluated the effectiveness of coping strategies used by students to stop their stalker's or cyberstalker's be-haviors. Such a study is needed because, as we discuss later, institutions of higher education have not adequately responded, if at all, to students who are stalked or who stalk fellow students.

The Psychological Toll of Stalking on Victims

Clinical and self-report studies of stalking victims have concluded that stalking causes an array of negative psychological and emotional problems (see Hall, 1998; Pathé & Mullen, 1997). The pervasiveness of fear, anger, and stress at not being able to control one's privacy is well documented (see Davis & Frieze, 2000). Not surprisingly, studies of college students have come to the same dismal conclusion: stalking has serious psychological and emotional consequences for student victims.

Westrup et al. (1999), for example, found that female victims suffered sig-nificant negative psychological effects because of being stalked. Stalking vic-tims reported more psychological symptoms compared to harassed or control groups of students. Victims of stalking also reported significantly higher lev-els of Post-Traumatic Stress Disorder symptoms relative to the harassed and control groups. Bjerregaard (2000) found that female victims were more like-ly to seek counseling than male victims. Although close to 6 percent of the women in Fisher et al.'s study (2002) became less trustful or more cynical of other, only 2.9 percent of the stalking victims sought psychological counsel-ing. This is significantly less than the 30 percent of stalked women in the NVAWS who sought counseling (and the 20% of stalked men who did) (Tjaden & Thoennes, 1998).

Implications for Campus Policy and Programs

Recognizing Stalking as a Crime

Stalking is a crime defined by laws that have been upheld by the courts as constitutional. It is a pressing issue that warrants recognition by campus ad-

ministrators so that appropriate policies and educational programs and services can be designed for stalking victims and perpetrators. There is also increasing evidence that cyberstalking among college students is of growing
concern in light of findings that most students own cell phones, computers,
and frequently visit social networking sites, which aid potential perpetrators
in locating students' whereabouts and increasing communication and surveillance. In these times when students are inundated with new technology –
much of which is encouraged by the college itself such as e-mail, Internet use,
online courses and materials, discussion boards – it is important for campus
administrators to better inform students of possible dangers and how they can
protect themselves from becoming a victim.

At this point, however, there is little evidence suggesting that college administrators recognize the seriousness of stalking victimization or perpetration
among students or the need to respond systematically. This is somewhat iron-
ic since over the last two decades campus administrators have addressed sexual victimization of college students, in part because schools have been held
civilly liable for these victimizations (Burling 2003). Also influential was passage of the *Jeanne Clery Disclosure of Campus Security Policy and Campus Crime
Statistics* (28 USC 1092) that requires Title IX schools to publish an annual security report which includes their crime statistics, such as forcible and nonforcible sex offenses and to establish a sexual assault policy that describes
many aspects of prevention (e.g., educational programs) and responses (e.g.,
procedures when a sexual assault happens, sanctions for offenders) to campus
sexual assault (see Kiss, 2013).

Despite recent gains, results from a national-level study of sexual assault
polices of institutions of higher education suggest that stalking has largely fall-
en outside the formal concerns of campus officials. Karjane, Fisher, and
Cullen (2001) reported that only 1.5 percent of all schools surveyed mentioned having a stalking policy in their sexual assault policies and an equally
small 1.5 percent reported having a separate stalking policy. When examining schools by type, four-year private nonprofit schools were most likely to
have a stalking policy mentioned in the content of their sexual assault policy
(3.6%), while four-year public schools were most likely to have a stalking policy separate from their sexual assault policy (3.7%). Even so, these are rather
small percentages among four-year schools. Most notably, 97 percent of all
four-year schools have not addressed stalking in mandated sexual assault materials that are distributed annually to students. One explanation could be that
since *The Clery Act* does not require reporting of stalking statistics, campus administrators feel they are under no legislative mandate to address stalking.
However, there is evidence of improvement in campus official's responses to
crime. In their study of universities in Florida, Truman and Mustaine (2009)
reported that 90 percent of the institutions mentioned stalking in their student

conduct code, and a majority had victim service units which defined stalking and gave advice as to what to do if being stalked.

Beyond the issue of publicly reporting stalking statistics is the matter of campus administrators recognizing the extent stalking victimization and perpetration happens to their students both on and off campus. Documenting the extent of stalking through the ease of a web-based victimization and perpetration survey can result in administrators more fully understanding the extent and nature of stalking among students. Such a survey can inform campus administrators about not only the characteristics of victims and stalkers and the negative toll these experiences have on students, but also which campus characteristics create opportunities for stalking to occur. With evidence-based information, administrators can be judicious in their approaches to addressing the extent and nature of stalking among their students.

Stalking Awareness and Education Policies and Programs

Assuming that the first step in effective public policy is recognizing that a substantial proportion of students are stalking targets and perpetrators, the next step is getting these issues on the active policy agenda. This second step includes the development of strategies for stalking awareness and education and mental health services. Caution should be exercised at this step so that administrators do not simply implement generic "crime prevention programs" or provide generic "mental health services" for students in a symbolic effort to "do something about the problem." As the research has shown, stalking presents unique challenges due to its repetitive nature, frequency and duration, and the ample opportunities presented by the physical campus setting and its operations, and students' lifestyle and routines, including high dating mobility.

These challenges, however, provide the opportunity for a comprehensive approach to addressing the needs of students (and faculty and staff, too) who have been stalked or have stalked someone. This comprehensive approach involves the entire campus community – students, as well as academic, housing, judicial or disciplinary affairs, counseling, medical, dining services, athletic, parking and other support staff – that can and should play a part in educating the campus community about the extent and nature of stalking among students, and working together to stop it. For example, residence hall personnel, professors, and campus security could be trained in how to identify stalkers who are looming in a location (e.g., on a dorm floor, outside a classroom, or in a parking area) and effectively intervene.

One way to increase awareness and education among the campus community is to incorporate the topic of "unwanted and repeated" pursuit behaviors into sexual awareness and prevention program and healthy dating programs at not only orientation sessions but also throughout the school year at strategic times (e.g., at the beginning of each academic term, during national sexual awareness week or month). Another means of disseminating information could be through *The Clery Act* mandated annual security report. A crucial element would be to use all educational materials to encourage victims to report stalking to residential hall personal, campus and law enforcement officials. Telling family, friends, roommates, and coworkers about the stalking and seeking their support can also provide added safety for the target by having additional "eyes and ears" watching and listening. Since the research is quite clear that stalking is psychological and even physically harmful, targets should be encouraged to seek counseling services and medical-related services. These clinical services, however, should be tailored to the specific needs of both the stalking target and perpetrator (see Ravensberg & Miller, 2003).

Another means to educating the campus community is to develop an antipursuit behavior or antistalking policy, similar to the sexual assault policy required by *The Clery Act,* or a sexual harassment policy. An antistalking policy could be included in the student and faculty code of conduct. Among the purposes of this policy would be to inform the stalking target of safety and procedural issues and the perpetrator to unacceptable behaviors that are subject to disciplinary and legal response. Included in this policy could be the state's legal definition of and penalties for criminal stalking, a description of the types of pursuit behaviors using campus setting examples, formal and legal redresses that victims can take both on and off campus to address (and hopefully stop) the pursuit behaviors, and a description of the school-based disciplinary sanctions (e.g. warning, dismissal). Formal actions can include documenting the location and times of the pursuit behaviors, saving all text communications, recording all telephone messages, and saving all gifts for criminal complaints. Information can also be provided that tells the victim that he or she has an option of filing a formal grievance or complaint against a student or campus employee perpetrator. Also, the antistalking policy could advise students that criminal stalking cases can be referred to the local law enforcement and prosecutor. Seeking help or treatment from counseling or medical staff should also be clearly included in such a policy.

Beyond the educational programming or antistalking policy, administrators need to think innovatively about how the campus setting and its operations may facilitate pursuit behaviors. This could range from access policies to buildings (especially residential halls) to rethinking the availability of student contact information on the web or assigning name-based email addresses. Also, with the technological advances found on and encouraged by most colleges (e.g., school/group Facebook pages, online discussion boards), there needs to be special attention placed on addressing how to limit the information accessed by would-be perpetrators.

Conclusion

The results from studies of college student stalking (and other student victimization studies) suggest that students do not exist in an ivory tower that protects them from crime (see Mustaine and Tewksbury, 2013). Recent cyberstalking research indicates that advances in technology (e.g. cell phones, computers, and social networking websites) allow college students to communicate and socialize in ways never imagined, including around the clock seven days a week (Henson et al., 2011). Stalking among college students, as we have noted, provides an opportunity for campus administrators to take a proactive approach to addressing stalking among their respective students. From a legal perspective, the courts have held campuses liable for "foreseeable" victimization (see Burling, 2003). Given the repeated nature of stalking and cyberstalking, the criterion for foreseeability may help to establish legal liability if campuses have not taken any procedural or substantive steps to address stalking and a stalking incident turns into a fatal attack. From an educational perspective, administrators should be concerned that many of their female students are stalking targets and many of their perpetrators are fellow students. Being stalked or stalking someone should not be included in the rising costs of attending college. If they are stalked, students should not have to cope alone without any support from the campus community.

NOTES

1. The range in the estimates reflects the degree of fear in the definition of stalking. The lower estimate is when respondents reported that the pursuit behavior made them feel a high level of fear. The upper estimate resulted in them being somewhat or a little frightened.

2. In this chapter, we limit our discussion to only those studies of college students that examined either legally defined or self-defined criminal stalking. We did not include studies that examined "unwanted pursuit behaviors" (see, for example, Langhinrichsen-Rohling, Palarea, Cohen, & Rohling, 2000) or "obsessive relational intrusion" (see, for example, Cupach & Spitzberg, 2004). Researchers have reported that both type of behaviors are prevalent among college students, yet we decided not to include them into our discussion of stalking as it is unknown if they would be legally defined or self-defined as stalking. This exclusionary decision on our part clearly points to the need for an acceptable definition and measurement of repeated pursuit behaviors if researchers are to advance the comparative stalking research (see Davis & Frieze, 2000; Fisher, 2001).

REFERENCES

Alexy, E. W., Burgess A. W., Baker, T., & Smoyak, S. A. (2005). Perceptions of cyberstalking among college students. *Brief Treatment and Crisis Intervention, 5,* 279–289.

Amar, A. F. (2006). College women's experience of stalking: Mental health symptoms and changes in routines. *Archives of Psychiatric Nursing, 20,* 108–116.

Aud, S., Hassar, W., Kena, G., Bianco, K., Fohlich, L., Kemp, J., & Tahan, K. (2011). The condition of education 2011 (NCES 2011–033). U. S. Department of Education, National Center for Education Statistics. Washington, DC: U.S. Government Printing Office.

Baum, K., Catalano, S., Rand, M., & Rose, K. (2009). *Stalking victimization in the United States.* Washington, DC: U. S. Department of Justice, Bureau of Justice Statistics.

Bjerregaard, B. (2000). An empirical study of stalking victimization. *Violence and Victims, 15,* 389–405.

Black, M. C., Basile, K. C., Brieding, M. J., Smith, S. G., Walters, M. L., Merrick, M. T., Chen, J., & Stevens, M. R. (2011). *The National Intimate Partner and Sexual Violence Survey (NISVS); 2010 Summary Report.* Atlanta, GA: National Center for Injury Prevention and Control, Center for Disease Control and Prevention.

Buhi, E. R., Clayton, H., & Surrency, H. H. (2009). Stalking victimization among women and subsequent help-seeking behaviors. *Journal of American College Health, 57,* 477–488.

Burling, P. (2003). *Crime on campus: Analyzing and managing the increasing risk of institutional liability* (2nd ed.). Retrieved from http://ww.nacua.org/onlinepubs/crimeon campus/CrimeonCampus.pdf.

Cass, A. I., & Rosay, A. B. (2012). College student perceptions of criminal justice system responses to stalking. *Sex Roles, 66,* 392–404.

Cohen, L., Kluegel, J., & Land, K. (1981). Social inequality and predatory criminal victimization: An exposition and a test of a formal theory. *American Sociological Review, 46,* 505–524.

Coleman, F. (1997). Stalking behavior and the cycle of domestic violence. *Journal of Interpersonal Violence, 12,* 420–432.

Cupach, W. R., & Spitzberg, B. H. (1998). Obsessional relational intrusions and stalking. In B. H. Spitzberg & W. R. Cupach (Eds.), *The dark side of close relationships* (pp. 233–263). Mahwah, NJ: Erlbaum.

Cupach, W. R., & Spitzberg, B. H. (2004). *The dark side of relationship pursuit: From attraction to obsession and stalking.* Mahwah, N. J.: Erlbaum.

Davis, K. E., & Frieze, I. H. (2000). Research on stalking: What do we know and where do we go? *Violence and Victims, 15,* 473–487.

Davis, K. E., Frieze, I. H., & Maiuro, R. (Eds.). (2002). *Stalking: Perspectives on victims and perpetrators.* New York: Springer.

Del Ben, K., & Fremouw, W. (2002). Stalking: Developing an empirical typology to classify stalkers. *Journal of Forensic Sciences, 47,* 152–158.

Dowdall, G. W. (2013). The role of alcohol abuse in college student victimization. In B. S. Fisher & J. J. Sloan III (Eds.), *Campus crime: Legal, social, and policy perspectives* (3rd ed.). Springfield, IL: Charles C Thomas.

Finn, J. (2004). A survey of online harassment at a university campus. *Journal of Interpersonal Violence, 19,* 468–483.

Fisher, B. S. (2001). Being pursued and pursuing during the college years: Their extent, nature, and impact of stalking on college campuses. In J. A. Davis (Ed.), *Stalking crimes and victim protection: Prevention, intervention, threat assessment, and case management* (pp. 237–238). Boca Raton, FL: CRC Press LLC.

Fisher, B. S., Cullen, F. T., & Turner, M. G. (2000). *Sexual victimization of college women.* Washington, DC: Department of Justice Statistics, National Institute of Justice, Bureau of Justice Statistics.

Fisher, B. S., Cullen, F. T., & Turner, M. G. (2002). Being pursued: Stalking victimization in a national study of college women. *Criminology and Public Policy, 1,* 257–308.

Fox, K. A., Nobles, M. R., & Fisher, B. S. (2011). Method Behind the Madness: An Examination of Stalking Measurements. *Aggression and Violent Behavior, 16,* 74–84.

Fremouw, W. J., Westrup, D., & Pennypacker, J. (1997). Stalking on campus: The prevalence and strategies for coping with stalking. *Journal of Forensic Sciences, 42,* 666–669.

Garbage (1996). #1 Crush [Recorded by Garbage]. On *William Shakespeare's Romeo + Juliet: Music from the Motion Picture* [CD]. Madison, WI: Capital.

Hakoama, M., & Hakoyama, S. (2011). The impact of cell phone use on social networking and development among college students. *The AABSS Journal, 15,* 1–20.

Hall, D. M. (1998). The victims of stalking. In J. R. Meloy (Ed.), *The psychology of stalking: Clinical and forensic perspective* (pp. 115–136). San Diego, CA: Academic Press.

Harris Interactive (2001). *Presenting: The class of 2001.* Retrieved from http://www.harrisinteractive.com/news/printerfriend/index.asp?NewsID=292.

Henson, B., Reyns, B. W., & Fisher, B. S. (2011). Security in the 21st century: Examining the link between online social network activity, privacy, and interpersonal victimization. *Criminal Justice Review, 36,* 253–268.

Hernandez, S. (2010). Ball State study shows college students' smartphone usage rising. Retrieved from http://www.bsudailynews.com/ball-state-study-shows-college-students-smartphone-usage-rising-1.2275899.

Hindelang, M. J., Gottfredson, M. R., & Garofalo, J. (1978). *Victims of personal crime: An empirical foundation for a theory of personal victimization.* Cambridge, MA: Ballinger.

Holt, T. J., & Bossler, A. M. (2009). Examining the applicability of lifestyle-routine activities theory for cybercrime victimization. *Deviant Behavior, 30,* 1–25.

Jordan, C. E., Wilcox, P., & Pritchard, A. J. (2007). Stalking acknowledgement and reporting among college women experiencing intrusive behaviors: Implications for the emergence of a "classic stalking case." *Journal of Criminal Justice, 35,* 556–569.

Junco, R., & Mastrodicasa, J. (2007). *Connecting to the Net Generation.* Washington, DC: National Association of Student Personnel Administrators.

Karjane, H. M., Fisher, B. S., & Cullen, F. T. (2001). *Campus sexual assault: How America's institutions of higher education respond.* Final Report. Washington, DC: National Institute of Justice, U.S. Department of Justice.

Kiss, A. (2013). The Jeanne Clery Act: A summary of the law and its evolution in higher education. In B. S. Fisher & J. J. Sloan (Eds.), *Campus crime: Legal, social, and policy perspectives* (3rd ed.). Springfield, IL: Charles C Thomas.

Kraft, E. M., & Wang, J. (2010). An exploratory study of the cyberbullying and cyberstalking experiences and factors related to victimization of students at a public liberal arts college. *International Journal of Technoethnics, 1,* 74–91.

Langhinrichsen-Rohling, J., Palarea, R. E., Cohen, J., & Rohling, M. L. (2000). Breaking up is hard to do: Unwanted pursuit behaviors following the dissolution of a romantic relationship. *Violence and Victims, 15,* 73–90.

Lauritsen, J. L., Sampson, R. J., & Laub, J. H. (1991). The link between offending and victimization among adolescents. *Criminology, 29,* 265–292.

LeBlanc, J. J., Levesque, G. J., Richardson, J. B., & Ladislav, H. B. (2001). Survey of stalking at WPI. *Journal of Forensic Sciences, 46,* 367–369.

Lewis, S. F., Fremouw, W. J., Del Ben, K., & Farr, C. (2001). An investigation of the psychological characteristics of stalkers: Empathy, problem-solving, attachment and borderline personality features. *Journal of Forensic Sciences, 46,* 80–84.

Logan, T. K., Leukefeld, C., & Walker, B. (2000). Stalking as a variant of intimate violence: Implications from a young adult sample. *Violence and Victims, 15,* 91–111.

Meloy, J. R. (1996). Stalking (obsessional following): A review of some preliminary studies. *Aggression and Violent Behavior, 1,* 147–162.

Miethe, T. D., & Meier, R. F. (1994). *Crime and its social context: Toward an integrated theory of offenders, victims, and situations.* Albany, NY: State University of New York Press.

Mullen, P. E., Pathé, M., Purcell, R., & Stuart, G. W. (1999). Study of stalkers. *American Journal of Psychiatry, 156,* 1244–1249.

Mustaine, E. E., & Tewksbury, R. (1999). A routine activity theory explanation for women's stalking victimizations. *Violence Against Women, 5,* 43–62.

Mustaine, E. E., & Tewksbury, R. (2013). The routine activities and criminal victimization of students. In B. S. Fisher & J. J. Sloan (Eds.), *Campus crime: Legal, social, and policy perspectives* (3rd ed.). Springfield, IL: Charles C Thomas.

Nobles, M. R., Fox, K. A., Piquero, N. L., & Piquero, A. R. (2009). Career dimensions of stalking victimization and perpetration. *Justice Quarterly, 26,* 476–503.

Pathé, M., & Mullen, P. E. (1997). The impact of stalkers on their victims. *British Journal of Psychiatry, 170,* 12–17.

Ravensberg, V., & Miller, C. (2003). Stalking among young adults: A review of the preliminary research. *Aggression and Violent Behavior, 8,* 455–469.

Reyns, B. W., Henson, B., & Fisher, B. S. (2012). Stalking in the twilight zone: The extent of cyberstalking victimization and offending among college students. *Deviant Behavior, 33,* 1–25.

Roberts, K. A. (2002). Stalking following the breakup of romantic relationships: Characteristics of stalking former partners. *Journal of Forensic Sciences, 47,* 1070–1077.

Salaway, G., Caruso, J. B., & Nelson, M. R. (2007). *The ECAR Study of Undergraduate Students and Information Technology, 2007.* Boulder, CO: EDUCAUSE, 2007. Retrieved from http://connect.educause.edu/library/abstract/TheECARStudyof Underg/45075.

Simpson, D. (1995). *Vig's atomic dustbin.* UK: Melody Maker.

Spitzberg, B. H., & Hoobler, G. (2002). Cyberstalking and the technologies of interpersonal terrorism. *New Media and Society, 4,* 71–92.

Spitzberg, B. H., & Rhea, J. (1999). Obsessive relational intrusion and sexual coercion victimization. *Journal of Interpersonal Violence, 14,* 3–20.

Tjaden, P., & Thoennes, N. (1998). *Stalking in America: Findings from the national violence against women survey.* Denver, CO: Center for Policy Research.

Truman, J. L., & Mustaine, E. E. (2009). Strategies for college student stalking victims: Examining the information and recommendations available. *American Journal of Criminal Justice, 34,* 69–83.

U.S. Department of Commerce, Census Bureau. (2011). Current Population Survey (CPS), October Supplement. Retrieved from http://nces.ed.gov/programs/coe/ indicator_ope.asp.

Westrup, D., & Fremouw, W. J. (1998). Stalking behavior: A literature review and suggested functional analytic assessment technology. *Aggression and Violent Behavior, 3,* 255–274.

Westrup, D., Fremouw, W. J., Thompson, R. N., & Lewis, S. F. (1999). The psychological impact of stalking on female undergraduates. *Journal of Forensic Sciences, 44,* 554–557.

Williams, S. L., & Frieze, I. H. (2005). Courtship behaviors, relationship violence, and breakup persistence in college men and women. *Psychology of Women Quarterly, 29,* 248–257.

Chapter 12

CRIME ON CAMPUS: SPATIAL ASPECTS OF CRIME AT A REGIONAL COMPREHENSIVE UNIVERSITY

MATTHEW ROBINSON AND SUNGHOON ROH

INTRODUCTION

If we knew *why* crime occurred, it would be easier to prevent because we could make efforts to reduce those factors thought to cause crime (Bohm, 2000). Similarly, if we knew *where* crime was likely to occur, it would be easier to prevent because we could focus efforts at those places where crime is most likely to occur (Rengert, Mattson, & Henderson, 2001). While neither approach – focusing on people or places – is necessarily superior to the other, it is fair to conclude that the place-specific approach has led to more effective crime prevention techniques (e.g., Paulsen & Robinson, 2004).

In this chapter, we utilize the place-specific approach by examining police statistics at a university campus in the Southeast United States. Our primary goal is to identify the places that host the most crimes, as reflected in campus crime data, in order to determine why some places have many crimes known to the police while others have few or none. Another goal is to suggest place-specific crime prevention strategies for those places that generate the most crime.

Previous studies at the same campus have shown there is very little serious criminal activity; students, faculty, and staff do not feel there is a "crime problem" on the campus; there are low levels of fear and perceived risk of victimization; and the campus is rated as "highly attractive" and "aesthetically pleasing" (see Mullen, Robinson, & Paulsen, 2001; Robinson & Mullen, 2001). While these previous studies have been useful to policy-makers in various ways – including demonstrating the high level of safety on the campus and identifying at least one significant crime problem (i.e., underage alcohol use and illicit drug use) – their main limitation is that they did not directly address the spatial aspects of crime on the campus. That is, the studies did not address *where* crimes most occur and what might explain the spatial variation on campus. Our current study attempts to overcome this weakness.

Literature Review

The literature on campus crime has historically been sparse but has grown significantly in the past decade. Specifically, a 2002 search for peer-reviewed articles utilizing the database, Criminal Justice Periodicals Index, found only 115 articles on campus crime, but a search in 2012 using the same database found 3,326 articles, most of them published since 2000.

As the chapters in this volume show, campus crime research addresses issues such as criminal victimization on college and university campuses, lifestyles and routine activities and criminal victimization, and potential crime prevention strategies that can be implemented to reduce or eliminate opportunities for criminality on campus (Armstrong, Hamilton, & Sweeney, 2006; Brantingham & Brantingham, 1994; Brinkley & Laster, 2003; Bromley, 1994; Cass, 2007; Clodfelter et al., 2010; Fisher, Sloan, Cullen, & Lu, 1998; Fox & Hellman, 1985; Henson & Stone, 1999; Jackson, Gilliand, & Veneziano, 2006; Johnson & Sigler, 1996; Moriarty & Pelfrey 1996; O'Kane, Fisher, & Green, 1994; Richards, 1996; Schwartz et al., 2001; Siegel & Raymond, 1992; Sloan, 1992, 1994; Tewksbury & Mustaine, 2003). Other studies address university obligations involving federal and state laws designed to increase safety on campus and inform the public about crimes on campus (Fisher & Sloan, 1993; Sloan, Fisher, & Cullen, 1997).

These previous studies demonstrate several notable realities about campus crime. First, levels of crime against persons on campus are less than that against the general population off campus. Second, the vast majority of campus crime involves property offenses, while violent crimes are rare. Third, the majority of students feel safe on campus even though perceptions of safety vary depending on student demographics and time/space correlates. Fourth, many victims of crime occurring on campus (especially property crimes) do not report the event to the police, making difficult a correct estimation of campus crime under the FBI's Uniform Crime Reports (UCR) system. Fifth, students' risky lifestyles (e.g. the use of alcohol and illicit drugs) increase their vulnerability to some forms of criminal victimization (Abbey, 2002; Abbey et al., 2001; Armstrong, Hamilton, & Sweeney, 2006; Cass, 2007; Clodfelter et al., 2010; Fisher et al., 1998; Jackson, Gilliand, & Veneziano, 2006; Robinson, 2004; Schwartz et al., 2001; Testa & Livingston, 1999; Tewksbury & Mustaine,

2003; Wechsler et al., 1995; Wechsler & Wuethrich, 2003).

An additional reality of crime generally (that has not been widely documented on college and university campuses) is that crime tends to cluster in some areas. In these areas, known as "hot spots" of crime, a very large amount (in relative terms) of crime occurs. In this chapter, we examine whether police statistics show that hot spots exist on one university campus. However, before we present our evidence, we first discuss the concept of "hot spots" of crime.

Hot Spots of Crime

Criminological research has identified places that host a disproportionate amount of crime (Brantingham & Brantingham, 1999; Sherman, Gartin, & Buerger, 1989; Sherman & Weisburd, 1995). A significant amount of research exists concerning hot spots of crime and their impact on criminal victimization. Specifically, research on hot spots has dealt with the crimes of burglary (Robinson, 1998a), auto burglary (Cochran & Bromley, 2002), liquor-related crime (Block & Block, 1995), homicide (Block & Christakos, 1995; Block & Block, 1998), street gang violence (Block & Block, 1995), gun violence (Sherman & Rogan, 1995), robbery (Braga, Hureau, & Papachristos, 2011), disorderly behavior (Koper, 1995), drug activity (Green, 1995; Weisburd & Green, 1995), and juvenile crime (Weisburd, Morris, & Groff, 2009).

Common hot spots of crime include street blocks near bars, alcohol outlets, and known drug selling areas (Gorman, Zhu, & Horel, 2005; Roncek & Maier, 1991), entertainment districts (Cochran, Bromley, & Branch, 2000), casinos (Stitt, Nichols, Giacopassi, 2003; Barthe & Stitt, 2007), some street segments in cities (Weisburd, Bushway, Lum, & Yang, 2004), a tiny fraction of all blocks in large cities (Braga, Hureau, & Papachristos, 2011), bus stops (Loukaitou-Sideris, 1999), many places where disorder is common (Braga, & Bond, 2008; Kochel, 2011), and even schools (Kautt, & Roncek, 2007).

Only a few published studies exist within educational institution settings that explore physical environmental features of crime hot spots. For example, O'Kane et al. (1994) found that about 40 percent of all auto-related crime occurred on only 12 percent of campus street segments, which were easily accessible to major thoroughfares. Astor et al. (1999) showed that the majority of violent events in high schools were concentrated in spaces with no guardians, such as hallways, dining areas, and parking lots. Rengert and Lowell (2005) showed that hot spots even exist within buildings on a university campus.

These hot spot studies are limited in terms of crime type and study setting. This is a particularly glaring omission in hot spot research considering the amount of crime – especially crimes against property that are most amenable to prevention efforts – that occurs on college campuses in any given year. It is likely that there are hot spots of campus crime because the environmental factors that may account for hot spots are prevalent on college campuses (e.g., a large amount of targets that are often unguarded in some locations, making those targets more attractive to offenders).

There are at least three kinds of hot spots, each of which potentially has a separate explanation (Clarke & Eck, 2006). First, crime generators attract "large numbers of people . . . for reasons unrelated to criminal motivation" (e.g., shopping areas, transportation hubs, festivals, and sporting events). Here, crime is attributable to the "large number of place users and targets." Second, crime attractors are places that provide "many criminal opportunities that are well known to offenders" so that those "with criminal motivation are drawn to such locales" (e.g., prostitution and drug areas, entertainment spots). Third, crime enablers provide "little regulation of behavior at places" so that "rules of conduct are absent or are not enforced" (e.g., a parking lot with no attendant).

Several theoretical perspectives can explain these three types of hot spots of crime: rational choice theory, routine activity theory, and crime pattern theory. According to rational choice theory, offenders engage in criminal acts only when they believe that the potential benefits outweigh expected costs by their criminal behaviors (Cornish & Clarke, 1986). Circumstances, situations, and opportunities heavily affect the decision-making process because the offender considers these factors in such a way as to produce the maximum net benefits expected from committing crimes.

Routine activity theory posits that crime requires three elements: motivated offenders, suitable targets (potential victims), and an absence of capable guardians (Cohen & Felson, 1979; Felson, 2002). The risk of crime increases when these three elements converge at the same place at the same time. In contrast, eliminating any one element results in no crime occurring. Routine activity theory has been mostly used to explain property crime when the property is a suitable target and when it is not protected by a capable guardian.

Finally, crime pattern theory combines rational choice theory and routine activity theory to explain the geographic distribution of crime (e.g., Brantingham & Brantingham, 1993; Eck & Weisburd, 1995). Crime pattern theorists assume that most offenders seek their crime targets within areas that are familiar to them. Serious offenders, like the rest of us, engage in noncriminal activities in their daily lives. As they engage in their daily routines, they come to recognize desirable targets for crime. It is in these areas that crime will most frequently occur.

According to crime pattern theory, triggering of a criminal event occurs by the presence of an opportunity that an offender comes upon in the course of a search (minimal or broad) depending on such factors as how well the offender knows the area). Nodes refer to where people travel to and from, paths are the main areas of travel in-between these nodes, and edges are the boundaries of areas where people engage in their activities (Clarke & Eck, 2006).

There have been numerous studies to explain campus crime with routine activity theory (Armstrong, Hamilton, & Sweeney, 2006; Cass, 2007; Clodfelter et al., 2010; Fisher & Wilkes, 2003; Jackson, Gilliand, & Veneziano, 2006; Mustaine & Tewksbury, 1998; Schwartz et al., 2001; Tewksbury & Mustaine, 2003; Volkwein, Szelest, & Lizotte, 1995; Wooldredge, Cullen, & Latessa, 1995). However, most of these studies focus on vulnerability to crime by focusing on victims' lifestyles rather than crime-prone spatial characteristics. This, too, can be conceived as a limitation to the body of literature on campus crime because physical features of the built environment play a large role in explaining where crime can cluster in hot spots, consistent with the crime prevention approaches of Crime Prevention Through Environmental Design (CPTED) and Situational Crime Prevention. In the next section, we discuss these two approaches to crime prevention.

Preventing Crime:
Environmental Design and Situational Actions

Alterations to the physical environment, such as increasing lighting, are examples of CPTED, which aims to "[identify] conditions of the physical and social environment that provide opportunities for or precipitate criminal acts . . . and the alteration of those conditions so that no crimes occur . . ." (Brantingham & Faust, 1976, pp. 289–292). CPTED thus involves the management, design, or manipulation of the physical environment to prevent crime (Crowe, 1991; Robinson, 1999b). On the university campus, CPTED most commonly takes the form of blue-light trails, increased lighting and security mechanisms, and other target hardening devices (e.g., locks, alarms) (Robinson, 1999b).

CPTED is similar to "situational crime prevention." Situational crime prevention is aimed at eliminating opportunities for crime. It includes opportunity-reducing measures that are targeted at specific forms of crime and aimed at increasing "the effort and risks of crime and reduce the rewards as perceived by a wide range of offenders" (Clarke, 1992, pp. 3–4).

There are at least 25 different approaches to crime prevention aimed at reducing opportunities for crime. The five major categories of situational crime prevention include increasing the difficulty of crime; increasing the risks of crime; reducing the rewards of crime; reducing provocations for crime; and removing excuses for crime (Clarke, 2001).

While CPTED and situational crime prevention generally involve changing the environment to reduce the opportunity for crime, they are aimed at
other outcomes as well. These include reducing fear of crime and perceptions
of crime risk, increasing the aesthetic quality of an environment (e.g., by reducing conditions of incivilities) and increasing the quality of life for law-abiding citizens, especially by reducing the propensity of the physical environment to support criminal behavior (Robinson, 1999b).

On many university and college campuses, where the risks of victimization
by serious violent crimes may be remote, relative to large and mid-size cities,
CPTED and situational crime prevention strategies may still be useful. Since
alterations to the physical environment of campus may make people feel safer
and less fearful, as well as increase the aesthetic quality of the surroundings,
CPTED and situational crime prevention have a place on campus. Further,
crime prevention efforts directed at hot spots of crime on campus should
greatly reduce the amount of crime on campus, given that most crimes on
campus (like off campus) likely occur in certain areas regularly. We believe
that focusing on hot spots of crime will reduce the majority of crime on campus.

Hot Spots of Crime on Campus: A Case Study

The current study examines the university police statistics (2004–2005) for
the most common crimes occurring on the campus of a major comprehensive
university in the southeastern United States. The goals of the study are to determine which places generate the most crimes known to the police and develop potential explanations as to why. We relate the findings to those from
the previous studies of the same university campus and pay special attention
to violations of drugs and alcohol, since they are related to other forms of
criminality. The study's explicit focus on the spatial aspects of the campus
crime make it unique. Although a significant amount of time has passed since
the completion of the study, little has changed on campus in terms of criminality; we discuss this more fully later in the chapter.

Study Location

The university under study – Appalachian State University – is located in
Boone, North Carolina, a town that, at the time of this study, was inhabited by
approximately 14,000 residents (not counting students). The university is located in a county that, at the time of the study, had only about 45,000 residents.
Given these population figures, it is not surprising that the town and the county have below average crime rates and especially very little violent crime. This

is because rates of street crime tend to be much higher in large and mid-size cities (Paulsen & Robinson, 2004). Thus, there is a wide perception that students at "Appalachian" are not threatened by the possibility of serious criminal victimization, either while they are on campus or while traveling throughout the town or county. Indeed, police statistics show that serious street crime is rare relative to larger towns and counties in the state and region.

This perception was shaken when, only 13 months apart, two Appalachian students were murdered in off campus drug deals that had gone wrong. The murders caused great concern on campus and significant attention was focused on criminal victimization of university students and the crime prevention techniques that could be implemented on campus to protect students and put people's minds at ease. This study was motivated, in part, by these murders.

Appalachian State is a major comprehensive public university that, at the time of the study, had approximately 14,000 students, and is one of 16 campuses of the state of North Carolina's university system. The university population has since grown to more than 17,000 students. As Appalachian is located in Blue Ridge chain of the Appalachian Mountains, its campus is surrounded by mountains, trees, and park-like features (e.g., streams, boulders, etc.). Previous studies of the campus show that users of the campus generally rate the campus as highly attractive. The university is more than 100 years old and serves mostly residential students from the surrounding counties and larger state of North Carolina.

Study Methodology

We contacted the University Police Department and requested the most recent campus crime statistics. The available data included two years of data (2004–2005) of calls for police service and police-initiated services for various types of crimes. The data were stored in police logs that were not computerized, not searchable, nor organized by crime type, location, date, time of day, or any other meaningful category. Thus, we had to sort through each daily log of crimes known to the police, hundreds of pages each with between one and 20 crimes per page. Although much has changed on the campus since the completion of this study, especially the construction of new buildings mostly on the center of campus, crime remains low, as will be illustrated later in the chapter.

We then made a list of campus crimes for each major crime indicated in the data. For example, going chronologically through the data, we listed each theft by location, date, and time. Then, we counted the total number of each type of crime to determine which types of crimes were most common on campus. This process introduces the possibility of error, as some crimes were listed more than once (often to update the case with new evidence or the passage of time as cases were solved or closed due to a lack of evidence). It is also possible that we did not receive every page of data from the Department. Because of this, our counts of campus crimes may not perfectly match those ultimately compiled by the University Police Department.

Police often combined counts of alcohol and illicit drug violations. For example, at one police response at a dorm, five citations were issued for alcohol use and illicit drug use. Since the police log did not specify how many citations were given for alcohol violations and how many were given for illicit drug violations, we were forced to count these violations as five alcohol violations and five illicit drug violations. We suspect this will tend to inflate the numbers of these offenses (although the data will still likely underestimate the true number of alcohol and illicit drug use violations on campus since most are not known to the police).

An additional limitation of the police data is that most criminal victimizations are not included in police data. Nationwide, less than 40 percent of serious criminal victimizations are captured in police data (Robinson, 2005). Thus, this study of crimes known to the police does not likely capture the majority of criminal victimizations on campus. However, in the absence of a university-wide victimization survey that addresses location of offenses, police data are the only data available for a study of campus crime locations. Further, most studies of place and crime utilize official crime statistics from police departments (Paulsen & Robinson, 2004).

With these limitations in mind, we next plotted campus crimes on maps of the university campus in order to identify those areas on campus that generated the most crimes as reflected in police statistics. Given that we did not have addresses for any of the crimes, including those that occurred inside dorms, academic buildings, and in parking lots, we could not plot exact locations of where the crimes occurred. Further, it was impossible to plot crimes that occurred on streets since the police data did not indicate where on streets the crimes occurred. The police data merely indicated from which streets calls originated (or on which street the offense occurred). The most common crime on streets was driving while intoxicated (DWI), and most of these were likely discovered by the police rather than initiated by a telephone call for service.

Given the nature of criminal victimization on campus, it was impossible to calculate criminal victimization rates based on the number of potential victims in each location. This is because there is no way to know how many potential victims and targets there were in each location during the 2004 and 2005 calendar years. For example, one dorm may have had more criminal violations than another dorm, simply because there were more people there, and/or because there were targets that were more suitable. We did contact the university's Department of Housing and Residential Life and learned that the average number of occupants in each dorm at the time of the study was 267 students, with very little variation in this number across the 19 living centers. Only five dorms had substantially less than the number of average students in residence (these dorms housed 109, 128, 172, 215, and 221 students), and only one dorm had substantially more (371 students). We discuss the implications of these numbers in the findings section. It was impossible to calculate crime rates based on the number of students living in each dorm, since this is not a suitable indicator of the number of potential victims and offenders in any given location.

Data included crimes known to the police on campus, on non-campus buildings or property, on public property, and in on campus residential facilities. We did not consider non-campus buildings outside town limits. Public property includes roads, thoroughfares, streets, sidewalks and parking facilities. Those that are off campus were also not considered. Thus, we only examined crime statistics on campus, in on campus residential facilities, and in public property located on campus.

Results and Discussion

MOST COMMON CRIMES ON CAMPUS. The most common crimes according to the police data in the two-year period of study (2004–2005) were theft, alcohol violations, drug violations, and vandalism. Table 12.1 shows the numbers of recorded offenses for each type of crime in 2004–2005.

These top four crimes on campus in 2004–2005 are similar to those from previous studies conducted on the same campus from 1997–2000. For example, findings from victimization surveys of space users on the same campus suggested that the most common crimes on campus were crimes involving legal and illegal drugs. Further, the most common self-reported form of criminal victimization on campus was for someone to offer the student some illegal drugs while on campus, followed by burglary, theft, and threats of violence (Robinson & Mullen, 2001).

More recent data from the university police department confirm that these crimes remain the most common crimes on campus through 2010 (Appalachian State University, 2012). We've also reported in Table 12.1 data on serious crimes only to demonstrate that these crimes have not increased since the original study (data on other crimes were not reported by the university police).

Police data also show that there were almost no violent crimes reported to the police. In 2004 and 2005, there were no murders or robberies, five sexual assaults, and 28 reported assaults (two students were murdered in 2005, but both were murdered off campus, as noted above). This, too, is nearly identical to the findings of the victimization surveys from previous years. In 2009

Table 12.1
Crimes Known to the Police (2004–2005 and 2009–2010)
at Appalachian State University

Type of Offense	2004	2005	Total	2009	2010	Total
Alcohol Violations	163	221	384	149	113	262
Arson	4	2	6	0	1	1
Assault	13	15	28	0	1	1
Breaking & Entering	17	13	30	22	21	43
Child Neglect	1	0	1			
Communicating Threats	14	12	26			
Disorderly Conduct	20	30	50			
Domestic Dispute	0	6	6			
DWI	31	29	60			
Forcible Fondling	2	0	2			
Forgery	1	1	2			
Fraud	6	5	11			
Hacking	1	0	1			
Harassment	12	21	33			
Harassing Phone Calls	17	17	34			
Hit and Run	14	22	36			
Illicit Drug Violations	116	139	255			
Inappropriate Behavior	2	1	3			
Indecent Exposure	1	0	1			
Motor Vehicle Theft	7	3	10	2	1	3
Murder	0	0	0	0	0	0
Peeper	0	1	1			
Possessing Stolen Property	3	3	6			
Property Damage	15	10	25			
Robbery	0	0	0	0	1	1
Sexual Assault	3	2	5	5	3	8
Solicitation	5	2	7			
Soliciting Sex	0	1	1			
Theft	159	148	307	136	150	286
Trespassing	9	13	22			
Vandalism	101	145	246			
Weapons	10	14	24	0	1	1

and 2010, the data show no murders, one robbery, eight sexual assaults, and only one aggravated assault.

It should be pointed out that while the police crime data have consistently revealed less than ten sexual assaults per year on campus (and typically less than five), two previous victimization studies conducted on campus estimated the number of sexual assaults to be far higher (Mullen, Robinson, & Paulsen, 2001; Robinson & Mullen, 2001). Thus, consistent with any town or city – and heightened by the fact that there is also a town Police Department that may take criminal complaints related to sexual assaults – the number of calls for service for the crime of sexual assault is likely a vast underestimate (Abbey et al., 2001). It is likely that many other crimes also go unreported, including some assaults, much theft and vandalism, and probably the vast majority of alcohol and illicit drug use.

HOT SPOTS OF CRIME ON CAMPUS. With these additional limitations in mind, we plotted crimes known to the campus police on campus maps to demonstrate visually, which areas of the campus were most likely to host criminal activity. Figures 12.1 through 12.6 show the campus crime maps.

In looking at the spatial distribution of crimes known to the police on campus, some important findings are evident. First, crime locations for illicit drug violations, alcohol violations, breaking and entering, assault, communicating threats, harassment, sexual assault, forcible fondling, vandalism, and theft are all concentrated largely at or near student dormitories. This finding is not unexpected as most student activity is centered in-and-around dormitories and thus victimization would also be expected to center around these dorms, consistent with routine activity theory and crime pattern theory (Brantingham & Brantingham, 1993; Cohen & Felson, 1979; Eck & Weisburd, 1995; Felson, 2002; Rossmo, 2000).

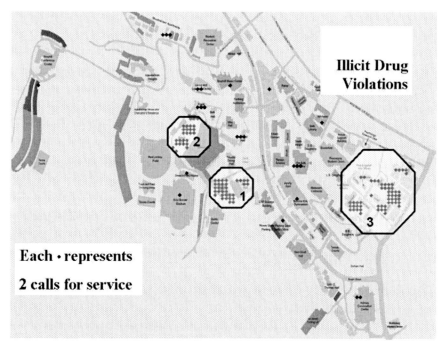

Figure 12.1. Hot spots of drug violations known to the police, 2004–2005.

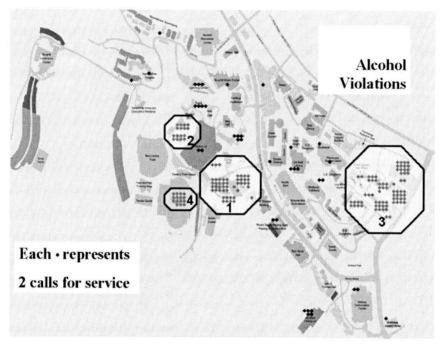

Figure 12.2. Hot spots of alcohol violations known to the police, 2004–2005.

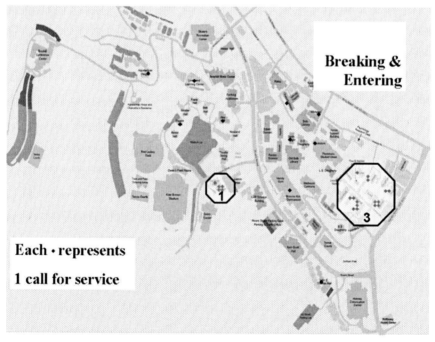

Figure 12.3. Hot spots of breaking and entering incidents known to the police,
2004–2005.

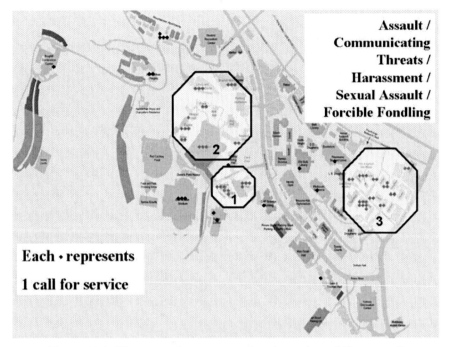

Figure 12.4. Hot spots of interpersonal violence (actual/threatened) known to the police, 2004–2005.

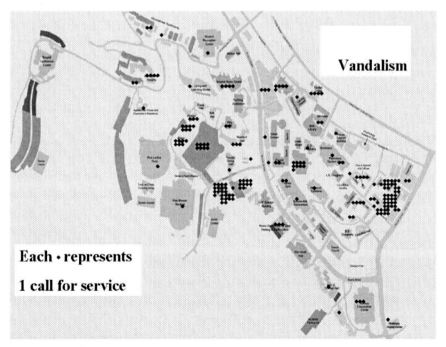

Figure 12.5. Acts of vandalism known to the police, 2004–2005.

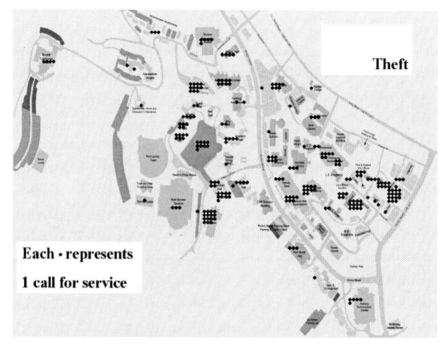

Figure 12.6. Thefts known to the police, 2004–2005.

Previous studies of student lifestyles show that students spend most of their time at or near their residences (Robinson, 1999a). Thus, it is generally at student dorms, their main nodes of activity, where most opportunities for crime exist. We consider all university dorms as "crime generators" because large numbers of students congregate there for a variety of reasons, including criminal behavior.

Second, high traffic areas between main parts of campus, such as near educational buildings and parking areas near pedestrian tunnels, also experience a moderate amount of crime, including thefts, vandalism, and crimes against automobiles (e.g., hit and run, property damage). This is also consistent with routine activity theory and crime mapping theory, as there are higher opportunities for crimes here due to the automobile and pedestrian traffic patterns at these places (Brantingham & Brantingham, 1993; Cohen & Felson, 1979; Eck & Weisburd, 1995; Felson, 2002; Rossmo, 2000). Essentially, it is reasonable to expect that the paths students and other users of campus space travel to and from their regular nodes of activities will host higher amounts of crime.

Third, there are three major places where crime clusters on campus for the crimes of illicit drug violations (Figure 12.1); alcohol violations (Figure 12.2); breaking and entering (Figure 12.3); and assault, communicating threats, harassment, sexual assault, and forcible fondling (Figure 12.4). The crimes of assault, communicating threats, harassment, sexual assault, and forcible fondling were grouped together because of the infrequent nature of each crime on campus and the similar nature of those crimes. That is, each is a crime that rarely occurs on campus and typically involves violence that is related to relationships between students (Carlson, 2005; Gover, 2004; Griffing et al., 2005; Lauritsen & Schaum, 2004; Thompson & Kingree, 2006).

The three places where these various crimes cluster are the main "hot spots" of crime on the campus. Another crime that tended to cluster in these same places, but far less frequently, was disorderly conduct. The three areas are dorms located around potential crime-generating environments. The first two areas are groups of dorms located across from the football stadium, its parking lots, and an open field known as "Duck Pond Field." Duck Pond Field is an area that is used by students for recreational and sporting activities, including drinking alcohol associated with football games, playing sports, and hanging out, as well as some illicit drug use associated with parties. As such, these two areas can also be considered crime attractors since they will regularly draw in students looking to use and abuse alcohol and other drugs as part of social gatherings.

HOT SPOTS OF CRIME ON CAMPUS: A CLOSER LOOK. The first area (labeled Area #1 in the figures) is the "Yosef Hollow Community," and is comprised of five dorms. One of these dorms is all male, whereas the rest are co-ed. One of the dorms houses the "Wellness Community," where use of drugs, alcohol, or tobacco products will result in removal from the dorm. The Wellness Community could possibly act as a social control on the behavior of those in this dorm. Interestingly, both the all-male dorm and the adjacent dorm housing the "Wellness Community," had a large amount of alcohol and drug violations, as well as acts of vandalism, theft, and disorderly conduct violations. None of the smaller dorms appeared in this group.

The second area (labeled Area #2 in the figures) is the "Stadium Heights Community," and is comprised of five dorms. One of these dorms is all-female, whereas the rest are co-ed. Interestingly, the all-female dorm had no alcohol or drug violations, and only a few acts of vandalism or theft. Similarly, the "Living Learning Center," which houses some academic "learning communities," had very few crimes known to the police, with the exception of theft, which fell within a campus hot spot. The Living Learning Center could also serve as a social control on the behavior of students in the dorm. The Stadium Heights Community is a hot spot of crime, even though three of the smaller dorms on campus are located in this cluster. The rate of crimes known to the police in these smaller dorms is likely roughly equivalent to those large dorms in Area #1.

The third area (labeled Area #3 in the figures) is the "Eastridge Community," and is comprised of five co-ed dorms. The community is located on the other side of campus, near a major thoroughfare and a university owned social club – an area that is also used by students for recreational activities, including concerts, dances, and other events where students twenty-one years and older are permitted to possess a six-pack of beer for each event (as such, this can be considered a crime attractor). These dorms are closest to this club facility and to other establishments off campus where students frequently hang out for social purposes (e.g., restaurants and bars).

Three other nearby dorms, part of the "Pinnacle Community" (which also includes an apartment complex located on the other side of campus up a mountain that houses married, single parent, graduate, and nontraditional students), are also near enough to the university social club to house a large number of alcohol and illicit drug violations, as well as acts of theft and vandalism. The largest dorm on campus is found in the Pinnacle community which hosts a large amount of crimes known to the police.

Yet, the one dorm in this area that houses university honors students (which is also the smallest dorm on campus), had no alcohol or illicit drug violations, no reported acts of vandalism, and only two reported thefts in a two-year period. Similarly, the apartment complex that houses older and married students had very few crimes known to the police relative to other housing locations on campus (despite being of average size relative to all dorms on campus). The small number of crimes known to the police at the small honors dorm is due in part to the relative size of the dorm; yet, its lower incidence of crimes known to the police (as well as those at the apartment complex which houses older and married students) if likely due to the nature of student population there. These places serve as social controls on potential maladaptive behavior.

The crimes of assault, communicating threats, harassment, sexual assault, and forcible fondling, occurred most often in the three hot spots of crime, as well. Alcohol violations also clustered at these places, in addition to a fourth place. This fourth place (labeled Area #4 in Figure 12.2) is the football stadium itself, another crime attractor. Almost all the incidents here occurred on game days inside the stadium, and thus this hot spot is situational rather than static.

Theft was most prevalent in the above four areas, but also occurred frequently at a few others places. Given the widespread nature of theft on campus, it was impossible to neatly identify hot spots and thus none are indicated in Figure 12.6. The location of theft on campus is the most unique, primarily because it appears to occur occasionally all across campus. The same is true for vandalism, which is why no hot spots of vandalism are indicated in Figure 12.5. The dispersal of theft and vandalism across the campus likely reflects the numerous opportunities that are present across university buildings.

The primary difference between the location of theft and vandalism from other crimes on campus is that they tend to occur more frequently in academic buildings on campus (e.g., classroom buildings) and student support buildings (e.g., student union), as well as at some athletic facilities (e.g., university gym). These are places where opportunities for crime abound and where guardianship is lower (especially at night) than in student residences. Alcohol and illicit drug violations tend to occur almost exclusively at and around certain dorms and the football stadium. Part of this owes itself to opportunity factors; students spend more time in their dorms and socializing at certain places than they do in class, and alcohol and illicit drug use are obviously more accepted at these places than in academic buildings on campus (Robinson, 1999a).

Other Findings of Interest

We found some additional outcomes that are of interest to our study of campus hot spots. First, not all student dormitories were characterized by a high level of crime, as newer student dormitories built farther from the center of campus experienced less reported criminal activity. The relative lack of criminal activity at these newer dormitories is probably due to their distance from the center of campus, making them both socially and physically isolated from the center of campus. Crime pattern theorists would say these dorms are out of the awareness space of most campus users, and are thus less prone to victimization.

Second, the crime of DWI almost universally occurred on one street. The street is a main thoroughfare through campus (the primary path used by students driving cars) that connects nearly every dorm with restaurants, bars, and other student-centered locations. It is safe to say that this street stands out as a DWI hot spot because it is the only main thoroughfare through campus and thus is the main area where police officers will look for intoxicated drivers.

Third, there is a high degree of consistency between findings from the previous studies of student fear of specific campus areas, perceptions of students of where crime occurs, and the location of reported crime on campus in the current study. In general, areas identified by students in previous studies of the campus involving where they were afraid to go because of criminal victimization are consistent with areas where reported crime is highest on campus, although campus tunnels under streets (a place where some students feared going) host literally no reported criminal activity, except the occasional act of vandalism (Mullen, Robinson, & Paulsen, 2001; Robinson & Mullen, 2001).

In the earlier studies, 88 percent of students surveyed felt that most crime occurred in dorms and parking lots, areas where the spatial analysis of reported crime shows have high concentrations of crime (Mullen, Robinson, & Paulsen, 2001; Robinson & Mullen, 2001). On the campus of study, students have an accurate understanding of where street crimes occur, at least based on police data.

Hot Spots of Crime on Campus: Potential Explanations

As for the hot spots on campus, it is not clear whether they occur because of enduring characteristics about targets which make them attractive or suitable to multiple offenders (the risk heterogeneity argument), or if they occur because of factors related to the initial victimization (the state-dependent argument). Is it because certain people and places are different in such that they that attract offenders, or because initial victimizations result in reinforcement for offenders (e.g., Everson, 2003; Farrell, Phillips, & Pease, 1995; Robinson, 1998b)?

In the case of the college campus, it is likely that the answer to each of these questions is "yes." That is, it is likely that some places on campus are hot spots of crime because of factors related to criminal opportunities and student lifestyles that are consistently present, meaning criminality will likely occur there consistently over time. These are probably crime generators. Some of these places might also be more likely to host criminality due to a "legend" or "reputation" as the "party dorm" or a "cool hang-out," regardless of who lives there. These are better understood as crime attractors. Clearly, a handful of dorms on campus, including the largest dorm, the all-male dorm, and the dorms that border the football stadium and the social club, have the largest number of crimes known to the police. Appropriately, these are also the dorms on campus that are known to be the "party dorms."

Applying community level factors that explain why some neighborhoods have higher crime rates than others to the issue of hot spots may also provide some explanation as to why some areas of a university campus have higher occurrences of crimes than others. Such factors include:

- Community composition (with higher rates of some types of people living in a community, crime rates are found to be higher);
- Community social structure (crime rates are also affected by the way in which inhabitants of an area interact);
- Oppositional culture (high crime neighborhoods are thought to be characterized by an "oppositional culture" or subcultural values that stem from frustration arising out of financial strains);

- Criminogenic commodities (rates of youth violence tend to be associated with the presence of places where alcohol use, drug use, and gun ownership are prevalent); and
- Social and physical disorder (high crime rate areas tend to be characterized by incivilities, which are signs that a neighborhood is in disarray) (Paulsen & Robinson, 2004; Sherman et al., 1998).

Social and physical disorder was not problematic anywhere on the ASU campus. Again, the campus is highly attractive and rated as aesthetically pleasing by space users. Further, there is no evidence that some places on campus are characterized by different levels of oppositional cultures although this is possible (for example, some dorms may attract different types of people than others). Again, the all-male dorm tends to have a higher level of crimes known to the police than many other dorms. Community composition factors may explain higher crimes known to the police on some areas of campus, as may community social structure factors. That is, some dorms on campus, for whatever reason, have a more pronounced reputation for partying behaviors.

Criminogenic commodities may very well vary by campus location, as alcohol, illicit drugs, and weapons possession may simply be higher in some locations than others based on who lives there. As noted earlier, part of this owes itself to the proximity of dorms to criminogenic locations such as the football stadium and university operated social clubs.

Implications for Crime Prevention

The findings of this study, based on crimes known to the police, show that there are some unique areas on campus that are most crime prone. Specifically, there are a few groups of dorms that generate the most known offenses for larceny, vandalism, breaking and entering, alcohol and illicit drug violations, assault, communicating threats, harassment, sexual assault, and forcible fondling, as well as disorderly conduct.

Interestingly, the places on campus indicated by 2004 and 2005 police data as the most crime-prone – the three main hot spots on campus – are the same places found to generate the most fear and perception of crime risk by previous studies of the university campus that utilized victimization surveys of students, faculty, and staff. If this means, as we think it does, that the location of criminality on campus is relatively stable, this offers some unique opportunities for prevention strategies aimed at breaking the cycle of crime in some locations on campus. That the place of crime has remained stable from 1997 to 2006 is important, especially considering that new students have come to campus and that the campus has been significantly developed (i.e., built up).

We were unable to determine if these areas of crime remained the same through 2010, the latest year for which data are available. But we suspect they are for, although new buildings have been erected on campus, the arrangement of dorms remains largely unchanged.

The crime of sexual assault, which is likely to be vastly underreported on college campuses (see Fisher et al., 1998), is not spatially clustered due to any particular environmental conditions, and it is likely that it occurs in the same locations where alcohol use and illicit drug use is most prevalent. Sexual assault and alcohol use are clearly linked (Abbey, 2002; Abbey et al., 2001; Fisher et al., 1998; Robinson, 2004; Testa & Livingston, 1999; Wecshler et al., 1995; Wechsler & Wuethrich, 2003). That the crimes of assault, communicating threats, harassment, sexual assault, and forcible fondling all occur with the greatest frequency in places where alcohol use is most widespread should lead to preventive action in these dorms.

The most significant problem on the ASU campus appears to be alcohol and illicit drug use. Since it appears that the same places that generate these offenses also generate the most incidents of other types of crimes, it is logical that alcohol and illicit drug use are driving these other criminal events, especially considering the student lifestyle (Robinson, 1999a). Young people often commit acts of stupidity – including disorderly conduct, vandalism, theft, assault, communicating threats, harassment, and more seriously, sexual assault – under the influence of drugs, especially alcohol (Robinson, 2004).

Alcohol is the one drug that would most likely lead to a psychopharmacological effect on criminality (Robinson & Scherlen, 2007). Because of the effects of the drug on the brain, as well as because of how it is consumed by young people and the setting in which it is consumed, alcohol is the one drug that is most likely responsible for the clustering of criminality at particular locations on campus. This warrants serious investigation into the effects that alcohol consumption has on criminality on this particular campus. Further, it warrants dedicated action on the part of the university administration to combat irresponsible alcohol use – especially by underage students – on the campus. This is not meant to de-emphasize the issue of illicit drug use on campus, which is the one crime that is likely most prevalent based on previous student surveys. Further, it is the illicit drug market that led to the murders of two students just more than one year apart.

Yet, even the Office of National Drug Control Policy has noted that when it comes to drugs and crime and mayhem, alcohol leads the pack (Robinson & Scherlen, 2007). At ASU, there was no evidence that students drink more alcohol than students on other campuses, or that they drink any differently. Still, this is the one drug that is most responsible for antisocial behavior and alcohol use clearly plays a meaningful role in the lives of a sizable portion of the student body throughout the year. Thus, one logical crime prevention strategy would be alcohol awareness campaigns directed at all students, and especially those who live in the particular dorms that comprise the hot spots of crime on campus.

Finally, other crime prevention strategies should be developed and implemented at the hot spots of crime on campus. Given that displacement is not likely to result, and that there is likely to be a diffusion of benefits, it makes very good sense to focus efforts on the areas that are most likely to host alcohol and illicit drug violations, theft, and vandalism (Clarke, 1998; Clarke & Weisburd, 1994; Cohen & Tita, 1999; Paulsen & Robinson, 2004). This would include the many well-tested efforts aimed at CPTED and situational crime prevention.

The strategies that would most likely be successful to reduce these crimes vary by type of crime. For example, a large number of thefts could be prevented by increasing student awareness of problem areas (e.g., the library, the gym) and encouraging students to maintain guardianship of their property at all times. A large amount of vandalism could be prevented by better securing construction sites on campus and increasing surveillability of other locations at night. And as noted above, much alcohol and illicit drug violations could be prevented by educating students about the dangers of irresponsible use and abuse, as well as giving students more opportunities for alternative forms of entertainment. Given the relationships between alcohol and illicit drug use and criminality, reducing alcohol and illicit drug use would likely reduce some thefts, acts of vandalism, disorderly conduct, assaults, communication of threats, acts of harassment, sexual assault, and probably breaking and entering.

REFERENCES

Abbey, A. (2002). Alcohol-related sexual assault: A common problem among college students. *Journal of Studies on Alcohol, 14,* 118–128.

Abbey, A., Zawacki, T., Buck, P., Clinton, A., & McAuslan, P. (2001). Alcohol and sexual assault. *Alcohol Health and Research World, 25.* Retrieved from http://www.athealth.com/Practitioner/ceduc/alc_assault.html.

Appalachian State University. (2012). *Jeanne Clery Disclosure of Campus Security and Crimes Statistics Act 2010.* Appendix C: ASU Campus Three Year Crime Statistics. Retrieved from http://police.appstate.edu/sites/default/files/AppendixC CleryCrimeStats2010.pdf.

Armstrong, E., Hamilton, L., & Sweeney, B. (2006). Sexual assault on campus: A multilevel, integrative approach to party rape. *Social Problems, 53,* 483–499.

Astor, R., Meyer, H., & Behre, W. (1999). Unowned places and times: Maps and interviews about violence in high schools. *American Educational Research Journal, 36,* 3–42.

Barthe, E., & Stitt, B. (2007). Casinos as "hot spots" and the generation of crime. *Journal of Crime & Justice, 30,* 115.

Block, C., & Block, R. (1995). *Street gang crime in Chicago: NIJ Research in brief.* Washington, DC: National Institute of Justice.

Block, C., & Block, R. (1998). Homicides in Chicago, 1965–1995 [Computer file]. 4th ICPSR version. Chicago, IL: Illinois Criminal Justice Information Authority. Ann Arbor, MI: Inter-university Consortium for Political and Social Research.

Block, C., & Christakos, A. (1995). *Major trends in Chicago homicide: 1965–1994.* Washington, DC: National Institute of Justice.

Bohm, R. (2000). *A primer on crime and delinquency theory.* Belmont, CA: Wadsworth.

Braga, A., & Bond, B. (2008). Policing crime and disorder hot spots: A randomized controlled trial. *Criminology, 46,* 577.

Braga, A., Hureau, D., & Papachristos, A. (2011). The relevance of micro places to citywide robbery trends: A longitudinal analysis of robbery incidents at street corners and block faces in Boston. *Journal of Research in Crime and Delinquency, 48,* 7–32.

Brantingham, P., & Brantingham, P. (1993). Environment, routine, and situation: Toward a pattern theory of crime. *Advances in Criminological Theory, 5,* 259–294.

Brantingham, P., & Brantingham, P. (1994). Surveying campus crime: What can be done to reduce crime and fear? *Security Journal, 5,* 160–171.

Brantingham, P., & Brantingham, P. (1999). A theoretical model of crime hot spot generation. *Studies on Crime and Crime Prevention, 8,* 7–26.

Brantingham, P., & Faust, F. (1976). A conceptual model of crime prevention. *Crime & Delinquency, 7,* 284–295.

Brinkley Jr., W., & Laster, D. (2003). Campus crime in Missouri: An analysis and comparison of crime in four-year colleges and universities. *Journal of Security Administration, 26,* 1–15.

Bromley, M. (1994). Correlates of campus crime: A nationwide exploratory study of large universities. *Journal of Security Administration, 17,* 37–52.

Carlson, B. (2005). The most important things learned about violence and trauma in the past 20 years. *Journal of Interpersonal Violence, 20,* 119–126.

Cass, A. (2007). Routine activities and sexual assault: An analysis of individual- and school-level factors. *Violence and Victims, 22,* 350–366.

Clarke, R. (1992). *Situational crime prevention: Successful case studies.* Albany, NY: Harrow and Hest.

Clarke, R. (1998). The theory and practice of situational crime prevention. Retrieved from http://www.edoca.net/Resources/Articles/Clarke_the_theory_and_practice_of_situational_crime_prevention.pdf.

Clarke, R., & Weisburd, D. (1994). Diffusion of crime control benefits: Observations of the reverse of displacement. *Crime Prevention Studies, 2,* 165–184.

Clarke, R. (2001). Rational choice. In R. Paternoster & R. Bachman (Eds.), *Explaining crime and criminals.* Los Angeles: Roxbury.

Clarke, R., & Eck, J. (2006). Crime analysis for problem solvers in 60 steps. Center for Problem Oriented Policing. Retrieved from http://www.popcenter.org/learning/60steps/index.cfm?stepNum=17.

Clodfelter, T., Turner, M., Hartman, J., & Kuhns, J. (2010). Sexual harassment victimization during emerging adulthood: A test of routine activities theory and a general theory of crime. *Crime & Delinquency, 56,* 455–481.

Cochran, J., & Bromley, M. (2002). Auto burglaries in an entertainment district: Patron perceptions of risks and precautionary behaviors. *Journal of Security Administration, 25,* 1–18.

Cochran, J., Bromley, M., & Branch, K. (2000). Victimization and fear of crime in an entertainment district crime "hot spot": A test of structural-choice theory. *American Journal of Criminal Justice, 24,* 189–201.

Cohen, J., & Tita, G. (1999). Diffusion in homicide: Exploring a general method for detecting spatial diffusion processes. *Journal of Quantitative Criminology, 15,* 451–493.

Cohen, L., & Felson, M. (1979). Social change and crime rate trends: A routine activity approach. *American Sociological Review, 44,* 588–608.

Cornish, D., & Clarke, R. (Eds.). (1986). *The reasoning criminal: Rational choice perspectives on offending.* New York: Springer-Verlag.

Crowe, T. (1991). *Crime prevention through environmental design: Applications of architectural design and space management concepts.* Boston: Butterworth-Heinemann.

Eck, J., & Weisburd, D. (1995). Crime places in crime theory. In J. Eck & D. Weisburd (Eds.), *Crime prevention studies: Crime and place* (pp. 1–34). Monsey, NY: Willow Tree Press.

Everson, S. (2003). Repeat victimization and "prolific" offending: Chance or choice? *International Journal of Police Science & Management, 5,* 180–194.

Farrell, G., Phillips, C., & Pease, K. (1995). Like taking candy: Why does repeat victimization occur? *British Journal of Criminology, 35,* 384–399.

Felson, M. (2002). *Crime and everyday life* (3rd ed.). Beverly Hills, CA: Sage.

Fisher, B., & Sloan III, J. (1993). University responses to the Campus Security Act of 1990: Evaluating programs designed to reduce campus crime. *Journal of Security Administration, 16,* 67–80.

Fisher, B., Sloan, J., Cullen, F., & Lu, C. (1998). Crime in the ivory tower: The level and sources of student victimization. *Criminology, 36,* 671–710.

Fisher, B., & Wilkes, A. (2003). A tale of two ivory towers: A comparative analysis of victimization rates and risks between university students in the United States and England. *British Journal of Criminology, 43,* 526–545.

Fox, J., & Hellman, D. (1985). Location and other correlates of campus crime. *Journal of Criminal Justice, 13,* 429–444.

Gorman, D., Zhu, L., & Horel, S. (2005). Drug 'hot-spots', alcohol availability and violence. *Drug and Alcohol Review, 24,* 507–513.

Gover, A. (2004). Risky lifestyles and dating violence: A theoretical test of violent victimization. *Journal of Criminal Justice, 32,* 171–180.

Green, L. (1995). Cleaning up drug hot spots in Oakland, California: The displacement and diffusion effects. *Justice Quarterly, 12,* 737–754.

Griffing, S., Ragin, D., Morrison, S., Sage, R., Madry, L., & Primm, B. (2005). Reasons for returning to abusive relationships: Effects of prior victimization. *Journal of Family Violence, 20,* 341–348.

Henson, V., & Stone, W. (1999). Campus crime: A victimization study. *Journal of Criminal Justice, 27,* 295–307.

Jackson, A., Gilliland, K., & Veneziano, L. (2006). Routine activity theory and sexual deviance among male college students. *Journal of Family Violence, 21,* 449–460.

Johnson, I., & Sigler, R. (1996). Forced sexual intercourse on campus: Crime or offensive behavior? *Journal of Contemporary Criminal Justice, 12,* 54–68.

Kautt, P., & Roncek, D. (2007). School as criminal "hot spots:" Primary, secondary, and beyond. *Criminal Justice Review, 32,* 339.

Kochel, T. (2011). Constructing hot spots policing: Unexamined consequences for disadvantaged populations and for police legitimacy. *Criminal Justice Policy Review, 22,* 350.

Koper, C. (1995). Just enough police presence: Reducing crime and disorderly behavior by optimizing patrol time in crime hot spots. *Justice Quarterly, 12,* 649–672.

Lauritsen, J., & Schaum, R. (2004). The social ecology of violence against women. *Criminology, 42,* 323–357.

Loukaitou-Sideris, A. (1999). Hot spots of bus stop crime: The importance of environmental attributes. *Journal of the American Planning Association, 65,* 83–95.

Moriarty, L., & Pelfrey, W. (1996). Exploring explanations for campus crime: Examining internal and external factors. *Journal of Contemporary Criminal Justice, 12,* 108–120.

Mullen, K., Robinson, M., & Paulsen, D. (2001). Crime on campus: Repeat criminal victimization and hot spots of crime. Paper presented to the annual meeting of the American Society of Criminology, November.

Mustaine, E., & Tewksbury, R. (1998). Predicting risks of larceny theft victimization: A routine activity analysis using refined lifestyle measures. *Criminology, 36,* 829–857.

O'Kane, J. Fisher, R., & Green, L. (1994). Mapping campus crime. *Security Journal, 17,* 172–179.

Paulsen, D., & Robinson, M. (2004). *Spatial aspects of crime: Theory and practice.* Boston: Allyn & Bacon.

Rengert, G., & Lowell, R. (2005). Combating campus crime with mapping and analysis. *Crime Mapping News, 7,* 1–5.

Rengert, G., Mattson, M., & Henderson, K. (2001). *Campus security: Situational crime prevention in high-density environments.* Cullompton, Devon, UK: Criminal Justice Press.

Richards, G. (1996). The security survey: Creating a proactive foundation for campus crime prevention. *Journal of Contemporary Criminal Justice, 12,* 45–53.

Robinson, M. (1998a). Accessible targets, but not advisable ones: The role of "accessibility" in student apartment burglary. *Journal of Security Administration, 21,* 29–43.

Robinson, M. (1998b). The time period of heightened risk for repeat burglary victimization. *British Journal of Criminology, 38,* 76–85.

Robinson, M. (1999a). Lifestyles, routine activities, and residential burglary victimization. *Journal of Crime and Justice, 22,* 27–56.

Robinson, M. (1999b). The theoretical development of crime prevention through environmental design (CPTED). *Advances in Criminological Theory, 8,* 427–462.

Robinson, M. (2004). *Why crime? An integrated systems theory of antisocial behavior.* Upper Saddle River, NJ: Prentice-Hall.

Robinson, M. (2005). *Justice blind? Ideals and realities of American criminal justice* (2nd ed.). Upper Saddle River, NJ: Prentice-Hall.

Robinson, M., & Mullen, K. (2001). Crime on campus: A survey of space users. *Crime Prevention and Community Safety: An International Journal, 3,* 33–46.

Robinson, M., & Scherlen, R. (2007). *Lies, damned lies, and drug war statistics.* Albany, NY: State University of New York Press.

Roncek, D., & Maier, P. (1991). Bars, blocks, and crimes revisited: Linking the theory of routine activities to the empiricism of "hot spots." *Criminology, 29,* 725–753.

Rossmo, K. (2000). *Geographic profiling.* Boca Raton, FL: CRC Press.

Schwartz, M., DeKeseredy, W., Tait, D., & Alvi, S. (2001). Male peer support and a feminist routine activities theory: Understanding sexual assault on the college campus. *Justice Quarterly, 18,* 623–649.

Sherman, L., Gartin, P., & Buerger, M. (1989). Hot spots of predatory crime: Routine activities and the criminology of place. *Criminology, 27,* 27–55.

Sherman, L., Gottfredson, D., MacKenzie, D., Eck, J., Reuter, P., & Bushway, S. (1998). *Preventing crime: What works, what doesn't, what's promising.* Retrieved from http://www.ncjrs.org/pdffiles/171676.pdf.

Sherman, L., & Rogan, L. (1995). Deterrent effects of police raids on crack houses: A randomized, controlled experiment. *Justice Quarterly, 12,* 755–781.

Sherman, L., & Weisburd, D. (1995). General deterrent effects of police patrol in crime "hot spots": A randomized, controlled trial. *Justice Quarterly, 12,* 625–648.

Siegel, D., & Raymond, C. (1992). An ecological approach to violent campus crime. *Journal of Security Administration, 15,* 19–29.

Sloan, J. (1992). Campus crime and campus communities: An analysis of crimes known to campus police and security. *Journal of Security Administration, 15,* 31–47.

Sloan, J. (1994). The correlates of campus crime: An analysis of reported crimes on college and university campuses. *Journal of Criminal Justice, 22,* 51–66.

Sloan, J., Fisher, B., & Cullen, F. (1997). Assessing the Student Right-to-Know and Campus Security Act of 1990: An analysis of the victim reporting practices of college and university students. *Crime and Delinquency, 43,* 148–168.

Stitt, B., Nichols, M., & Giacopassi, D. (2003). Does the presence of casinos increase crime? An examination of casino and control communities. *Crime and Delinquency, 49,* 253–284.

Testa, M., & Livingston, J. (1999). Qualitative analysis of women's experiences of sexual aggression: Focus on the role of alcohol. *Psychology of Women Quarterly, 23,* 573–589.

Tewksbury, R., & Mustaine, E. (2003). College students' lifestyles and self-protective behaviors: Further considerations of the guardianship concept in routine activity theory. *Criminal Justice and Behavior, 30,* 302–327.

Thompson, M., & Kingree, J. (2006). The roles of victim and perpetrator alcohol use in intimate partner violence outcomes. *Journal of Interpersonal Violence, 21,* 163–177.

Volkwein, J., Szelest, B., & Lizotte, A. (1995). The relationship of campus crime to campus and student characteristics. *Research in Higher Education, 36,* 647–70.

Wechsler H., Dowdall G., Davenport A., & Castillo, S. (1995). Correlates of college student binge drinking. *American Journal of Public Health, 85,* 982–985.

Wechsler H., & Wuethrich, B. (2003). *Dying to drink: Confronting binge drinking on college campuses.* New York: Rodale Books.

Weisburd, D., Bushway, S., Lum, C., & Yang, S. (2004). Trajectories of crime at places: A longitudinal study of street segments in the city of Seattle. *Criminology, 42,* 283–321.

Weisburd, D., & Green, L. (1995). Policing drug hot spots: The Jersey City drug market analysis experiment. *Justice Quarterly, 12,* 711–735.

Weisburd, D., Morris, N., & Groff, E. (2009). Hot spots of juvenile crime: A longitudinal study of arrest incidents at street segments in Seattle, Washington. *Journal of Quantitative Criminology, 25,* 443–467.

Wooldredge, J., Cullen, F., & Latessa, E. (1995). Predicting the likelihood of faculty victimization: Individual demographics and routine activities. In B. S. Fisher & J. J. Sloan (Eds.), *Campus crime: Legal, social, and policy perspectives* (2nd ed.) (pp. 133–122). Springfield, IL: Charles C Thomas.

Part III

THE SECURITY CONTEXT
OF CAMPUS CRIME

Part III

THE SECURITY CONTEXT
OF CAMPUS CRIME

INTRODUCTION

For more a decade or more, postsecondary institutions have faced a series of challenges, some relatively constant, others of a completely new variety. Spurred in part by *Clery* mandates, colleges and universities have undertaken large-scale efforts to address campus security by developing explicit policies designed to enhance campus safety and security. Meeting legislative and/or judicial mandates creates both issues and opportunities for postsecondary administrators, not to mention campus security and law enforcement personnel.

One of the ongoing issues facing postsecondary administrators is developing and implementing *effective* programs and strategies, as well as coordinated responses to, campus crime. For example, they may implement strategies that focus on crime control through environmental design; through the use of rapidly advancing information technology; or by using more proactive-oriented or intelligence-based strategies for patrolling the campus. Administrators may also emphasize educating students on the pitfalls of high-risk lifestyles involving the use of recreational drugs and alcohol. Administrators must also confront the growing menace of *high-tech crimes* in which students are often involved as offenders *and* victims. Further, administrators face organizational, operational, and tactical issues when their attention turns to policing the campus community. Finally, because no strategy is 100 percent effective at preventing on-campus victimizations, administrators must also design and implement policies or programs that provide assistance to students unfortunate enough to experience a crime, particularly those experiencing various forms of sexual assault and stalking.

Part III presents four chapters that examine the security context of campus crime. These chapters include discussions of not only "traditional" issues such as how campus law enforcement can be more effective at preventing campus crime, but also new directions they can take. Finally, the daunting challenges posed by high-tech crimes which allow perpetrators to potentially victimize thousands of students, faculty members, and staff in a single incident now occupy an ever increasing amount of administrators' time.

In Chapter 13, Max Bromley reviews the evolution of campus law enforcement in the U.S. In the chapter, Bromley not only traces the history of campus policing from Colonial America to the present, he presents a solid case for why the 24/7 college campus with its youthful, multiracial and ethnicity identity and multiple functions – education, residential, and entertainment – requires campus law enforcement to move beyond traditional, rapid-response-oriented policing and toward proactive, problem-solving, community-based orientation. His case study of the University of South Florida's efforts to implement such a model for the campus police department shows both the problems and the successes inherent in fundamentally altering not only the organizational structure of a campus police department, but its culture as well.

Chapter 14, by Eugene Paoline and John Sloan, explores new directions in campus law enforcement as agencies attempt to move beyond community-oriented policing or COP. Paoline and Sloan discuss the components of COP but also extend their discussion to include current innovations in the tactics of campus police that include use of information technology and human intelligence. The chapter also highlights the potential benefits of these innovations to campus law enforcement.

As presented in Part II, alcohol use and abuse on college campuses are well-established correlates of student victimization. In Chapter 15, by Andrea Allen and Scott Jacques, the two criminologists explore how campus law enforcement responds to the challenges posed by students drinking on campus. Using qualitative analyses of episodes of the cable television series *Campus PD,* Allen and Jacques explore various themes found in the episodes, as well as the attitudes of campus officers toward their jobs and the students they police, and how officers use different tactics to address drunken students, some of whom have engaged in relatively serious offending.

We conclude Part III with a chapter by Samuel McQuade titled "High-Tech Abuse and Crime on College and University Campuses: Reflections on What Is Occurring, Why It Is Occurring, and What Can Be Done." In the chapter, McQuade focuses attention on "new" types of campus victimization – those involving technology. He explains how computing and telecommunication advances, including the Internet and cell phones, have created opportunities for campus personnel and computer networks to be vulnerable to victimization. McQuade shows how different types of attacks pose new security challenges for campus IT departments, as well as campus police. In conclusion, he discusses how campuses can address high-tech abuses and crimes through a variety of strategies such as active sanctioning of offenders, educating and training the campus community to protect information systems, and using technological advancements to prevent or counter computing and telecommunication abuses and attacks.

The chapters in Part III provide both historical and contemporary insight into how the changing dynamics of college campuses and opportunities for crime influence the operational and organizational structures of 21st century campus security operations. Chapter authors educate readers about how and why changes have occurred, while reminding us that "locking 'em up" is not the only perspective needed to understand (and hopefully reduce) campus crime. Rather, through greater coordination and integration of various units on the college campus, successful efforts can be taken to help reduce the risk of on-campus victimizations.

Chapter 13

THE EVOLUTION OF CAMPUS POLICING: AN UPDATE TO "DIFFERENT MODELS FOR DIFFERENT ERAS"

Max L. Bromley

INTRODUCTION

College campuses in America have undergone tremendous change over the last 50 years. This change has resulted in some observers suggesting that campuses today are often "cities within cities" (Bromley & Territo, 1990). Smith (1995) noted it is not surprising that, as campuses have changed and grown, so too have the number of serious crimes occurring on them. While there is evidence suggesting that property crimes far outnumber violent crimes on campuses (Bromley, 1992; Fernandez & Lizotte, 1995; Lewis & Farris, 1997), institutions of higher education (IHEs) must still be prepared to provide a high level of security for their communities. Therefore, today's campus executives recognize the necessity of having campus police forces available to provide most of the same services rendered by police departments in similar-sized municipalities (Atwell, 1988). Additionally, like their municipal counterparts, campus police agencies are increasingly adopting Community-Oriented Policing (COP) as their organizational model and basing their practices on COP principles.

Before discussing campus-based community policing efforts, it is first useful to review the development of campus police from an historical perspective. The next four sections of the chapter undertake that task by describing the various eras of campus policing from their humble beginnings to becoming "a part of the fabric of higher education" (Sloan, 1992). Subsequently the chapter identifies and discusses the challenges facing campus police arising from the complex nature of the modern college campus. Later the chapter describes how campus police agencies have incorporated COP into their common practices. The chapter concludes with a case study of one university police department's experiences with implementing COP.

The Evolution of Campus Policing

The Watchman Era: 1700s–1800s

In early Colonial times, various personnel ranging from college presidents, to faculty members, and sometimes-even janitors performed security functions at American colleges and universities. These individuals were responsible for enforcing often-lengthy lists of rules and regulations developed in an attempt to govern student lives while at school. Additional concerns with respect to security on campus included "the avoidance of fires and the protection of property from straying animals and irate town folk" (Gelber, 1972, p. 16). Some IHEs used college professors to monitor student behaviors in dormitories and sometimes in the dining halls (Proctor, 1958; Rudolph, 1962). Brubacher and Willis (1968) cited examples from the mid-1800s where colleges used students to help enforce discipline and policies. Witsil (1979, p.7) noted that late in the nineteenth century ". . . some colleges created an 'Office of Proctor,' a designation for a university police officer, who was responsible for helping discharge disciplinary duties at the university."

It was not until 1894, however, that the first "official" campus police officers appeared when Yale University hired New Haven police officers to patrol its campus. The institution had experienced a series of bloody confrontations between students and townspeople and irate citizens demanded the campus do more to police student behavior. Following the recommendations of a committee composed of campus and city officials, two New Haven police officers began patrolling the Yale campus on a routine basis (Powell, 1981). Powell (1981) noted that these officers were so successful in their endeavors that the Yale campus eventually accepted them as part of its institutional setting.

The Campus Security Era: 1900 – mid-1960s

The primary focus of campus security departments and their officers during the early part of the twentieth century continued to be on two primary areas: (1) student misconduct and, (2) property protection. According to Esposito and Stormer (1989), officers during this era wore the two hats of "campus watchman" and assistant deans of students. Powell (1981) wrote that alcohol consumption was a campus problem, as it was elsewhere in the United States in the late 1920s and 1930s and that much of the property destruction and other student disturbances during the 1940s and 1950s on campus were often alcohol related. Thus, the role of "monitoring" student conduct role by campus security officials continued well into the twentieth century.

Following World War II, American colleges experienced tremendous growth in student population and institutional size. The G. I. Bill made it possible for large numbers of returning veterans to attend college for the first time and created great impetus for the extension of higher education throughout the United States. According to Shoemaker (1995), this growth in campus population led to other typical community problems including crime. The existing campus security departments were often ill prepared for the rapidly changing college environment.

During the 1950s and early 1960s, campus security departments remained organizationally attached to physical plant departments, reflecting the continued emphasis on their role in protecting campus and personal property. According to Kassinger (1971), this administrative arrangement failed to recognize what was needed in terms of professional law enforcement on the growing college campuses. Sloan (1992) noted that, during this time, many campus security directors and campus security officers were former city or military police and thus had professional law enforcement experience. Hiring ex-municipal police officers would be one of several steps taken by university administrators in an attempt to upgrade the quality of campus security services.

A second organizational approach used by some IHEs was for them to have security departments organizationally linked to the Dean of Students office (Powell, 1981). This reflected another emphasis often placed on the security department's role, that of student conduct enforcer. It was also during the 1950s and early 1960s that the Higher Education Section of the Campus Safety Association and the International Association of Campus Security Directors would be formed (Gelber, 1972). The International Association of Campus Security Directors would later evolve into the International Association of Campus Law Enforcement Administrators (IACLEA) recognized today as the primary professional organization for campus police chiefs and other high-ranking officials.

The Era of Professionalization: Late 1960s – Early 1980s

Events of the late 1960s and 1970s, including major civil disturbances and the anti-Vietnam war movement, led to dramatic change in the organizational structure and role of campus security departments in higher education. Social change related to the civil rights movement and protests, both violent and non-violent, often created problems for college presidents who frequently found their existing campus security departments ill prepared to deal with these serious issues. While some IHEs summoned local law enforcement agencies to assist during these times, the approach often led to an exacerbation of the conflict (Skolnick, 1969). McDaniel (1971) suggests university officials' failure to handle campus disorders was because they lacked a professionally trained campus police department.

Leaders seeking to change the role of the campus police recognized that for campus law enforcement to be truly effective it would have to a assume a role consistent with the educational expectations of higher education while simultaneously adopting the best practices of law enforcement. Individuals such as Bill McDaniel of Wayne State University, Ed Kassinger of the University of Georgia, Richard Bernitt of Michigan State University, and Bill Tanner of Florida State University, were part of the leadership seeking professionalism in campus policing (Sims, 1971). These emerging leaders recognized that campus policing needed a new model, one that would eventually find a home in the higher education community and one that became what Sloan (1992) referred to as the "birth of the modern campus police department." Key to this model was training off campus officers by local and state police academies; such training would provide legitimacy to campus law enforcement.

During the 1970s and through the 1980s, the professionalization of campus policing would further accelerate. The 1970s new state statutes passed that granted to public colleges and universities the right to have sworn officers on their staff (Gelber, 1972). During the 1980s, experts explicitly recognized campus police departments were operating as professional law enforcement organizations. They found these agencies: (1) had become more organizationally autonomous; (2) resembled municipal departments in structure and operations; (3) enhanced education and training levels for their officers; (4) developed career paths for personnel; and (5) had become an accepted part of campus life at American colleges and universities (Peak, 1988, 1995; Sloan, 1992).

Experts noted other similarities developing between campus and municipal police agencies. Jacobs and O'Meara (1980) observed the equipment and technology (e.g., handguns, riot helmets, and tape recording devices) that campus police routinely used was comparable to that used by city police. The 1980s saw the introduction of nonlethal weapons, such as pepper spray to campus police (Sloan, 1992). Peak (1988, 1989) found many campus departments during the 1980s had rank structures and organizational hierarchies that closely resembled those found in local police departments. Likewise, membership in national police organizations, achieving accreditation status, and supporting professional growth of campus police officers through additional training were also indicators of the continued professionalization of campus police. When Bromley and Reaves (1998a) compared campus and municipal police departments on a variety of operational and human resource issues using U.S. Justice Department data, they found additional evidence supporting the notion that strong parallels exist between campus police and their municipal counterparts.

The Community Era of Campus Policing: Late 1980s – Present

During the 1980s and 1990s, the evolution of campus police continued because of influences both internal to, and outside of higher education. The sheer growth in the number of students enrolled in IHEs and ever-increasing number of colleges and universities were obvious influences. According to *The Digest of Education Statistics* (1991), by 1990 there were approximately 14 million students attending college (triple the number of students that attended college in 1960) and almost 3,500 IHEs (up approximately 1,500 institutions since 1960). Today, the largest of the campuses, (those with enrollments of 25,000 students and above) often have daily on-campus populations that exceed 50,000 people; usually have large special events centers and/or football stadiums on their property; often have medical centers or hospitals on campus; and nearly half have a nuclear facility on its campus (Reaves & Goldberg, 1996).

Given this growth, it is not surprising that reports of serious crimes occurring on college campuses were common during the last few decades (see Lederman, 1994, 1995). If the 1970s saw the development of campus policing as a profession, the 1980s saw its maturation as a profession (Bordner & Petersen, 1983; Peak, 1988; Sloan, 1992). Some authorities have even suggested that by the 1980s campus communities had come to expect full service policing from campus departments (Atwell, 1988). Legal scholars, such as Smith (1989), noted that the threat of serious campus crime had become very real and thus gave impetus to insuring that campus police had full law enforcement authority and responsibility.

In addition to the growing recognition that a full-service campus police agency would be the best choice to handle crime and security challenges brought about by the growth and increasing complexity of IHEs, forces outside the campus boundaries would further influence the changing campus police model. The legal arena would provide a two-pronged impetus for the evolving campus police profession.

During the 1980s victims or their families filed a series of well-documented, highly publicized, and successful lawsuits against colleges and universities alleging that inadequate campus security contributed to the death or injury of the victims. Smith (1988, 1995), Bromley (1992), and others, documented the impact these high-profile civil lawsuits had on college and university executive decision makers. Rightly or wrongly, litigants viewed the campus police department as the primary organizational entity charged with insuring a safe and secure campus. Therefore, the courts would exert pressure on campus executives to have adequate security programs in place, starting with a professional full-service police agency.

Congress and state legislatures also played a role in the continued professionalization of campus police. At both the federal and state levels of government more attention than ever was focused on campus crime. Although research suggested many campuses are actually safer than their surrounding communities (Bromley, 1992; Fernandez & Lizotte, 1995), when a homicide or a rape occurs on a college campus citizens, the courts, and even lawmakers have strong reactions. Congressional passage of the *Student Right-to-Know and Campus Security Act of 1990* (now known as the *Jeanne Clery Disclosure of Campus Security Policy and Campus Crime Statistics Act*), and enactment of statutes in fourteen states (Seng, 1995) resulted in new policies requiring institutional disclosure of campus crime and arrest data and security policy information (Seng, 1995; Smith, 1995). These statutory requirements, in turn, had a direct impact on campus police organizations; legislative mandates gave additional emphasis to the responsibilities of the campus police.

One could thus argue that given the successful lawsuits brought against IHEs combined with "campus crime" statutes enacted by a variety of legislative bodies, the standard of "adequate security" on the college campus became much higher than that required of a municipality. If that argument is accurate, the role of campus police should continue to evolve to meet those expectations. There is simply no municipal parallel to the legal and legislative mandates now required of campus police agencies.

Given the relatively high expectation of providing adequate security, coupled with the increasing complexity of IHEs, campus police have continued to evolve in the mid 1980s and beyond. It was simply not sufficient to adopt a professional/crime control model within the campus community. Since the 1980s, many police agencies in America have been reshaping their philosophy and direction toward "community policing" (Goldstein, 1987). While many definitions exist for this new model, Trojanowicz and Carter (1988) observed that two key aspects of COP is that it is proactive and looks to reduce not only crime but also fear of victimization. Other characteristics of the COP model include a closer degree of cooperation between police and community members in finding ways to mutually deal with crime. In this evolving model, the police actively are involved with the community and often assign officers to specific locations for long periods to work closely with community members.

As previously noted, campus police have traditionally served a unique role within the campus environment. Not only are the campus police expected to provide professional law enforcement services, they also routinely interact with law-abiding campus community members such as students, staff, and faculty. Peak (1995) suggested the campus police view campus community members as "clients" who are served. Clearly, this relationship between the campus police and its community clients provides a framework for the development and implementation of community-oriented policing practices. Later in this chapter, examples of these practices will be described in some detail.

The preceding sections identified the various eras in the continuing evolution of campus policing. Each era reflected the role of the campus police at a particular historical point. To understand the currently evolving campus-policing model, it is first necessary to examine the uniqueness of the contemporary campus community. As Peak (1995) suggested, because the campus community is relatively small geographically and inhabited by a somewhat transitory but educated population, the context presents campus police an opportunity to experiment with and be innovative in their practices. The following section examines the uniqueness of the campus community and explores whether campus policing will evolve using a more flexible, adaptive approach to fulfill its role – namely COP.

The Modern College Campus: A Challenge for Campus Police

While the nature and extent of crime on college campuses is an important factor in determining the provision of campus police services, there are other major factors to consider when assessing how campus police are organized, as well as their tactics. This section provides an overview of the various features of a typical residential college or university campus, such as population demographics, its structural characteristics, and activities that individually and collectively affect the delivery of campus police services. Campuses may also vary according to utilization of campus facilities, and by whether people consider the location a "main" or "branch/satellite" campus. The following subsections describe these factors and the challenges they present to campus police.

The Nature and Extent of Campus Crime

Over the past several decades, there has been a growing body of research regarding the nature and extent of crime occurring on college campuses. Media sources have highlighted the most serious types of violent crime, such as sexual assault and homicide, occurring on campus (Lederman, 1993, 1995; Lively, 1996, 1997; Ordovensky, 1990; Palmer, 1993). While such violence does occur, and law enforcement should aggressively investigate such incidents and should be publicly reported, other authorities note that campuses are not necessarily as dangerous as portrayed in the media (see Brantingham, Brantingham, & Seagrave, 1995).

The majority of crimes reported to campus police are property-related offenses (Bromley, 1992; International Association of Campus Law Enforcement Administrators, 1995; Lizotte & Fernandez, 1993; Reaves & Goldberg, 1996; Sloan, 1994). With respect to sexual assault, research has long shown this crime is often unreported to police officials (Territo, Halsted, & Bromley, 1998). Hart (2003) using National Crime Victimization Survey (NCVS) data, found that between 1995 and 2000, only 12 percent of college women who were victims of rape/sexual assault reported the crime to police. Hart (2003) also found that non-strangers committed 74 percent of the rapes/sexual assaults perpetrated against college students, a finding with obvious implications for campus police. Hart (2003) did find, however, college students experienced a lower rate of violent (rape, robbery and aggravated assaults) victimization compared to nonstudents ages 18–24. Finally, Hart (2003) reported that most student victimization occurred off campus.

The results of studies such as Hart's are important to the campus police in their efforts to educate campus community members regarding potential violence. It is also important for campus administrators to know as much as possible about the nature and extent of crime on their respective campuses. Data from crime reports, victimization surveys, and from campus departments such as student health services and victims' services can be useful in developing proactive police services shaped by extent victimization patterns revealed (Bromley & Fisher, 2002).

Demographic Features of College Campuses

The modern American postsecondary education institution's complexity is partially due to factors such as the size of enrollment and the number of facilities present on campus. Its complexity is also a function of additional variables such as the demographics of its community members, structural aspects of its campus and the nature of ongoing activities on that campus. Understanding these factors and projecting future changes in them will have an impact on the ability to provide adequate police services to the university community.

A comprehensive campus security program must take into account a student population containing more women than men or a rapidly growing minority population. It must also consider an expansion in international student enrollment or an increase in "nontraditional" students coming to campus to start or continue their education. Additionally, the number of "night students" and the division of full-time and part-time students on the campus will be important considerations in determining overall security plans for a campus. According to Fernandez and Lizotte (1995), the diversity of a campus population directly affects security resources and potential risk.

Physical Features of College Campuses

A comprehensive security policy must also take into account the physical characteristics of a campus. For example, some campuses are public and therefore are relatively "open" to campus community members as well as nonaffiliates. Other institutions are privately controlled and more restrictive in allowing public access to facilities and limiting hours of operation of those campus facilities. Whether a campus is "residential" in nature or predominantly "commuter" would likewise be of importance in campus policing issues and will certainly influence an institution's security planning.

Lizotte and Fernandez (1993) noted that security strategies and crime prevention education and programming efforts must take into account the previously mentioned demographic and physical factors. For example, Fernandez and Lizotte (1995) found that certain common crimes, such as rape and larceny, occur more frequently on residential campuses than on commuter campuses. On the other hand, they reported that commuter campuses have higher rates of motor vehicle theft.

The geographic location of a college is also important in underscoring the diverse nature of many campuses. Brantingham et al. (1995) have noted that specific campus locations directly affect a campus's overall crime rate. Because urban campuses often border large neighborhoods, the pool of prospective offenders would be large and thus such campuses might have higher crime rates than campuses located in rural settings. Research by Fox and Helman (1985) supported this hypothesis. They found crime rates of urban campuses were higher if the campus was located adjacent to a lower socioeconomic demographic area within a city (see also Brantingham et al., 1995).

Utilization of the Campus

Brantingham et al. (1995) suggested IHEs can be described based on the degree students, faculty, and staff utilized the campus and its facilities. Brantingham et al. (1995) hypothesized that utilization of the campus and its facilities will be associated with daily macro-movement patterns of campus community members. The campus "user" categories they developed included "major," "moderate," and "minimal" user. At one end of the user-continuum, "major users" are students who make daily use of the campus as a residence or class/study facility and who attend many extracurricular activities there. A "major user" campus would be one with a large residential population, a significant number of classroom facilities, sports complex for football or basketball, and a multipurpose facility for concerts and plays. Brantingham et al. (1995) suggested the "major user" type campus should experience higher crime rates compared to the other categories of college campuses. At least one study supports associating the "major user" type of higher rates of campus crime. Specifically, in a study of college faculty victimization at a single urban institution, Wooldridge, Cullen, and Latessa (1995) found faculty members increased the risk of victimization when they were frequently on campus at night and on weekends making use of facilities.

At the other end of the user category continuum, the "minimal user" campus is one where students or staff members come to campus only when attending class or working and engages in few other on-campus activities. Brantingham et al. (1995) suggested less victimization would occur on a "minimal user" type campus. Therefore, in security planning for an institution, the campus police should take into consideration how people use a campus and its facilities on a typical day.

UTILIZING CAMPUS FACILITIES. As campus police develop their security plans, they need also consider the number, complexity, and function of different facilities on the campus. As noted earlier, Reaves and Goldberg (1996) found that some of the largest campuses have medical centers/hospitals and special events centers attracting thousands of visitors/patrons. These facilities also draw on and off campus clientele. Similarly, a large sports stadium or basketball arena also draws on and off campus visitors. Hosting numerous large-scale public events or serving large numbers of medical patients requires customized police responses that go well beyond normal day-to-day police operations.

Persons unfamiliar with today's college environments might be surprised to see the number of nonacademic facilities providing essential daily services to campus constituents and guests. For example, today's college campuses have retail food service operations such as Subway® or Burger King®, credit unions serving as comprehensive banks, and convenience-type stores providing round-the-clock service for on-campus residents. Automated Teller Machines (ATMs) are often located on college campuses and large parking garages accommodate parking needs and save valuable horizontal campus property. While each of these facilities provides useful services to campus community members and visitors, they also represent potential risks as crime targets.

Main vs. Branch and Satellite Campuses

Lanier (1995) suggested an additional consideration in campus security planning involves accounting for sites in addition to a "main campus." One example would be the University of South Florida (USF) whose main campus is located in the suburbs of Tampa and enrolls 37,000 students including over 5,000 on-campus residents. A second, smaller nonresidential campus is located in a downtown St. Petersburg business district. U.S. Highway 41 (a major north/south corridor) divides a third campus located in Sarasota. This campus is located immediately adjacent to a regional airport and has a small residential population. Finally, USF has another campus that shares physical facilities with a community college in Lakeland, Florida. Security planning for USF thus must not only consider the general needs of the campuses, such as selecting security systems for buildings, but must also consider the unique needs of each campus.

When considering the appropriate level of police services for a "main" or "branch/satellite," campus decision makers need to consider virtually all of the previously mentioned factors (e.g., population demographics, structural features, types of facilities). For example, if a "branch" campus offers primarily evening classes to older students, this presents a different challenge to the police than a "main" campus that has several thousand residential students. The demographic and physical characteristics of the "main" or "branch" campus will also drive, to some extent, the nature and delivery of crime prevention/public education programs.

The Evolving Community-Oriented Policing Model on College Campuses

The diverse and complex nature of the current college environment contributes to the challenge of providing appropriate police services. As described below, many campus police agencies either have adopted or are adopting COP due to its flexibility and adaptability to the campus context. Successful municipal police agencies recognize that there may be considerable variation between the crime rate and quality of life issues in different neighborhoods and COP practices allow them to "tailor" their responses according to specific needs. Campus police must likewise recognize various factors, such as those identified in this section, that influence the nature and variety of campus police services.

For example, if a campus slowly changes from primarily a "minimal user" category institution to one that adds several thousand resident students, the change has serious implications for the police in terms of types of crimes, educational outreach efforts, and crime prevention efforts. Should a campus decide to extend its programs in an effort to offer more evening or weekend courses, build more 24-hour recreational facilities, or add an on-campus day care center, the campus police will face additional challenges. As change in higher education is continuous and inevitable, so, too, will be subsequent challenges confronting campus police officials. Anticipating and planning for the changes and using creative approaches to policing on campuses will be major contributors to the continuing evolution of campus policing. The strength of COP as a model for campus police is that its flexibility allows departments to change to meet the changing safety and security needs of the campus.

Viewing the Campus as a Community

We have seen that the complexity of the contemporary campus community has implications for both campus law enforcement planning and practice. Further, modern campuses may be viewed as "communities within communities" or as distinct entities. Sloan and Fisher (1995) have argued that while there may be some differences between a campus community and a typical nonacademic community, they are similar in a number of ways. For example, most campuses have a fixed geographic location (Sloan & Fisher, 1995) where fences, distinctive entryways, and signage delineate campus-specific property and create boundaries (even if only symbolic) between the campus and surrounding areas. Even at urban campuses located in downtown areas of larger cities, there is usually an effort made to separate campus property from the surrounding area.

Additionally, the campus community members have common ties in a level of social interaction (Sloan & Fisher, 1995). Residential students live and often eat in common areas. Commuters may belong to student organization or honor societies or attend extracurricular events on the campus. Faculty members usually have offices arranged according to their discipline or department; they work together on committees; belong to university governance groups; and attend cultural or sporting events with fellow faculty members and students. Support staff members frequently work in teams, socialize in break rooms, and likewise take advantage of campus special events. Students often stay at a given college four or five years, while some staff and faculty members spend their entire careers at one institution. The investment of time, mental and physical energy on the part of campus community members also contributes to a sense of "community."

An Overview of Community-Oriented Policing

If the "typical" college campus is a community, then campus police must adopt appropriate philosophical, organizational, and tactical orientations. COP affords campus departments the opportunity to do so. According to Peak and Gensor (1999), in the mid-1980s many municipal police departments began moving from a reactive, incident-driven approach to policing to one that demonstrates a greater willingness to work in collaboration with key community stakeholders in order to reduce crime and to improve the quality of life. Thus, the police become "problem solvers" working in collaboration with neighborhood residents to address not only crime but quality of life issues, at least some of which are also tied to levels of crime in the community (e.g., abandoned buildings serving as "crack houses"). This change in the overall philosophy of policing has been steadily evolving for the last 20 years.

While it is not without its critics (e.g., Zhao, Lorvich, & Thurman, 1999), there is a growing body of research demonstrating that COP practices are prevalent in many police agencies across the country. For example, according to a recent Bureau of Justice Statistics report (Reaves, 2008), a majority of police agencies serving cities of all population categories had full-time community policing officers, the number of these officers had steadily increased since 1997, and 56 percent of responding agencies indicated they provided COP training to new recruits while in the police academy.

In addition to noting that municipal police agencies practice community policing, Cochran, Bromley, and Landis (1999) suggested many sheriffs' departments might be well suited for involvement in community policing. As elected officials, most sheriffs understand the need to work effectively with community members. If the Office of the Sheriff is an "open system," there is a continuous flow of information between the agency and the community. Sheriffs must be concerned with both crime and quality of life issues important to citizens, thus making a COP philosophy almost a necessity. Discussion now turns to the applicability of a COP philosophy on a college campus.

Beyond Traditional Policing for Campuses

Some authorities suggest that in order to provide adequate security consistent with the overall mission of an institution of higher education, the campus needs more than the traditional practices of a professional police department. Jacobs and O'Meara (1980, p. 293) emphasized the need to include community members in providing safety on campus ". . . students, faculty, and employee involvement in the issues of crime and deviancy should be emphasized. Security forces should articulate the special norms and institutional patterns of the university." Early in the professional development of campus policing, leaders, including McDaniel (1971), Kassinger (1971), and Sims (1971), emphasized the importance of the "service" role of campus police officers. These leaders argued that campus police should emphasize their service role over that of their law enforcement role to gain long-term acceptance within the academic setting.

To underscore the service role, some campus departments combined police, traffic/parking, and environmental safety services under the organizational title of a Public Safety Department. Michigan State University, the University of Georgia, Pennsylvania State University, Florida State University, and the University of South Florida are examples of major universities that developed the "department of public safety" concept in the early days of the professionalization of campus policing. One could view the concept of a public safety department as an important predecessor of today's COP efforts on college campuses in much the same way "team policing," practiced in the 1970s, preceded today's municipal COP operations. Gelber (1972), and Bordner and Peterson (1983) noted the emphasis placed by campus police on crime prevention efforts and similar community service. Providing public education programs and having officers routinely interact with campus community members while engaged in foot patrol were a part of campus police actions long before the term COP was formally instituted in city departments (Jackson, 1992).

Campus police agencies can initiate crime-prevention efforts, a major part of the COP philosophy, by utilizing nondepartmental resources. For example, to enhance controls over certain campus facilities, departments such as physical plant, housing, and student services can work with the police to achieve that end (Esposito & Stormer, 1989). Bromley and Territo (1990) suggested that creating a "team approach" that includes departments such as the General Counsel's Office, the Provost, the Vice President for Business, the physical plant, facilities planning, and residence life, in addition to the police, is a preferred way to develop a comprehensive plan with respect to campus security. COP principles emphasize just such a collaborative approach to creating a safer campus.

Brug (1984), Greenburg (1987), and Peak (1995) have noted that the college campus environment provides a fertile environment for the initiation of COP efforts. Given the general openness to change and willingness to try new ideas found on most college campuses, it is reasonable that a COP model of policing would be a good fit.

Operationalizing COP on Campus

COP appears to offer to campus police the opportunity for continued professional development in an environment – the college/university campus – that encourages innovation and creativity. This approach goes beyond simply responding to calls for service in a professional and timely manner but seeks to involve community members in mutually identifying problems and solutions. In a survey of local chiefs and sheriffs, the National Institute of Justice (1995, p. 2) identified common operational practices that are part of community policing:

- Permanent neighborhood-based offices or stations.
- Designation of "community" or neighborhood police officers.
- Foot patrol as a specific assignment or periodic expectation.
- Regularly scheduled meetings with community groups.
- Specific training and interagency involvement in problem identification and resolution.
- Use of regulatory codes to combat drugs/crime.

As the following examples illustrate, campus police can operationalize virtually all of these practices in a college community. Bromley (2006), in a survey of campus police departments, found that 56 percent of the departments assigned officers to permanent geographic locations, while 72 percent had one or more designated "community officers" on staff. Officers assigned to foot patrol were found in almost 94 percent of the departments, while bike patrol assignments were found in nearly 75 percent of the same agencies (Bromley, 2006). Territo et al. (1998) suggested that placing officers on foot patrol and on bicycles "humanizes" the police and enhances communication between officers and the community; walking or riding the campus creates numerous opportunities for officers to have positive interaction with members of the campus community.

Regarding practices such as routinely meeting with community members and training citizens in identifying problems and resolving them, Bromley (2006) found campus departments were involved in these practices. For example, approximately 31 percent of the departments surveyed had formed "problem solving relationships" with community members and close to 21 percent had actually trained faculty, staff, and students in problem solving techniques.

Using existing regulatory codes and involving nonpolice agencies in crime prevention and quality of life issues are also recognized practices on many college campuses. Stormer and Esposito (1989) and Bromley and Territo (1990) noted that a close relationship can be developed between the campus police and other departments, such as physical plant, student life, residence life, and the general counsel's office, to develop an overall strategy of crime prevention. Further, student governments on many campuses also work with campus police on making campuses safer by establishing student escort programs and installing emergency phones throughout the campuses (Bromley, 1995).

To expand COP practices, campus police departments may develop mutually satisfying relationships academic departments at the institution. Brantingham et al. (1995) and Sloan and Fisher (1995) have provided detailed descriptions of how academic departments can assist campus police in assessing campus security and the perceived risk/fear of victimization among their community members. Academic departments can assist campus police in conducting campus security surveys, including assessing, locks, lighting in public spaces, landscape design, and building architecture. These departments can also assist the campus police department in developing public education/crime prevention materials and a mechanism for timely release of news regarding campus crime and related information. Multiple academic disciplines (e.g., criminal justice, sociology, architecture, urban planning, and mass communication) may be involved with the campus police in these efforts. University provosts, administrative vice presidents, and deans of students can further foster community policing on a campus in much the same way that a city manager or city mayor can do so at the local level of government.

According to Peak (1995), the campus environment uniquely allows the campus police to try philosophical and tactical innovation. While it seems natural that campus police would continue to evolve in the new era of COP, the question remains of how a campus police department brings about planned change. The following section describes how one campus developed and implemented its COP efforts.

Implementing COP on the Campus: A Case Study

The University of South Florida

The University of South Florida (USF), located in Tampa, Florida, opened in 1960 and had an enrollment of 30,000 students in 1991 prior to the implementation of COP at USF. The University currently has 200 degree programs at all levels, including bachelors, masters, doctorate, and professional (e.g., M.D.). It is the principal public university for the Tampa Bay region.

Today the student population is quite diverse, with students coming from every state in the nation and more than 100 foreign countries. Approximately 29 percent of the student body consists of minority group members (e.g., African American, Hispanic, and Asian). Approximately 60 percent of the students are women. Located on over 1,700 acres, USF has a major outpatient clinic, two hospitals, an elementary school, a hotel, and a 10,000-seat multipurpose facility in addition to its traditional academic and general-purpose buildings. It also has 25 miles of roads within its boundaries and nine public entry points (Staehle, 2003).

The University Police Department

The University of South Florida Police Department (USFPD) provides a full range of public safety services to the campus community 24 hours a day, seven days a week on the Tampa Campus. The State of Florida certifies all University Police officers after completing minimum standards training from the Regional Police Training Academy. General services provided by the University Police include car, foot and bicycle patrol, investigation of all misdemeanors and felonies, traffic enforcement, accident investigation, special events management, and crime prevention programs.

The Implementation of COP at USF

Prior to implementing COP at USF, the USFPD long had a reputation for professionalism and for being "community oriented." However, department officials in 1992 made a conscious decision to take additional steps to strengthen the relationship between the department and the campus community. With the department's five-year plan, they established a formal goal to "develop and implement community-oriented policing (COP) throughout the university police department." The department took a number of steps to achieve that goal, as described below.

COP TRAINING. In the Spring of 1992, the Department hired professors from Anthropology and from African American Studies to conduct a series of two-day workshops on cross-cultural communication for all university police personnel. Prior to facilitating these workshops, the two professors spent a significant amount of time reviewing COP materials in order to develop their sessions within the context of the COP philosophy. Participants suggested creating a quality management committee composed of representatives of all university police operational sections. This group became instrumental in enhancing internal communication, reviewing new policies, and developing a revised mission and value statement for the Department that are consistent with COP efforts.

During the Summer of 1992, the Associate Director and the Captain for Police Operations attended a COP workshop conducted by the International Association of Chiefs of Police (IACP). The workshop provided attendees an overview of national COP trends and helped attendees formulate additional plans of action for their departments.

Three law enforcement trainers from Michigan, including Chief Bruce Benson of the Michigan State University Campus Police who had considerable experience with community policing in the campus context provided specialized COP training for all university police personnel. These sessions provided participants concrete examples of how COP was being used in other agencies. The trainers also provided leadership training for all first line supervisors within the department.

COMMUNITY SURVEY. Next, the department developed a community survey to identify perceptions held by university community members regarding university police services and to assess the priority assigned to such services. The department also planned to survey its personnel to determine the priority they would assign to same services. Subject experts from the University Counseling Center, University office of Resource Analysis and Planning, and the Office of Student Affairs previewed and evaluated the survey instrument, based on their input the department revised the instrument and then conducted the survey. The racial/ethnic composition of the respondents paralleled the overall demographics of the university at that time.

Information gained from the survey helped university police command staff in implementing COP. In-service training sessions and public education programs addressed significant differences in the expectation of service delivery between the police officers and community members.

DEPARTMENT REORGANIZATION AND GEOGRAPHIC DEPLOYMENTS. The department then reorganized itself with a more decentralized management structure, consistent with COP principles. The department selected new patrol shift lieutenants who directly supervised their individual units. The department selected the lieutenants based primarily on their knowledge of and commitment to COP principles and their recognized ability as problem solvers. Further, the department revised not only its employee performance evaluation standards to reflect COP principles, but standardized questions used for applicants during the selection process to be more consistent with COP.

The department also assigned its uniformed patrol officers to specific geographic areas of the campus for them to become more familiar with the people living and/or working in the area. The department expected the officers would be more involved in problem solving and not merely respond to calls for service within their geographic areas.

Additionally, the department assigned two full-time university police officers as "community policing specialists" in student residence halls for a one-year period. One of specialists' goals was to work closely with residence hall staff and to serve as in-house liaisons to residents on a daily basis. The Department of Residence Hall Services actually provided office space for the officers in the residence halls.

Finally, all police personnel, in conjunction with their immediate supervisors, developed an individual "community policing project" for the following year. The department's management team reviewed these projects to insure that they met one of two COP criteria: (1) they sought to improve the quality of life within the university or (2) they sought to reduce crime on campus.

Responding to the Challenges: The COP Experience at USF

Described above were some of the unique challenges confronting campus police administrators. Since the early 1990s, the USF Police Department met many of these challenges but was able to remain flexible and adaptive in its approach to providing police services by continuing its COP practices.

For example, today the USF main campus has over 5,000 resident students compared to approximately 3,000 in 1992. The Residential Officer Program, which assigns a full-time officer and other rotating patrol officers to residence halls, has received office space, administrative support, and other resources from the Division of Residence Life which now seen the officers as an integral part of student resident hall life.

Another example of the value of practicing a COP-based organizational philosophy occurred immediately following the terrorist attacks of September 11, 2001. By this time, the student body had experienced a significant increase in nonnative students who had arrived from over 100 foreign countries. COP officers from the University Police Department worked very closely with the Office of International Student Life in the days after 9/11 to provide information and reassurance to foreign students. Because of COP efforts, a partnership developed between the two departments that resulted in enhanced communication.

Presently, 60 percent of the students at USF are women, another example of a potential challenge regarding safety on the campus. Once again, working within the COP framework, the department initiated the nationally recognized *Rape Aggression Defense* (RAD) system. RAD is a comprehensive safety course for women, which combines the elements of awareness, prevention, and risk reduction with hands-on self-defense training. The proactive program has become so popular that the Physical Education Department, a COP partner, now offers it as a two-hour credit course.

One other example involves the vast growth in facilities on the USF campus. Today the campus has over 200 academic and support facilities. As part of the "team approach" used in community policing, a police department representative in consultation with the university's Facilities Planning Division reviews all new building proposals and major renovation projects at USF. This process helps to identify possible security concerns and allows security enhancements before construction ever begins.

While a campus department can implement COP in a variety of ways, the foregoing example illustrated the comprehensive approach that a department must take to accomplish that end. As today's campuses grow in size and complexity, change will be inevitable and challenges will be formidable. Within the context of providing a broad-based service-oriented approach to policing and security on a twenty-first century campus, campus police departments already practicing COP may best be positioned to anticipate and prepare for further change. The college campus setting which fosters innovation and changes would seem a good environment for campus policing to continue its evolution. Long before the concept "community-oriented policing" was invented, forward thinking campus police leaders understood the need to be proactive, community-involved, and service-oriented in their approach to providing police services. These same overarching principles are just as important in today's complex higher education environment and, as such, provide a framework for COP initiatives both now and in the near future.

Campus Policing in the First Decade of the Twenty-first Century

As the first ten years of the twenty-first century have passed, it is now appropriate to review the extent to which campus policing has further evolved. The continued movement towards the implementation of COP initiatives on the part of campus police agencies is shown in the most recent Bureau of Justice Statistics (BJS) report (Reaves, 2008) on campus law enforcement policies and practices. Select highlights of the community policing activities of campus law enforcement agencies at public four year campuses include the following (Reaves, 2008, p. 7):

- campus officers being included in developing campus security policy – 73 percent;
- officers being assigned geographically – 59 percent;
- departments having partnerships with citizen groups – 51 percent;
- departments having student ride-along programs – 49 percent;
- departments having a written community policing plan – 38 percent;
- departments involved in problem-solving projects – 39 percent.

COP has traditionally placed an emphasis on police agencies meeting routinely with various constituent groups to share information and to work collectively to solve community problems. Once again, the BJS report on campus law enforcement shows a commitment to this strategy. According to Reaves (2008, p. 7), campus law enforcement routinely works with various constituent groups on campus (note the percent figure represents the percentage of responding agencies indicating they routinely worked with the named organization to solve one or more problems on campus):

- student housing groups – 86 percent;
- faculty/staff organizations – 83 percent;
- student organizations – 83 percent;
- fraternity/sorority groups – 64 percent;
- advocacy groups – 52 percent;
- domestic violence prevention groups – 52 percent.

Finally, the BJS report provides a third data set that demonstrates the commitment to COP efforts on the part of campus law enforcement agencies during the first decade of the century. These data show the percentage of agencies that have a full-time unit or specifically designated personnel to address the following problems or tasks (Reaves, 2008, p. 17): crime prevention – 88 percent; rape prevention – 85 percent; drug education – 79 percent; self-defense training – 75 percent; alcohol education – 75 percent; community policing – 71 percent; victim assistance – 67 percent; stalking – 68 percent; student security patrol – 55 percent; bias/hate crime – 55 percent.

One true measure of organizational commitment to any concept is the willingness of its administrators to show support by assigning specific responsibility for operationalizing the function to a person or unit. The data above would seem to indicate the majority of public four-year campus police agencies have continued to be involved in COP policies and practices as we enter the twenty-first century.

It would appear that COP initiatives will continue to play an important role in the on-going evolution of campus policing for the immediate future. In addition, the first decade of the twenty-first century has experienced unforeseen, major traumatic events which may have altered campus policing policies and practices for decades to come. Specifically, two events of extreme violence would serve as major catalysts for changes in campus policing. The first event, of course, was the horrific terrorist attacks of September 11, 2001. The second was the unprecedented murders of 33 persons and wounding of 15 others on the Virginia Tech campus in 2007.

The Impact of September 11, 2001 on Campus Policing

Significant changes at all levels of law enforcement have been made as a result of September 11, 2001. The Department of Homeland Security was formed, major formal legislation has passed and funding priorities changed. One priority given to all agencies of law enforcement was to become involved in counterterrorist activities. New multiagency task forces would involve federal, state, municipal, and often campus police organizations. There would be a new mandate for every agency to be involved in intelligence collection, analysis, and sharing. New organizational units within police departments would be formed to support various counterterrorist functions. The long-term effects on policing of September 11, 2001 are still being analyzed (Davis et al., 2010). Some have questioned how community policing activities will be affected by the emerging and on-going emphasis on homeland security functions (Lee, 2010).

American institutions of higher education also had to deal with the aftershock of September 11th. There had already been several attacks on ten IHEs in America by domestic terrorists, such as the Animal Liberation Front (Burke, 2000). Now, the scope of potential attacks would be expanded to involve other terrorist groups (Nelson, 2001; Mojica, 2001). As Bromley (2005, pp. 37–371) has noted, there are a variety of reasons why colleges and universities might be considered potential targets for terrorists, including:

- Most college campuses take pride in allowing relatively easy public access to campus grounds and many on-campus facilities. Campuses usually have multiple public entrances that are open 24 hours a day, seven days a week. In addition to having the normal complement of students, faculty, and staff, colleges and universities frequently have numerous vendors, service providers, and visitors on their campuses on a daily basis.
- The academic tradition of most campuses places a high premium on the freedom of movement and general accessibility to campus buildings and other facilities. This freedom must be balanced with the need to provide a reasonable level of security.
- Given the public nature of many universities, terrorists may be well aware of the vast number of ongoing chemical and biological research projects being conducted on campuses throughout the United States. Many of these projects are funded by the U.S. government and could be very attractive to potential terrorists.
- Some universities may be considered attractive targets based on the sheer size of their student enrollment. On a given day when classes are in session, many large universities may have on-campus populations in excess of 50,000 people. The level of shock following a terrorist attack on a college campus that resulted in thousands of youthful casualties would be significant and long lasting. Large crowds in attendance at high-profile on-campus athletics events or concerts could also be very attractive as targets to potential terrorists.
- There is also the possibility terrorist organizations could try to recruit college students, who might be disgruntled. This tactic was used successfully in the past by groups such as Students for a Democratic Society (SDS), Weather Underground, and the Iranian Student Association. Some more recent stories of "home grown" members of terrorist organizations have surfaces in various American cities.

Given the complex nature of modern IHEs and their communities, many institutions developed task forces comprising persons with both institutional knowledge and appropriate expertise to evaluate their current level of security. While the campus police would play major roles in those task forces, some campuses used broad representation from key faculty, staff, and student organizations to ensure appropriate steps were taken to protect individual rights of community members while understanding the responsibility of all to contribute to the safety of the campus (Bromley, 2005, p. 372).

The changes to the policies and practices of campus police organizations following the terrorist attacks would be evident in a variety of ways. For example, a review of articles written for the *Campus Law Enforcement Journal* after September 11, 2001 reveals the new priority given to preventing and responding to potential terrorist acts by campus police agencies. This journal is considered the primary communication vehicle for the thousand members of the International Association of Campus Law Enforcement Administrators. The journal serves as an outlet for campus police practitioners to share their innovations and activities with other professionals. Therefore, it usually reflects the "hot topics" of the current timeframe. The new concerns presented to all in campus law enforcement post-September 11 would bring new challenges in the "homeland security era." For example, new training in the prevention of and response to acts of suspected terrorism would be emphasized. Better communication with local, state, and federal police agencies would be moved to the forefront. Articles written post-September 11th would reflect these and other topics.

In order to assist police agencies (including campus police), the Department of Homeland Security established the National Incident Management System (NIMS). This program was developed to assist agencies with sharing of information as well as to improve responses to major emergencies. NIMS protocols include: consistency of response; common approach to management of such incidents; and commonality of nomenclature.

According to Peak, Barthe, and Garcia (2008), the campus police provided the following data regarding their policies and practices relating to NIMS: Have policies on NIMS protocols – 71 percent; agencies in fact using NIMS – 77 percent; had conducted training in dealing with potential terrorist threats – 71 percent; and had received federal funding to assist in antiterrorist efforts – 7 percent.

Finally, in his national survey of campus law enforcement departments conducted for the U.S. Bureau of Justice Statics, Reaves (2008, p. 7) also found considerable evidence of the homeland security role now being assumed by these agencies. A brief summary is found in Table 13.1.

The Impact of the Virginia Tech Mass Murders on Campus Policing

The first decade of the twenty-first century had a second major act of tragic violence that would, once again, profoundly affect IHEs and their police Agencies. The extreme incident was, of course, the killing of 33 people and wounding of 15 more on the campus of Virginia Tech University in 2007 by

Table 13.1
Type of Homeland Security Implemented by Campuses

Type of Activity	Percent of Public Institutions
Emergency preparedness plan	94%
Met with campus administrators	91%
Disseminated information	71%
Terrorism response plan	70%
Emergency preparedness exercises	63%
Intelligence-sharing agreements	65%
Held campus meetings	61%
Culturally diverse partnerships	48%
Campus anti-fear campaign	25%

a lone gunman who had a record of mental health issues. While other acts of major violence have occurred on college campuses, none have had the stunning and far reaching impact of the Virginia Tech tragedy. Campus police would once again be compelled to review their policies and practices to meet a new set of expectations of their roles and responsibilities.

The tragedy at Virginia Tech was initially being investigated in a dorm as an isolated incident. When the killer moved to other parts of the campus to continue his violence, neither the police nor other campus officials were adequately prepared for either the violent acts or criticisms to follow. Once again, the role of the campus police would become the subject of inquiry and some changes would follow.

The Virginia State Crime Commission was directed by the state legislature to study campus safety, including: current policies and procedures; the nature of criminal offenses at Virginia IHEs; the use of best practices for campus safety nationally; and the need to develop statewide procedures to disseminate information pertaining to campus safety to IHEs (HJR Final Report, 2006, p. 1). According to McBride (2010), 11 other states also established statewide task forces to review campus safety conditions. McBride's subsequent analysis of these eleven task force reports revealed major commonalities, among them the recommendations that:

- Institutions should annually review the adequacy of resources devoted to campus safety, security and mental health services for students and employees.
- Many campus executives and officials lack adequate emergency management training (especially in terms of Incident Command System [ICS] and NIMS).
- Campus emergency plans should be reviewed and tested annually.
- Existing methods of mass emergency communication should be evaluated in terms of redundancy and effectiveness.

- Campus safety and security officers should be given extensive training as emergency first responders and as crisis intervention team members.

The federal government would also become directly involved in the review of the issues that were raised by the Virginia Tech tragedy. Numerous meetings were conducted involving representatives from the IME community, law enforcement, and mental health care providers. The latter groups would provide important input as Seung Hui Cho, the Virginia Tech student who had done the shootings, had a known history of mental health issues. In June 2007, there was issued (by select federal agencies) the "Report to the President on Issues Raised by the Virginia Tech Tragedy." Subsequently in 2010, the U.S. Secret Service, U.S. Department of Education, and the Federal Bureau of Investigation published their follow-up report. This report, by Drysdale, Modzeleski, and Simmons (2010), frankly acknowledged that identifying, assessing and managing violence risk at IHEs were difficult tasks. They specifically mention that "law enforcement, mental health, student affairs and legal professionals must provide incredible service and unique and often challenging circumstances" (p. iii).

The report also suggested that IHEs create threat assessment teams (Drysdale, Modzeleski, & Simmons, 2010, p. 27). These teams typically comprise representatives from various departments within the college or university, including academic affairs, student affairs, the IHE's legal counsel, mental health services, and public safety. IHE threat assessment teams seek to thoroughly evaluate persons of concern who may pose a potential risk of violence and generally engage in a three-step process that includes: identifying individuals whose behavior causes concern or disruption on or off campus affecting IHE members, such as students, faculty, or other staff; assessing whether the identified individual possesses the intent and ability to carry out an attack against the IHE or members of the IHE community, and if the individual has taken any steps to prepare for the attack; and managing the threat posed by the individual to include disrupting potential plans of attack, mitigating the risk, and implementing strategies to facilitate long-term resolution.

Each of these objectives has implications for campus police leaders and their operational personnel. For example, since the Virginia Tech tragedy, many campuses have reviewed and revised their policies and technology to provide members of the community with "timely warnings" about potential dangers.

Additionally new policies must be developed to guide campus police officials, and additional training will be required in topics, such as dealing with recognizing and responding to persons exhibiting mental health difficulties and responding to "active shooters" such as Seung Hu Cho. Of critical importance will be the establishment of channels of on-going communication among all IHE departments playing a role in providing campus security. As

Drysdale et al. (2010, p. 25) noted:

> IHEs must then establish an infrastructure capable of providing the neces-
> sary services, support and protection to students, staff, and others who may
> have contact with the IHE. Looking at the protection side alone, as a mini-
> society, IHEs must contend with the full range of crimes committed by or
> against its members.

Conclusion

Since September 11, 2001, some authorities have speculated that policing
in America has changed from being community-oriented to a more protective
"militarized" role (Peak, 2012). This view also raised the concern whether the
legalistic, strict enforcement militaristic approach can co-exist with the more
service-oriented community policing philosophy. As argued in a previous section of this chapter, the campus police role has been affected by the terrorist
attacks of September 11th. Likewise, the more aggressive response by campus
police to active shooters is at least partially explained by the Virginia Tech
tragedy. Many campus police agencies today have ready access to high-pow-
ered weapons to be used in these responses; these were virtually nonexistent
a decade ago. Today, when an IHE is "locked down" due to a threat of extreme violence, campuses look more like military installations than secure institutions of higher learning.

Executive-level campus leaders learned during the first part of the twenty-
first century that their institutions were no longer sanctuaries safe from natural disasters, terrorist threats, and acts of extreme interpersonal violence. The
role of the campus police has been expanded to help IHEs prevent, respond
to, and recover from emergencies not envisioned ten years ago. According to
Altizer, Corbett, and Harris (2010), 38 percent of the universities responding
to a recent survey indicated the campus emergency management office was
under the jurisdiction of the campus police department. This fact also reflects
an expanded campus police role and scope of authority and activities.

It remains to be seen exactly how the campus police role will further
evolve. Given the high level of community/police interaction at most IHEs,
the COP model may still be flexible enough to provide the best framework
for campus police operations. Developing strong partnerships with other key
student, faculty, and staff groups should continue to be a point of emphasis for
campus police. Gathering information, preventing serious incidents, and developing problem-solving approaches to resolve acts of extreme violence
should still be viable within campus communities. Given the general cohe-
siveness of most campuses, community policing should continue to emphasize the problem-solving response to contemporary issues (Peak et al., 2010).
The challenge will continue to be how to use the community-oriented ap-

proach, but still be ever vigilant and prepared to react to the possible tragedies that campuses will likely continue to experience at some level. It is likely that as IHEs grow in size and complexity, so too, will the roles of the campus police. Paoline and Sloan (2003) note that campus police are among the most numerous forms of specialized police and, therefore, it is important for researchers to continue their systematic study of the profession's evolution. This is a reasonable recommendation certainly worth pursuing.

REFERENCES

Altizer, A., Corbett, C., & Harris, S. (2010). Emergency management on campus: Where should it reside? *Campus Law Enforcement Journal, 40,* 27–29.

Atwell, R. (1988). *Memorandum regarding campus security.* Washington, DC: American Council on Education.

Bess, W., & Horton, G. (1988). The role of campus law enforcement. *Campus Law Enforcement Journal, 19,* 35–36.

Bordner, D., & Petersen, D. (1983). *Campus policing: The nature of university work.* Lanham, MD: University Press of America.

Brantingham, P., Brantingham, P., & Seagrave, J. (1995). Crime and fear of crime in a Canadian university. In B. S. Fisher & J. J. Sloan. (Eds.), *Campus crime: Legal, social, and policy perspectives* (pp. 123–155). Springfield, IL: Charles C Thomas.

Bromley, M. (1992). Campus and community crime rate comparisons: A statewide study. *Journal of Security Administration, 15,* 49–64.

Bromley, M. (1995). Securing the campus: Political and economic forces affecting decision-makers. In B. S. Fisher & J. J. Sloan (Eds.), *Campus crime: Legal, social, and policy perspectives* (pp. 214–227). Springfield, IL: Charles C Thomas.

Bromley, M. (1996). Policing our campuses: A national review of statutes. *American Journal of Police, 15,* 1–22.

Bromley, M. (2005). Planning for campus security after September 11: One university's experience. In L. Snowden & B. Whitsel (Eds.), *Terrorism: Research, readings and realities* (pp. 369–379). Upper Saddle River, NJ: Pearson-Prentice-Hall

Bromley, M. (2006). Comparing campus and municipal police community policing practices. *Journal of Security Administration, 26,* 37–50.

Bromley, M., & Fisher, B. (2002). Campus policing and victim services. In L. Moriarty & M. Dantzker (Eds.), *Policing and victims* (pp. 133–158). Upper Saddle River, NJ: Prentice-Hall.

Bromley, M., & Reaves, B. (1998a). Comparing campus and city police operational practices. *Journal of Security Administration, 21,* 41–54.

Bromley, M., & Reaves, B. (1998b). Comparing campus and municipal police: The human resource dimension. *Policing: An International Journal of Police Strategies and Management, 21,* 534–546.

Bromley, M., & Territo, L. (1990). *College crime prevention and personal safety.* Springfield, IL: Charles C Thomas.

Brubacher, J., & Willis, R. (1968). *Higher education in transition.* New York: Harper and Row.

Brug, R. (1984). Cal-Poly maximizes use of students. *Campus Law Enforcement Journal, 14,* 41–42.

Burke, R. (2000). *Counterterrorism for emergency responders.* Boca Raton, FL: Lewis.

Caldwell, A. (2010). Farooque Ahmed arrested for plotting DC terrorist attack. Retrieved from http://www.huffingtonpost.com/2010/10/27/farooque-ahmed-arrested-f_n_774841.html.

Cochran, J., Bromley, M., & Landis, L. (1999). Officer work orientations, perception of readiness and anticipated effectiveness of an agency-wide community policing effort within a county sheriff's office. *Journal of Police and Criminal Psychology, 14,* 43–65.

Davis, L., Pollard, M., Ward, K., Wilson, J., Varda, D., Mansell, L., & Steinberg, P. (2010). *Long-term effects of law enforcement post 9/11 focus on counterterrorism and homeland security.* Los Angeles: Rand Corporation.

Digest of educational statistics. (1991). Washington, DC: United States Department of Education.

Drysdale, D., Modzeleski, W., & Simons, A. (2010). *Campus attacks: Targeted violence affecting institutions of higher education.* Washington, DC: U.S. Secret Service; U.S. Department of Homeland Security; Office of Safe and Drug Free Schools, U.S. Department of Education; and Federal Bureau of Investigation.

Esposito, D., & Stormer, D. (1989). The multiple roles of campus law enforcement. *Campus Law Enforcement Journal, 19,* 26–30.

Fernandez, A., & Lizotte, A.J. (1995). An analysis of the relationship between campus crime and community crime: Reciprocal effects? In B. S. Fisher & J. J. Sloan (Eds.), *Campus crime: Legal, social, and policy perspectives* (pp. 79–102). Springfield, IL: Charles C Thomas.

Fox, J., & Hellman, D. (1985). Location and other correlates of campus crime. *Journal of Criminal Justice, 13,* 429–444.

Gelber, S. (1972). *The role of campus security in the college setting.* Washington, DC: United States Department of Justice.

Goldstein, H. (1987). Toward community oriented policing: Potential, basic requirements, and threshold questions. *Crime and Delinquency, 33,* 6–30.

Greenburg, M. (1987). Harnessing campus humanism for sake of public safety. *Campus Law Enforcement Journal, 17,* 41–42.

Hart, T. (2003). *Violent victimizations of college students.* Washington, DC: United States Department of Justice, Bureau of Justice Statistics.

International Association of Campus Law Enforcement Administrators. (1995). *Campus crime report, 1991–1993.* Hartford, CT: IACLEA.

Jackson, E. (1992). Campus police embrace community based approach. *The Police Chief, 59,* 62–64.

Jacobs, J., & O'Meara, V. (1980). Security forces and the transformation of the American university. *College and University, 31,* 283–297.

Kassinger, E. (1971). Alternative to chaos: The need for professionalization of campus law enforcement. In S. Sims (Ed.), *New directions in campus law enforcement: A handbook for administrators* (pp. 1–13). Athens, GA: The University of Georgia Center for Continuing Education.

Lanier, M. (1995). Community policing on university campuses: Tradition, practice, and outlook. In B. S. Fisher & J. J. Sloan (Eds.), *Campus crime: Legal, social, and policy perspectives* (pp. 248–264). Springfield, IL: Charles C Thomas.

Lederman, D. (1993, January 20). Colleges report 7,500 violent crimes on their campuses in first annual statements required under federal law. *The Chronicle of Higher Education*, pp. A32–A43.

Lederman, D. (1994, February 2). Crime on the campuses: Increases in reported robberies and assaults. *The Chronicle of Higher Education*, pp. A31–A41.

Lederman, D. (1995, February 3). Colleges report rise in violent crime. *The Chronicle of Higher Education*, pp. A31–A42.

Lee, J. (2010). Policing after 9/11: Community policing in an age of homeland security. *Police Quarterly, 13,* 347–366.

Lewis, L., & Farris, E. (1997). *Campus crime and security at postsecondary education institutions.* Washington, DC: United States Department of Education, National Center for Education Statistics.

Lively, K. (1996, April 26). Drug arrests rise again. *The Chronicle of Higher Education,* p. A37.

Lively, K. (1997, March 21). Campus drug arrests increased 18 percent in 1995: Reports of other crime fell. *The Chronicle of Higher Education,* p. A44.

Lizotte, A., & Fernandez, A. (1993). *Trends and correlates of campus crime: A general report.* Albany, NY: Consortium of Higher Education Campus Crime Research.

McBride, J. T. (2010). Virginia Tech task force reports. *Campus Law Enforcement Journal, 40,* 21–23.

McDaniel, W. (1971). Law Enforcement: The Officer as the Educator. In O. Sims (Ed.), *New directions in campus law enforcement: A handbook for administrators.* Athens, GA: The University of Georgia, Center for Continuous Education.

Mojica, S. (2001). Putting the Pieces Back Together. *Campus Safety Journal, 9,* 14–15.

National Institute of Justice Research Review. (1995). *Community policing strategies.* Washington, DC: United States Department of Justice.

Nelson, T. (2001). Incident Management. *Campus Safety Journal, 9,* 11–13.

Nichols, D. (1987). *The administration of public safety in higher education.* Springfield, IL: Charles C Thomas.

Ordovensky, P. (1990, December 3). Students easy prey on campus. *U.S.A. Today,* p. 1A.

Palmer, C. (1993, April 21). Skepticism is rampant about the statistics on campus crime. *The Chronicle of Higher Education,* p. B1.

Paoline, E., & Sloan, J. (2003). Variability in the organizational structure of contemporary campus law enforcement agencies: A national-level analysis. *Policing: An International Journal of Police Strategies and Management, 26,* 612–639.

Peak, K. (1988). Campus law enforcement. A national survey of administration and operation. *Campus Law Enforcement Journal, 19,* 33–35.

Peak, K. (1989). Campus law enforcement in flux: Changing times and future expectations. *Campus Law Enforcement Journal, 19,* 21–25

Peak, K. (1995). The professionalization of campus law enforcement: Comparing
campus and municipal law enforcement agencies. In B. S. Fisher & J. J. Sloan III
(Eds.), *Campus crime: Legal, social, and policy perspectives* (pp. 228–245). Springfield
IL: Charles C Thomas.

Peak, K. (2012). *Policing in America: Challenges and best practices.* Upper Saddle River,
NJ: Prentice-Hall.

Peak, K., Barthe, E., & Garcia, A. (2008). Campus policing in America: A twenty-year
perspective. *Police Quarterly, 11,* 239–260

Peak, K., & Barthe, E. (2010). Policing educational spaces: Status, practices and challenges. In C. Cranford (Ed.), *Spatial policing: The influence of time, space and geography on law enforcement practices* (pp. 137–158). Durham, NC: Carolina Academic
Press.

Peak, J., & Gensor, R. (1999). *Community policing and problem solving: Strategies and practices.* Upper Saddle River, NJ: Prentice-Hall.

Powell, J. (1981) *Campus Security and law Enforcement.* Woburn, MA: Butterworth.

Powell, J., Pander, M., & Nielsen, R. (1994). *Campus security and law enforcement* (2nd
ed.). Boston: Butterworth-Heinemann.

Proctor, S. (1958). *The University of Florida: Its early years.* Unpublished doctoral dissertation, University of Florida, Gainesville, FL.

Reaves, B. (2008). *Campus law enforcement 2004–2005.* Washington, DC: U.S. Department of Justice.

Reaves, B. (2010). *Local police departments, 2007.* Washington, DC: U.S. Department of
Justice.

Reaves, B., & Goldberg, A. (1996). *Campus law enforcement agencies, 1995.* Washington,
DC: U.S. Department of Justice.

Rudolph, F. (1962). *The American college and university: A history.* New York: Random
House.

Seng, M. (1995). The *Crime Awareness and Campus Security Act:* Some observations, critical comments, and suggestions. In B. S. Fisher & J. J. Sloan (Eds.), *Campus crime:
Legal, social, and policy perspectives* (pp. 38–52). Springfield, IL: Charles C Thomas.

Shoemaker, E. (1995). Non-traditional strategies for implementing community oriented policing. In International Association of Campus Law Enforcement Administrators (Eds.), *Community policing on campus* (pp. 25–36). Hartford, CT: IA-
CLEA.

Sims, O. (1971). *New directions in campus law enforcement: A handbook for administrators.*
Athens, GA: The University of Georgia Center for Continuing Education.

Skolnick, J. (1969). *Politics of protest.* Washington, DC: United States Government
Printing Office.

Sloan, J. (1992). The modern campus police: An analysis of their evolution, structure,
and function. *American Journal of Police, 11,* 85–104.

Sloan, J. (1994). The correlates of campus crime: An analysis of reported crimes on
university campuses. *Journal of Criminal Justice, 22,* 51–62.

Sloan, J., & Fisher, B. (1995). Campus crime: Legal, social, and policy perspectives. In B. S. Fisher & J. J. Sloan (Eds.), *Campus crime: Legal, social, and policy perspectives* (pp. 3–22). Springfield, IL: Charles C Thomas.

Smith, M. (1988). *Coping with crime on campus.* New York: Macmillan.

Smith, M. (1989). *Campus crime and campus police: A handbook for police officers and administrators.* Asheville, NC: College Administration Publications, Inc.

Smith, M. (1995). Vexations victims of campus crime. In B. S. Fisher & J. J. Sloan (Eds.), *Campus crime: Legal, social, and policy perspectives* (pp. 25–37). Springfield, IL: Charles C Thomas.

Staehle, R. (2003). Personal communication, October 17, 2003.

Territo, L., Halsted, J., & Bromley, M. (1998). *Crime and justice in America: A human perspective* (5th ed.). Newton, MA: Butterworth-Heinemann.

Trojanowicz, R., & Carter, D. (1988). *The philosophy and role of community policing.* East Lansing, MI: National Center for Community Policing.

Virginia State Crime Commission. (2006). *HJR final report: Study on campus safety.* Richmond, VA: Virginia State Crime Commission.

Witsil, J. (1979). Security at Princeton is low-keyed. *Campus Law Enforcement Journal, 9,* 6–7.

Wooldridge, J., Cullen, F., & Latessa, E. (1995). Predicting the likelihood of faculty victimization: Individual demographics and routine activities. In B. S. Fisher & J. J. Sloan (Eds.), *Campus crime: Legal, social, and policy perspectives* (pp. 133–122). Springfield, IL: Charles C Thomas.

Zhao, J., Lorvich, N., & Thurman, Q. (1999). The status of community policing in American cities: Facilitators and impediments revisited. *Policing: An International Journal of Police Strategies and Management, 22,* 74–92.

Chapter 14

COMMUNITY-ORIENTED POLICING (COP) ON COLLEGE CAMPUSES: NEW DIRECTIONS?

Eugene A. Paoline, III and John J. Sloan, III

INTRODUCTION

Over the last three decades, the philosophy of American policing has undergone substantial change. No longer operating within the so-called "professional model" that dominated American policing for the better part of the twentieth century and which stressed random and reactive patrol, rapid response to calls for service, and an emphasis on law enforcement and crime control (Fogelson, 1977; Maguire, 1997; Monkkonen, 1981; Reiss, 1992), Community-Oriented Policing (COP) has required American police departments to shift the philosophical, operational, and tactical orientation of their agencies (Cordner, 1996, 1997; Maguire & Mastrofski, 2000; Paoline & Sloan, 2003; Rosenbaum, 1994).

COP proponents argue this model not only helps control crime but also addresses the alienation from the police commonly felt by members of urban communities (Skogan & Hartnett, 1997). As such, COP represents a radical departure from the past, due to it emphasizing, among other considerations, decentralization and despecialization of organizational functions; the empowerment of line personnel (patrol officers); community partnerships; and problem solving (see Cordner, 1996; Maguire, 2002).

As discussed below, COP has involved multiple levels of reform, beginning with the underlying philosophy of the role of the police in the community and ending with specific tactics used by beat officers. COP has found favor with both academic police researchers and many municipal police departments, both large and small. For example, according to the most recent Bureau of Justice Statistics' *Law Enforcement Management and Administrative Statistics* (LEMAS) survey (Reaves, 2010), 47 percent of all local police departments deployed full-time community policing officers, although among departments serving a population of at least 50,000 residents, the percentage was much greater (71%). Thus, COP continues to be a feature of American police despite its critics (e.g., Bayley, 1988; Herbert, 2006; Manning, 1984, 1988, 1989), and the emergence of additional innovations such as comparative statistical analyses (COMPSTAT; see Dabney, 2010; Eterno & Silverman, 2010; Willis, 2011) that have permeated local police departments. Importantly, for purposes of the present discussion, campus police departments have embraced COP and it appears to be the primary organizational model for the vast majority of campus police agencies (Bromley, 2003, 2007).

This chapter examines COP as an organizational model for campus police departments. We begin the chapter with an overview of COP and discuss its key components. Second, we examine the extent campus agencies have adopted COP by reviewing several case studies of its implementation and results of a national-level study. Next, we examine why, given the history and unique context of campus police, COP is a reasonable organizational model for campus police departments to adopt. We conclude the chapter by discussing recent changes in the landscape of campus communities and the implications of these changes for campus police agencies.

Community-Oriented Policing: An Overview

The origins of COP can be traced to two publications occurring several years apart but which have become linked as forming COP's foundation: Goldstein (1979) and Wilson and Kelling (1982). Goldstein presented a strong argument that urban police needed to focus less on quickly responding to calls for service and more on neighborhood and community problems that give rise to crime, disorder, and fear. Instead of being reactive and focusing on rapid responses to calls for service – as had been the dominant theme in policing for decades – Goldstein (1979) called on the police to be more proactive and "problem oriented." This shift in orientation, argued Goldstein, would result in greater interaction and cooperation between the police and the community. In turn, generous benefits would accrue the police, such as enhancing its legitimacy in the public eye, individual officers developing stronger ties to the communities they were policing, and making departments more effective and efficient.

Wilson and Kelling (1982) developed the now famous "broken windows" thesis which suggests crime, neighborhood disorder, and citizen fear of victimization worked in combination to devastate communities. They used the example of a broken window left unrepaired in a building; soon, they argued, more broken windows would appear signaling prospective offenders that "no one in the community cared" enough to fix them. This "lack of care" opens the door for offenders to engage in even greater levels of lawlessness, fueling greater levels of neighborhood disorder and fear. Wilson and Kelling argued that if the police were to have any chance of making a difference, they had to work *with* the community and attack the "broken windows." In other words, before the police could address high levels of crime, they first had to address the problems that plagued high-crime neighborhoods and could only do so by collaborating with the community (see also Skogan, 1990).

While approaching the same problem from different angles, the two articles reached the same conclusion: reactive-based, calls-for-service oriented, top-down focused organizational models had failed, and a new model was needed. Importantly, this model would need to bring together the police and the community to address the problems that give rise to crime, disorder, and fear, and create partnerships between the police and the community to address them.

During the 1980s, academic researchers and police practitioners alike debated what Zhao, Lovrich, and Thurman (1999) called the "promises and challenges" of COP, particularly whether it represented something "real" or was mere "rhetoric" (Greene & Mastrofski, 1988). Helping fuel this debate was publication of several case studies, the results of which were widely disseminated by the National Institute of Justice, alleging the successes of COP in Flint, Michigan (Trojanowicz, 1982); Houston, Texas (Brown & Wycoff, 1987); and Newport News, Virginia (Eck & Spelman, 1987). For some of its critics (e.g., Greene & Mastrofski, 1988), these case studies merely showed the benefits of foot patrol for reducing crime or how changes in other tactics used by beat officers would benefit communities and not the utility of COP in achieving its stipulated goals.

Zhao et al. (1999) suggest the 1990s marked a "third wave" of COP development where widespread acceptance and implementation of COP occurred (see also Zhao, Thurman, & Lovrich, 1997). The Clinton Administration played a crucial role because it strongly supported COP and pressed Congress to pass (which it did) the *Violent Crime Control and Law Enforcement Act* in 1994 which authorized federally subsidized funding to hire 100,000 new community police officers by local law enforcement agencies, and created the federal Office of Community Oriented Policing Services (the COPS Office). The Justice Department charged the COPS Office with coordinating and supervising community oriented policing programs nationwide, which it has now done for over a decade.

Through the start of the twenty-first century, some researchers suggested that COP initiatives were "the preferred form of quality management strategies employed" to address such issues as officer productivity, agency responsiveness, and the quality of police services provided to the public (Cochran, Bromley, & Swando, 2002, p. 508). Supporters claimed COP addresses these issues because the model involves multifunctionality, coproduction, partnership, decentralization, a flat organizational hierarchy, despecialization, and proactiveness (Skogan & Hartnett, 1997).

Despite its widespread acceptance, confusion remains among scholars and practitioners alike as to whether COP is a philosophy, an operational model, a tactic, or something else entirely. The following section addresses this issue.

The Components of COP

There is no consensus definition of COP (Eck & Rosenbaum, 1994), which is one of the biggest criticisms levied against COP supporters. Critics argue that if one cannot define COP, how can one know if a department has actually implemented it and how can its effectiveness be evaluated? Cordner (1996) tried to answer this criticism by presenting a comprehensive explanation of COP, including its key dimensions – philosophical, strategic, tactical, and organizational – and the various subcomponents of each dimension.

CORDNER'S (1996) DISCUSSION OF COP. Cordner's discussion begins by exploring the philosophical dimension of COP. According to Cordner (1996, p. 2), the philosophical dimension of COP ". . . includes the central ideas and beliefs underlying community policing. Three of the most important . . . are *citizen input, broad function,* and *personal service.*" *Citizen input* involves citizens having a say in how the department operates and how it responds to the community's security and safety needs. Cordner suggests departments can use specific methods to enhance citizen input including advisory boards at different levels within the agency ranging from the individual beat to the highest levels of the command structure; community surveys; use of Internet homepages and email communication; and town meetings. Each technique is designed to bring together individual officers, department administrators, and citizens, and creates specific opportunities for citizens to have input into department operations at a variety of levels, from a specific beat to the entire agency.

Broad function points to the fact that policing under COP is viewed as a broad-based activity that involves officers:

> . . . working with residents to enhance neighborhood safety. This includes resolving conflicts, helping victims, preventing accidents, solving problems, and fighting fear as well as reducing crime through apprehension and enforcement. Policing is inherently a multi-faceted government function; arbi-

trarily narrowing it just to call handling and law enforcement reduces its effectiveness in accomplishing the multiple objectives that the public expects police to achieve. (Cordner, 1996, p. 3)

Activities such as pursuing traffic safety through a combination of enforcement and engineering efforts; reducing drug abuse through public education and enforcement; reducing fear of victimization (particularly when it is not justified by actual victimization risk) through high-interaction patrols and enforcement of nuisance statutes relating to public panhandling or urban camping; providing services to domestic violence victims and implementing mandatory arrest policies (if appropriate); and participating in zoning/rezoning decisions to address public safety and traffic issues would all come under the umbrella of broad function police activities.

According to Cordner (1996, p. 4), the *personal service* component emphasizes that police are not bureaucrats, nor should they behave like them:

> [Personal service] is designed to overcome one of the most common complaints that the public has about government employees, including police officers – that they do not seem to care and that they treat citizens as numbers, not real people. Of course, not every police-citizen encounter can be amicable and friendly. Nevertheless, whenever possible, officers should deal with citizens in a friendly, open, and personal manner designed to turn them into satisfied customers. This can best be done by eliminating as many artificial bureaucratic barriers as possible, so that citizens can deal directly with 'their' officer.

Cordner (1996) suggests officers can enhance personal service by issuing business cards to victims, complainants, and witnesses and using pagers and voice mail so citizens can directly contact them. Cordner also suggests that departments can adopt slogans and symbols (e.g., mission statements, value statements) to reinforce the importance of providing personal service to the public.

THE STRATEGIC DIMENSION OF COP. The strategic dimension links the philosophical beliefs and values of COP to specific programs and policies. Three important strategic elements include *reorienting operations, emphasizing prevention,* and *focusing on geography.*

Reorienting operations includes departments (and officers) relying less on motorized patrol and more on face-to-face interaction with citizens. An important objective here is to replace "ineffective or isolating operational practices (e.g., motorized patrol and rapid response to low priority calls) with more effective and more interactive practices" (Cordner, 1996, p. 4). Additionally, as part of reorienting their operations, departments can find more efficient ways of performing necessary traditional functions (e.g., handling emergency calls and conducting follow-up investigations) to save time and resources that are then redirected to more community-oriented activities (Cordner, 1996). Examples of reorienting operations include increased reliance on foot and other forms of patrol (e.g., bicycle or mounted); differential patrol (e.g., delayed response, telephone reporting, walk-in reporting); and different investigative responses tailored to meet the needs of different types of cases, rather than automatically assigning detectives to follow up on all cases.

Emphasizing prevention focuses on making crime prevention a routine part of every officer's daily activities. Cordner (1996, p. 5) suggests the following as activities geared toward prevention:

- *Situational Crime Prevention* – the most promising general approach to crime prevention that involves tailoring specific preventive measures to each situation's specific characteristics.
- *CPTED* – many departments have become involved with CPTED – Crime Prevention Through Environmental Design – which focuses on changing the physical characteristics of a location that make it conducive to crime.
- *Community Crime Prevention* – many departments now work closely with individual residents and with groups of residents in a cooperative manner to prevent crime (e.g., block watch).
- *Youth-Oriented Prevention* – many departments have implemented programs or collaborated with others to provide programs designed to prevent youth crime (e.g., recreation, tutoring, and mentoring programs).
- *Business Crime Prevention* – many departments work closely with businesses to recommend personnel practices, retail procedures, and other security measures designed to prevent crime.

Finally, Cordner (1996, p. 6) suggests "Community policing adopts a geographic focus to establish stronger bonds between officers and neighborhoods . . . to increase mutual recognition, identification, responsibility, and accountability." Cordner points out that while departments traditionally assign officers to a *physical space* (a beat), their accountability has been almost exclusively *temporal* (during a particular shift). COP changes the focus from the temporal to the geographic by having departments use methods such as permanent beat assignments for officers; by creating "lead officers" responsible for problem identification and coordination of the efforts of all officers assigned a specific beat during a 24-hour period; implementing "cop of the block" where a beat is subdivided into smaller areas of individual accountability so that although every officer has general responsibility for a beat, each officer also has special responsibility for a smaller area within it; creating mini-stations or storefront stations; and assigning detectives as "area specialists" to handle all investigations in a particular area, rather than specializing in one type of case (e.g., burglary) arising throughout the department's jurisdiction.

THE TACTICAL DIMENSION OF COP. According to Cordner (1996, p. 6), the tactical dimension of COP "ultimately translates ideas, philosophies, and strategies into concrete programs, tactics, and behaviors," and suggests that the three most important tactical elements of COP include *positive interaction, partnerships,* and *problem solving.*

While policing inevitably involves negative contacts between officers and the public (e.g., traffic stops, stopping citizens on suspicion, or issuing orders to desist), COP seeks to offset these negative contacts as much as possible with positive contacts between officers and citizens. As Cordner (1996, p. 6) puts it:

> Positive interactions have several benefits, of course: they generally build familiarity, trust, and confidence on both sides; they remind officers that most citizens respect and support them; they make the officer more knowledgeable about people and conditions in the beat; they provide specific information for criminal investigations and problem solving; and they break up the monotony of motorized patrol.

Departments seeking to enhance positive interactions between officers and citizens can use a variety of methods to achieve that goal. For example, when handling routine calls for service, rather than officers rushing to clear the call and return to patrol, they spend extra time with citizens to create a more positive experience for them. Officers can also attend neighborhood association or block association meetings to show their commitment to the neighborhood. Such interaction can also provide additional benefits to officers, such as information from citizens on problems with which the officer is unfamiliar. Finally, instead of concentrating patrol on "public places or spaces," officers can stop and talk with people so their patrol now focuses less on *watching* people and more on *interacting* with them.

Key to the success of COP are *active partnerships* between police and other agencies, and citizens, in which the parties work together to identify and solve problems. Cordner (1996) suggests citizens can take a greater role in public safety than has been typical over the past few decades, and other public and private agencies can leverage their resources and authority toward solving public safety problems. While mindful of the fact there are legal and safety limitations on how extensive a role citizens can play in "co-producing" public safety, Cordner (1996, p. 6) argues ". . . it is a mistake for the police to try to assume the entire burden for controlling crime and disorder." Using "citizen police academies" to train citizens to patrol their neighborhoods; enforcing building codes; being involved with nuisance abatement; and working with landlords and tenants, are just a few of the ways that officers can partner with citizens to address problems.

The final component of the tactical dimension of COP is *problem solving,* which Cordner (1996, p. 7) explains as follows:

> Community policing urges the adoption of a *problem solving* orientation toward policing, as opposed to the incident-oriented approach . . . Naturally, emergency calls must still be handled right away and officers will still spend

much of their time handling individual incidents. Whenever possible, however, officers should search for the underlying conditions that give rise to single and multiple incidents. When such conditions are identified, officers should try to affect them as a means of controlling and preventing future incidents. [O]fficers should strive to have more substantive and meaningful impact than occurs from 15-minute treatments of individual calls for service.

Cordner (1996, p. 7) offers the following as "promising approaches" to problem solving:

- *The SARA Process* – many departments use the SARA model (scanning, analysis, response, assessment) as a guide to the problem solving process for all kinds of crime and non-crime problems.
- *Guardians* – when searching for solutions to problems, it is often helpful to identify so-called "guardians," people who have an incentive or the opportunity to help rectify the problem (e.g., property owners or school principals).
- *Beat Meetings* – some departments utilize meetings between neighborhood residents and their beat officers to identify problems, analyze them, and brainstorm possible solutions.
- *Hot Spots* – many departments analyze calls for service to identify locations that have disproportionate numbers of calls arising from them and then do problem solving to try to lower the call volume in those places.
- *Multi-Agency Teams* – some jurisdictions use problem solving teams comprised not just of police, but also of representatives of other agencies (public works, sanitation, parks and recreation, code enforcement, etc.) so that an array of information and resources can be brought to bear once problems are identified.

THE ADMINISTRATIVE DIMENSION OF COP. The final dimension of COP, according to Cordner (1996, p. 8), is the administrative, that Cordner describes as follows:

It is important to recognize an Organizational Dimension that surrounds community policing and greatly affects its implementation. [T]o support and facilitate community policing, police departments often consider a variety of changes in organization, administration, management, and supervision. The elements of the organizational dimension are not really part of community policing per se, but they are frequently crucial to its successful implementation.

Cordner (1996, p. 8) suggests the three most important elements of the administrative dimension of COP are *structure, management,* and *information.*

Cordner (1996, p. 8) argues that restructuring police agencies to facilitate and support implementation of the philosophical, strategic, and tactical elements is one of the most important aspects of COP. Departments can facilitate this restructuring by using the following processes and activities:

- *Decentralization* – departments can delegate authority and responsibility more widely so that commanders, supervisors, and officers can act more independently and be more responsive.
- *Flattening* – departments can reduce the number of layers of hierarchy to improve communication and reduce waste, rigidity and bureaucracy.
- *Despecialization* – departments can reduce the number of specialized units and personnel so that more resources are devoted to direct delivery of services to the general public.
- *Teams* – A department's efficiency and effectiveness can improve by getting employees to work together as teams to perform work, solve problems, or look for ways of improving quality.
- *Civilianization* – Departments can reclassify positions currently held by sworn personnel so non-sworn personnel may hold them. Doing so allows both cost savings and better utilization of sworn personnel.

Management, according to Cordner (1996, p. 9), involves styles of leadership and supervision that emphasize organizational culture and values over written rules and formal discipline. Although COP does not advocate abandoning formal rules, its orientation is such that managers resort to them much less often to maintain control over subordinates. Practices consistent with this new orientation include mission statements guiding departments' decision-making. Departments would also make continuous use of strategic planning to insure resources and energy remain focused on achieving the department's mission and adhering to its core values. Supervisors spend more time "coaching" and mentoring subordinates than simply reviewing their paperwork or enforcing rules. The department empowers subordinates by rewarding them for reasonable risk-taking behavior that furthered larger organizational goals. Superiors use selective discipline, whereby disciplinary processes distinguish intentional from unintentional errors and between employee actions violating core values versus those that merely violate technical rules. By using these methods, departments can successfully integrate a new style of management that facilitates the type of organizational change necessary for implementing COP.

Finally, Cordner (1996, pp. 9–10) suggests that "doing" COP and managing it effectively requires departments to compile and then use certain types of *information* that have not traditionally been available in most, if not all, police departments. In the never-ending quality versus quantity debate, for example, community policing tends to emphasize quality. This emphasis on quality reveals itself in many areas, such as avoiding traditional "bean-counting" procedures (such as arrests made or tickets issued) to measure success, and focusing on how well officers handle calls, rather than how quickly they are handled. Further, the geographic focus of community policing increases the need for detailed information based on neighborhoods (or even blocks) as the unit of analysis. The emphasis on problem solving highlights the need for information systems that aid in identifying and analyzing a variety of community-level problems.

Several aspects of police administration under COP that have implications for information include:

- *Performance Appraisals* – individual officers can be evaluated on the quality of the their community policing and problem solving activities, and perhaps on results achieved, instead of on traditional performance indicators (tickets issued, arrests made, calls handled, etc.).
- *Program Evaluation* – police programs and strategies are evaluated more on their effectiveness (outcomes, results, quality) than their efficiency (effort, outputs, quantity).
- *Departmental Assessment* – the police agency's overall performance can be measured and assessed on the basis of a wide variety of indicators (including customer satisfaction, fear levels, problem solving, etc.) instead of a narrow band of traditional indicators (reported crime, response time, number of arrests, etc.).
- *Information Systems* – an agency's information systems need to collect and produce information on the whole range of the police function, not just on enforcement and call-handling activities, in order to support more quality-oriented appraisal, evaluation and assessment efforts.

In summary, Cordner (1996) addressed the "devil in the details" of COP by comprehensively discussing what he viewed as the key dimensional aspects of COP and the subcomponents of each dimension. He also provided specific examples of methods departments could use to implement the key dimensions of COP. Cordner's description provides a sound foundation to understanding what COP is, the changes that must occur to implement it, and the strategies and activities that will bring COP to the community.

Importantly, Cordner (1996, p. 1) also described what COP is *not*. He argued, for example, that COP is *not* a panacea – the answer to all the problems facing any one department. He does, however, suggest that COP is one possible answer to *some* of the problems modern police agencies face and that it may be *an* answer to *some* of the problems facing any one department.

He also argues that COP is *not* completely new; that some departments or individual officers reported they had already been doing it or even that they had *always* practiced COP. While this may be true, there are specific aspects of community policing that *are* new and very few agencies can factually claim they have fully adopted the entire gamut of COP.

Third, Cordner argued that COP is not "hug a thug" – it is not antilaw enforcement or anticrime fighting. COP does not seek to turn police work into social work, but is in fact even more serious about reducing crime and disorder than has been the superficial brand of incident-oriented "9-1-1policing" that most departments have been doing the past few decades.

Finally, Cordner argued that COP is not a "cookbook" that contains an ironclad and precise definition of community policing, nor a set of specific activities that *must* always be included. Rather, COP presents to agencies a set of universally applicable principles and elements, but is flexible enough to realize that their implementation must vary because jurisdictions and police agencies have differing needs and circumstances.

Given this review of the components of COP, the immediate question becomes the extent COP "makes sense" for campus law enforcement agencies, given their history, organizational characteristics, and general mission. We address that question in the next section.

COP: A Contemporary Model for Campus Law Enforcement

One could argue the campus police are better positioned than municipal police to implement COP. Generally, in comparison to major municipal police agencies, campus police agencies have relied to a larger degree on a proactive, crime-prevention approach. Bordner and Peterson (1983), Gelber (1972), and Peak (1995) all have argued that campus police traditionally overemphasized their "service-related" duties compared to their law enforcement duties, and relied more on foot patrol, resulting in greater interaction between them and students, faculty, and staff. These historical forces are certainly favorable to the development of a COP-based model that formalized their importance.

Chief Eric Jackson at the University of North Texas Police Department has presented what he sees as the "key" aspects of traditional law enforcement, community policing, and campus policing (Jackson, 1992). Table 14.1 presents his schematic, showing how the police mandate, police authority, the police role, police/community relations, and political considerations, operate to place campus police in a favorable position to implement COP.

As shown in Table 14.1, Jackson sees major similarities between COP and campus policing, including such keys as the role of the community in crime control, department accountability, and in the authority granted the agency. Indeed, Jackson's point is that because of its context, the issues campus law enforcement faces are far similar to those relating to community policing than to the traditional, reactive-based law enforcement of the 1950s and 1960s and thus make it easier for campus agencies to formally adopt the tenants of COP.

As Bromley (2007) and others (Bordner & Peterson, 1983; Gelber, 1972; Peak, 1995; Sloan, 1992) have reported, campus police agencies have undergone a metamorphosis during the past 50 years, adopting organizational and

Table 14.1
A Comparative Analysis of Police Models

Philosophy	Traditional Law Enforcement	Community Policing	Campus Policing
Police Mandate	Control crime via rapid response deterrence, apprehension	Control crime as means to insure community order, peace, and security	Law enforcement and disciplinary actions as means of control to insure campus order, peace, and security
	Reactive policing	Preventive policing	Preventive & reactive policing
Police Authority	Authority from law	Authority from society & community granted through law	Authority primarily from faculty, staff and students; granted through regulations and law
	Agency of the criminal justice system	Agency of municipal government and community	Agency of the university administration and campus community
Police Role	Legally defined/ limited by law	Socially defined, expanded role	Environmentally defined
	Distinct and separate from citizens	Legal and social agencies	Legal, educational and social agencies
	Law enforcement officers/professional crime fighters	One of a number of agencies of order	Peacekeeping/ educational professionals
	Addresses crime only	Addresses crime and social problems that affect crime	Addresses crime and environmental problems that affect crime
Relationship Between Community & Police	Passive role	Active role	Active role
	Supportive but adjunct to police	Shared responsibility for crime and social order	Shared responsibility for crime and social order
	Community as system of support	Community as client	Community as client
Politics	Apolitical	Political: mediate interests	Political: mediate interests & take advocacy role
	Police and political issues kept separate	Responsible to community and political representatives	Responsible to community and board of trustees
	Fiscal accountability primarily	Policy and operational accountability	Total accountability

Source: Adapted from Jackson (1992) cited in Lanier (1995).

operational characteristics that echo those found in local agencies (see Paoline & Sloan, 2003). The question is, however, to what extent have campus police agencies *actually* adopted COP as their organizational model? What evidence is there that "COP on campus" is in operation?

Evidence of COP on Campus

Several case studies reveal that major universities in the U.S. have adopted COP. For example, the Director of Public Safety at Michigan State University (MSU) strongly endorsed the community policing concept for campus police in the late 1980s and fully implemented COP with all Department of Public Safety (DPS) officers in 1987 (Trojanowicz, Benson, & Trojanowicz, 1988). The plan involved dividing the MSU campus into three large segments and assigning "teams" comprised of command and line officers to specific districts in each segment. The teams actively recruited students and staff to assist with the program. They also set up "mini-stations" in the larger dormitories, conducted surveys and needs-assessments to determine the most pressing problems in each area, and jointly developed strategies and solutions with students and campus employees.

The campus police at the University of Washington at Seattle also implemented community policing in the late 1980s/early 1990s. Unlike Michigan State University, officers at the University of Washington make extensive use of bicycle patrols as part of their community policing strategy. The department reported successes with improved public relations, decreased response time, increased patrols of secluded areas, lowered operating expenses, and a boosting of officer morale while improving officers' physical health (Espinosa & Wittmier, 1991).

Virginia Commonwealth University (VCU) and its nearly 50 sworn officers implemented community policing in the early 1990s (see Carlson, 1991). The plan called for officers to organize Local Management Groups comprised of university members who regularly met to devise ways to increase positive interaction between students and the police, and who developed and distributed a survey to help identify specific problem areas. Second, the department revised patrol officer job descriptions and hiring criterion to reflect COP principles. The department recruited student volunteers to staff a Corps of Preventive Specialists (COPS) and serve on a campus watch program. Training in the principles of COP and officer evaluation based on those principles also became central to the VCU community policing effort. Finally, similar to the MSU model, the department divided the VCU campus into eight sectors with officers assigned to specific areas on a permanent basis. Officers were responsible for "designing, initiating, and maintaining various crime-prevention programs within their assigned sectors" (Carlson, 1991, p. 23).

The University of Alabama at Birmingham (UAB) is another university that implemented a community policing strategy on its campus during the 1990s. As part of the implementation process, the department created multiple "precincts" that are housed in the large, on-campus hospital and in two of the on-campus dormitories. Officers routinely patrol campus on foot and using bicycles. They also organized a "campus watch" program led by a crime prevention specialist and staffed by volunteers drawn from the ranks of students, faculty members, and staff.

The University at Albany, State University of New York's ATLAS (Athletics, Team Building, Leadership, And Mentoring for Student Athletes) program incorporated a university police officer liaison to partner with student athletes and team officials with the aim of addressing behavioral problems among college athletes, in particular football team members (Williams, 2011). The liaison not only worked with athletes and team officials on the home campus, but also traveled with the team to other universities, in serving as a counselor and mentor. This problem-solving initiative defined core problem areas for the team (i.e., assaults, domestic violence, and sexual offenses), and also incorporated assessments of efforts in terms of police incident reports, campus judicial officer referrals, mentoring program evaluations, leadership development evaluations, and overall program evaluations (Williams, 2011, p. 23).

Finally, Bromley (2007) chronicled a near decade-long initiative to implement COP on the campus of the University of South Florida. Bromley included discussion of how the department addressed the philosophical, strategic, tactical, and administrative dimensions of COP and overcame multiple implementation hurdles. While a case study of single department at a single university, it nonetheless offered insightful commentary on the inherent difficulties associated with organizational change.

Beyond anecdotal evidence illustrating that COP is operating on campus police departments across the country, systematic evidence gleaned from the Bureau of Justice Statistics' 2004–2005 Campus LEMAS survey (Reaves, 2008) provides additional insight. Across a national sample of four-year institutions serving populations of 2,500 or more students, the survey revealed that 69 percent of campus police departments had incorporated community policing elements into their policies, and 59 percent had assigned personnel to specific geographic areas on campus (Reaves, 2008). Moreover, in disseminating crime-related information to community "partners" with a vested interest in such issues, Reaves (2008) reported that a substantial number of campus law enforcement agencies regularly met with faculty/staff (84%), students (83%), student housing groups (84%), fraternities and sororities (57%), and other law enforcement agencies (88%).

Thus, both anecdotal and national-level data show that COP has apparently become an organizational model adopted by many campus police departments in this country. More specifically, these agencies report they have adopted both administrative and tactical aspects of COP, and in doing so sought to bridge gaps that may have existed between the agency and the campus community. Campus agencies' large scale adoption of COP likely shows that in the context of campus law enforcement, COP presents an organizational model that readily fits these agencies' core missions and values. However, new developments are occurring that may alter, at least at the tactical level, some of COP's well practiced activities.

COMPSTAT: A New Model for Campus Agencies?

Given that campus police agencies tend to mimic the organizational structures of their municipal counterparts (see Bromley, 2003; Paoline & Sloan, 2003), contemporary innovations, and corresponding new policing models developed by local agencies could certainly be expected to take shape on college campuses – just as COP did. One innovation in particular, COMPSTAT (comparative statistics) is currently being embraced by many municipal police departments across America, and in some instances, may be supplementing COP. In fact, in the only national study of COMPSTAT implementation, Weisburd et al. (2003) found that one-third of local police departments with 100 or more sworn personnel endorsed COMPSTAT (or a program similar in design), with an additional one-fourth of the agencies planning to do so.

The COMPSTAT model, in many ways, incorporates features from both the professional model and COP. As Dabney (2003, p. 36) explains:

> . . . the Compstat model is defined by three fundamental facets: (1) realigning police operations according to four core management principles (gathering accurate and timely intelligence, designing effective strategies and tactics, the rapid deployment of personnel and resources, and relentless follow-up and assessment), (2) decentralizing command decision-making and resource allocation to geographic districts, and (3) the identification and internalization of clearly stated departmental objectives.

At the core of the data-driven COMPSTAT model is the utilization of crime analysis and crime mapping (Eterno & Silverman, 2010). Interestingly, according to Reaves (2008), over one-half (51%) of campus law enforcement agencies surveyed had upgraded their technology to support analysis of campus community problems, and over one quarter (28%) of the agencies utilized computers for crime mapping. As such, many campus police departments (circa 2004–2005) apparently are in the early stages of reorganizing themselves to incorporate COMSTAT approaches to address crime on campus.

Unlike the transition from the professional model to COP, adoption of COMPSTAT does not necessarily have to come at the expense of COP, as arguments (e.g., Willis, 2011) have been made that both can co-exist and actually serve to promote greater legitimacy in the eyes of the public. One primary difference between COP and COMPSTAT, however, is that COMPSTAT targets specific types of crime. According to Willis (2011), COMPSTAT tends to focus on the reduction of serious crime, while COP aims to address broader, quality of life issues. While campus police aim to address quality of life issues under the COP model, recent serious criminal events (e.g., mass shootings, sexual assaults) actually provide an arena for campus agencies to adopt COMSTAT (Schafer et al., 2010). Should the landscape of college campuses continue to change with respect to increases in serious crime, we might see a COMSTAT approach supersede the COP model.

Conclusion

Although no longer new, and despite its critics, community-oriented policing (COP) remains part of many American police organizations (Reaves, 2010). Concurrently, campus police agencies have seemingly embraced COP as their primary operating philosophy and organizational model. That this is the case should be of little surprise, since campus police are in an excellent position to successfully implement community policing. For one, in comparison to their municipal agency counterparts, campus police are more reliant upon proactive, preventive measures. Campus police are also, in general terms, in a position to have greater interaction with their "clients" compared to major municipal departments. Finally, their proximity to an environment of higher education affords them not only greater flexibility and room for innovation (such as using volunteer and paid students – see Brug, 1984), but also allows them to be exposed to the most current philosophical and pragmatic police practices.

While some municipal police departments might be transitioning "out" of COP with the introduction of recent COMPSTAT approaches, the cohesive "community" nature of the college campus might still tend to favor the former model over the latter. At the same time, changing dynamics with respect to potentially serious criminal events might warrant mimicking by campus police once again. As such, COMPSTAT approaches could easily be utilized by campus police, but not necessarily at the cost of COP. Willis's (2010) argument regarding the integration of community policing (which focuses on sharing crime information externally with citizens) and COMPSTAT (which focuses on sharing information about crime internally) into a single operating philosophy to enhance police legitimacy seems like a perfect fit for the campus environment. For now, such changes are merely speculative, but something to surely monitor.

REFERENCES

Bayley, D. (1988). Community policing: A report from the devil's advocate. In J. Greene & S. Mastrofski (Eds.), *Community policing: Rhetoric or reality* (pp. 225–237). New York: Praeger.

Bromley, M. (2003). Comparing campus and municipal police community policing practices. *Journal of Security Administration, 26,* 37–50.

Bromley, M. (2007). The evolution of campus policing: Different models for different eras. In B. S. Fisher & J. J. Sloan (Eds.), *Campus crime: Legal, social, and policy perspectives* (2nd ed.) (pp. 280–303). Springfield, IL: Charles C Thomas.

Brown, L., & Wycoff, M. (1987). Policing Houston: Reducing fear and improving service. *Crime and Delinquency, 33,* 71–89.

Bordner, D., & Peterson, D. (1983). *Campus policing: The nature of university police work.* Lanham, MD: University Press of America.

Brug, R. C. (1984). Cal Poly maximizes use of students. *Campus Law Enforcement Journal, 14,* 45–46.

Carlson, W. (1991). Community policing at Virginia Commonwealth University: Designing strategies for a campus environment. *Campus Law Enforcement Journal, 21,* 22–25.

Cochran, J., Bromley, M., & Swando, M. (2002). Sheriff's deputies' receptivity to organizational change. *Policing: An International Journal of Police Strategies and Management, 25,* 507–529.

Cordner, G. (1996). *Principles and elements of community policing.* Washington, DC: National Institute of Justice.

Cordner, G. (1997). Community policing: Elements and effects. In R. Dunham & G. Alpert (Eds.), *Critical issues in policing: Contemporary readings* (pp. 401–418). Prospect Heights, IL: Waveland Press.

Dabney, D. (2010). Observations regarding key operational realities in a Compstat model of policing. *Justice Quarterly, 27,* 28–51.

Eck, J., & Spelman, W. (1987). Who ya' gonna call: Police as problem busters. *Crime & Delinquency, 33,* 31–52.

Eck, J., & Rosenbaum, D. (1994). Effectiveness, equity, and efficiency in community policing. In D. Rosenbaum (Ed.), *The challenge of community policing: Testing the promises* (pp. 3–26). Thousand Oaks, CA: Sage.

Eterno, J., & Silverman, E. (2010). The NYPD's COMPSTAT: Compare statistics or compose statistics. *International Journal of Police Science & Management, 12,* 426–449.

Espinosa, G., & R. Wittmier. (1991). Police bicycle patrols: An integral part of community policing. *Campus Law Enforcement Journal, 21,* 10–13.

Fogelson, R. (1977). *Big city police.* Cambridge, MA: Harvard University Press.

Gelber, S. (1972). *The role of campus security in the college setting.* Washington, DC: United States Government Printing Office.

Goldstein, H. (1979). Improving policing: A problem-oriented approach. *Crime and Delinquency, 25,* 236–258.

Greene, J., & Mastrofski, S. (1988). *Community policing: Rhetoric or reality.* New York: Praeger.

Herbert, S. (2006). *Citizens, Cops, and Power: Recognizing the Limits of Community.* Chicago: The University of Chicago Press.

Jackson, E. (1992). Campus police embrace community-based approach. *The Police Chief, 59,* 63–64.

Lanier, M. (1995). Community oriented policing on college campuses: Tradition, practices, and outlook. In B. S. Fisher & J. J. Sloan (Eds.), *Campus crime: Legal, social, and policy perspectives* (pp. 246–263). Springfield, IL: Charles C Thomas.

Maguire, E. (1997). Structural change in large municipal police organizations during the community policing era. *Justice Quarterly, 14,* 547–576.

Maguire, E. (2002). *Organizational structure in large police organizations: Context, complexity, and control.* Albany, NY: SUNY Press.

Maguire, E., & Mastrofski, S. (2000). Patterns of community policing in the United States. *Police Quarterly, 3,* 4–45.

Manning, P. (1984). Community policing. *American Journal of Police, 3,* 205–227.

Manning, P. (1988). Community policing as a drama of control. In J. Greene & S. Mastrofski (Eds.), *Community policing: Rhetoric or reality* (pp. 27–46). New York: Praeger.

Manning, P. (1989). Community policing. In R. Dunham & G. Alpert (Eds.), *Critical issues in policing* (pp. 419–445). Prospect Heights, IL: Waveland Press.

Monkkonen, E. (1981). *Police in urban America.* New York: Oxford University Press.

Paoline, E. III, & Sloan, J. III (2003). Variability in the organizational structure of contemporary campus law enforcement agencies: A national level analysis. *Policing: An International Journal of Police Strategies and Management, 26,* 612–639.

Peak, K. (1995). The professionalization of campus law enforcement: Comparing campus and municipal law enforcement agencies. In B. S. Fisher & J. J. Sloan (Eds.), *Campus crime: Legal, social, and policy perspectives* (pp. 228–245). Springfield, IL: Charles C Thomas.

Reaves, B. (2008). *Campus law enforcement, 2004–05.* Washington, DC: Office of Justice Programs, U.S. Department of Justice.

Reaves, B. (2010). *Local police departments, 2007.* Washington, DC: Office of Justice Programs, U.S. Department of Justice.

Reiss, A. (1992). Police organization in the 20th century. In M. Tonry & N. Morris (Eds.), *Modern policing* (pp. 51–97). Chicago: University of Chicago Press.

Rosenbaum, D. (1994). *Community policing: Testing the promises.* Thousand Oaks, CA: Sage.

Schafer, J., Heiple, E., Giblin, M., & Burruss, G. (2010). Critical incident preparedness and response on post-secondary campuses. *Journal of Criminal Justice, 38,* 311–317.

Skogan, W. (1990). *Disorder and decline: Crime and the spiral of decay in American cities.* New York: The Free Press.

Skogan, W., & Hartnett, S. (1997). *Community policing: Chicago style.* New York: Oxford University Press.

Sloan, J. (1992). The modern campus police: An analysis of their evolution, structure, and function. *American Journal of Police, 11,* 85–104.

Trojanowicz, R. (1982). *An evaluation of the neighborhood foot patrol program in Flint, Michigan.* East Lansing: Michigan State University, National Center for Community Policing.

Trojanowicz, R., Benson, B., & Trojanowicz, S. (1988). *Community policing: University input into campus police policy-making.* East Lansing, MI: National Neighborhood Foot Patrol Center.

Weisburd, D., Mastrofski, S., McNally, A., Greenspan, R., & Willis, J. (2003). Reforming to preserve: COMPSTAT and strategic problem solving in American policing. *Criminology & Public Policy, 2,* 421–456.

Williams, R. (2011). ATLAS: A community policing response to adverse student athlete behaviors. *Campus Law Enforcement Journal, 41,* 21–27.

Willis, J. (2011). Enhancing police legitimacy by integrating Compstat and community policing. *Policing: An International Journal of Police Strategies and Management, 34,* 654–673.

Wilson, J., & Kelling, G. (1982). Broken windows: The police and neighborhood safety. *Atlantic Monthly, 243,* 29–38.

Zhao, S., Thurman, Q., & Lovrich, N. (1997). Community policing in the U.S.: Where are we now? *Crime and Delinquency, 43,* 345–357.

Zhao, S., Lovrich, N., & Thurman, Q. (1999). The status of community policing in American cities. *Policing: An International Journal of Police Strategies and Management, 22,* 74–92.

Chapter 15

POLICING ALCOHOL-RELATED CRIME AMONG COLLEGE STUDENTS

Andrea Allen and Scott Jacques

*The one thing about alcohol that's universal with all
age groups is that bad decisions come along with it, with
intoxication. Everything that we respond to around here,
there's alcohol or some form of intoxication that's a part of it.*

– Officer RC, University of Cincinnati PD

INTRODUCTION

Alcohol is connected to illegal behavior in two broad ways. One is through *alcohol crime,* which refers to prohibited acts of alcohol consumption, possession, distribution (e.g., buying, selling, or giving), and manufacturing (e.g., brewing one's own supply). Examples of alcohol crime include underage drinking, operating a motor vehicle while intoxicated (i.e., DUI), or using a fake ID to purchase alcohol. Alcohol crime is distinct from *alcohol-related crime,* which is the focus of this chapter. Although there are three types of alcohol-related crime, the most common of them all is the *psychopharmacological* relationship (Goldstein, Brownstein, Ryan, & Bellucci, 1997). This is when an intoxicated person commits an offense or is victimized (Goldstein, 1985). For example, an intoxicated person at a bar may try to leave without paying the tab, get in a fight, steal a glass, sexually harass someone, write on the bathroom stall, or urinate on the wall.

Drinking and related offenses are a prominent feature of college life on and off campus. National estimates suggest 65 percent of full-time college students consumed alcohol in the last 30 days (e.g., Johnston, O'Malley, Bachman, &

343

Schulenberg, 2011; American College Health Association, 2012). Research shows that students who frequently consume alcohol are more likely to offend and be victimized than less frequent drinkers or abstainers (Siegel & Harriss, 1992). This relationship applies to a number of crime types, including assault, rape, sexual assault, vandalism, public disorder, and indecency offenses like public urination and public nudity (Fisher, Sloan, Cullen, & Lu, 1998; Mustaine & Tewksbury, 1998; NIAAA, 2002; Wechsler, 2001; Wechsler, Davenport, Dowdall, Moeykens, & Castillo, 1994). The American College Health Association's *National College Health Assessment* (ACHA-NCHA) survey of 27,774 students at 44 postsecondary institutions (ACHA, 2012) reported that within the last year, two of every one hundred college students physically injured another person or had sex without consent with another person due to drinking. Other studies (e.g., CASA, 1994) find that that approximately 95 percent of all violent offenses committed on campuses involve alcohol.[1]

Students' alcohol-related offending and victimization place a heavy burden on campus law enforcement officials. According to the ACHA-NCHA, 2 percent of college students had contacts with police for reasons related to intoxication (ACHA, 2012). The U.S. Department of Education's *Campus Safety and Security Data* (USDOE, 2010)[2] is a comprehensive source of information on annual rates of on-campus arrests and disciplinary actions of persons attending colleges and universities. In 2010, according to the data, there were 30,839 arrests and 178,747 disciplinary actions for liquor law violations on campuses.[3] Arrests for other offenses included 2,664 sex offenses, 1,051 robberies, 1,782 assaults, 18,598 burglaries, and 688 arsons. It is likely that many of these "other crimes" also involved alcohol because it has been implicated in 95 percent of all campus crimes (Sloan, 1994).

Despite the availability of basic statistics on arrests for alcohol crime and related offenses, we know very little about how campus police officers view these problems or how best to police them. To explore those issues we draw on excerpts from the television show *Campus PD* to illustrate police officers' "common sense" (Geertz, 1983) beliefs about college students' drinking and its relation to offending and victimization. As described more fully below, these beliefs are natural, simple, accessible, and important because they guide officers' actions (Geertz, 1983). We conclude the chapter by discussing how police have traditionally addressed alcohol-related crime among college students and suggest alternatives to that model.

Analyzing *Campus PD*

To shed light on policing alcohol-related crime among college students, we make use of – what is to our knowledge – the only publicly available data source for the subject: scenes from the television series *Campus PD* aired by the cable television channel G4. This show is similar to the classic series *Cops* where a camera crew follows patrolling officers to get their thoughts on crime and justice, and video record them responding to calls for service. In *Campus PD,* the focus is on officers' interactions with American college students, both victims and offenders.

At the time of this writing, the complete first three seasons of *Campus PD* were available for purchase on iTunes. We do not know exactly when each season was recorded, but some sense of this is gained from knowing the episodes were aired in 2009, 2010, and 2011, respectively. These three seasons include a total of 36 episodes. Six of the episodes focus only on spring break venues, so we excluded them from our analysis. This left 30 episodes and a total of 113 scenes for us to analyze. For each scene, we coded the university where the crime occurred; whether the officers' involvement was proactive or reactive; whether municipal and/or university police were involved; reason for initial contact with the student(s); if alcohol was present; the alcohol-related crimes investigated; and the sanction for each crime (e.g., verbal or written warning, sanction, or arrest). Noteworthy is that of the 113 scenes, 71 (63%) of them involved some form of alcohol-related crime.[4] The beginning of each scene would usually show an officer saying what he or she thinks about crime and/or students; when relevant to alcohol-related crime we transcribed these words verbatim.[5] Our findings are based on these qualitative accounts as well as descriptions of the scenes.

Before presenting our findings, we should point out that in some respects a limitation of using *Campus PD* scenes as data is they overwhelmingly involve municipal police; only 10 percent of the incidents involve campus police. It is also unclear what percent of the scenes occur on or off campus. With that said, one should not infer that municipal police involvement with college students or student involvement in off campus crimes are without consequence for university life. Whether students realize it or not, by enrolling in institutions of higher learning, they agree to a student code of conduct which often includes a clause stating that criminal offenses can be punished by the school. For example, the University of South Carolina has a policy allowing it to take disciplinary action against students involved in offense committed on *or* off campus (Student Affairs Policy, 2010). Such a situation is illustrated in several *Campus PD* scenes. In one scene from the second season of *Campus PD,* Chico State University students who held an unruly party off campus were called into a school conduct hearing and punished accordingly (1-4-2).[6] In a second season scene, University of Cincinnati students faced academic probation for their first offense and academic suspension (with forfeiture of tuition payments) if a second offense occurred (2-14-1). Offenses that are more serious may result in immediate expulsion. Thus, the actions of both municipal and campus police officers, who are on and off campus, affect the lives of students.

Findings from *Campus PD*

When police respond to calls for service involving possible crimes their actions are guided by law, of course, but also by their personal beliefs (Klinger, 1997). As described in the excerpts below, alcohol-related crime among students is a common concern for officers. They believe students inevitably get drunk, mainly because they lack maturity, and their intoxication makes them frequent targets for, and perpetrators of, crime. After presenting officers' beliefs in their own words and describing a few scenes of alcohol-related crime, we discuss their implications for the study of "common sense beliefs" as first described by Geertz (1983).

Cops, College Students, and Alcohol

Police officers strongly associate drinking with college life. They perceive this relationship to be "natural." When described, officers' beliefs have an air of "of-courseness" (Geertz, 1983). In one scene from the first season of *Campus PD,* an officer from the Cincinnati Police Department said: "Up here because it's the college life, the parties, the frat parties, the sorority parties, there's a lot more . . . drinking" (1-10-3; Officer OB, Cincinnati PD). Another officer from the Montclair (NJ) Police Department explained: "Obviously, with the college in town and a few colleges outside of [town], we have a problem with the excessive amount of drinking" (3-1-2; Lieutenant JL, Montclair PD).

The police believe "[t]he majority of kids that go to school get caught in a routine of excess drinking" (3-6-4; Officer HL, Pullman PD). They suggest excessive drinking is common among students because they lack maturity: "A lot of these students are new to living on their own, and they're enjoying the freedom, and unfortunately they don't have the maturity to deal with the alcohol" (2-16-4; Patrolman SJ, Conway PD). While university students are physically adults, police officers tend to think of them as children: "Let's face it – most of the students here are away from home for the first time, so even though they're adults, maturity wise they're nothing more than big kids" (3-7-4; Lieutenant MF, Cincinnati PD).

Some officers believe college student immaturity is a new phenomenon that is generational: "When you look at some of the students, some of the situations they get themselves in, sometimes I shake my head and it's like I'll say, 'Wow, this is a new generation'" (1-5-2; Officer TV, Cincinnati PD). One theory of the current generation's behavior held by some police officers is that this age cohort has been overly cared for and protected by their parents. They have thus failed to learn some important life lessons, especially about accountability: "It's a generational thing. These kids right now they're 18, 19, 20,

21, 22 years old. That age group, in my opinion, and it's just my opinion, is that they feel like they can do what[ever] they want and get away with what they want because they've been coddled their whole life or whatever the case is" (1-2-1; Officer TF, Chico PD).

Cops, College Students, and Alcohol-Related Crime

One reason that officers are concerned with students' alcohol consumption is because they perceive involvement with alcohol increases the chance for victimization: "The students get out here and they get so drunk and it can hurt them. I mean they can . . . become a victim or . . . they can get alcohol poisoning . . ." (2-14-1). Police officers understand that students may dislike them for "ruining a good time," but the officers' goal is to deter bigger problems than that: "We're not against the students having parties and having fun . . . We're here to ensure . . . they're not victims" (1-1-1; Officer MB, Cincinnati PD). Intoxication not only enhances the risk of victimization, but also makes it more difficult to solve cases and punish offenders: "Every Friday and Saturday night you get some kind of assault where someone gets hurt and they're too drunk to even tell you what happens" (2-3-3; Officer BK, Cincinnati PD).

Police officers also express the belief that students' drinking increases the likelihood of their breaking the law. Simply put, "[a] lot of people do stupid things while under the influence of alcohol" (3-10-3; Officer HL, Pullman PD). In one scene of *Campus PD,* for example, a severely inebriated student was caught breaking and entering into a residential building that he mistakenly believed to be the home of a friend. When police found him, he was sitting on the foyer floor with blood all over his face and hands, apparently the consequence of breaking door glass. He then proceeded to vomit and was then handcuffed (3-3-3).

Alcohol crime and alcohol-related offenses involving college students are a "big deal" for officers: "I'd say probably one of the biggest problems we have surrounds alcohol consumption because almost all of the calls we go to involves someone that's been drinking" (3-8-2; Officer DH, Pullman PD). Officers' explanation of this high frequency of offending is that "students get too intoxicated and it affects their judgment. They think they can do things that they really can't" (2-15-4; Officer BE, Cincinnati PD). Officers also seem to perceive that the relationship between drinking, poor judgment, and law-breaking applies to many different types of crime, including violence, destruction, theft, and disorderly conduct.

ALCOHOL-RELATED VIOLENCE. Alcohol intoxication is a known facilitator of violence, defined as the use or threatened use of physical force against another person (Boles & Miotto, 2003; Parker & Auerhahn, 1998). As one Montclair Police Department officer succinctly summed it up: "Some people when they're under the influence of alcohol they act violent. . . . It's really no different with the college kids [from other adults]" (3-2-2; Lieutenant JL, Montclair PD). Given the popularity of drinking among college students, it is perhaps not surprising that police officers regularly respond to fights involving students: "Just because we're dealing with college students doesn't mean that they can't be dangerous, and can't be a danger to us and others" (3-6-4; Officer HL, Pullman PD). Violence is especially likely to occur on weekend nights in high population density areas: "This is . . . the city and at 1:30 at night you just now have the mix of intoxicated adults and intoxicated kids, and you can pretty much bank on a fight breaking out here very, very shortly" (1-3-3; Officer RC, University of Cincinnati PD).

ALCOHOL-RELATED DESTRUCTION OF PROPERTY. Crimes involving the destruction of property or damage to it, such as vandalism, commonly involve college students. For example, in a scene from the first season of *Campus PD,* an alcohol-related case of vandalism at a pizza restaurant involving a college student was handled by police one night. The rear of the restaurant had an outdoor patio with a wooden roof. In the scene, the owner found a group of college students drinking on top of the roof. Worse, they were jumping up and down causing the roof to bow. The owner was shown flagging down an officer on routine patrol and explaining the problem to her. The officer then spoke with the offender who was wearing a shirt with the phrase "Jesus Loves This Guy" written on it. The owner of the establishment seemingly felt different and had the suspect arrested for criminal damaging of property (1-10-2).

ALCOHOL-RELATED THEFT. Theft is the illegal taking of the property of another, and is a very commonly occurring crime both on and off campus. Intoxicated students seem especially inclined to commit this kind of offense. In one scene from the 3rd season of *Campus PD,* a Marquette (MI) police officer told the audience that:

> [on] [t]he midnight shift everything is alcohol-related for the most part. You rarely talk to somebody that's not intoxicated. Drunk college kids walking back from the bars or from parties, if something's not bolted down or tied down, it winds up getting damaged or stolen. (3-6-3; Patrolman GK, Marquette PD)

In one case documented on *Campus PD,* an officer on routine patrol is driving along and sees an intoxicated young woman walking across the street wearing an orange construction cone as a hat. The officer asks her where she is going with it and she nonchalantly replies "just walking to my house." He tells her to put it back and she says, "It's a cone – are you kidding me right now?" After arguing with the cop, she eventually does what he asked (3-6-3).

ALCOHOL-RELATED DISORDERLY CONDUCT. Disorderly conduct includes public disturbances of all sorts. In one scene from the second season of *Cam-*

pus PD, an officer is shown on routine patrol riding down "Main Street" and is clearly amazed at what he sees occurring. He is heard asking rhetorically, "Is this guy actually [urinating] on the sidewalk here?" The officer then stops the perpetrator who clearly understood why he had been stopped: "Because I was [urinating] on Main Street. Not something you should do." He was then arrested and transported to jail (1-8-2).

House parties involving students are the most frequent scene of alcohol-related crime depicted in *Campus PD.* In part, this is because these events bring together alcohol, a large group of people (many of whom are underage), and a lack of mature guardianship. This convergence of factors is a perfect storm for drunken and disorderly behavior, especially loud noise: "One of the biggest problems we have . . . with the university is we get some pretty big parties. Obviously you get that many people together, they've been drinking, it's gonna be loud, it's gonna be a little rambunctious, and it doesn't take long for us to get called" (3-2-1; Corporal JF, Marquette PD). Since neighbors typically desire their neighborhoods to be peaceful and quiet, they quickly call police when house parties become disorderly: "With college kids we deal with a lot of loud parties and intoxication. If it's a huge party with 50 people, it's just obnoxious, then we'll break it up right there even if it's the first time we've been there" (3-8-4; Officer PB, Las Cruces PD).

ALCOHOL-RELATED MIXING OF CRIMES. One possible unintended consequence of disrupting loud or disorderly house parties is that other crimes may arise as students become angry over having their party broken up. Officers appear to believe that breaking up loud parties can lead to crimes of destruction or violence, as explained by a San Marcos (CA) officer:

> There been times during in the past where a party's been broken up and police vehicles have been damaged or beer bottles been thrown at them, or people urinating on the cars, so on those calls – the party calls – it's department policy to dispatch two officers to almost every call just for safety. (1-4-1; Officer RH, San Marcos PD)

At the extreme, student parties may turn into violent riots when police intervene (see Madensen & Eck, 2006). One such instance was described in detail by an officer with the City of Chico (CA):

> Toward the end of the night when people have been to a party or two that's been shut down, they sometimes tend to become a little more resistant, a little more intoxicated, and willing to express their opinion a little bit more . . . . There's nights I'd be more than happy to not go to any more parties. I've done it throughout my career at Chico. You always got to be on your toes, always got to be paying attention to what's going on, looking out for bottles and people that take a shot at you . . . We've had riots in town before. Always seems to be they revolve around a couch fire. The last time we had a riot it was a party that had 300 or 400 college kids in it and as the party was

letting out they kind of took over the street, and an officer drove by, they started throwing items at the police car, started chanting, next thing you know somebody dragged a couch into the middle of the street and lights it on fire and now it causes a riot. And unfortunately we had to go in and get that to disperse. (1-7-1, 1-9-2, 1-9-4; Officer JD, Chico PD)

Common Sense Policing

The above stories of alcohol-related crime are just a few examples of those aired on *Campus PD*. As seen on the show, alcohol intoxication is often involved in other crimes, such as fraud, trespassing, jaywalking, driving violations, obstruction of justice, interfering with police business, and resisting arrest. The above excerpts reveal some police officers' beliefs about students' drinking, offending, and victimization. Municipal and campus police officers generally seem to believe students drink excessively because they lack responsibility and – once they are drunk – fall prey to offenders and commit all sorts of offenses themselves.

According to Geertz (1983), such beliefs are "common sense." In normal life (i.e., outside academia), common sense is "life in a nutshell" or a "matter-of-fact apprehension of reality" (Geertz, 1983, p. 75). From a scholarly perspective, common sense is much more than that. "It is, in short, a cultural system" a set of specific beliefs about the world and its workings (Geertz, 1983, p. 76). Members of groups all have a "common sense" understanding of the world, but what is common sense *differs* from one group to the next. To illustrate: while police may believe college students get drunk because they are immature, college students may get drunk because they believe doing so is fun. Thus members of the two groups hold much different "common sense" views of the same phenomenon.

Although what constitutes common sense on the part of group members varies, the *characteristics* of common sense beliefs do not. According Geertz (1983), these cultural systems share certain traits. First, a belief is considered *natural* if people think it is "of course" true. Second, a belief is seen as *practical* when it guides action. Third, a belief is *thin* if it is simple. Finally, a belief is *accessible* if anyone can learn it. Police officers' "common sense" beliefs about alcohol-related crime among students embody these four traits. They believe it is "natural" for college students to get drunk and, in turn, be victimized or offend because they are immature. This belief set is simple (i.e., thin), easy to learn (i.e., accessible), and practical in the sense it guides officers' actions. For example, officers believe it acceptable to stop, investigate, detain, or disperse intoxicated students – even when they are not breaking the law – because their intoxication increases the chance of a crime occurring. Right or wrong, intoxicated students may be brought "to the police department because they're *probably* going to make poor choices" (3-10-3; Officer HL, Pullman PD, emphasis added). Officers' common sense tells them that by paying attention to one group of individuals – namely drunk students – they can deter, detect, and (in some instances) punish a multitude of offenses.

Methods of Policing Alcohol-Related Crime by Students

What police officers fail to talk about on *Campus PD* is the way they attempt to control alcohol-related crime: by either engaging in routine patrol until they encounter an incident by chance or being dispatched to a particular location. These actions characterize traditional, reactive-based tactics in which police officers engage. Routine patrol is also the dominant police tactic, at least in the United States. Although not discussed by officers, it is clear to anyone who watches *Campus PD* that routine motorized patrol is the primary tactic police use to manage alcohol-related crime among students with a few exceptions. However, as critics have shown, reactive patrol is generally considered the least effective way to reduce crime (e.g., Weisburd & Eck, 2004).

Three potentially more effective tools campus police have available include community-oriented policing (COP), problem-oriented policing (POP), and hot spots policing (HSP) (see Weisburd & Eck, 2004). Although distinct, these models share certain characteristics. Below, we suggest how campus and municipal police could employ these methods on and around university grounds to reduce alcohol and alcohol-related crimes among students.

Community-Oriented Policing (COP)

COP is an organizational model for police departments that promotes the use of community partnerships and problem-solving techniques to proactively address and reduce conditions that facilitate crime, social disorder, and fear of victimization (COPS, 2012). There are three interlinked components of this model. One is fostering community partnerships between the police, other government agencies, and nongovernmental institutions and organizations (e.g., private businesses, the media). Another is corporate transformation, which involves restructuring the agency in a way conducive to the development of community partnerships and the implementation of proactive problem solving.[7] The third is problem solving via proactive and systematic identification of crime problems through the process known as the SARA model – scan, analyze, respond, assess. The tactics used by COP include knock and talks, foot patrol, establishment of local "cop shops," hotlines, neighborhood revitalization, block watch groups, and the use of treatment and prevention programs (Mazerolle, Soole, & Rombouts, 2006, 2007).

To address alcohol and related crimes, police can adopt several strategies. Using a COP-based approach, it is essential that the police not rely solely on arrest as the primary means to address lawbreaking; community involvement and partnerships are a must. First, officers could work with campus organizations to inform them of the dangers of drinking, including the fact alcohol use increases not only the risk for criminal victimization but also the chance of breaking various laws. Forming liaisons with Greek organizations is especially important since fraternity and sorority members are known to frequently binge drink (Wechsler, 1996, 2001), which increases the chance of offending and victimization (NIAAA, 2002). Second, officers can increase foot patrols at times and at places where large numbers of intoxicated students are routinely present (e.g., Friday and Saturday evenings around dormitories) to deter both alcohol and alcohol-related crime. Finally, police could encourage residence hall advisors (RAs) to take steps to deter drinking in dorms through preventative and reactionary steps. The rationale for this measure is that by reducing alcohol consumption, reductions in alcohol-related crime will naturally follow.

Problem-Oriented Policing (POP)

POP is similar to COP but more focused and practical in application. It directs officers to identify specific problems, through the SARA model (Scan/Analyze/Respond/Assess), and develop tailor-made strategies for response (Weisburd & Eck, 2004). This approach, like COP, insists that officers utilize external sources (e.g., government agencies, community services) to help address crime problems, but reduces creating partnerships with community members as crucial. Components of POP include concentrating on high-call locations, collaborating with government and other private agencies as well as community service providers, using mediation rather than solely arrest, reducing opportunities for crime, and using civil and criminal law to control public nuisances. The importance of POP is that it emphasizes the use of external partnerships in tandem with law enforcement tactics like high visibility policing to disrupt offending by making it riskier or – in the case of displacement – inconvenient and less beneficial (Harocopos & Hough, 2005). Recent developments of POP have begun to use a "pulling levers" strategy, which relies on partnerships with external agencies and the use of data-driven approaches that target specific hot spots locations and repeat offenders who are made aware that their offending will come to an end by their own choice or, if not, through incapacitation (see Corsaro, Brunson, & McGarrell, 2010; Corsaro, Brunson, & McGarrell, forthcoming; Frabutt, Gathings, Hunt, & Loggins, 2006; Kennedy, 1997; Kennedy & Wong, 2009).

Using a POP approach, police would first work to identify areas where al-cohol and alcohol-related crimes occur most often. Next, they would devise a plan of action that addresses how the unique features of these areas facilitate offending and victimization. They could, for example, engage in high visibil-ity policing to reduce opportunities for would-be offenders. Or, the police could employ a "pulling levers" approach where officers would aggressively tackle repeat alcohol and alcohol-related offenders, but rather than cite or ar-rest them, officers would refer these students to student disciplinary proceed-ings. Under this strategy, offenders are targeted using noncriminal sanctions involving a combination of benefits and punishments to shape behavior. The benefits could take a number of forms, such as suspension of sanctions if the student enrolled in an alcohol diversion program or that refocused the stu-dent's time toward school and away from substance use. To deter recidivism, it could be made clear to students that repeat offending would result in seri-ous sanctions including loss of tuition assistance, academic suspension, or even expulsion.

Hot Spots Policing (HSP)

A final strategy available to campus officers is HSP. This model relies on identifying specific micro-locations at which there are exceedingly high levels of crime and, in turn, focusing police resources there. Hot spots may be a "sin-gle address, a cluster of addresses close to one another, a segment of a street block, an entire street block, or two, or an intersection" where a dispropor-tionate amount of crime is occurring (Taylor, 1998, p. 3). Tactics are geo-graphically focused and vary in duration, intensity, and types. Examples in-clude crackdowns – a dramatic increase in police presence at a specific pub-lic locale; raids of private property; street sweeps in which a stretch of space is cleared through searches of suspicious persons; and buy-busts or reverse stings in which undercover officers engage in trade with drug traders for the purpose of collecting evidence (see Jacobson, 1999; Mazerolle et al., 2007; Worden, Bynum, & Frank, 1994).

Police could first identify hot spots of alcohol and alcohol-related crime lo-cations on campus. For instance, a study by Robinson and Roh (2007) found that dorms are hot spots for both types of crimes. Once hot spots are identi-fied, officers could then conduct crackdowns at these places, such as through vehicular checkpoints leading into and out of the area. Another strategy could involve the campus police forming an alcohol enforcement unit where offi-cers in plainclothes patrol bars and taverns operating near campus to identi-fy underage drinkers and detect alcohol-related problems (Schafer, 2005).

Conclusion

This chapter demonstrated that police handle a variety of alcohol-related crimes in which college students are involved as offenders and victims. What is apparent is that police officers view alcohol and alcohol-related crimes in a commonsensical way: it is "natural" that college students drink; therefore, they become involved in crime as victims and offenders and should be policed accordingly – even when they are yet to commit an offense. As shown in *Campus PD,* routine patrol is the traditional tactic police use to respond to student involvement with alcohol and alcohol-related crime, but it is perhaps the least effective strategy among those available (see Weisburd & Eck, 2004).

Despite the high frequency of drinking and alcohol-related crimes among students, research has yet to tell us what are in fact, the best, "good enough," and worst tactics the police can use to address these problems *in the college campus context.* Relatedly, we do not know whether campus and municipal police handle such incidents differently and, if so, how, why, and to what effect. Addressing these gaps in our knowledge has obvious practical implications for reducing the negative consequences of students' drinking. At this point, however, there are more questions than answers. As more research is conducted to determine which tactics are most effective at reducing alcohol-related crime among college students, best practices may finally emerge and the problem be significantly reduced.

NOTES

1. College students are not the only people whose intoxication is known to affect crime. Generally, in locations where excessive drinking occurs, there is usually greater potential for crime. Research consistently demonstrates that ". . . when violent behavior is associated with a substance, that substance is, overwhelmingly, alcohol" (Parker & Auerhahn, 1998, p. 306). A study of homicides in New York City, for instance, found alcohol was involved in more murders than any other drug (Goldstein et al., 1997). A study in the United Kingdom found that only heroin and crack cocaine had a larger relationship to crime than did alcohol (Nutt, King, & Phillips, 2010). Time and again, research consistently finds that alcohol has a strong effect on levels of both offending and victimization (see e.g., Boles & Miotto, 2003; Brecklin & Ullman, 2010; Felson & Burchfield, 2004; Lasley, 1989; Felson, Savolainen, Aaltonen, & Moustgaard, 2008; Felson, Teasdale, & Burchfield, 2008; Graham, Bernards, Wilsnack, & Gmel, 2011; Mustaine & Tewksbury, 1998; Parker & Auerhahn, 1998).

2. Of course, these arrest statistics do not include crimes not reported to police (the "dark figure of crime") and thus the actual frequency of the offenses could be considerably larger.

3. Results are based on 3,905 colleges and universities within the 50 states and the District of Columbia with enrollment over 500 and student residential facilities. Institutions included only public or private nonprofit and for profit, four-year schools.

4. These scenes involve areas around 11 universities that, in the show at least, were handled by 12 police departments – the extra department being accounted for by the one and only university PD involved in the series. If not self-evident, we must point out these cases or departments are unlikely to be a random sample. We do not know how or why some universities were chosen for taping and agreed but not others, nor do we know why some scenes appeared on air but others did not. Thus, the findings from this study may or may not be generalizable to other times and places but the extent to which they are is unknown.

5. Some of the transcriptions we present are not actually direct quotes. For example, we did not include pauses or "you know."

6. The notation that follows each quote or descriptive story represents its season-episode-scene. For example, scene 3 from episode 2 in season 1 would be denoted as 1-2-3. When quoting an officer, his or her name, initials, job title, and department are provided.

7. This may involve modifying the organizational structure, utilizing information systems and technology to track data, recruiting and training personnel, and the geographic assignment of officers.

REFERENCES

American College Health Assessment. (2012). *American College Health Association National College Health Assessment (ACHA-NCHA II): Reference group executive summary fall 2011.* Hanover, MD: American College Health Association.

Boles, S. M., & Miotto, K. (2003). Substance abuse and violence: A review of the literature. *Aggression & Violent Behavior, 8,* 155–174.

Brecklin, L. R., & Ullman, S. E. (2010). The role of victim and offender substance use in sexual assault outcomes. *Journal of Interpersonal Violence, 25,* 1503–1522.

Community Oriented Policing Services (COPS). (2012). *Community policing defined.* Retrieved from http://www.cops.usdoj.gov/default.asp?item=36.

Corsaro, N., Brunson, R. K., & McGarrell, E. F. (2010). Evaluating a policing strategy intended to disrupt an illicit street-level drug market. *Evaluation Review, 34,* 513–548.

Corsaro, N., Brunson, R. K., & McGarrell, E. F. (forthcoming). Problem-oriented policing and open-air drug markets: Examining the Rockford pulling levers deterrence strategy. *Crime & Delinquency,* 1–23. Doi: 10.1177/0011128709345955.

CASA Commission on Substance Abuse at Colleges and Universities. (1994). *Rethinking rites of passage: Substance abuse on America's campuses.* New York: Columbia University.

Felson, R., & Burchfield, K. (2004). Alcohol and the risk of physical and sexual assault victimization. *Criminology, 42,* 837–859.

Felson, R., Savolainen, J., Aaltonen, M., & Moustgaard, H. (2008). Is the association between alcohol use and delinquency causal or spurious? *Criminology, 46,* 785–808.

Felson, R., Teasdale, B., & Burchfield, K. B. (2008). The influence of being under the influence: Alcohol effects on adolescent violence. *Journal of Research in Crime and Delinquency, 45,* 119–141.

Fisher, B. S., Sloan, J. J., Cullen, F. T., & Lu, C. (1998). Crime in the ivory tower: The level and sources of student victimization. *Criminology, 36,* 671–710.

Frabutt, J. M., Gathings, M. J., Hunt, E. D., & Loggins, T. J. (2006). *High Point West End Initiative: Project description, log, and preliminary impact analysis.* Greensboro: University of North Carolina at Greensboro, Center for Youth, Family and Community Partnerships.

Geertz, C. (1983). *Local knowledge: Further essays in interpretative anthropology.* New York: Basic Books.

Goldstein, P. J. (1985). The drugs/violence nexus: A tripartite conceptual framework. *Journal of Drug Issues, 15,* 493–506.

Goldstein, P. J., Brownstein, H., Ryan, P. J., & Bellucci, P. A. (1997). Crack and homicide in New York City: A case study in the epidemiology of violence. In C. Reinarman & H. G. Levine (Eds.), *Crack in America: Demon drugs and social justice* (pp. 113–30). Los Angeles: University of California Press.

Graham, K., Bernards, S., Wilsnack, S. C., & Gmel, G. (2011). Alcohol may not cause partner violence but it seems to make it worse: A cross national comparison of the relationship between alcohol and severity of partner violence. *Journal of Interpersonal Violence, 26,* 1503–1523.

Harocopos, A., & Hough, M. (2005). *Drug dealing in open-air markets.* Washington, DC: U.S. Department of Justice.

Jacobson, J. (1999). *Policing drug hot-spots.* London: Home Office.

Johnston, L. D., O'Malley, P. M., Bachman, J. G., & Schulenberg, J. E. (2011). *Monitoring the future: National survey results on drug use, 1975–2010, Volume II, College students & adults ages 19-50.* Ann Arbor, MI: Institute for Social Research, The University of Michigan.

Kennedy, D. (1997). Pulling levers: Chronic offenders, high-crime settings, and a theory of prevention. *Valparaiso University Law Review, 31,* 449–484.

Kennedy, D. M., & Wong, S. L. (2009). *The High Point Drug Market Intervention Strategy.* Washington, DC: U.S. Department of Justice, Office of Community Oriented Policing Services.

Klinger, D. A. (1997) Negotiating order in patrol work: An ecological theory of police response to deviance. *Criminology, 35,* 277–306.

Madensen, T. D., & Eck, J. E. (2006). *Student party riots.* Problem-Specific Guide Series, No. 39. Washington, DC: U.S. Department of Justice, Office of Community Oriented Policing Services.

Mazerolle, L., Soole, D. W., & Rombouts, S. (2006). Street-level drug law enforcement: A meta-analytical review. *Journal of Experimental Criminology, 2,* 409–435.

Mazerolle, L., Soole, D., & Rombouts, S. (2007). Drug law enforcement: A review of the evaluation literature. *Police Quarterly, 10,* 115–153.

Mustaine, E. E., & Tewksbury, R. (1998). Specifying the role of alcohol in predatory victimization. *Deviant Behavior, 19,* 173–199.

National Institute on Alcohol Abuse and Alcoholism. (2002). *A call to action: Changing the culture of drinking at U.S. colleges.* Rockville, MD: author.

Nutt, D. J., King, L. A., & Phillips, L. D. (2010). Drug harms in the UK: A multicriteria decision analysis. *Lancet, 376,* 1558–65.

Parker, R. N., & Auerhahn, K. (1998). Alcohol, drugs, and violence. *Annual Review of Sociology, 24,* 291–311.

Robinson, M., & Roh, S. (2007) Crime on campus: Spatial aspects of calls for service at a regional comprehensive university. In B. S. Fisher & J. J. Sloan III (Eds.), *Campus crime: Legal, social, and policy perspectives* (2nd ed.) (pp. 231–255). Springfield, IL: Charles C Thomas.

Schafer, J. A. (2005). Negotiating order in the policing of youth drinking. *Policing, 28,* 279–300.

Siegel, D., & Harriss, R. C. (1992). An ecological approach to violent crime on campus. *Journal of Security Administration, 15,* 19–29.

Sloan, J. J. (1994). The correlates of campus crime: An analysis of reported crimes on college and university campuses. *Journal of Criminal Justice, 22,* 51–61.

Student Affairs Policy. (2010). Alcohol policy and guidelines for the university community. Retrieved from http://www.sc.edu/policies/staf302.pdf.

Taylor, R. B. (1998). *Crime and small-scale places: What we know, what we can prevent, and what else we need to know.* Washington, DC: National Institute of Justice.

U.S. Department of Education. (2010). *Campus Safety and Security Data Analysis Cutting Tool.* Retrieved from http://ope.ed.gov/security/index.aspx.

Weisburd, D., & Eck, J. (2004). What can police do to reduce crime, disorder, and fear? *Annals of the American Academy of Political and Social Science, 593,* 42–65.

Wechsler, H. (1996). Alcohol and the American college campus: A report from the Harvard school of public health. *Change, 28,* 20–25.

Wechsler, H. (2001). *Binge drinking on America's college campuses.* Cambridge, MA: Harvard University School of Public Health.

Wechsler, H., Davenport, A., Dowdall, G., Moeykens, B., & Castillo, S. (1994). Health and behavioral consequences of binge drinking in college: A national survey of students at 140 campuses. *The Journal of the American Medical Association, 272,* 1672–1677.

Worden, R. E., Bynum, T. S., & Frank, J. (1994). Police crackdowns on drug abuse and trafficking. In D. L. MacKenzie & C. D. Uchida (Eds.), *Drugs and crime* (pp. 95–113). Thousand Oaks, CA: Sage.

Chapter 16

HIGH-TECH ABUSE AND CRIME ON COLLEGE AND UNIVERSITY CAMPUSES: REFLECTIONS ON WHAT IS OCCURRING, WHY IT IS OCCURRING, AND WHAT CAN BE DONE

Samuel C. McQuade, III

INTRODUCTION

A book that focuses on campus crime presupposes that colleges and universities matter, which they do. That postsecondary institutions matter is especially true in the disciplinary areas of computer science, computer engineering, and the more recent field of information technology (IT) where, since WWII, colleges and universities have been at the forefront of research and development in computers. Postsecondary institutions' partnerships with other schools, the private sector, and with federal agencies resulted in tremendous advances in computing. Many of these advances had profound effects on society and literally transformed people's lives, particularly in accessing, using, and disseminating information. The problem is that these innovations have a dark side that involves criminal victimization of not only postsecondary institutions, but their students, faculty members, and staff.

Computer science and engineering-based activities present unique opportunities for individuals to both perpetrate and be the victims of "high-tech" crime. It is now possible for a college student to sit in her dormitory and systematically steal the identities of fellow students, deface websites, or crash computer networks. This possibility underscores the reality that cybercrime or "[the] use of computers or other electronic information technology devices via information systems . . . to facilitate illegal behaviors" (McQuade, 2006a, p. 16) causes *real* harm, not just harm limited to cyberspace. However, two caveats are in order because traditional forms of crime increasingly involve innovative use of information technology (IT): (1) strict interpretation of what constitutes a cybercrime relies on determining that consummate act(s) prohibited by law or policy could *not* have been done without using an IT device online; and (2) technological evolutions in IT-related deviancy, including abuse and criminality matter only to the extent that postsecondary institutional and criminal justice capabilities are not organized to effectively prevent and respond to such incidents.

In reality, people occupying physical space on college campuses use tangible devices to create, access, distribute, or otherwise use information for illicit purposes including to commit cybercrimes such as computer hacking, identity theft, consumption and distribution of child pornography, pirating of copyrighted software, music, and movies, and cyberbullying (where such activities are illegal). No organizational environment offers greater opportunity for cyber-enabled abuse and illegal behavior than do postsecondary institutions. They are attractive targets, given their large numbers; students, faculty members, and staff include potentially large numbers of relatively uninhibited users who are lax in their security; and colleges and universities often provide broadband/high-speed systems capabilities and inherently open rather than more securely compartmentalized information system architectures.

This chapter provides a "high-tech" perspective to new forms of IT-enabled abuse and crime occurring on American college and university campuses, regardless of whether harmful effects are directed at, or experienced by, individuals or groups (e.g., students, faculty members, or staff), by campus information systems, or by institutions as a whole. The chapter is divided into three sections, and begins with a brief history of computing on college campuses and how such activities fueled early forms of computer-enabled abuse. Analysis is also presented of how emerging IT-enabled crime drives perceptions about, and the labeling of, what constitutes "crime," and how society is organizing for the investigation, prosecution, and prevention of these new crimes. Section two of the chapter focuses on the ways high-tech crime occurs on college and university campuses, describes the predominant forms of campus crime enabled with IT, and examines how technological aspects of attacks to information systems lead to victimization. Stressed here is the interplay between off- and online victimization and offending – how students and others increasingly interact with and learn to use IT for both legitimate and illicit purposes, even as IT may cloud moral clarity about committing certain kinds of abuse or crime. Crucial here is how social networks, though steadily less infatuating and ordinary, are changing how users merge their on- and offline activities for work, play, and education. The chapter concludes by presenting three imperatives facing higher education: (1) educate students, staff, and faculty in how to be safe, secure, and responsible online; (2) lead by example, using best practices for protecting information systems against data breaches and other forms of abuse and crime; and (3) increasingly amalgamate physical and cyber security/safety units and operations.[1]

A Brief History of IT-Enabled Abuse and Crime on Campus

Early Computing and Computer Abuse on Campuses

Colleges and universities have always been at the forefront of computer-related and enabled research and education, as well as computer-related abuse, crime, and victimization. Especially since WWII and the Space Race that followed, computers enjoyed increasing prominence on college and university campuses as a subject of academic study, and as a means of research and education. Funded by the military, university electrical engineering researchers developed first generation (mainframe) computers during the 1940s and 1950s to design computerized rocket, missile, and other weapons' guidance systems. Industry funding to universities followed during the 1960s for development of computerized accounting and banking technologies. By the early 1970s, "supercomputers" of the day, principally housed at major research universities such as MIT, supported increasingly complex data analysis in military, space flight, and healthcare research, as well as in support of banking and financial services management. Throughout these periods, early forms of computer abuse and computer crime, such as computer hacking, also emerged on or from within college campuses and later in society as college graduates, increasingly competent in using computers, entered the workforce.

Since the 1980s, many computing and telecommunications inventions and innovations, including the Advanced Research Projects Agency Network (ARPANET), the Internet, and the World Wide Web, progressively transformed society. Technological changes created new opportunities for imaginative and computer savvy offenders who tended to be bright young males, usually without criminal records, who were curious about and drawn to computers. Many of these individuals enrolled in increasingly popular computer science programs offered by two- and four-year colleges and universities. A few of these students helped establish a computer "hacker" subculture that espoused technological creativity and exploration through free and unlimited access to information (Levy, 1984).[2] This subculture affected computing norms on campuses across the country then and now, especially at technological institutes, and involved mischievous computing pranks played out on college and university campuses worldwide. As computing continued to expand during the 1980s, governments began enacting computer crime laws that specifically prohibited trespassing into computer networks or exceeding permissions to access areas within them, and unauthorized copying, altering, or destroying of electronic data stored on networked computers.

Thus, computers were transforming higher education in fundamental ways. Like other sectors in society, colleges and universities steadily adopted information systems to support their business operations. Computers enabled creation of both distance learning courses and high-tech classrooms that feature dynamic visual and audio displays, recording, and interactive learning experiences, combined with Internet connectivity, and a variety of real-time teaching methods. Meanwhile students, staff, and faculty increasingly carry their own mobile electronic devices including laptop computers, tablets, and smart phones that are radically changing the technological, social, and cultural environments of higher education.

Today, thousands of colleges and universities, occupied by millions of young adults who often grew up using IT devices while in K-12 schools, and/or as the primary users of computers and cell/smart phones in their homes, provide technological opportunities integral to virtually every aspect of campus life and operations. Increasingly dependent upon IT are classroom instruction, research and development, resident life and extracurricular student activities including Web accessible entertainment like electronic gaming and music/movie downloading services, as well as academic and human resources administration, media and alumni relations, and community outreach. Many campuses now provide for viewing online content tailored for the screens of smaller "smart phones" Indeed, rating and comparing campuses based on technological capabilities is a chief consideration among prospective students – and their parents – seeking advanced and cost-beneficial education. An institution deemed among the "most wired" in the country has now become almost as important as the size of its endowment.

Conceptual Evolution and Labeling of High-Tech Crime

With technological advances in society comes the recognition of new forms of off-and-online deviancy. Most forms of deviancy that harm people in some way are destined to be criminalized or at least regulated. In the U.S., local, state-level, and the federal governments promulgate laws and regulations intended to prevent, mitigate, and counter technology-enabled harm. Within the realm of cybercrime, hacking, digital pirating, distributing malware, spamming, and cyberbullying, all represent behaviors that evolved from new to adaptive to ordinary phases and divergent forms of crime commanding legal intervention (McQuade, 2006b). Conceptions of social constructs for new forms of abuse and crime, and subsequent labeling, defining, and categorizing of them are necessary to update methods of investigation and prevention, and formulate policies needed for administering information systems within organizations as well criminal justice systems throughout society. McQuade (2006, pp. 10–18) paralleled contemporary understanding of cybercrime with Sutherland's (1940) conceptualization and later diffusion of the concept "white-collar crime" which now encompasses a host of illegal behaviors involving the victimization of consumers, employees, and corporations. Like white-collar crime, constructs of IT-enabled crime have evolved for over 50 years with interested observers sequentially labeling them as "computer abuse," "computer crime," "computer-related crime," "high-tech crime," and "electronic crime." Other constructs such as "corporate crime," "economic crime," and "transnational organized crime" also developed as computing, telecommunication, and transportation technologies radically changed illicit activities committed with computers and interoperable electronic devices Each new form of crime resulted in not-so-distinct forms of victimization, exacerbating conceptual confusion surrounding IT-enabled abuse, crime, and victimization. By 1995, overlapping conceptions of increasingly high-tech crime raised concern in academic and policy circles about definitional dilemmas surrounding IT-enabled crimes (National White Collar Crime Center, 1996). Ensuing debate occurred over whether labeling crime constructs was even useful, given that deviancy and crime evolve technologically and in the process are naturally conceived in more or less accurate ways.

Debate notwithstanding, recognition, labeling and responding to new forms of high-tech crime continues. This process is both useful and inevitable, although it does challenges researchers, practitioners, and policymakers to recognize, accept, and address this reality as they attempt to better understand, respond to, and prevent high-tech crimes both on college and university campuses and elsewhere. As progress is made, we ought not be overly concerned about general labels for IT-enabled abuse and crimes, although adoption of the term "cybercrime" to represent abusive, illicit, and illegal behaviors facilitated with IT via information systems is currently apt (McQuade, 2006, pp. 10–18).

What is also important is that our current conception of IT-enabled offending on college and university campuses is not limited to behaviors explicitly prohibited by law or institutional policy. As previously indicated laws and regulations change with innovations in technology-enabled abuse, as people experience new forms of harm. Eventually, change in policies and procedures follow, bringing organizations into statutory and regulatory compliance. As of this writing most states have criminalized "cyberbullying" to penalize intentional repeated online embarrassment, harassment, intimidation, stalking, or threats. Colleges and universities are following suit by proscribing cyberbullying in their Acceptable Use of Information Systems Policies. Consequently, students are being held accountable for this form of misconduct even if the incident is not referred to law enforcement agencies for investigation and possible prosecution as a crime. Just as in the past, we now conceptualize and label offending and victimization according to the technological underpinnings that made the behaviors possible. What has long been regarded simply as traditional face-to-face "bullying," today involves all kinds of online cyberbullying. As technology advances, new conceptions, constructs, and terms will likely be needed to capture the essence of innovative, harmful, and interrelated sets of behaviors occurring in society, inclusive of those that occur on college and university campuses.

High-Tech Crime and Abuse on College Campuses

Predominant Forms of High-Tech Crime on Campuses

Currently, there are seven predominant forms of IT-enabled abuse and cybercrime occurring on college campuses and via campus-based computer networks including: (1) writing and distributing malicious code (e.g., viruses, worms, Trojans, adware/spyware, or spam); (2) disrupting computer services such as excessive unauthorized use of network resources or launching denial of service attacks; (3) computer spying and intrusions, including hacking into networks or exceeding authorized permissions; (4) fraudulent schemes and data or device theft, including credit card fraud and identity theft; (5) unauthorized or illegal file sharing (e.g., piracy of software, music, movies, and electronic games); (6) academic and scientific misconduct, including using computers to plagiarize, buy/steal papers, fake research findings, or post inappropriate content to websites, chat forums, or blogs; and (7) cyberbullying. Note that this list is not comprehensive and that within each category are several technologically distinct types of abusive/criminal behaviors.

Technological Aspects of Cyber Attacks Leading to Victimization

Understanding and managing IT-enabled abuse, crime, and victimization occurring on college campuses requires recognizing several technological aspects of appropriately using or misusing information systems and devices capable of processing, exchanging, and storing data. *Systems* include wired/wireless computer controlled telecommunications networks such as campus intranets that connect servers or the Internet and allow computers and other electronic IT devices to send and receive data. *Devices* include desktop, laptop, tablet, and mini-computers, as well as combination scanner/copier/fax machines, and cell/smart phones. Such devices are increasingly smaller, lighter, and therefore more portable, which makes them easier to possess and conceal for clandestine purposes required to carry-out illicit activities. IT devices are also more affordable, interoperable, have greater processing speed and memory capacity, and are capable of more extensive multitasking (e.g., simultaneous Web browsing, listening to music, and sending or receiving text messages).

There are ten technological aspects of high-tech abuse and crime that complicate understanding and managing them, both on campus and elsewhere. First, consider that IT-enabled abuse and crime occurs when offenders use systems and/or devices to invade and possibly damage the technology and/or other property of another, including data. This scenario generally plays out as technological competitions pitting the capabilities of offenders against those of potential victims. Such scenarios are consistent with the basic principles of routine activities theory (Cohen & Felson, 1979) which suggest that a crime occurs when motivated (and capable) offenders have identified suitable targets that lack capable guardians to stop them. These competitions also explain evolutions in crime as the result of technology innovation their adoption for illicit purposes, and the diffusion of systems, tools, and techniques throughout society (McQuade, 2006b).

Second, college campuses create physical environments in which illicit use of electronic devices can be easily concealed and detectable only with electronic monitoring. A person using a digital phone to send a text message may be returning a friendly note or sending a threat, but in either case may do so in public in an unsuspicious manner and thus causes no notice that abuse or crime is occurring. Consequently, IT-enabled crimes are difficult to notice using conventional means of detection and more difficult to prevent using ordinary crime prevention strategies like neighborhood, business, or campus watch programs. Nearly everyone on college campuses possesses portable electronic devices that can be used under various circumstances to facilitate high-tech abuse or crime without raising suspicion.

Third, cybercrime often damages student, faculty member, or staff software or hardware. Attacks of systems and devices may result in their destruction or manipulation, and/or copying and distribution of confidential or personal data that allows for additional abuses or crime. For example, after losing personal data to hackers, victims of identity theft typically have their personal information sold online via clandestine markets before their financial accounts are drained and their credit ruined (Skorwonski, 2012). Victims may also be revictimized in other ways stemming from loss of their personal data, money, and credit rating, including denial of positions requiring security clearances or being improperly arrested for crimes allegedly perpetrated by them (Synovate, 2003). Subsequent crimes and victimization continue as long as offenders can tap funds through electronic means; unless and until victims correct their financial records; and until their names are cleared. Inadequately protected databases containing confidential information allow identity theft and other types of high-tech crime to occur.

Fourth, data also exist in hardcopy and analog forms that scanners can convert to digital form. Computer hackers learn about their targets, such as particular users or servers through ongoing intelligence-gathering of security-related, personal, or other confidential information. Armed with these valuable data often acquired in prior attacks, offenders are then free to perpetrate various high-tech crimes against people or organizations.

Fifth, like traditional crime, different IT-enabled abuse and cybercrime often occur together in the course of a single event or as a result of ongoing criminal activity. These offenses differentially affect students, staff, and faculty members, as well as groups and organizations, depending on the relative strength of available defensive technologies. Each additional system identified, targeted, and successfully attacked likely contains different kinds and amounts of information. In turn, the value of this information varies and depends on attackers' combined knowledge, skill, motivation, available resources, and access to technological systems (Parker, 1998). Personal information (e.g., financial, health, and academic records) are all potentially valuable sources of intelligence for committing abuse or crimes against data owners as well as targeting other individuals, information systems, and facilities.

To illustrate, on March 11, 2005, an intruder stole a laptop computer from an office on the campus of the University of California at Berkeley. University officials were extremely worried because the device contained sensitive personal information for nearly 100,000 students, student applicants, and alumni. Ten years earlier, UC Berkley had experienced a hacking incident resulting in the loss of confidential information for hundreds of thousands of California residents involved in research commissioned by the state's Department of Social Services (see Liedtke, 2005). Because many other colleges and universities have experienced similar thefts and hacking incidents along with other types of high-tech crimes, leading observers have concluded college campuses may be *the* most vulnerable organizations to breaches of information security (Marklein, 2006a).

Sixth, cybercrimes always involve physical actions combined with cyber transactions. Regardless of the IT used and types of assets targeted, there are tangible aspects to what perpetrators do – cybercrimes do not occur solely within the amorphous realm of cyberspace. Rather, human beings occupying physical space and using tangible devices connected to wired or wireless devices perpetrate cybercrime including sophisticated hacking, the release of malicious software programs, and denial of service attacks involving remotely controlled "bots."[3] In accordance with classic crime investigation theory, law enforcement officials can collect, analyze, and trace physical and cyber-based clues left by high-tech offenders. The challenge for investigators is to place a specific offender in control of a keyboard or other input device within the time and at the location from which an attack was initiated. Fortunately, trained investigators employing computer forensic techniques in combination with traditional evidence collection methods can nearly always achieve this goal if sufficient expertise is brought to bear. But relatively few colleges or universities have sufficient computer forensic resources readily available. Very few campuses currently have dedicated information security officers much less those capable of undertaking computer forensics investigations. Typically, only criminal case evidence referred to local law enforcement agencies and meeting threshold circumstances warranting prosecution will ever be queued for digital forensics analysis.

Seventh, offenders using any number of IT systems and devices can launch attacks either sequentially or simultaneously against targets located in many on- or off-campus locations. Offenders can launch attacks in relatively high-to-low-tech ways, from within particular facilities or network environments that are co-occupied by victims or they can launch attacks from outside a facility or computer network by disguising the source of messages and/or defeating firewalls and password protections intended to keep intruders out. In spring of 2012, the University of Pittsburgh with 29,000 students experienced dozens of bomb threats that were posted in buildings and sent via anonymous email servers (to disguise the origins and authors). For three months campus life, classes, and studies were disrupted by an expanding number of threats even as university officials along with local, state, and federal law enforcement agencies including the FBI investigated (Remizowski, 2012). Although an on-line group called "The Threateners" took responsibility and offered to cease making threats if university officials removed a controversial $50,000 reward for information leading to arrests in the case (Huffington Post, 2012), the threats ceased following the April 11, 2012 arrest of Mark Lee Krangle, 65, of Croton-On-Hudson, New York who was "charged with harassment and making terroristic threats" in connection with the case (Dezayas, 2012). However, the official investigation continues as of this writing. This case reveals that cybercrimes can be committed by insiders – students or employees – or outsiders It is also true that offenders can make it appear an attack originated from anywhere in the world when, in reality, the attacks originated from within a victim's geographic and network environment. The University of Pittsburgh case also demonstrates how cyber threats, including instances that cause fear but not actual consequences (e.g., no explosives found or detonations occurring), can nonetheless result in disruptions in the physical and virtual lives of thousands.

Eighth, as in traditional crime, victims are often targeted, manipulated, and fooled by offenders who know them personally or come to know enough about them through intelligence gathering to establish a relationship based on trust (Parker, 1998, pp. 148–150; McQuade, 2006, pp. 114–117). Social engineering for the purpose of manipulating people into revealing personal information is common online. "Friending" among Internet users poses new opportunities for being socially engineered, which is especially worrisome because thousands are fooled every day into revealing personally sensitive information by increasingly authentic-appearing (but bogus) websites. College students who grew up amidst a digital youth culture where browsing, texting and "sexting" (i.e., the exchanging of pornographic images of oneself with one's partner) are especially vulnerable to online victimization and offending via social engineering (see McQuade et al., 2009, pp. 12–17). Members of that culture expect one another to connect, be connected, and remain linked with one another and with strangers through whom they seek career access and advancement. But the inextricability of social and mobile computing for personal and professional development purposes, combined with inexperience, indiscretion, overconfidence, and/or lax security attitudes means that tech-savvy college and university students face new risks of being manipulated online (see Angwin, 2006). In May of 2006, for example, the website www.bad-jocks.com received national media attention after posting photos depicting partially nude male and female athletes from numerous colleges or universities allegedly participating in hazing rituals. Revelations that such foolishness documented on social media sites and later discovered by prospective employers, combined with the reality that employers use such information to eliminate prospective employees from serious consideration, should give pause to students to imprudently participate in activities intended to be private (see Bell, 2011; Bennett, 2011; Kutzer-Rice, 2011). Ultimately, as a population, college-aged students are vulnerable via chat, websites (especially personal profiles), blogs, gaming forums or any other type of online forum through which they can reveal or have personal confidential information betrayed. After all, the more users go online the more exposed their systems, devices and data are to being compromised even if online "friends" could be completely trusted.

Ninth, social engineering underscores the reality of human factors related to both the offensive and preventive aspects of cybercrime. Cybercrimes are committed by people using IT which is analogous to the expression that "Guns don't kill people, people kill people." Even so-called automated crimes carried out by self-morphing bots are, in reality, programs coded by individuals who make mistakes and are vulnerable to all the usual human entrapments that trip up criminals (e.g., bragging about their exploits, indiscreetly spending of large amounts of illicit money, and leaving physical or cyber clues to their identity, etc.). From a preventive standpoint, most users, despite their increasing awareness about cybercrime remain largely ignorant or naïve about their personal or their institution's vulnerability because they do not understand the computing and technical aspects of information security. For example, malware threats that once applied only to the operating systems of computers now extend to smart phones. Additional problems include failing to use and routinely change "strong" nonalphanumeric passwords, failing to encrypt sensitive data even though "locked down" behind firewalls, and blindly trusting insiders who may be negligent or disloyal when it comes to protecting their devices and storage media.

Finally, being victimized does not necessarily mean being harmed only as the result of behaviors proscribed by law or institutional policy all of which must continually be updated. Rather, high-tech victimization appropriately includes abusive behaviors that cause any harm to individuals, groups, or organizations. This includes direct, indirect, and tertiary harm, and applies especially to campuses where computing by students is ubiquitous but may encourage unethical use of technology. For example, student plagiarism of copyrighted work may not rise to the level of violating state or federal copyright law but can cause considerable harm to the original author, especially if the violating student's paper finds its way onto the Web without proper attribution. Similarly, a faculty member who uses his or her college-issued computer during business hours to email family pictures to coworkers is not violating law, but may well be violating institutional computer use policies by denying other users of the network needed bandwidth for legitimate school purposes. This situation is analogous to victimless crime, where theoretically, harm accrues to the community at large by willing participants' actions. Other forms of cyber abuse, such as Web page defacement and cyberbullying, may not constitute crimes in a given legal jurisdiction, but can harm victims in various ways. Cyberbullying, for example, has since resulted in suicide among adolescents and young adults (see case descriptions by McQuade, Colt, & Meyers, 2009).

Off- and Online Victimization and Offending Interplay

Millions of potential victims and thousands of perpetrators are technologically and behaviorally intertwined through use of campus facilities and information systems. This makes it difficult to neatly separate relatively high-to-low-tech offending and victimization occurring on campuses. For example, students who illegally pirate software, music, or movies via peer-to-peer (p2p) networks are likely violating copyright laws. But they are periodically also victimized as a result of their downloading malicious code embedded in the downloaded files that may damage their systems, their data, or lead to other crimes being committed against them. If not detected and quarantined, their now infected computers or other electronic device potentially exposes an entire campus network to infection, infiltration, and other forms of harm, thus extending victimization through technology.

Consider the following hypothetical scenario:

> Scott slides open his Palm Treo 650 as his computer crime professor continues a lecture on social penetration theory. The smart phone connects to the campus wireless network through an SD adaptor, allowing him to sign onto an instant messaging service without using his free cellular service subscriber minutes. Pretending to take notes, he silently starts a chat session with his friend Mike, joking about the pornographic videos of Mike's ex-girlfriend Sally that Mike had previously posted online without her knowledge a week earlier as revenge for their breakup. Later, back in his dorm, Mike begins downloading the latest episodes of *Family Guy* through BitTorrent, while resuming his chat with Scott who is now in a sociology class still pretending to take notes. Down the hall from Mike, Amy, who is also online with Scott, helps feed the *Family Guy* episode that Mike just sent to several friends. In the process, she posts the link to BitTorrent along with her course schedule to her MySpace page, which is automatically sent to Brian's laptop via an RSS feed. Amy does not know Brian, but he certainly knows a lot about her, and he smiles at his luck as he reads her course schedule and plans his next social engineering move . . .

On campuses replete with systems and devices, the forgoing scenario is not farfetched. Research indicates a majority of students on campuses periodically misuse computers or other electronic devices to (1) buy papers, cheat on exams, or plagiarize the work of other people; (2) post to websites or chat forums derogatory information about their classmates or professors; (3) harass, threaten, or solicit sex online; or (4) pirate and also redistribute copyrighted software, music, and movies (McQuade & Castellano, 2004). Obviously some of these result in primary, secondary, or tertiary harm, and thus contribute to overall levels of victimization occurring on campuses and via information systems. This effectively extends and amalgamates social interactions and social computing on campuses and within surrounding communities to physical *and* cyberspace occupied by students, staff, and faculty. In short, possible locations and spaces in or through which high-tech abuse and crime can occur are boundless, yet geographic locations still matter because people occupy facilities, grounds, or vehicles whenever they are using systems and devices.

Evidence for technological and behavioral interplay between high tech offending and victimization by and among college students in particular has much to do with social learning theory (Fream, 1993; Rogers, 2001). This further underscores the importance of off- and online interactions. What students do not know about high-tech abuse and crimes from which they can benefit personally, they often find out shortly after arriving on campuses filled with

IT, technologically well-informed peers and unprecedented ability to access information about innovative offending methods. This situation is likely being exacerbated by media coverage of innovative high-tech crimes (Fream, 1993), which now effectively includes a multitude of websites, chat rooms, and blogs specializing in high-tech offending content. The result is that high-tech victims and offenders on campuses frequently know each other in the flesh or through social computing interactions. Indeed, one-third to one-half of students of all ages surveyed in primary, secondary, and higher education report they knew the offender prior to the cyber attack, abuse, or crime in which they were victimized (McQuade & Sampat, 2008; McQuade & Castellano, 2004).

The Extent and Impact of IT-Enabled Crime on Campuses

An important question yet addressed in the chapter is how much high-tech abuse and crime occurs on campuses and what is their social and economic impact. Unfortunately, a dearth of research reveals relatively little about the extent of high-tech offending in society, much less the social, psychological, and economic impacts experienced by victims. What is known about the extent and impact of IT-enabled crime on college campuses is even more limited. This lack of knowledge stems from: (1) inconsistent conceptualizations of IT-enabled crime and flawed research methodologies used to study it; (2) victim unawareness that they have been attacked or reluctance to report crimes for any number of reasons; (3) violent and traditional property crimes being the priorities of campus officials; (4) insufficiently trained and equipped campus security or police officers who may also be indifferent about high-tech crimes or intimidated by technical aspects of cybercrimes; (5) exclusion of many specific IT-enabled crimes in national and state crime reporting systems and reports (e.g., the National Incident Based Reporting System – NIBRS) to which colleges and universities may voluntarily contribute crime data; and (6) continually changing IT and associated threat capabilities available to those who would use computers or other types of electronic devices for illicit purposes.

Despite these obstacles and the near absence of funding to study IT-enabled crime, studies have been undertaken. While most have usually involved convenience samples of students, a few have employed large random samples, rigorous data analysis, and the testing of specific theories to determine causes and correlates of illicit, unethical, abusive, and/or criminal use of computers.

The first of these studies was by Hollinger (1989), who surveyed 1,774 undergraduate students at a southern university about software piracy and computer hacking. Hollinger found a relatively large number of students admitted to participating in various types of computer-aided offending behavior. Specifically, during a 15-week semester, 10 percent of respondents reported they pirated software and 3.3 percent of students reported they had violated another person's account/files/privacy. Fifty percent of those respondents said they did so only once during the semester in question, 11.1 percent reported they had committed one of these two offenses at least once, and 2.1 percent reported doing both activities. Skinner and Fream (1997) expanded Hollinger's study by asking 581 students about their lifetime, past year, and past month behavior involving: (1) software piracy, (2) guessing passwords, (3) gaining unauthorized access merely to browse data, (4) gaining unauthorized access to change data, and (5) writing/using virus-like programs. Skinner and Fream concluded that aspects of social learning theory (e.g., differential reinforcement/punishment, definitions, and sources of imitation) were significant explanations for computer crime.

McQuade and Castellano (2004) built on these and other studies using a survey of 873 randomly selected students at the Rochester Institute of Technology. That survey examined perceptions, attitudes, and experiences, including 20 types of IT-enabled offending. Table 16.1 and Table 16.2 summarize some of the interesting victimization and offending data from McQuade and Castellano (2004).

Major findings of this study revealed that: (1) large numbers of respondents reported having experienced a large variety of cybercrimes as both victims and/or offenders, though with the exception of pirating, rates and patterns of offending were quite low; and (2) college students rarely use strong passwords and infrequently change passwords despite periodically sharing their passwords with fellow students or others who are unauthorized to access information systems administered by their institution. In addition, a factor analysis involving 20 types of online abuse clustered with statistical significance

Table 16.1

Self-reported Victimization by College Students in Year Prior to Study

Type of Victimization	No. of Student Victims	Percent of Respondents
Harmed by Malicious Code	435	48%
Denial of Service	115	13.8%
Online Harassment	149	17.1%
Received Online Threat(s)	68	7.9%
Cyber Stalking	52	6.1%
Hacking	99	12.3%
Stolen Equipment	23	2.7%
Identity Theft	55	6.5%
Other Fraud	27	3.2%
Other	20	2.4%

Table 16.2
Percent of Self-reported Offending by College Students

Offending in 12 months prior to survey:	Never	1-10 Times	11-30 Times	31+ Times
Unauthorized music file sharing	24.5%	14.6%	7.4%	53.5%
Unauthorized move file sharing	42.1%	22.2%	11.4%	24.4%
Unauthorized software file sharing	39.9%	36.9%	9.2%	14.0%
Obtained someone's credit card # without their knowledge	99.5%	.5%	0%	0%
Used credit card without permission	99.8%	0.2%	0%	0%
Plagiarized	92.9%	6.6%	0.2%	0.2%
Copied and inappropriately used someone else's computer code	93.1%	6.4%	0.2%	0.2%
Purchased paper and turned in as an assignment	99.0%	1.0%	0%	0%
Used a computer or other IT device to cheat on school assignment	94.2%	5.3%	0.2%	0.2%
Used a computer or other IT device to cheat on an exam	96.9%	2.8%	0.2%	0.1%

Table 16.3
Scale, Scale Items and Descriptive Statistics for Online Abuse

Offender Group	Factor Loadings	Descriptive Statistics
HACKERS		
Disrupted or denied computer services	.958	Alpha = .9008
Disclosed computer security flaws/vulnerabilities	.962	Mean = .1959
Wrote and released computer viruses	.916	St. Dev. = .6769
HARASSERS		
Gave out password of another person	.827	Alpha = .9021
Harassment	.935	Mean = .935
Threats	.953	St. Dev. = .6861
PIRATES		
Unauthorized music file sharing	.817	Alpha = .8470
Unauthorized movie file sharing	.911	Mean = 6.632
Unauthorized software file sharing	.864	St. Dev. = 5.004
ACADEMIC CHEATS		
Plagiarized	.828	Alpha = .7461
Use IT device to cheat on school assignment(s)	.920	Mean = .2188
		St. Dev. = .5577
DATA SNOOPS		
Guessed a password access system	.788	Alpha = .8081
Gained unauthorized access just to look	.840	Mean = .2566
		St. Dev. = .6119

Table 16.4
Bivariate Correlations Among Types of Online Abusers

	HACKERS	HARASSERS	PIRATES	ACADEMIC CHEATS	DATA SNOOPS
HACKERS	1.00				
HARASSERS	.852	1.00			
PIRATES	.397	.380	1.00		
ACADEMIC CHEATS	.703	.703	.356	1.00	
DATA SNOOPS	.695	.685	.399	.575	1.00

into the five offender groups.[4] As summarized in Table 16.3 and Table 16.4, hackers, harassers, pirates, academic cheats, and data snoops explained 58.39 percent of the variance among the 20 forms of online abuse asked about in the survey.

McQuade and his colleagues conducted additional self-report surveys of randomly selected college students between 2004 and 2006 including: (1) an online survey of 574 incoming first-year RIT students; (2) a comparative study of 509 SUNY Brockport students that used the same instrument used at RIT in April, 2004; and (3) a program evaluation survey of 449 RIT students, split evenly between individuals who used and did not use a free music downloading service provided by the university. Although detailed findings from these studies have not yet been published, highlights further reveal the nature and extent of high-tech abuse and crimes committed by and among students:

- Offending behavior and victimization experiences of students at large private technological institutes versus small-to-medium sized general education colleges do not vary to any appreciable extent (McQuade, Gorthy, & Linden, 2006);
- Social learning theory is a powerful explanation of IT-enabled offending; campus alternative education sanctions and other disciplinary actions less than academic suspension have little deterrent effect on students' illegal file sharing (McQuade & Fisk, 2006);
- Students who engage in IT-enabled offending often specialize in specific types of abusive or illegal behavior (McQuade & Castellano, 2004);
- Students vary considerably in their ethical attitudes towards IT-enabled abuse and crime. For example, students regard using a computer or other electronic device to facilitate academic dishonesty or violate copyright laws as being less wrong than harassing or threatening someone

online, and much less wrong than using IT to commit fraud (McQuade & Linden, 2006).

These and other studies confirm the need for greater attention to on-campus, IT-enabled abuse and crime and suggest new avenues of research for investigators. Readers should understand that empirical evidence about the true nature, extent, and impacts of high-tech campus crime remains very limited. Fortunately, a growing number of researchers are paying attention to these issues. Perhaps one day government agencies, corporations, or foundations may sponsor funded research into behavioral aspects of high-tech offending on college and university campuses.

Three Imperatives for Higher Education

Educate Campus Communities to be Safe, Secure, and Responsible Online

The challenge facing colleges and universities is to combine high-tech education with intervention strategies to combat high-tech abuse and crime that continues to evolve and which is possibly increasing in both incidence and prevalence on college campuses. Two- and four-year institutions in the U.S. commonly offer programs of study in computer science, software engineering, IT systems administration, and similar specializations. Increasingly, academic institutions are also offering courses, if not entire programs of study, that focus on information security, computer/cyber crime, and computer forensics. This is rather paradoxical given that the computer-related inventions and innovations that have benefited society enormously have also led to new forms of criminality. Now, the founding institutions that made those advances possible are not only undertaking new research but also providing education and training to protect information systems. It seems that society has come full cycle.

Ironically, such research and education is geared towards a generation of students who grew up using computer devices, often without adequate supervision or training in information security or cyber ethics. In the series of computer use and ethics studies described earlier, McQuade and colleagues at RIT found most of today's college students not only grew up with computers in their homes, they were usually the primary users of those devices at ten years of age. In general, they were strongly encouraged and supported by parents who, although encouraging the use of computers for a variety of activities, failed to supervise adequately the use of IT devices. Lacking systematic cyber ethics and information security/safety-related education or training, today's college students are generally prone to IT-enabled offending and victimization. For many students, this reality may be exacerbated given powerful computers and high-speed Internet connectivity available on most campuses and combined with youth cultures that embrace actively using electronic devices for almost every imaginable activity – certainly for coursework, research, and chatting with friends, as well as for online shopping and various forms of entertainment such as watching/viewing downloaded music/movies, playing electronic games, and viewing of legal pornography – in some extreme cases the latter activities reportedly having detrimental effects on students' grades, employment responsibilities, and personal relationships (see McQuade, 2006, pp. 153–155).

Higher education officials and faculty, working collaboratively across academic departments and campus services offices must embrace a new national education and workforce training imperative to raise awareness, knowledge, understanding, and skills for enhanced Internet safety, information security, and cyber ethics among students, faculty, and staff. It is the combination of education and training for all campus IT users in these subject areas, combined with efficacious technology solutions that will ultimately lead to prevention of cybercrime on campuses and their social computing environments.

Lead by Example to Better Protect Information Systems

Since 2005, the Privacy Rights Clearinghouse has documented 635 publically disclosed data breach incidents at U.S. educational institutions. Although this list includes some breaches experienced by local school districts, the vast majority occurred at higher education institutions including community colleges, technical institutes, and four-year colleges and universities. Breaches reveal that the number of records containing confidential information (i.e., records containing a person's social security number, date of birth, or financial account data) accessed or disclosed without authorization ranged from a few dozen to hundreds of thousands *per incident*. The largest such breach was experienced by The Ohio State University, which in December of 2010 began notifying up to 760,000 current and former students and employees, plus businesses that had provided services to the school, that confidential personal information including social security numbers may have been compromised by a hacking incident (Pyle, 2010). But this was not the first breach experienced by OSU. In 2008, a vendor doing work for the school's student health-insurance plan mistakenly stored 18,000 names of current and former students on a computer open to the Internet. Two years earlier, hackers had gained access to social security numbers, addresses, and data on medical treatments of 60,000 student patients of the campus health care center. "That breach followed an attack on a network server containing data on 300,000 Ohio University alumni and donors, including 137,000 social security numbers. The university's Innovation Center also was hacked, leading to the exposure of intellectual property files, e-mails, and Social Security numbers" (Pyle, 2010).

OSU is not alone among college and universities that have experienced data breaches, too often from not heeding best practices for due care and diligence long advocated by the managed information security sector. The following examples of data breaches are merely three egregious among dozens of recent institutions that disclosed unauthorized accessing of records containing personal information of individual students, faculty, staff, alumni, donors or others (Privacy Rights Clearinghouse, 2012):

- February 15, 2012 University of North Carolina at Charlotte 350,000 records:

" . . . Around 350,000 people had their Social Security numbers exposed. Financial information was also exposed. A system misconfiguration and incorrect access settings caused a large amount of electronic data hosted by the University to be accessible from the Internet. One exposure issue affected general University systems over a period of about three months. A second exposure issue affected the college of engineering systems for over a decade."

- January 20, 2012 Arizona State University (Tempe) 300,000 records:

"ASU shutdown its online computer system after discovering a breach. An encrypted file containing user names and passwords was downloaded on Wednesday, January 18 by an unauthorized party. All online services were suspended until the night of Thursday, January 19. Students and staff will be required to enter new passwords to access their accounts since there is a chance that some information could have been compromised."

- November 11, 2011 Virginia Commonwealth University 176,567 records:

"Hackers were able to access a Virginia Commonwealth University (VCU) computer server. It contained files with the personal information of current and former VCU and VCU Health System faculty, staff, students, and affiliates. Suspicious files were discovered on the server on October 24. It was taken offline and subsequent investigation revealed that two unauthorized accounts had been created on a second server. While the first server did not contain personal data, the second server did and had been compromised through the first server. Data included either a name or eID, Social Security number, and in some cases, date of birth, contact information, and various programmatic or departmental information."

Data breaches can be costly and reflect poorly on all organizations regardless of the extent to which managers and IT professionals can be legitimately blamed for not employing sound information security practices. This is especially true for academic institutions that maintain complex computing environments with hundreds-to-tens of thousands of authorized users and symbolize the highest of professional standards and integrity; and that endear trust from students (and parents) to educate while exacting enormous tuition and/or housing fees along with expectations for protecting privacy as now required by law. In April 2012, the University of Hawaii settled a class action law suit "stemming from five data breaches over a three-year period that affected nearly 96,000 individuals. The settlement [at a cost of approximately $550,000] will provide those affected with two years of free credit monitoring and credit restoration services, according to a statement from the university. The settlement affects students, faculty, alumni, university employees, and others whose data was exposed in the five breaches from 2009 to 2011" (Roman, 2012).

Due in no small part to failures among academic institutions to prevent breaches of legally protected data, " . . . forty-six states, the District of Columbia, Puerto Rico, and the Virgin Islands have [since 2002] enacted legislation requiring notification of security breaches involving personal information" (National Conference of State Legislatures, 2012). To comply with legislative requirements, some colleges and universities with advanced information security policies, procedures, and technology now use personal identity finder software to routinely and automatically scan connected device hard drives of faculty and staff to detect, alert, and even delete protected data such as student names, social security numbers, and dates of birth. Such tools are helpful but insufficient given the larger cyber abuse and cybercrime threats that campuses now experience. Broader thinking and more aggressive action is required, commensurate with enormous public trust, numbers of affected people at risk and contemporary still-increasing costs of higher education. Colleges and universities that rely on sound policies and practices to comport with legal requirements for information security and online privacy increasingly do so guided by recognized standards. "Established by EDUCAUSE and Internet2 in July 2000, the Higher Education Information Security Council (HEISC) mission is to improve information security, data protection, and privacy programs across the higher education sector through its working groups of volunteers and professional EDUCAUSE staff that coordinate activities and collaborate with partners from government, industry, and other academic organizations" (EDUCAUSE, 2012). Other entities, such as the National Institute of Standards and Technology (NIST), are also available. Structured within the U.S. Department of Commerce, NIST, beginning in 2002, has operated a Computer Security Division and Computer Security Resource Center to guide development, implementation, and practices for information security and national critical information infrastructure protection. Detailed information and assistance available to government, private and nonprofit organizations, including academic institutions, may be accessed online via the website www.csrc.nist.gov (NIST Computer Security Division, 2012). Similarly, "the International Standards Organization (ISO) is the world's largest developer of voluntary International Standards. International Standards give state of the art specifications for products, services and good practice, helping to make industry more efficient and effective" (ISO, 2012). Its standards for information security are specifically geared towards advancing as well as protecting international trade. Many countries, including the U.S., strive to dovetail national standards for information security with widely used ISO standards. Of further special mention is the Information Technology Infrastructure Library (2012):

> ITIL is a set of practices for IT service management (ITSM) that focuses on aligning IT services with the needs of business. In its current form (known as ITILv3 and ITIL 2011 edition), ITIL is published in a series of five core publications, each of which covers an ITSM lifecycle stage. ITILv3 underpins ISO/IEC 20000 (previously BS15000), the International Service Management Standard for IT service management, although differences between the two frameworks do exist. ITIL describes procedures, tasks and checklists that are not organization-specific, used by an organization for establishing a minimum level of competency. It allows the organization to establish a baseline from which it can plan, implement, and measure. It is used to demonstrate compliance and to measure improvement. The names *ITIL* and *IT Infrastructure Library* are registered trademarks of the United Kingdom's Office of Government Commerce (OGC) – now part of the Cabinet Office. Following this move, the ownership is now listed as being with HM Government rather than OGC.

The significance of ITIL for academic institutions is its recognition that colleges and universities are effectively businesses that must provide information services as a core function reliably and on budget, and that information security and privacy constitute critical aspects of a much larger enterprise responsibility. Heretofore adopted mainly by large transnational corporations and government agencies within the United Kingdom, leading academic institutions in the U.S. are also embracing ITIL standards as a means of incorporating information security, as well as prevention and investigation of online abuse and cybercrimes, into a larger management conceptualization of what academic institutions must do relative to IT administration. For example, the Rochester Institute of Technology (RIT) has fully adopted ITIL. Having sent IT managers for ITIL training, the university now categorizes IT threats and incidents requiring attention into four types of priority responses. RIT is also developing evaluative metrics to monitor progress and success across a full range of IT services provided to the university. The large point here is that information security management is and must be increasingly integral to enterprise-level IT administration, hence of equal importance to institutional recruiting, course management, finance, and other vital IT-dependent core functions of institutions. Gone are the days when secure computing was an add-on risk management responsibility; "infosec" to prevent campus-related cyber abuse and cybercrime cannot be a spectator sport!

Amalgamated Offices for Information Security, Policy Development, and Training

Prior to computerization, campus security consisted almost entirely of uniformed officers protecting the institution's physical assets through installing and monitoring locks, lighting, and alarm systems; promoting pedestrian, vehicle, and personal safety; and conducting preventative patrols while making students and campus employees more aware of crime possibilities. Campus police officers commissioned with arrest power also investigated crimes occurring on college and university property and traditionally maintained close working relationships with law enforcement agencies in surrounding jurisdictions. These and many other functions remain extremely important.

In recent years, hundreds of campuses throughout the U.S. have created Information Security Offices. Often these are organized within Information Technology Services (ITS) divisions or risk management units. Analogous to traditional campus security offices, these information security or "infosec units" concentrate on installing technological safeguards; monitoring network environments; and generally preventing, detecting, and responding to situations that threaten information systems. Depending on designated mission responsibilities, available resources, and expertise, infosec units may also participate in procurement activities for system upgrades; provide cybercrime prevention training for students, faculty, and staff; investigate system abuses and cybercrimes; and support development and enforcement of campus policies and procedures pertaining to responsible use of IT and systems.

Given the apparent prevalence of IT-enabled abuse and crimes occurring on campuses, combined with institutional dependence on IT for every aspect of campus life and business operations, infosec units now provide essential services of equal importance to traditional physical security and policing services. The fact that crime on campus now runs the gauntlet from low-to-high tech and involves both the physical and cyber worlds, amalgamating the functions of traditional campus security offices with dedicated infosec units makes sense. Typically, however, postsecondary institutions continue to separate these functions, both organizationally and operationally: "cops" do their thing while "cyber sleuths" theirs. There is little, if any, recognition that IT-enabled abuse of systems and devices frequently occurs over time by students, faculty and staff both on- and offline, and from on- and off-campus locations. For better organizing and operational purposes, it is useful to conceptualize a new campus security paradigm as a Venn diagram in which illicit activities may occur strictly via networks or in physical places without using IT systems or that crossover into the cyber and physical realms simultaneously. To put it another way, innovative and traditional crime increasingly involves illicit use of IT and related networks. Therefore, both the organization and its delivery of traditional security and policing functions must similarly evolve to address human behaviors that play out via physical and cyber realms. To remain effective, campus security and policing must become as seamless as the IT systems that enable illicit behaviors to be committed in increasingly high tech ways.

Sanctioning and Technological Solutions to Network Security and Prevention

Institutions must address IT-enabled abuse and cybercrimes on college campuses through active sanctioning of offenders and with technological solutions. Historically, colleges and universities have used administrative offices and programs to address student academic and nonacademic misconduct involving inappropriate physical, mental, emotional, or sexual abuse. Institutions seek to prevent such problems by developing written policies that specify inappropriate behaviors and sanctions the institution may impose for the behavior. Institutions address such misconduct, including that involving inappropriate use of IT, through mediation services, disciplinary hearings, and alternative education courses required of students who violate rules. Institutional sanctions, including academic suspension and expulsion, for unacceptable use of IT devices and network resources including online harassment, unauthorized downloading via p2p networks, copyright infringement, and violations of privacy proscribed in laws such as the federal *Family Education Rights and Privacy Act* (FERPA) and the *Digital Millennium Copyright Act* (DMCA) are designed to educate, prevent, and deter future violations.

Campuses also rely on a variety of information security and network monitoring technologies to prevent, detect, and respond to misconduct involving IT. These include contracting for services that automatically update operating systems, software applications, and malware definitions; hardware and software firewall and network traffic monitoring programs; and other programs that filter, block, or otherwise quarantine suspicious files or access to particular Web content, such as p2p sites known to facilitate the illegal downloading of software, music, or movies. IT administrators assign unique Internet Protocol (IP) addresses to fixed or portable computers authorized to connect to campus networks (e.g., those located in computing labs, libraries, or owned by students, etc.), which allows officials and investigators to monitor and/or analyze computing activities accomplished with specific devices. Virtual privacy networks (VPNs) now allow authorized users from off-campus locations to connect securely to campus networks over the Internet. Institutions can configure technology-enabled password management processes requiring using strong passwords to access campus networks (e.g., those consisting of 12 or more randomly selected alphanumeric characters) and changing passwords on a regular basis. Many campuses are also eliminating social security numbers as a basis of student identification, encrypting data stored or transmitted over its networks, rapid fire email alert systems to warn of new malware releases, and restricting access to data based on authorized user security levels (Marklein, 2006b). And they are increasingly coordinating to stay abreast of emerging threats to information security and best practices for its protection with government agencies, private sector firms, and nonprofit organizations such as EDUCAUSE. However, as previously indicated, human factors (i.e., knowledge and capabilities of campus IT professionals, offenders and potential victims) have much to do with the effectiveness of passwords and other technological solutions to high-tech misbehavior.

Conclusion

More than half a century since computer abuse originated on American college and university campuses and following decades of ongoing improvements in higher education for using, learning with, and securing information systems, society now finds itself more than ever connected and dependent on critical information infrastructure. At the same time, cybercrime, enabled by exponentially increasing Internet access and use of IT devices throughout the world, is steadily increasing and continuously evolving with respect to technological complexity. As cybercrime becomes more complex, it also becomes more difficult to understand, prevent, and develop adequate responses to (McQuade, 2006). This chapter described ten aspects of IT-enabled abuse and crime that complicate preventing, detecting, monitoring, managing, and responding to cybercrime and threats to information security and cyber safety on college and university campuses.

Having been the original test-bed and an enduring source for computing and telecommunications inventions and innovations leading to their amalgamation, American colleges and universities now experience many forms of IT-enabled abuse and crimes. For many campuses, copyright infringement via students' pirating of movies, music, and software remains a large challenge as evidenced by notifications received respectively from entities such as the Motion Picture Association of America (MPAA), the Recording Industry Association of America (RIAA), and the Business Software Alliance. Production companies and other types of firms are increasingly taking their own initiative to notify IT administrators of suspected pirating originating from college campuses. When it comes to plagiarism as academic cheating and violating of copyright laws, a sense of anonymity may pervade college students especially among international students whose cultural and academic backgrounds seemingly condone permissiveness rather than caution and respect for intellectual property. Instances involving students possessing or distributing child pornography are rare, but do occur. Posting of obscene language and sexually tinged activities on social computing forums also occurs, despite the potential for students to jeopardize future employment with companies and organizations that increasingly browse online for evidence of an applicant's poor judgment, immaturity, or worse.

Social computing combined with mobile computing has simultaneously expanded and merged physical and cyber environments through which crime may now occur at any time and involve people engaged in most anything online regardless of location. Dormitories, libraries, athletic facilities, and traditional or virtual classrooms, as well as open spaces, are now ripe for cybercrime to occur within them. Yet given limited sources of funding combined with relatively few scholars expressing interest in, or possessing sufficient training in criminology, security management, and IT, relatively little information has been generated about the nature or extent of cybercrime on college campuses, nor of the social and economic impacts of cybercrime on postsecondary institutions. This remains true even as hundreds of colleges and universities in the last decade have experienced embarrassing, costly, and damaging breaches of information system security and data loss. Phishing schemes that employ apparently valid websites to fool people into revealing confidential personal information – including passwords needed to access information systems – haunt IT administrators who fear students, faculty, staff, and alumni being duped via social engineering.

The chapter also identified three imperatives involving higher education efforts to address cybercrime. First, institutions must educate students, staff, and faculty in online safety, security, and responsibility. Such efforts are already enjoying success at postsecondary institutions certified as Centers in Academic Excellence (CAE) in information security. Laudable with respect to building national capacity for protecting critical information infrastructure, the truth is that all users – not merely future information security professionals and their employing organizations – deserve to be safe and secure online and all users must ultimately learn to protect their systems, devices, and data. If higher education does not systematically address these expectations by insuring future members of the workforce are knowledgeable about and skilled in the use of IT devices and applications, who will?

A second imperative is that academic institutions must lead by example using best practices for protecting information systems against data breaches and other forms of online abuse and crime. Hundreds of publically disclosed breaches of information systems in recent years undermine trust and confidence of students, parents, and policymakers in the ability of institutions to protect confidential information as increasingly required by state and federal laws and regulations. Data breaches are also costly in financial and political terms. Repeat offenses experienced by a few institutions are especially disconcerting, especially given readily available expert resources and professional development opportunities extended through entities such as EDUCAUSE, HEISC, NIST, and ITIL.

Third, increasing levels of IT-enabled online abuse and crime, along with technological evolution in this realm, combined with the reality that both cybercrime and traditional (offline) forms of crime and security violations are occurring on campus, underscore a need for colleges and universities to increasingly merge their physical and cyber security/safety units and operations. Conceptual and operational fusion of these entities is a logical extension of the changing nature of offending and organizational capacities to respond and intervene. Economies of scale in services provided can be realized and may also be increasingly required if fiscal budgets, such as those being experienced in public higher education, are further constrained or scrutinized. Put differently, information and campus security professionals must increasingly become one in the same because this is what institutions need. The same holds true for policing agencies and security firms, but higher education can and should lead the way. We have come a long way and made many important improvements since the emergence of "computer abuse" more than 50 years ago. More needs to be done.

NOTES

1. Space constraints severely restrict the depth of my discussion and incorporation of examples throughout the chapter. IT-enabled crimes on college and university campuses are a subset and extension of innovative and harmful behaviors increasingly occurring throughout the modern world. These behaviors threaten users of computers and other types of electronic devices, as well as all members of modernizing societies increasingly dependent on critical information infrastructures.

2. Within non-technical communities the word "hacker" refers to a person who cracks passwords or otherwise defeats security measures in order to break into computer networks. However, the term "hacker" is controversial and may, among programmers and other IT professionals, connote expertise in cracking systems for good or necessary as well illicit purposes. So whereas "black hat hackers" are commonly regarded as cyber criminals, white hat hackers specialize in discovering and reporting security vulnerabilities as a way to improve the security of networks, devices, and data while raising public awareness about the growing importance of information security.

3. "Internet bots, also known as web robots, WWW robots, or simply bots, are software applications that run automated tasks over the Internet. Typically, bots perform tasks that are both simple and structurally repetitive at a much higher rate than would be possible for a human. The largest application of is in what is known as "web spidering," in which an automated script fetches, analyzes, and files information from web servers. Bots may also be implemented where a response speed faster than that of humans is required (e.g., video gaming bots and auction-site robots) or less commonly in situations where the emulation of human activity is required, for example, chat bots (bots are used for commercial as well as malicious purposes). Recently bots have been used for search advertising, such as Google Adsense" (retrieved from http://en. wikipedia.org/wiki/ Internet_bot).

4. Analytical procedures of McQuade and Castellano (2004) were as follows: Internal structures of self-reported computer abuse identified through a series of a principal components factor analysis. Varimax rotation was performed. The decision regarding the number of factors to retain was assisted by a scree plot of the eigenvalues, as well as the Kaiser-Normalization Rule, which retains factors with eigenvalues greater than one. Internal consistency reliability evidence was obtained by computing the Cronbach alpha statistic for each identified scale. Scale items were examined to determine if their deletion would result in an improved reliability level; items were retained or excluded based on improvements in resulting reliability levels.

REFERENCES

Angwin, J. (2006). Parental guidance: How safe are the top social networking sites for teens? We take them for a test run. Retrieved from http://online.wsj.com/public/article/SB115333833014811453-LjMFsXTCUjSigIarp2FhC0Y_TSs_20060822.html?mod=tff_main_tff_top.

Armour, N. (2006). Blogs, photo sites give everyone a peek at athletes' lives. Retrieved from http://sportsillustrated.cnn.com/2006/more/wires/05/26/2080.ap.bad.jocks.adv27.1331/index.html.

Bell, M. (2011). More employers using firms that check applicants' social media history. Retrieved from http://www.washingtonpost.com/lifestyle/style/more-employers-using-firms-that-check-applicants-social-media-history/2011/07/12/gIQAxnJYGI_story.html.

Bennett, S. (2011). 91% of employers use Twitter, Facebook and LinkedIn to screen job applicants. Retrieved from http://www.mediabistro.com/alltwitter/social-media-job-screening_b15090.

Cohen, L. E., & Felson, M. (1979). Social change and crime: A routine activity approach. In Joseph E. Jacoby (Ed.), *Classics of criminology* (pp. 66–74). Prospect Heights, IL: Waveland Press.

Dezayas, H. (2012). Police arrest man at airport for threatening Pitt professors. Retrieved July 12, 2012, from http://plum-oakmont.patch.com/articles/police-arrest-man-for-threatening-pitt-professors.

Educause. (2012). Cybersecurity initiative. Retrieved from http://www.educause.edu/focus-areas-and-initiatives/policy-and-security/cybersecurity-initiative/about.

Fream, A. (1993). The prevalence and social learning predictors of computer crime among college students. Unpublished master's thesis. University of Kentucky.

Hollinger, R. C. (1993). Crime by computer: Correlates of software piracy and unauthorized account access. *Security Journal, 4,* 2–12.

Hollinger, R. C., & Lanza-Kaduce, L. (1988). The process of criminalization: The case of computer crime laws. *Criminology, 26,* 101–126.

Huffington Post. (2012). University of Pittsburgh bomb threats finished now that 'the threateners'" demands are met, email says. Retrieved from http://www.huffingtonpost.com/2012/04/24/pitt-bomb-threats-finished_n_1448956.html.

International Standards Organization. (2012). What is ISO? What we do. Retrieved from http://www.iso.org/iso/about.htm.

Kutzer-Rice, R. (2011). Social media: The newest background check. Retrieved from http://www.smartertechnology.com/c/a/Social-Business/Social-Media-The-Newest-Background-Check/.

Levy, S. (1984). *Hackers: Heroes of the computer revolution.* New York: Doubleday.

Liedtke, M. (2005). Stolen UC Berkeley laptop exposes personal data of nearly 100,000. Retrieved from http://www.detnews.com/2005/technology/0503/30/tech-132193.htm.

Marklein, M. (2006a). Colleges are textbook cases of cybersecurity breaches. Retrieved from http://www.usatoday.com/tech/news/computersecurity/hacking/2006-08-01-college-hack_x.htm.

Marklein, M. (2006b). The new learning curve: Technological security. Retrieved from http://www.usatoday.com/tech/news/computersecurity/hacking/2006-08-01-college-security_x.htm.

McQuade, S. (2006a). *Understanding and managing cybercrime.* Boston: Pearson Education.

McQuade, S. (2006b). Technology-enabled crime, policing and security. *Journal of Technology Studies* (January 1). Reprinted by International Library of Criminology, Criminal Justice and Penology – second series (2009).

McQuade, S., Colt, J., & Meyer, N. (2009). *Cyber bullying: Protecting kids and adults from online bullies.* Westport, CT: Praeger.

McQuade, S., & Sampat, N. (2008). *RIT Survey of Internet and At-risk Behaviors.* Rochester, NY: Rochester Institute of Technology.

McQuade, S., & Fisk, N. (2006). *Social interactions for learning high tech crime: An empirical analysis of social learning and deterrence theory correlates.* Unpublished manuscript. Rochester Institute of Technology.

McQuade, S., & Linden, E. (2006). *College student computer use and ethics: An empirical analysis of self-reported unethical behaviors.* Unpublished manuscript. Rochester Institute of Technology.

McQuade, S., Gorthy, M., & Linden, E. (2006). *High tech crimes on college campuses: A comparison of offending and victimization at RIT versus SUNY Brockport.* Unpublished manuscript. Rochester Institute of Technology.

McQuade, S. (2005). IT-enabled offending and victimization by and among RIT students: Implications for student services, education and training. Presented to the Student Affairs Division at the Rochester Institute of Technology, August 17, 2012.

McQuade, S., & Castellano, T. (2004). Computer aided crime and misbehavior among a student population: An empirical examination of patterns, correlates, and possible causes. Paper presented at the 2004 Annual Meetings of the American Society of Criminology, Nashville, TN.

National Council of State Legislatures. (2012). Data breach law summary. Retrieved from http://www.ncsl.org/issues-research/telecom/security-breach-legislation-2012.aspx.

National White Collar Crime Center. (1996). *Proceedings of the Academic Workshop.* Washington, DC: Bureau of Justice Assistance.

NIST Computer Security Division. (2012). *Services of Computer Security Resource Center.* Retrieved from http://csrc.nist.gov/.

Parker, D. (1998). *Fighting computer crime: A new framework for protecting information.* New York: Wiley Computer.

Privacy Rights Clearinghouse. (2012). Chronology of data breaches in educational institutions. Retrieved from http://www.privacyrights.org/data-breach/new.

Pyle, E. (2010). Server hacked at OSU; 760,000 affected – Personal data of faculty, students are at risk; free credit protection offered. Retrieved from http://www.dispatch.com/content/stories/local/2010/12/16/server-hacked-at-osu-760000-affected.html.

Remizowski, L. (2012). String of bomb threats reaches University of Pittsburgh chancellor. Retrieved from http://articles.cnn.com/2012-04-11/us/us_pennsylvania-school-threats_1_bomb-threats-buildings-campus-life?_s=PM:US.

Rogers, M. (2001). *A social learning theory and moral disengagement analysis of criminal computer behavior: An exploratory study.* Unpublished manuscript. University of Manitoba, Winnipeg, Manitoba.

Roman, J. (2012). University breach settlement approved. Retrieved from http://www.bankinfosecurity.com/university-breach-settlement-approved-a-4685.

Skowronski, J. (2012). Who's stealing your credit card data? Retrieved from http://money.msn.com/credit-cards/article.aspx?post=c26c8de1-716c-48e0-870f-0d19318f179a.

Skinner, W., & Fream, A. (1997). A social learning theory analysis of computer crime among college students. *Journal of Research in Crime and Delinquency, 34,* 495–519.

Sutherland, E. H. (1940). White-collar criminality. In J. E. Jacoby (Ed.), *Classics of criminology* (pp. 20–25). Prospect Heights, IL: Waveland Press.

Synovate, (2003). *FTC identity theft survey report.* Washington, DC: Federal Trade Commission.

POSTSCRIPT

In 1990, Congress passed and President George H. W. Bush signed into law the *Student Right to Know and Campus Security Act of 1990*. Hailed by some as an effective tool in the fight against campus crime, the legislation forced postsecondary institutions participating in Title IV federal financial aid programs to finally "come clean" with their crime statistics and security policies and "do something" about campus crime. Additionally, during the 1990s, several states passed their own "campus crime" legislation and passed legislation that enabled colleges and universities to create campus police departments staffed by sworn peace officers. Congress subsequently amended the legislation several times, including renaming it the *Jeanne Clery Disclosure of Campus Security Policy and Campus Crime Statistics Act* (henceforth, *Clery*) and enhancing its unfunded mandates.

Both federal and state legislation during the 1990s sparked much interest and activism in campus crime and security. During this time, the first edition of *Campus Crime: Legal, Social, and Policy Perspectives* was published – making it among the first edited collections of scholarly works specifically devoted to campus crime and security issues. Further, research on campus crime that began in the late 1980s gained momentum during the 1990s and continued into this decade as social scientists became increasingly interested in campus crime and safety. Federal funding also became available to postsecondary institutions to develop and strengthen security and investigation strategies to address violence against college women, namely domestic violence, dating violence, sexual assault, and stalking on campuses. These monies also could be used to develop and strengthen victim services in cases involving such crimes against women on campuses. Scholars from a variety of disciplines, including the social sciences, law, and public health, continued to publish studies that described and explained the magnitude and the dynamics of on-campus student victimization and critically questioned the effectiveness of both state and federal campus crime legislation.

Other parties were also actively engaged in furthering the safety and security interests of college students. For example, Security On Campus, Inc. (now

387

the *Clery Center for Security on Campus*) became the leading national advocate and watchdog for "doing something" about campus crime, including providing information on campus crime and security via its website, helping student victims and their parents find "justice," lobbying Congress for further changes to federal legislation, and conducting training for campus officials responsible for filing compliance documents. Additionally, the past 15 years has seen the courts become more actively involved in litigation involving on-campus victimization of students by holding postsecondary institutions liable under civil law and awarding victims and/or their families damages.

Further, during the 1990s the U.S. Justice Department funded three large-scale, national-level studies of college student victimization experiences and one national-level study of postsecondary institutional compliance with federal legislation; reports and scholarly articles arising from these studies were also published. The U.S. Department of Education expanded its role in this arena during the 1990s and into this decade by making campus crime data available to the public via a special website. The agency also undertook multiple high-profile investigations of alleged *Clery* noncompliance that resulted in record fines being imposed on two universities. The Department also published a handbook in 2005 for schools to assist them in complying with *Clery* stipulations (the handbook was revised in 2011). Finally, in 2011, the agency's Civil Rights Division issued a ruling that college and university disciplinary proceedings involving alleged peer-on-peer sexual violence occurring on campus would be governed by an evidentiary standard of "beyond a preponderance of the evidence." By any measure, these examples represent a great deal of activity geared toward "doing something" about campus crime.

Yet, as the chapters comprising the third edition of this volume indicate, many of the same issues that activists, legislators, postsecondary administrators, and social scientists began addressing during the 1990s either remain unresolved or the solutions implemented have been shown wanting. As a result, the legislative and judicial branches of government, social scientists, and security officials continue to focus their attention on campus crime and security. Concurrently, over 6,000 Title IV eligible postsecondary institutions in this country address ongoing challenges involving compliance with state and federal legislation, civil lawsuits filed by crime victims, and other emerging issues such as stalking, high-tech abuse and crimes, and information technology security. Two decades after Congressional passage of the *Campus Security Act*, the center of attention continues to be "doing something" about crime at postsecondary institutions, fueled in no small part by high-profile mass shootings that occurred at Virginia Tech, Northern Illinois University, and the University of Alabama at Huntsville. However, as at least one chapter in this volume points out, attempts at "doing something" have too often resulted either in passage of "symbolic" legislation and/or the implementation of policies or programs that had little substantive impact on campus safety or security.

The collected works in this volume present a present-day picture of the three contexts of campus crime – legal, social, and security – and some of the policy issues associated with them. While answers to basic questions asked during the early 1990s such as "how much crime is there on college campuses?" and "to what degree have postsecondary institutions complied with federal campus crime legislation?" have been at least partially answered, lacking from the "doing something" momentum are questions about the *effectiveness* of what is "being done." Simply put, answers to the question "what works?" are much needed to move from "doing something" about campus crime to "*effectively* doing something" to prevent and therefore, reduce the opportunity for campus crime.

Postsecondary institutions have "come a long way" in their efforts to address campus crime. Yet, as the chapters show, they still have a ways to go. While postsecondary institutions have made gains in their efforts to "come clean" with their crime statistics; developed and implemented security policies that, at least on the surface, address some of the problems they face; and continue to address compliance and other issues arising from federal and state legislation, many tasks remain unfinished. Questions concerning the extent, nature, causes, and effects of campus victimization and fear of victimization remain largely unanswered. Legislation, both at the federal and state level, may be more symbolic than real, and continues to be criticized by academics and advocacy groups alike. New "models" of policing that move beyond so-called "community-oriented policing" are being experimented with by campus law enforcement, as are new ways to better use information to fight both traditional forms of crime as well as "new crimes" such as cybercrime. Finally, new issues in security involving the use and abuse of information technology – issues that few could have imagined in 1990 – threaten to supplant "traditional" security concerns on college campuses.

As we argued in the first and second editions of this volume, campus administrators must realize that addressing the problem of crime on their campuses involves interdepartmental cooperation. More than 15 years later, evidence of such cooperation remains mixed at best and nonexistent at worse. Just as when the first and second editions of this volume were published, the need continues for advocacy groups to push postsecondary institutions to do more to adequately respond to campus crime, in particular institutional responses to the survivors of on-campus sexual violence. Postsecondary administrators need also take better advantage of crime prevention designers – who use evidence-based approaches to create programs – and program evaluators – who use sophisticated quantitative and qualitative methods to assess both program processes and outcomes – many of whom are faculty members and graduate students at their respective schools. Granted, real progress has occurred on many fronts and we have generally moved past postsecondary administrators trying to cover up the reality of the crime and security challenges they face. That being said, we continue to hope that postsecondary administrators do not lose focus and enhance the pace with which they use the expertise and data available on their campuses to address the legal, social, and security contexts of campus crime and security. By doing so, administrators can develop and implement policies and programs that are both evidence-based and routinely evaluated (and revised accordingly), rather than developing responses that are politically and legally expedient but to the best of our current state of campus crime and security knowledge, largely ineffective in addressing each one.

NAME INDEX

391

Z

SUBJECT INDEX